DISCARDED

# Mozambique
## a country study

Foreign Area Studies
The American University
Edited by
Harold D. Nelson
Research completed
April 1984

On the cover: Elements of Mozambique's national flag. The book symbolizes education, the gun represents defense and vigilance, and the hoe stands for the peasantry and agricultural production.

Third Edition, 1984; First Printing, 1985

**Library of Congress Cataloging in Publication Data**

Main entry under title:

Mozambique: a country study.
   (Area handbook series) (DA pam/Headquarters,
Department of the Army; 550–64)
   "Research completed April 1984."
      Bibliography: p.
      Includes index.
      1. Mozambique. I. Nelson, Harold D. II. American University
(Washington, D.C.). Foreign Area Studies. III. Series. III. Series: DA
pam; 550–64.
DT453.M64 1985            967´.9        85–6027

Headquarters, Department of the Army
DA Pam 550–64

For sale by the Superintendent of Documents, U.S. Government Printing Office
Washington, D.C. 20402

# Foreword

This volume is one of a continuing series of books prepared by Foreign Area Studies, The American University, under the Country Studies/Area Handbook Program. The last page of this book provides a listing of other published studies. Each book in the series deals with a particular foreign country, describing and analyzing its economic, national security, political, and social systems and institutions and examining the interrelationships of those systems and institutions and the ways that they are shaped by cultural factors. Each study is written by a multidisciplinary team of social scientists. The authors seek to provide a basic insight and understanding of the society under observation, striving for a dynamic rather than a static portrayal of it. The study focuses on historical antecedents and on the cultural, political and socioeconomic characteristics that contribute to cohesion and cleavage within the society. Particular attention is given to the origins and traditions of the people who make up the society, their dominant beliefs and values, their community of interests and the issues on which they are divided, the nature and extent of their involvement with the national institutions, and their attitudes toward each other and toward the social system and political order within which they live.

The contents of the book represent the views, opinions, and findings of Foreign Area Studies and should not be construed as an official Department of the Army position, policy, or decision, unless so designated by other official documentation. The authors have sought to adhere to accepted standards of scholarly objectivity. Such corrections, additions, and suggestions for factual or other changes that readers may have will be welcomed for use in future new editions.

William Evans-Smith
Director, Foreign Area Studies
The American University
Washington, D.C. 20016

# Acknowledgments

The authors are grateful to those individuals in various governmental, international, and academic organizations who gave of their time, data, special knowledge, and authoritative perspective on Mozambique. In this regard, particular recognition is due Luís B. Serapião, associate professor in the African Studies Research Program at Howard University, Washington, D.C. Gratitude is also extended to members of the Foreign Area Studies support staff who contributed directly to the production of this book. These persons include Denise Ryan, Andrea T. Merrill, and Dorothy M. Lohmann, who edited the manuscript; Harriett R. Blood and Gustavo Adolfo Mendoza, who prepared the graphics; Gilda V. Nimer, librarian; Ernest A. Will, publications manager; Eloise W. Brandt and Wayne W. Olsen, administrative assistants; Margaret Quinn, typist; Dan Bress, photocomposer; and Kathryne Kozak and Joanne Morgan, indexers.

The aesthetic touches that enhance the book's appearance are the work of Marty Ittner, whose illustrations appear on the cover and the title pages of the chapters. The inclusion of photographs has been made possible by the generosity of various individuals and public and private agencies. The authors acknowledge their appreciation especially to those persons who contributed original camera work not previously published.

# Contents

*Robert Rinehart*

PRECOLONIAL HISTORY—Early Population Movements—The Arabs and the Swahili Coast—The Shona Dynasties—PORTUGUESE HEGEMONY—The Passage to
India—The Portuguese on the Swahili Coast—Portuguese
Expansion up the Zambezi—The Rise of the Prazos—Chal-
lenges to the Portuguese Presence in East Africa—Mozam-
bique in the Eighteenth Century—Portuguese Administration
in the Early Nineteenth Century—The Slave Trade—The
Ngoni Migrations—The Downfall of the Prazeros—THE
MODERN COLONIAL ERA—Portugal and the European
Scramble for Africa—Gungunhana—Portuguese Penetration
of the Northern Interior—The Chartered Companies—The
Colonial Regime—World War I and the Zambezi Rebellions—
Salazar and the Colonial Statute of 1930—The New State—
THE RISE OF AFRICAN NATIONALISM—Founding of the
Front for the Liberation of Mozambique—War of Liberation:
The Initial Phase—The Cahora Bassa Project—Final Phase of
the Liberation War—INDEPENDENT MOZAMBIQUE—
The Transitional Government—Independence—The FRE-
LIMO Regime—Foreign Relations—A Change of Direction

*Irving Kaplan*

PHYSICAL SETTING—Terrain and Drainage—Climate—
DEMOGRAPHY—Age and Sex Structure—Densities and
Rural-Urban Distribution—ETHNICITY—Language—Ethnic
Groups—Interethnic Relations—THE SOCIAL ORDER—
Local Rural Structures—Urban and National Structures—RELI-
GION—Religious Affiliation—Religion, the Party, and the
State—EDUCATION—HEALTH

*Donald P. Whitaker*

ECONOMIC OVERVIEW — AGRICULTURE — Land
Resources and Use—Livestock—Fisheries—Forestry—MIN-

ING—MANUFACTURING—ENERGY SOURCES—Wood
and Coal—Electric Power—Petroleum—TRANSPORTA-
TION—Railroads—Roads—Ports—Civil Aviation—Pipelines—FOREIGN TRADE AND BALANCE OF PAY-
MENTS

GOVERNMENT INSTITUTIONS AND THE PARTY—The
Constitution—The President and the Council of Ministers—
The People's Assembly—Elections—Local Government—
The Legal System—FRONT FOR THE LIBERATION OF
MOZAMBIQUE—Ideology and Program—Party Structure—
Mass Associations—Role of the Information Media—POLI-
TICS—New Economic Directions, 1980-83—Reforms of the
Fourth Congress of FRELIMO—Opposition to FRELIMO—
FOREIGN RELATIONS—Neighboring Black African
States—South Africa—Portugal—Other West European
Countries—The United States—Communist Countries

STATE OF NATIONAL SECURITY—The Mozambican
National Resistance—External Concerns—THE ARMED
FORCES—General Development—Place in the National
Life—Manpower: Sources and Quality—Defense Spending—
Mission, Organization, and Training—Foreign Military Assist-
ance—PUBLIC ORDER AND INTERNAL SECURITY—
The Police—The Prison System

## List of Figures

# Preface

This study replaces the *Area Handbook for Mozambique*, which was published in 1977, two years after the country had achieved independence from Portugal. That event had followed a decade of guerrilla activity by the Front for the Liberation of Mozambique (Frente de Libertação de Moçambique—FRELIMO) against the Portuguese colonial government. Coming to power as Black Africa's first avowed Marxist-Leninist government, FRELIMO set about transforming the country into a socialist state with assistance from the Soviet Union and other communist nations. Concurrently, Mozambique became a haven for black nationalists opposing the white minority governments in neighboring Southern Rhodesia (later independent Zimbabwe) and South Africa.

In the seven years since 1977, Mozambique's quest for political stability and economic development have come under attack by anti-Marxist insurgents of the Mozambican National Resistance movement in a persistent campaign of destabilization, aided and encouraged by South Africa. The impact of this so-called hidden war on Mozambican society in particular and on southern Africa in general has warranted a fresh look at the young sovereign state and its precarious role in world affairs.

*Mozambique: A Country Study*, like its predecessor, seeks to provide a compact and objective exposition of the country's dominant social, economic, political, and national security institutions and, hopefully, to give the reader some appreciation for the forces involved in contemporary Mozambican history. In presenting this new study, the authors have relied primarily on official reports of governmental and international organizations, journals, newspapers, and materials reflecting recent field research by scholarly authorities. Detailed information on many aspects of the society were not always readily available, however, and gaps in the data as well as varying interpretations of certain matters existed among some of the sources consulted. Where appropriate, these gaps and differences have been noted in the text. Should readers require greater detail on core area topics, the authors have noted the availability of amplifying materials in bibliographic statements at the end of each chapter. Full reference to these and other sources used or considered are included in the detailed Bibliography.

Place-names generally have been spelled in accordance with those published by the United States Board on Geographic Names in its current Gazetteer No. 109, *Mozamibique*, published in June 1969. Soon after independence in 1975, the FRELIMO government began to substitute African place-names for the Portuguese names that had been used earlier. Although probably an incomplete list, the new names that have become apparent are reflected where appropriate in this study (see table A). The authors are aware that variations exist between Portuguese and English sources for the spellings of the country's numerous ethnic groups. Moreover, different spellings may occur for a given ethnic group whose members live in more than one of the adjacent countries of southern Africa. The spelling of ethnic names is consistent throughout this book, but the more important alternatives are pointed out in Chapter 2.

Before national independence Mozambique's internal administrative subdivisions were known as districts. In 1975 these first-order units became provinces, which were further subdivided into districts.

An effort has been made to limit the use of foreign and technical words and phrases in this study. When this has been inappropriate, such terms have been defined where they first appear in any chapter or reference has been made to the Glossary, which is included at the back of the book for the reader's convenience.

All measurements are presented in the metric system. A conversion table will assist those readers who may not be familiar with metric equivalents (see table 1, Appendix).

## Table A.    Revised Geographic Names, 1984

| New Name | Former Name | Entity |
|----------|-------------|--------|
| Maputo | Lourenço Marques | Province[1] |
| Sofala | Beira | -do- |
| Manica | Vila Pery | -do- |
| Nampula | Moçambique | -do- |
| Maputo | Lourenço Marques | National capital and province capital |
| Xai-Xai | João Belo | Province capital |
| Lichinga | Vila Cabral | -do- |
| Pemba | Porto Amélia | -do- |
| Chimoio | Vila Pery | -do- |
| Angoche | António Enes | Town[2] |
| Cantandica | Vila Gouveia | -do- |
| Chicualacuala | Malvernia | -do- |
| Chilembene | Aldeia da Madragoa | -do- |
| Chokwe | Trigo de Morais | -do- |
| Cuamba | Nova Freixo | -do- |
| Guija | Vila Alferes Chamusca | -do- |
| Lupichili | Olivença | -do- |
| Macaloge | Miranda | -do- |
| Mahlazene | Santa Comba | -do- |
| Matola | Vila Salazar | -do- |
| Manjacaze | Muchopes | District |
| Cahora Bassa | Cabora Bassa | Gorge and dam |

[1] Under Portugese rule, first-order administrative units were called districts.

[2] António Enes was also the name of the second-order administrative division in which the town is located.

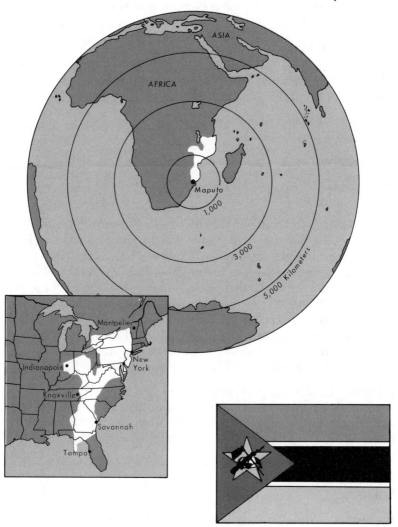

## Country

**Formal Name:**   People's Republic of Mozambique.

**Short Form:**   Mozambique.

**Term for Citizens:**  Mozambicans.

**Capital:**  Maputo (named Lourenço Marques, until 1976)

**Flag:**  Three broad horizontal stripes of green, black, and yellow separated by small white stripes; on left, open book and crossed rifle and hoe within yellow star superimposed on large red triangular field.

**Independence Achieved:**  June 25, 1975.

# Geography

**Size:**  799,380 square kilometers; about twice the size of California.

**Topography:**  North of Zambezi River valley narrow littoral (often less than 30 kilometers wide) give way to low plateaus and hills and then to eastward extension of Central African highlands manifested in several disconnected highland zones. South of Zambezi, littoral extends farther inland—more than 300 kilometers between 22⁰ and 24⁰ south latitude—taking up almost entire width of country except for isolated highlands in far west and eastern extension of Central African highlands. Littoral lowland and marshes thus make up about 44 percent of terrain, most of it in region south of Zambezi and Save rivers.

**Climate:**  Largely tropical; marked wet (October to April) and dry seasons. Wet season and higher temperatures coincide; rainfall and temperature generally lower and more uncertain in far south, which is more susceptible to both drought and flooding than rest of country.

# Society

**Population:**  Mid-1983 population estimated at 13.1 million. Well over 90 percent rural. Population density greatest near coastal urban centers.

**Ethnic Groups and Languages:**  Numerous Bantu languages, each divided into several dialects, linked to equivalent number of ethnic categories; larger categories have several sections. Early 1980s estimates ranked ethnic categories according to size as Macua-Lomue (sometimes considered as two separate groups), Tsonga, Lower Zambezi cluster (consisting of several diverse groups), Shona (major components: Manyika and Ndau), Islamic Coastal group, Chopi, Maravi (several independent groups), Yao, Maconde, and Ngoni (small scattered groups of South African origin).

**Religion:** In 1983 great majority of Africans, 60 to 65 percent, adherents of indigenous religions. Less than 15 percent of total professed Roman Catholicism; more than 5 percent Protestants of various denominations; another 5 percent belonged to African independent churches; roughly 12 percent of total were Sunni Muslims. Constitution grants right to practice (or not to practice) religion; regime's relations with religion, particularly with Roman Catholic church, have been cool.

**Education:** Almost all schools operated by the state; total conversion to free state-run system ultimate goal. Not all children able to attend school, but most of those aged six to nine were in four-year primary school in 1984. Trained teachers in short supply. Enrollment in seven-year, three-cycle secondary schools increasing since national independence, but only small proportion of Mozambicans of secondary-school age attended classes, especially beyond first two-year cycle. Proportion of young women dropped sharply at secondary level, the women having reached marriageable age. In 1984 Eduardo Mondlane University was sole domestic source of higher education. Before independence adult literacy rate probably under 10 percent; by early 1980s about 25 percent. Rate markedly higher for males than for females.

**Health:** Medical practice fully socialized; emphases on preventive health care, immunization, hygiene, sanitation, and nutrition delivered by equivalent of China's "barefoot doctors" and paramedics. Fully trained physicians and nurses still minimal in early 1980s; most physicians foreigners on temporary duty. Two mass health campaigns since independence—one for immunization against measles, diphtheria, tetanus, typhus, poliomyelitis, and smallpox; the other for community sanitation, principally latrine building. Success of both campaigns initially substantial but variable. Inadequate nutrition exacerbated by drought-induced famine, a major problem in early and mid-1980s.

## Economy

**Salient Features:** Agriculture and transportation services principal sectors. Largely rural population engaged mainly in subsistence production but also responsible for important share of cash crops. Commercial production of cash crops in 1984 by some private operations, but mostly by state farms. Export of agricultural commodities, earnings from transit traffic with neighboring countries, and wages of migrant labor in South Africa main sources of foreign exchange. Industry of some importance, but activities seriously hampered by shortages of managerial, technical, and labor skills after massive departure of Portuguese between 1974 and 1977. In 1984 production generally had not regained 1973 base-year levels. Government restructuring economy along Marxist-Leninist lines, but practical considerations have produced mixed economy of state, collective, and private sectors.

**Agriculture:** Crop production, forestry, and fishing occupy about two-thirds of labor force; 80 to 90 percent of population dependent in some way on agricultural sector for livelihood. Principal food crops: cassava, maize, rice, millet, sorghum, beans, peanuts, potatoes, bananas, and citrus fruit.

**Mining and Manufacturing:** In 1984 mining accounted for only small percentage of gross domestic product (GDP—see Glossary) despite presence of major reserves of coal, beryllium, and tantalite. Manufacturing diverse, largely import-substitution manufacturing sector; included food processing, tobacco products, textile manufacture, production of miscellaneous consumer goods, cement and chemicals production, oil refining, and tire manufacture.

**Energy:** Domestic sources of energy: wood, coal, and hydroelectric power. All petroleum products imported. Major Cahora Bassa dam first-phase power station began operations in 1975; capacity in 1984 about 1,500 megawatts. Most of power production designed for sale to South Africa. Wood and charcoal primary sources of energy for rural population.

**Foreign Trade:** Negative trade balance at independence increased rapidly throughout 1978 and remained at high level through early 1980s. Principal exports: cashew nuts and products, shrimp, petroleum and petroleum products, tea, cotton, sugar, timber, coal, cement, and tires. Principal imports: raw materials and supplies, about half (in value terms) crude oil and petroleum products; equipment and spare parts; food; and manufactured consumer goods. Principal sources of imports: United States, Portugal, Britain, France, Italy, Netherlands, German Democratic Republic (East Germany), Federal Republic of Germany (West Germany), and Brazil. Principal buyers of exports: United States, East Germany, West Germany, Netherlands, Kenya, Portugal, and Japan.

**Currency:** Until June 1980 the Mozambique escudo, consisting of 100 centavos; from June 1980, the metical, also 100 centavos. At the time of changeover one escudo/metical official equaled about US$0.035 (US$1 equaled 28 escudos/meticais). In April 1984 one metical equaled US$0.023 (US$1 equaled 41 meticais).

**Fiscal Year:** Same as calendar year.

## Transportation

**Railroads:** Some 3,100 kilometers; track almost entire 1.067-meter gauge. Three separate main systems originating in ports of Maputo, Beira, and Nacala constructed mainly to carry transit traffic to and from neighboring countries; branch from Beira line also serving coal mines in Tete Province.

**Roads:** In 1982 approximately 27,200 kilometers of national and regional roads; 4,600 kilometers of asphalt; 22,560 kilometers of graded earth. Additionally, 12,500 kilometers of unimproved dirt roads.

**Ports:** Three major ocean ports: Maputo, Beira, and Nacala; all under extensive rehabilitation and improvement in 1984. About six small ports used for coastal traffic; six others in state of disrepair.

**Civil Aviation:** State-owned Mozambique Air Lines (Linhas Aéreas de Moçambique—LAM) responsible for regular domestic, regional, and international service. National Air Transport and Services Company (Empresa Nacional de Transporte e Trabalho Aéreo—TTA) responsible for local, light-aircraft service between provincial and district capitals and crop dusting. International airports at Maputo and Beira; some 30 other airfields having hard-surface runways; numerous small, scattered airstrips.

## Government and Politics

**Government:** At national independence, Constitution created single-party state in which all power vested in Marxist-Leninist movement known as Front for the Liberation of Mozambique (Frente de Liberatação de Moçambique—FRELIMO). In 1984 president of FRELIMO chaired Council of Ministers (cabinet), which exercised authority over domestic and foreign affairs. People's Assembly of 226 deputies indirectly elected on FRELIMO recommendation to meet semiannually and ratify actions proposed by government. Permanent Commission of 14 assembly members enacted laws when assembly was not in session. Major policy decisions reached by party, carried into effect by government; most senior government officers held both high party and state positions simultaneously.

**Administrative Divisions:** Governors appointed by president to administer 10 provinces; administrators designated by governors to head 112 districts and 894 localities. Provincial, district, and locality people's assemblies presided over by governors and administrators. Supervision over local government bodies exercised by provincial and local FRELIMO committees.

**Judicial System:** People's tribunals at provincial, district, and locality levels staffed by judges and permanent jurors representing the people; serious economic and security charges heard by Revolutionary Military Tribunal. Ministry of Interior can confine without trial those deemed political, or social misfits.

**Politics:** Since 1977 political activity formally committed to revolutionary system under communist vanguard party, FRELIMO. Control over government and party exercised by party's 11-member Political Bureau, whose composition remained virtually unchanged since war of liberation. Politics embody both African nationalist and orthodox Marxist-Leninist tendencies apparently successfully reconciled by President Samora Moises Machel. Most sectors of economy nationalized after independence, but economic failures have dictated less dogmatic course since 1980. Fourth Party Congress (1983) reconfirmed earlier policy, encouraging private retail shops and small industry, favoring individual family farms over state farms, and seeking foreign investment. Persistent threat to FRELIMO rule and national security posed by Mozambican National Resistance (Resistência Nacional Moçambicana—RNM, sometimes known as RENAMO).

**Foreign Relations:** Generally aligned with Soviet Union and militant, leftist Third World countries on major international issues; regional and bilateral relations guided by more pragmatic policies. Effort launched in early 1980s to restore close ties with Portugal and strengthen relations with Western Europe and United States. To ease long-standing differences, Mozambique and powerful neighboring South Africa entered into economic negotiations in early 1984; signed security agreement, known as Nkomati accord, committing both countries to prevent use of their territory for violence and aggression against each other.

## National Security

**Armed Forces:** In 1984 armed forces, known as People's Forces for the Liberation of Mozambique (Forças Populares da Libertação de Moçambique—FPLM) consisted of regular conventional force of at least 26,700 personnel, including army of about 25,000; air force of roughly 1,000; and navy of approximately 700. Unconventional elements included People's Militia of approximately 30,000 and Border Guard of some 6,000. Registration mandatory for all men and women over age of 18; selective conscription for two-year periods of active duty.

**Major Tactical Units:** Army organized into one tank brigade (Presidential Guard) and eight or nine motorized infantry brigades (each composed of two to four infantry battalions of 300 to 400 troops and armored, artillery, and support battalions). Air force of six fighter-interceptor and forward ground attack squadrons, two helicopter squadrons, one transport squadron, and one training squadron. Navy organized to provide border surveillance on Lake Nyasa and limited coastal patrol. Weapons inventory included nearly 200 Soviet-built T-34, T-54, and T-55 tanks; at least 60 Soviet-built combat aircraft (MiG-17s, MiG-19s, and MiG-21s); and about 14 aging light coastal patrol craft of Soviet, Portuguese, and Dutch origin.

**Major Military Suppliers:** No known domestic arms industry; most military matériel supplied by Soviet Union and Eastern Europe; some weapons left behind by Portuguese taken over by FPLM. Training and advisory assistance provided by Soviet Union, East European countries, African front-line states (see Glossary), Democratic People's Republic of Korea (North Korea), China, Cuba, and Portugal.

**Defense Spending:** In 1982 Ministry of Defense budget equivalent of US$177.4 million, approximately 29 percent of total government expenditures.

**Internal Security Forces:** National Service of People's Security (Serviço Nacional de Segurança Popular—SNASP) of approximately 1,500 men and women acted as secret police agency in matters of internal security; aided in surveillance and intelligence gathering by units of People's Vigilance Groups, numbering about 300,000. People's Police of Mozambique (Polícia Popular de Moçambique—PPM), smaller than SNASP but of unknown personnel strength, responsible for public order in urban centers.

**Military Treaties:** Twenty-year treaty of friendship and cooperation, containing standard military commitment clause, signed with Soviet Union in 1977; Nkomati accord, defining nonaggression pact with South Africa, signed in March 1984.

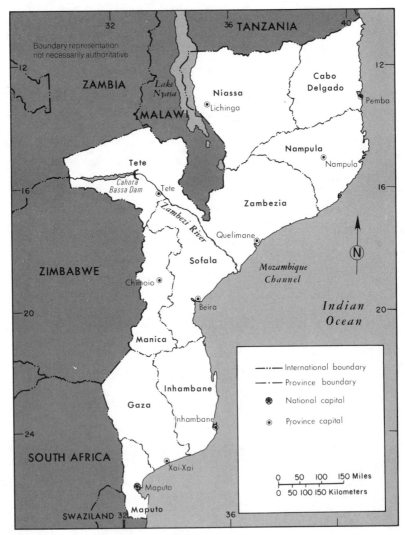

Figure 1. Mozambique, 1984

# Introduction

UNLIKE MOST AFRICAN countries whose independence from foreign domination in the twentieth century has provided an opportunity for national development, Mozambique has remained an international battleground. Gone are the Portuguese administrators and troops who controlled, intimidated, and exploited this southern African territory before it gained sovereign status in mid-1975; but success achieved in the decade-long struggle for freedom has not yet brought all the rewards envisioned by the victors. Instead, foreign influence and pressure from other sources have replaced the authority once wielded by the Portuguese, and Mozambique's independent government is mired down in an effort to combat and control a persistent insurgency that increasingly has threatened the political and economic stability of the young nation.

The problems that have beset Mozambicans cannot be attributed solely to colonial legacy, although many of them had their genesis in that long-lasting experience. Of undeniable significance has been the country's strategic location, vast coastline, and good ports on the Indian Ocean (see fig. 1). Much of the restricting disarray has resulted from efforts to deal with the aftermath of the pre-1975 relationships with its powerful white supremacist neighbors: South Africa and the breakaway British colony of Southern Rhodesia, which did not become black-ruled Zimbabwe until early 1980.

During the Portuguese colonial era in southern Africa, Mozambique and Angola, its fellow colony on the opposite side of the continent, played an important role as buffer territories in the so-called white redoubt, an area where white minority regimes stood shoulder to shoulder in defiance of the pressing demands for majority rule by numerically preponderant black populations. During that time Portugal itself was a developing country that faced great domestic distress. Lisbon's determined interest in preserving its African holdings was largely one of economics, a situation that found the metropolitan government exploiting its colonial possessions to the extent of declaring them "overseas provinces" that were officially designated integral parts of the European motherland. The faltering Portuguese economy thus reaped profit from the African colonies' productive output, which, in exchange for the buffer role against a rising tide of anticolonialism among black-ruled countries, was subsidized to a great extent by South Africa. Until 1975 it was not uncommon to see signs in Mozambique's capital city of Lourenço Marques (present-day Maputo) that declared "Here is Portugal." But as one observer has pointed out, they should more appropriately have read, "Here is South Africa."

Portugal's economy was perennially too weak to develop Mozambique's vast potential, and none of Lisbon's series of governing regimes really attempted to do so. Instead, they remained content to take whatever economic fallout they could from the territory while permitting it to become increasingly dependent on its wealthier white-ruled neighbors. That dependence rested in part on the existence of rail transportation links between South Africa and landlocked Southern Rhodesia on the one hand and Mozambique's Indian Ocean ports on the other, a system that proved lucrative for the colonial administration but was developed largely with South African assistance to serve that country's needs. The focus on transportation links that served South Africa's rich Witwatersrand mining region and Southern Rhodesia's need for surface connections with the outside world led to a failure to construct domestic transport routes running northward in Mozambique, a shortcoming that militated against a sense of unity within the colony—and one that had yet to be overcome in 1984.

Moreover, Mozambique had long relied on South Africa for imports of food, consumer goods, oil, and raw materials, and its struggling economy was heavily dependent on that wealthy southern neighbor for foreign exchange earnings. Much of this capital came from the large quantity of mineral and other commodity exports shipped over the rail line from the South African province of Transvaal to the port at Lourenço Marques as well as from the smaller shipments of petroleum products and spare parts arriving there on the way to South Africa. Technical assistance was provided by South Africans to keep the rail line and port operating for the mutual benefit of both parties.

Other economic ties established during the colonial era were also of significance. One dating from the early twentieth century involved the use of large numbers of Mozambican migrant laborers in South African gold mines. Under a formal arrangement, the Portuguese government received a substantial portion of the workers' wages in gold at the official rate and then paid the migrant laborers in local currency, retaining the gold for its own uses. This pattern persisted after the price of the precious metal on the world market far exceeded the official rate, enabling the

Portuguese—and the independent Mozambican government for awhile—to profit from the difference.

Still another link established with South Africa in the 1970s was the giant hydroelectric complex at Cahora Bassa on the Zambezi River. Constructed by a consortium organized and financed with major assistance from the government in Pretoria, the facility—the world's fourth largest—operated under Portuguese control to provide electric power primarily for South Africa, which sold some of it back to users in southern Mozambique, particularly the capital city.

Of equal economic importance to the Portuguese administration was Mozambique's attraction as a pleasurable tourist haven for white South Africans seeking respite from the stern rules imposed at home by their confining apartheid system. South African and Rhodesian whites flocked to relax at the seaside resorts, and the Portuguese reaped the profit. All considered, Mozambique was often described as a service economy for these two neighboring countries.

The government that came to power when Mozambique achieved independence on June 25, 1975, was controlled by the leaders of a movement known as the Front for the Liberation of Mozambique (Frente de Libertação de Moçambique—FRELIMO), which had long engaged in guerrilla warfare against Portuguese rule. Samora Moises Machel, head of the movement that had been transformed into the new republic's sole political party, became the first president. The country the Machel government inherited, however, was one of the poorest and least developed in Africa. The mass of its people were illiterate, lacked modern skills, and had never achieved a sense of national unity. Moreover, the new government inherited a colonial economy, one based essentially on agriculture that had been developed to supply cheap raw materials to Portugal and a small domestic market that had served as an outlet for Portuguese-manufactured products.

The kind of economic policies pursued during the colonial era had neglected domestic development, notably in the rural African sector. Relatively little had been done to exploit the country's mineral resources or to create an infrastructure that would support a relatively self-sufficient, integrated economic system capable of absorbing a growing population into productive employment. On the contrary, the nature of the colonial economy, the related social objectives of such an economy, and the Portuguese government's regulatory control and fiscal activities tended on balance to retard such development. The domestic economy was very limited, and few Africans had been provided the opportunity to acquire technical skills or managerial experience.

In contrast with the sanguine expectations expressed in 1972–73, the country on the eve of independence faced grave economic problems, epitomized by the estimate made by the transition government that Mozambique would have at its disposal only enough foreign exchange to cover the cost of one week's supply of vital imports. The financial crisis deepened after national sovereignty was proclaimed. By the end of 1976 only a few thousands of the former population of 250,000 white Portuguese remained. The hordes who left took with them vitally needed skills, and a massive flight of capital preceded them.

The political changes that occurred when the liberation movement came to power had a profound effect on southern Africa. Early in FRELIMO's history as an anticolonial movement, its leaders had espoused socialism as an integral part of their doctrine, and in time they proclaimed themselves Marxist-Leninists. The expressed goals and attitudes of the common people and much of the party cadre, however, were populist and nationalist. After instituting its hold on national authority, FRELIMO adopted rhetoric and actions that were dominated by two themes: an intention to establish a society guided by the principles of "scientific socialism" and an avowed commitment to engage actively in the elimination of white minority regimes in southern Africa. This stance attracted international interest, particularly in view of the socialist ventures on the continent that had faltered during the 1960s and the trouble Tanzania had undergone with a similar experiment in the early 1970s. Mozambique thus became something of a bellwether when it announced that it would be Africa's first Marxist state. Its measure of success—or failure—was expected to have a marked impact on the future of socialism in Africa.

The reaction from white-ruled neighboring countries was both immediate and predictable. As long as Portugal had exercised colonial control over Mozambique, the white-minority regime of Ian Smith in Southern Rhodesia had visualized itself as a defender of the white redoubt against both Marxism and radical black nationalism. When their eastern neighbor abandoned its buffer role in that region of the privileged few and announced its Marxist conversion, the Rhodesians were faced with the reality of a new enemy. The confrontation between the two antagonists began with Mozambique providing a haven and launching point for guerrilla operations against the Smith regime, particularly by the Zimbabwe African National Liberation Army (ZANLA), the military arm of Robert Mugabe's Zimbabwe African National

Union (ZANU). The lengthy and thinly populated border area enabled ZANLA forces to expand their operations, and for a time Mozamibican territory provided a shelter for the guerrillas as well as for growing numbers of civilian refugees seeking to escape the fighting. But Mozambique's strained economy was ill-prepared to absorb this added burden, and the situation was exacerbated when Rhodesian forces not only pursued ZANLA guerrillas across the border and sought to destroy their camps but also attacked the villages of civilian refugees and launched strikes against Mozambican facilities. In March 1976 Machel ordered his country's border with the western neighbor closed, seizing valuable Rhodesian rolling stock and cutting off access to the ports of Maputo and Beira, which left the Rhodesians without surface links to the outside world except over the longer and more expensive rail and road routes to ports in South Africa.

The Smith regime responded through the concerted action of its Central Intelligence Organization (CIO) and sympathetic Portuguese who had fled Mozambique before its independence. To gather information on ZANU and its guerrilla army that was infiltrating Southern Rhodesia, the CIO established and supplied a group of Mozambicans who had become dissastisfied with the Machel government and were resentful of its Marxist ideology and actions. Operating from bases on the Rhodesian side of the border, the group was well supplied by the Smith regime with weapons and other gear, including radio equipment with which to broadcast anti-FRELIMO appeals to Mozambicans. The CIO benefited from the effort, and the infiltrators capitalized on an opportunity to create disaffection among rural countrymen. Before long, what had started as a clandestine intelligence operation to aid Southern Rhodesia had blossomed into a nascent insurgency by a growing band of dissidents that proclaimed itself the Mozambican National Resistance (Resistência Nacional Moçambicana—RNM).

Most of the insurgents' hit-and-run operations during this period were limited to the provinces adjacent to the 600-kilometer border separating Mozambique and Southern Rhodesia. Many of them were directed against the so-called reeducation camps the Machel government had established to provide political indoctrination for recalcitrant citizens. The camps' spartan conditions and grim disregard for human rights made then natural targets for the RNM and its disaffection campaign. Eventually, the movement—also known in some circles as RENAMO—mounted raids against the republic's vulnerable rail, road, power, and communications lines as well as the state farms and communal villages that had been established by FRELIMO to cope with development needs. The international media referred to the situation as Mozambique's "hidden war," but Machel and his government refused to give the RNM recognition, calling its actions merely those of "armed bandits."

When Smith's white-ruled Southern Rhodesia was transformed into black-ruled Zimbabwe under Mugabe in April 1980, the RNM's support base for operations and training was shifted to South Africa. The government in Pretoria, which had provided some clandestine assistance during the RNM's Rhodesian phase, willingly assumed responsibility for the insurgents' continued activity. At stake was the need to halt attacks against South Africa's apartheid system by black nationalists of the African National Congress (ANC). Mozambique's role as a safe haven for ANC forces was well-known to the South Africans, and Pretoria's backing of the RNM was recognized as a ready instrument for retaliatory pressure against Machel and his Marxist compatriots.

Since Mozambican independence, the Pretoria regime had exerted great pressure on the economic front. By 1977 South Africa's annual requirement for Mozambican laborers in the mines was reduced from more than 100,000 men to about 40,000, and in 1978 the lucrative payments in gold calculated at the official rate for the workers' services previously sent to the government in Maputo were discontinued. Lost revenues equivalent to US$2.6 billion that resulted from this action were about twice the amount Mozambique had borrowed from international lending institutions to shore up its sagging economy. In addition, South Africans steadily reduced their use of Mozambican rail and port facilities by roughly 9 million tons a year. The profitable tourist trade once provided by the southern neighbor virtually dried up.

But the undeclared war by force of arms took an even greater toll on the Machel government's precarious position. By 1984 the insurgents were active in all of the country's 10 provinces. Their strength had grown to about 12,000 combatants, and efforts to contain their activity had occupied the attention of most of the government's armed forces. To the damage inflicted by the RNM, superior South African strike forces added sporadic attacks in retaliation for ANC-sponsored violence in South Africa. During 1982–84 the cost to the Mozambican government of all military action was roughly equivalent to the total value of the country's exports, and the external debt was mounting. The price in human terms throughout the countryside was even more telling. The RNM in many cases took advantage of FRELIMO's inability to protect and respond to the common people's needs, and the insurgents won sympathetic reaction to whatever stop-gap measures they employed to win converts to their cause. Hunger thus became a ready ally.

In a country where nearly 90 percent of its 13.1 million people were dependent on agriculture for a living, the government's attempt to install a Marxist system had not succeeded, and many mistakes had been made. Without a strong industrial base upon which to build, "scientific socialism" had little meaning for hungry Mozambicans. Nature also had not looked favorably on the experiment. A drought-induced famine that persisted in much of the country throughout the early and mid-1980s brought death by starvation to many thousands and threatened millions more. Debilitating diseases followed, and hordes of Mozambicans fleeing the drought sought refuge in Zimbabwe in ever-increasing numbers. In other areas a violent cyclone played havoc with agricultural crops, inundated villages, and destroyed elements of the transport infrastructure. In early 1984 many knowledgeable observers felt that the republic was on the verge of economic collapse.

In the face of this disarry, Machel's stance became more pragmatic and less doctrinaire. Realizing that his country's burdened economy required heroic life-saving measures, he made overtures to Western nations for assistance. Some aid was forthcoming but not in the vast amounts that were necessary. Foreign investment that could underpin the stricken republic's development needs largely were stalled by the insurgency and its threat to political stability.

More in desperation than because of a change of heart, Machel was compelled to make a deal with the neighboring country whose apartheid system he had so long opposed. Having few alternatives, his government entered into a far-reaching nonaggression pact with South Africa, an agreement known to the world as the Nkomati accord. Signed on March 16, 1984, the accord was formulated and negotiated with the quiet encouragement of the United States and has been hailed as both a diplomatic triumph and a solution to the unrest in southern Africa. Others have insisted that the agreement simply reflected Mozambique's desperate economic status. At the most basic level, the accord has meant that Mozambicans must cease their support of the ANC's terrorist actions against South Africa and that, in turn, South Africans must refrain from aiding and abetting the RNM's insurgency against Mozambique. Economic cooperation was also envisaged in the agreement.

The Machel government expects the security pact to lead to

new agreements on trade, energy exchange, and tourism as well as increased South African investment in, and use of, Mozambican ports and rail facilities. But the potential relief from economic chaos has its price, and that cost could create other problems for the Machel regime. In exchange for the relaxation it so badly needs on the military front, Mozambique must face the likelihood of becoming once again a service sector for South Africa. This stance could alienate other black-ruled front-line states (see Glossary) and weaken their concerted efforts to reduce economic dependence on South Africa and to hasten the advent of majority rule there.

In the first six months after the conclusion of the Nkomati accord, the insurgency in Mozambique presisted. A number of observers attributed the continuing military action to the level of supplies that had been amassed by the RNM in anticipation of the nonagression agreement between the governments in Maputo and Pretoria. Consultations between those two regimes explored the destabilizing effect of the ongoing insurgency, and meetings between Mozambican officials and RNM representatives were arranged with South African assistance. On October 3, 1984, Roelof F. ("Pik") Botha, South Africa's foreign minister, announced an accord between the two contending Mozambican factions in which the RNM had recognized Machel's authority and had agreed in principle to negotiate an end to the eight-year-old war.

But the road to peace was to be a bumpy one. In mid-October the Mozambican Council of Ministers called for a rapid and unambiguous implementation of the South African-brokered cease-fire agreement in order to allow the objectives of the Nkomati accord to be achieved. An early RNM hope for a coalition government in Maputo apparently had been ruled out by Machel's negotiators, and the question of how to accommodate the ambitions of the insurgents and their leaders after a cease-fire was still unresolved. As charges and countercharges were hurled by both sides, the negotiations in Pretoria assumed an on-again-off-again pace. Meanwhile, in Mozambique the fighting intensified. As October drew to a close, reconciliation with the insurgents and an end to the costly "hidden war" remained elusive.

Regardless of the outcome, in late 1984 the future of "scientific socialism" in Marxist-led Mozambique appeared to be undergoing significant modifications. The foothold established there by the Soviet Union when the Portuguese colonial empire collapsed in 1975 had deteriorated to more of a toehold. Despite Moscow's importance as a supplier of military matériel and training that had backed FRELIMO's armed forces, the situation had become more complicated. Mozambique's changing needs were more economic than military, and the Kremlin appeared unwilling—or unable, perhaps—to respond favorably. That, too, represented something of a respite for South Africa—and the Western world.

October 1984

Harold D. Nelson

# Chapter 1.    Historical Setting

VASCO DA GAMA

*Statue of Vasco da Gama on Ilha de Moçambique*

MOZAMBIQUE'S HISTORICAL DEVELOPMENT has to a large extent been conditioned by geography. The country is divided laterally into three regions—the north, the Zambezi River basin, and the south—each of which is historically differentiated. Consequently, piecing together Mozambique's past entails the consideration of several parallel regional histories and the study of groups active in them at different times. Each region's history was marked by the migrations of Bantu-speaking peoples who coalesced into distinct but often shifting ethnic clusters. There was no other unifying factor in Mozambique's history in the precolonial period, and the separate histories of the country's regions are more closely shared with those of neighboring nations than they are with one another.

The common theme found in Mozambique's history during the colonial period was the extension of Portuguese commercial and political influence in the interior with the cooperation of some African groups and against the resistance of others. Colonial policy deliberately discouraged the development of a comprehensive African identity in Mozambique. Many Portuguese saw their presence bestowing a civilizing influence on backward peoples, a mystique that gave them a mission apart from economic interests in defending their position in Africa. This apparently benevolent attitude was belied by a record of brutal exploitation and the treatment and policies that relegated all but the small number of Africans who chose to assimilate Portuguese values to a status of inferiority in their own country.

As early as the eighth century A.D., Mozambique's coast had attracted Arab merchants who established permanent settlements there and traded with Africans in the interior for ivory, gold, and slaves. The Portuguese navigator Vasco da Gama made landfall on the same coast in 1498 during his first passage to India. Nine years later, other Portuguese occupied the Muslim settlement on the Ilha de Moçambique, initiating a presence in that part of Africa that would last more than four and one-half centuries. The island's name, which is conjectured to have been derived from Musa al Biq, an Arab shaykh who once ruled there, was eventually applied to the territory for which it became the administrative center. The Portuguese enclaves in Mozambique formed part of an expansive maritime empire. Gold from mines on the Zimbabwe plateau was brought by traders to the coast and transferred to India, where it was used to purchase the spices that were the source of Portugal's prosperity in the sixteenth century. But in Mozambique the Portuguese sought the advantage of empire without assuming the burdens, preferring to let out responsibility for defending and administering its sphere of influence to African allies, to tenants of the Portuguese crown settled on great estates, and in the nineteenth century to chartered companies. It was only in the twentieth century that Portugal succeeded in making good its historical claims in Mozambique and began to exert effective control over the country's interior regions. Even then, African discontent over the excesses of colonial rule, exemplified by the forced recruiting of labor, boiled over into serious rebellion. The authoritarian regime of Portuguese prime minister António de Oliveira Salazar inaugurated a policy in the 1930s of integrating the economies of Portugal and its overseas territories, centralizing colonial administration in Lisbon, and encouraging settlement in Mozambique by Europeans.

Portugal refused to follow other European powers in the gradual withdrawal from their colonial empires in Sub-Saharan Africa in the 1950s and 1960s. The demand for self-determination in Mozambique had been slow in emerging. Movements opposing continued Portuguese rule came together in the 1960s, however, under the Marxist-oriented Front for the Liberation of Mozambique, which initiated a war of liberation to force Portugal to relinquish colonial control. The Portuguese departure, when it came, however, resulted from the military coup in Portugal that overthrew the government there in April 1974 rather than from the liberation front's limited but strategically important successes in Mozambique.

Mozambique became fully independent on June 25, 1975, and the liberation front's leader, Samora Moises Machel, assumed the presidency of the one-party state. He and a small group of close associates were dedicated, in Machel's words, to making Mozambique "the first fully Marxist state in Africa," but among the important tasks confronting the regime was to promote the kind of national consciousness that history had largely denied the country. Although continuing to stress Marxist-Leninist ideology, Machel would demonstrate himself to be both pragmatic and flexible in the years after independence.

## Precolonial History

Because the precolonial period in Mozambique's history did not terminate at the same date in all parts of the country, the term *precolonial* refers to the period in any given area before the establishment of steady, significant interaction between its African population and the Portuguese. Because the Portuguese presence in Mozambique, which dates from the beginning of the sixteenth century, was confined for nearly four centuries to the coast and lower Zambezi valley, other parts of the country remained free of direct colonial influence—in many cases until the early twentieth century.

Archaeological projects undertaken since independence promise to shed more light on the history of the African peoples of Mozambique before the arrival of the Portuguese, but the record of the precolonial period still must be sought primarily in Arab chronicles, reports of European visitors, oral traditions, and linguistic evidence, or inferred from archaeology in neighboring countries. Serious gaps remain, leading to widely conflicting interpretations.

### Early Population Movements

Bushmanoid hunters and gatherers, ancestors of the Khoisani peoples, were probably the only inhabitants of the area included in modern Mozambique until the arrival of the first Bantu-speaking peoples sometime before the fourth century A.D. Their small nomadic bands were eventually displaced or absorbed by the steady southward and eastward migrations of the ironworking Bantu speakers, whose sedentary agricultural communities took root in most parts of Mozambique over the next several hundred years. New Bantu-speaking migrants and invaders continued to enter the region well into the nineteenth century, constantly modifying patterns of settlement. The movements of African peoples are difficult to chart, however, before the sixteenth century, when the Portuguese had established a presence on the coast of Mozambique (see fig. 2).

The Maravi (or Malawi), for instance, were first mentioned by Portuguese sources as occupying the land between the Luangua and Shire rivers north of the Zambezi. Evidence suggests that these Maravi were a warrior elite whose ancestors had expanded out of the Shaba region (in present-day Zaïre) in the fourteenth century and established hegemony over a broad area west of Lake Nyasa in present-day Malawi and Zambia. Their paramount chief controlled the ivory trade north of the Zambezi with Arab merchants who carried the tusks downriver to the Indian Ocean ports.

During the period that corresponded with successful Portuguese efforts to supplant the Arabs along the Zambezi, several Maravi tributary states were established along its northern bank

5

in the Tete area and in the Shire River valley. These kingdoms, as they evolved, were decentralized and easily subject to fragmentation. According to their traditions, the Maravi were the first of their kind to come into the region, but this assertion appears to have been made to give force to their claim to the land of earlier Bantu inhabitants, like the ancestors of the Macua-Lomue people, whom they either subjugated or drove before them.

The Macua-Lomue were composed of a number of different groups that had probably lived in the Zambezi region since before the tenth century. Their basic unit of social organization was the clan, and there was no political unit among them larger than the individual village, governed by a chief and a council of elders. Later, under pressure from the Maravi, the Macua in some instances formed confederations of chiefdoms, some of which were initiated by the sixteenth-century Maravi overlords from whom many Macua chiefs still trace their lines.

Farther to the north, the Maconde lived in isolation and were spared contact with the Arabs and, until the nineteenth century, with the Portuguese. By contrast, the Yao extended their range southward from the Lake Nyasa region in the eighteenth century to take better advantage of the ivory and slave trade with the Arabs. In part to counter advancing Portuguese influence, the Yao converted to Islam in the late nineteenth century.

On the Zambezi's south bank below Tete were the Tonga. Their history in the precolonial period is obscure, but the groups to which the name was applied do not appear to have constituted a homogeneous ethnic cluster at that time. The name itself denoted a conquered or subject people, a condition reflected in their political structure. The Tonga chieftaincy was confined to members of the Chilendje clan, which is believed to have been descended from a warrior elite that invaded the region and imposed its rule on an ethnically unrelated population. Between the Zambezi basin and the Limpopo River lay lands first settled in the tenth and eleventh centuries by the Shona-speaking peoples, whose range eventually extended west to east from the Kalahari Desert across the Zimbabwe plateau to the sea. In Mozambique their history is inextricably bound with that of the Shona dynastic states, which in the sixteenth and seventeenth centuries extended their control or influence over much of the Zambezi basin region (see The Shona Dynasties, this ch.).

Three major groups—the Tonga (to be distinguished from the Tonga of the Zambezi basin), the Chopi, and the Tsonga— were formed in the region south of the Búzi and Revuè rivers

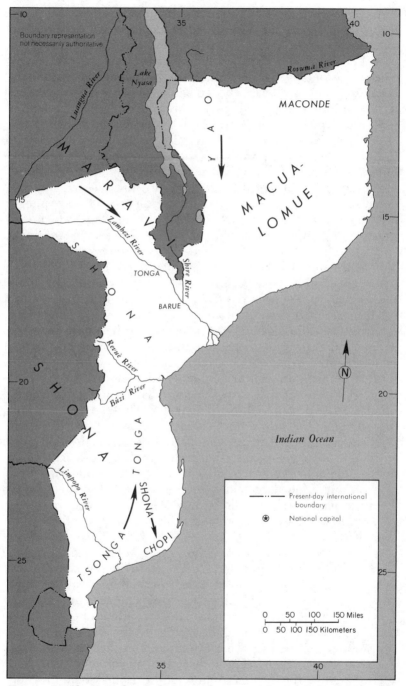

*Figure 2. The Peopling of Mozambique in the Precolonial Period*

through a process of migration and assimilation that may have begun as early as the fourth century and continued into the nineteenth century. Both the Tonga and the Tsonga originated from lineage groups that had detached themselves from larger clusters belonging to the Southeast Bantu linguistic group in Natal and the Transvaal. The Tonga knew of no larger political unit than the village-sized chiefdom but nonetheless carried on well-organized commerce with Arab traders on the coast.

At some point during the fifteenth century, the Tonga living in the coastal region north of the Limpopo were conquered by Shona warriors, who intermarried with them. Shona customs, including veneration of their god, Mwari, prevailed among the newly integrated population and, in deference to the newcomers, the Shona-Tonga community rejected circumcision, which was practiced by other Tonga. During the next century, several sizable and relatively powerful chiefdoms appeared in the area.

As a result of internal stresses, possibly associated with land inheritance, some lineage groups—later known collectively as the Tsonga—broke from the main body of the Sotho people during the seventeenth century and either were forcibly expelled or struck out to find an independent existence in a new location. Although they favored the highland areas in the interior for settlement, Tsonga expansion in southern Mozambique continued until the eighteenth century, when it was stemmed by the Portuguese. Pressure on their own western flank from the Sotho and others fostered statebuilding among the Tsonga to consolidate manpower and ensure a more effective defense. Likewise, their political and military organization gave the Tsonga a decided edge in their campaigns against the Tonga. Following a pattern of events similar to that which had led the Tsonga to undertake their original migration, larger lineage groups tended to break away from the main group to which they were attached in southern Mozambique, conquering new land for settlement and creating separate chiefdoms.

In the northern portion of the areas that they occupied, the Tsonga completely assimilated the Tonga. In the south, however, Tsonga language and customs were imposed on a substructure that remained essentially Tonga. The Tonga escaped total absorption and survived in some areas as a distinct ethnic cluster largely because of the protection given them by the Portuguese (see Mozambique in the Eighteenth Century, this ch.). As among the Zambezi Tonga, their name indicated a subservient status and was applied by the Tsonga to those of the group whom they did not absorb.

8

Around the year 1700 the Tsonga intruded into the Shona-Tonga region. Their warriors, however, like the Shona before them, merged into the much larger existing population, introducing in the process their cult of witchcraft and reviving the practice of circumcision. It was the Tsonga-influenced Shona-Tonga who became known as the Chopi, southern Mozambique's third major ethnic group. In alliance with the Portuguese, the Chopi resisted further Tsonga expansion in the region.

### The Arabs and the Swahili Coast

References in medieval Arab documents, confirmed by archaeological evidence, indicate that Muslim traders had set up outposts on the coast of East Africa as early as the eighth century. Other settlements founded by Arab and Persian merchant princes are traced to the tenth and eleventh centuries. These towns, stretching from the Benadir coast in Somalia to Sofala in Mozambique, became links in an extensive commercial network connecting East Africa with Southwest Asia and the Indies.

Arab traders trekked inland to exchange ceramics, cloth, glass, beads, salt, and metal goods, including weapons, for gold, palm oil, rhinoceros horn, and the most sought-after commodity, ivory. They concluded treaties with African chiefs, sometimes offering military assistance in exchange for guarantees of an unhindered flow of goods. Two principal routes were developed to the interior—one up the Zambezi and the other, more important, route leading inland from Sofala. Arab vessels also made regular trading expeditions to Delagoa Bay. Goods acquired in trade were collected in warehouses in Sofala and then transported to Kilwa (in present-day Tanzania), the hub of Arab trade in East Africa, from where they were shipped to their destinations overseas, usually in India.

Although the sultan of Kilwa exercised a loose hegemony over the Arab towns and theoretically held a monopoly over their trade, they gradually developed as autonomous sultanates and shaykhdoms, competing fiercely for a larger share of the region's commerce. Tradition held that the five towns on the northern Mozambique coast—Moçambique, Sancul, Sangage, Angoche, and Quelimane—were founded by exiles from Kilwa in the late fifteenth century to escape the sultan's monopoly, but they almost certainly would have been based on earlier Arab settlements on those sites. The coral reefs, sandbars, and mangrove swamps along the coastline also made it an ideal location for smuggling and piracy.

A major step in expanding trade in the interior was taken in the fifteenth century, when fairs were first held at permanent depots established along the Zambezi and other important rivers inland as far away as Mashonaland in present-day Zimbabwe. Large quantities of ivory and gold leaf were brought to the nearest fair by the Maravi or Shona at appointed times and exchanged for the goods stored by Arab traders in the depots. The fairs also proved advantageous for African rulers, who could thereby control their end of the trade and levy taxes on tusks and gold sold to the traders.

Over time, a distinctive Islamic culture resulted in the coastal region from contacts, including intermarriage, between Arab settlers and Africans. Physical and cultural integration were accompanied by the evolution of the Swahili (from the Arabic word meaning "coastal") language, which served as the lingua franca of the East African littoral, as well as becoming the mother tongue of the mixed Arab-African population.

### The Shona Dynasties

By the eleventh century a clan of the Karanga cluster had achieved ascendancy over a loose confederation of Shona chiefdoms. The clan's prominence was based not only on its military prowess and accumulated wealth in cattle but also on the reputation of its priests as oracles of the spirit world. A king chosen from the clan led the confederacy's military elite in battle and was entitled to collect tribute from subject groups. He symbolized the unity of the Shona people through the royal cult of Mwari, the creator and the sustainer of life.

The center of the royal clan's influence was at Great Zimbabwe, a vast walled complex near the city of Masvingo in present-day Zimbabwe. More than 150 *madzimbabwe* (stone enclosures; sing., *zimbabwe*) of this kind were constructed by the Shona over a period of several centuries in Mozambique and Zimbabwe as administrative centers, markets, and religious shrines. The stone enclosures were also utilized as assembly points for the military expeditions and as corrals for cattle collected by them in tribute from subject groups. The quantities of glassware, ceramics, and other luxury items imported by the Arabs in exchange for ivory and gold were intended for conspicuous consumption by the royal court and the elite of the *madzimbabwe*, but wealth and status were determined by the size of a chief's herd and retinue of dependents.

In the fourteenth century, the Mbire, a lineage that provided hereditary priests of the royal cult, established themselves as paramount chiefs (*vamambo;* sing., *mambo*) in the region around Great Zimbabwe. About 1450 Nyatsimba Mutota, a *mambo* of that line, ordered the removal of the royal court from its traditional seat and led his warriors toward the Zambezi, bringing the river's upper basin and the northern plateau under his control. He commemorated the conquest by taking the title *munhumutapa* (pillager), which was passed on to his successors and adopted as the name of his dynasty and the kingdom its members ruled. Mutota may have abandoned Great Zimbabwe because diminishing resources in the area were inadequate to support its large population, estimated to have exceeded 20,000, but the move northward to the Zambezi also allowed him to take greater advantage of opportunities for trade. His son, Matope Nyanyenwe, subdued most of central Mozambique, extending Munhumutapa dominion southward to the Save River, but he and his successors exhibited little interest in exerting direct political control over so broad an area. Their empire was decentralized; the territory of the various groups owing allegiance to the Munhumutapa was divided into a number of tributary kingdoms governed by chosen members of the royal clan or court favorites who exercised almost complete political autonomy. They were bound to the Munhumutapa, however, by fealty derived from the royal cult and by carefully monitored economic arrangements.

A tributary king's authority to rule, for instance, was symbolized by a flame kindled at the royal court and bestowed on him by the Munhumutapa. When a vassal died, the fire that burned at his court was extinguished, and a new flame was brought from the Munhumutapa for his successor. The tributary's primary duty to his nominal sovereign, however, was to act as the Munhumutapa's commercial agent and enforce the royal monopoly on trade. Ivory and gold, as well as cattle and grain, it was said, were gifts of Mwari and could only be exchanged or used with the approval of the god's representative, the Munhumutapa. It was by religious sanction, therefore, rather than by right of conquest or political sovereignty that the Munhumutapa could claim a monopoly on trade. A percentage of the tusks brought to the fairs was paid as a tax into the royal warehouses. The gold put on the market, usually in the form of leaf, was extracted from royal mines. All transactions with the traders from the coast were carried out by royal agents, and all imported goods were distributed by them at the Munhumutapa's direction. Likewise, it was the Munhumutapa who, for a price, granted the concessions required by the merchants to engage in trade within his empire. He was also responsible for regulating the weights and measures used at the fairs and determined the price of commodities traded there.

When he left Great Zimbabwe, Mutota had entrusted the

Karanga heartland, which included the sacred enclosure, to Changa, one of his chieftains. Changa's dynasty, called the Changamire (in an adaptation of the Arabic title amir, or prince), competed successfully with rival branches of the royal clan and extended its dominions, eventually to the point of challenging the Munhumutapa. The Changamire kingdom, like its predecessor, was a confederation of tribute-paying territories ruled by chieftains related to the royal lineage.

In 1490 Changa captured the *zimbabwe* of the Munhumutapa, Mukombero, and had him put to death. Changa, in his turn, was killed several years later in fighting with Mukombero's son, Chikuyo Chisamarengu, who had claimed his father's title. Hostilities between the two Shona dynasties continued under Changa's successor, who tried to alienate tributary kings from their allegiance to the Munhumutapa and disengage the kingdoms in central Mozambique from his empire. As a consequence, civil war became endemic in that region, allowing rulers like the Mokombe of Barue to assert their independence. The Munhumutapa, in the meantime, concentrated on protecting their trade with the Arabs and with the newly arrived Portuguese.

## Portuguese Hegemony

In its origins, Portugal's overseas expansion in the fifteenth and sixteenth centuries was a direct extension of the Christian reconquest of Spain from the Moors. In 1415 Portuguese knights had undertaken the first of many campaigns in Morocco that was considered a necessary preliminary to the final assault on Granada, the remaining Muslim bastion in Spain that was reinforced from Morocco. Plans were also discussed for linking with the fabled Christian kingdom of Prester John, supposedly located on the far side of Africa, to attack the Moors from the rear. In the process the Portuguese intended to open a new passage to the Indies, break the Muslim monopoly on the spice trade, and gain access to the African gold fields, which they had learned of from Arab sources and identified as the mines of King Solomon mentioned in the Bible. Some of the same crusading zeal that had gone into fighting the Moors was transferred to this new enterprise.

### The Passage to India
New discoveries followed close upon one another as Portuguese navigators moved systematically down the West African coast. In 1487 Bartolomeu Dias reached the Cape of Good Hope,

but a decade went by before another expedition was outfitted to complete the eastern passage to India around the southern reaches of Africa. Late in 1497 Vasco da Gama rounded the Cape of Good Hope with a small fleet and early the next year dropped anchor in Delagoa Bay. Proceeding up the coast, his ships stopped at the Muslim town of Moçambique. The Portuguese were impressed by the houses, harbor facilities, and ships they found there, but after an altercation with the local shaykh, they turned their guns on the town and bombarded it. The same fate awaited Mombasa some weeks later. After stopping at Malindi, da Gama sailed across the Indian Ocean to the Malabar coast of India, completing a 15,000-kilometer voyage that proved the feasibility of the eastern route.

After the first successful passage, Portuguese expeditions were sent out to India on a regular schedule. In 1500 Pedro Alvares da Cabral's outbound fleet was blown off course and made landfall in Brazil. Reporting the discovery, he continued to his original destination. On the return voyage, some of Cabral's ships called at Sofala, where inquiries were made about the gold trade with the Munhumutapa.

### The Portuguese on the Swahili Coast

On the basis of prospects opened up by da Gama and Cabral, the Portuguese determined to seize control of the Indian Ocean trade from the Arabs. In a series of decisive engagements, da Gama and other Portuguese commanders within a few years had swept Muslim fleets from the sea, ensuring Portuguese naval supremacy in the region for almost 100 years. A string of military strong points and commercial depots was constructed to protect the developing trade network and secure the lines of communications back to Portugal. In 1505 Francisco de Almeida was dispatched from Portugal to subdue the Swahili coast and establish bases there. Stopping first at Sofala, Almeida reached an agreement with the shaykh, allowing the Portuguese a share in the gold trade, and left behind a lieutenant to manage a depot where trade goods could be stored for exchanges with the Africans. Some months later, however, the Portuguese took advantage of a dispute with Arab traders to seize the town.

Meanwhile, Almeida sailed up the coast and burned Mombasa, the center of Arab opposition to the Portuguese. News of the attack persuaded the sultan of Kilwa to save his people from a similar fate by paying tribute and opening the port to the Portuguese. Almeida's demonstration of force was complemented by an alliance concluded with the sultan of Malindi, who was the enemy of Mombasa's ruler. In 1507 the Portuguese occupied the Ilha de Moçambique, which became the headquarters for their operations in East Africa. By 1510 they controlled the flow of commerce out of every major port from Sofala to Mogadishu.

Once the Swahili coast had been secured, the Portuguese were able to extend their sphere of influence across the Indian Ocean and beyond. In 1510 Afonso d'Albuquerque arrived as Portuguese viceroy in the East, making Goa in India the seat of his administration. In quick succession he seized Hormuz and Muscat to control the entrance to the Persian Gulf and Malacca to dominate the route to the East Indies. All of these Portuguese outposts, including those on the Swahili coast, were part of the State of India and came under the jurisdiction of the viceroy at Goa. His officers in East Africa, however, exercised considerable discretionary authority. Officials at Moçambique were initially well-connected merchant adventurers commissioned for three years by the Portuguese crown and paid a fixed sum on their departure from Portugal to cover operationg expenses. From this purse, officers met the expense of their garrison, maintained warehouses and harbors, and provisioned ships that laid over in their port. At the end of a term, accounts were settled, and the remainder was remitted to the viceroy. As compensation, the captain kept the income derived from a monopoly granted by the king on certain trading rights in his jurisdiction.

The Portuguese crown exercised monopoly on external trade in this vast maritime empire. Under a licensing system, the crown assumed direct management of trade and took its "royal fifth," or share of the profit, on all chartered commercial ventures. As had the Arab merchants whom they displaced, the Portuguese stored the gold and ivory brought from the interior at the Sofala depot. From Sofala and other ports under Portuguese control, the goods taken in trade were sent to the central depot at Moçambique (as the Arabs had delivered them to Kilwa), and from there they were convoyed annually to Goa, where the ivory and gold were used to purchase spices in the East Indies. Cargoes of this commodity were then shipped to Portugal for marketing in Europe.

Attempts by the Portuguese to trade in the interior consisted for many years of individual efforts carried out by a few adventurous *sertanejos* (backwoodsmen). The depot at Sofala was largely dependent, therefore, on the goods brought to it from the interior by Muslim traders. The Portuguese essentially tried to channel this traffic into routes that were advantageous to their interests. This policy, however, made it all the more profitable for Muslim traders to divert gold and ivory from established routes by offering better terms to the Africans than those of the Portuguese. Muslim settlements that defied the Portuguese monopoly were sacked in retaliation, and several expeditions were conducted in the interior to drive away unauthorized traders. The effects of these measures tended to be short-lived, however, and made enemies of the African chiefs who traded with the Muslims.

Because it combined an excellent harbor situated within closer reach of Indian ports, the settlement of Moçambique proved in the long run to be a better center than Sofala for resupplying ships and for transshipment of cargoes. As administrative center for East Africa, it was also the seat of the Council of the Straits Fleet, which was responsible for regulating maritime activity in the region. In 1552 the Portuguese began construction of the fortress of São Sebastião on the island. Built with granite brought from Portugual, it was intended to symbolize the permanence of the Portuguese presence in East Africa.

Portugal's aim was to control commerce rather than acquire territory, and the State of India was more a business enterprise than a colonial empire, consisting essentially of naval bases and trading depots. In East Africa, however, the Portuguese soon realized that it was necessary to secure access to the sources of trade in the interior, as well as to the outlets on the coast, if they were to eliminate Muslim competition.

### Portuguese Expansion up the Zambezi

The first Portuguese to penetrate deeply into the East African interior was António Fernandes, a *sertanejo* who journeyed up the Zambezi in 1515 and visited at the Munhumutapa's *zimbabwe* in Mashonaland. Their meeting was amicable and led to the establishment of formal Portuguese-Shona trade relations.

Expansion up the Zambezi began in earnest in 1531, when the Munhumutapa awarded the Portuguese concessions at the fairs at Sena and Tete. Permanent depots were set up at these locations that included a church and a stockade, as well as warehouses. In the next few decades, long-established Muslim traders were supplanted at other fairs, putting the Portuguese in an increasingly favorable position upriver (see fig. 3). These fairs continued to be regulated by the Munhumutapa, however, and the movement of the Portuguese beyond them was strictly forbidden, denying the traders direct access to the gold mines. The Portuguese imitated the custom of the Muslim traders in nominating a single officer, the captain of the gates (*capitão dos portas*), to represent their interests and to settle disputes under the law of a particular market. If he approved the nominee, seconded by the

Portuguese captain general at Moçambique, the Munhumutapa conferred authority on him to act in his name. Initially, this authority was exercised only over other Portuguese, but the rule of the captains gave the fairs a stability that encouraged the growth of permanent settlements, and consequently their jurisdiction was extended to cover Africans as well.

In 1561 the Jesuit missionary Gonçalo de Silveira made his way to the Munhumutapa's court, where he introduced Christianity and baptized the Munhumutapa Negomo along with several hundred of his household. Negomo received the Christian name Sebastião in emulation of the reigning king of Portugal. Soon after, however, Muslim traders, in league with soothsayers who had fallen from favor after the Munhumutapa's conversion, appear to have convinced Negomo that the Portuguese priest was a spy seeking to find the location of the gold mines, and they conspired to have him killed.

Silveira's murder was made the pretext for a Portuguese military expedition organized in Lisbon and led up the Zambezi by Francisco Barreto in 1572 to punish the Munhumutapa and seize the gold fields in Mashonaland. Barreto's small army, composed of 600 Portuguese harquebusiers and some African auxiliaries, routed the Shona, estimated by the Portuguese to have numbered 10,000 warriors, in a three-day pitched battle, but Barreto became ill and was unable to proceed to his objective. However, agreements were extracted from Negomo by Barreto and, after his death, by his lieutenant, Vasco Honem, by which the Munhumutapa conceded the supervision of trade at the fairs to the Portuguese captains and also allowed them to undertake mining operations, but still as agents of the Munhumutapa. The Portuguese were also granted special rights for trading and mining in Manicaland, although the Munhumutapa no longer exercised any authority there. In return, the Portuguese pledged to aid him in putting down a revolt by the Tonga and in bringing Manicaland and other rebellious provinces back to their allegiance. Small groups of Portuguese soldiers would thereafter accompany the Munhumutapa's forces on their campaigns. Similar treaties, offering military assistance in exchange for commercial concessions, were concluded with individual chiefs, who like the Munhumutapa became increasingly dependent on Portuguese firepower and Portuguese-led slave armies for their security. Barreto's expedition in 1572, however, would remain the only military effort undertaken by a large number of Portuguese troops in Mozambique until the late nineteenth century.

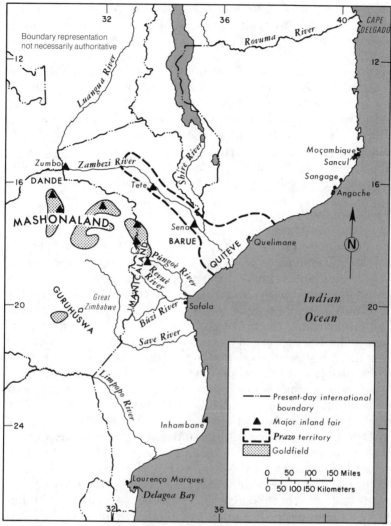

*Figure 3. Portuguese Penetration of the Interior, Sixteenth to Eighteenth Centuries*

Increased political involvement and military intervention in the Munhumutapa kingdom and its tributaries followed directly from the treaty obligations entered into by the Portuguese to protect their trading interests with the Shona. In 1607 Negomo's succeessor, Gatsi Rusere, concluded a treaty with the captain general of Moçambique, turning over all mineral rights in his realm to the Portuguese in recognition of their support for his

claim to the role of Munhumutapa. There were conflicting interpretations of the treaty, however, and when Nyambo Kaparidze,
leader of a rival branch of the royal family, became Munhumutapa
in 1623, he repudiated the agreement made by his predecessor.
In the civil war that followed his accession, Kaparidze was
defeated by his Portuguese and Shona enemies and in 1629 was
deposed in favor of Mavura Mhande, the Portuguese-backed candidate, who accepted the status as vassal of the Portuguese crown.
Not only were Portuguese at the fairs exempted from his law
thereafter, but their captains were also given authority to tax his
African subjects. Furthermore, large tracts of land were put at the
disposal of the crown to distribute to Portuguese settlers.

### The Rise of the Prazos

After the Munhumutapa ceded his title to the land in 1629,
the Portuguese crown granted estates to settlers according to a
semifeudal system of land tenure that pertained in Portugal.
Legally the land remained the property of the crown but was
leased for a fixed period of time, usually three lifetimes with the
possibility of renewal if the terms of the lease had been fulfilled.
During that time, the *prazeros* (lease holders) were expected to
provide for the defense of the property with the income derived
from it. They were also granted the use of the labor from the property's inhabitants, over whom they exercised judicial authority.

Property was acquired in a variety of ways, new methods
evolving as conditions changed. Many prospective *prazeros* were
granted the land of rebel chiefs whom they had to conquer in
order to take possession. Other land was taken from weak chiefs
through intimidation and extortion or was offered to the Portuguese in exchange for the promise of asylum by chiefs defeated
and pursued by the Munhumutapa. Still other *prazos* (leaseholds)
were created to consolidate military alliances against the Munhumutapa's enemies. The *prazos* proliferated in areas in the Zambezi basin where disruption resulting from the civil wars had been
the greatest, but substantial holdings were also located in the
Quelimane area.

By whatever means they obtained land from the African
chiefs, the *prazeros* received with it all their prerogatives and
responsibilities, just as earlier the leaders of conquering African
warrior elites had taken the place of chiefs whom they had
supplanted. In effect, the *prazeros* had become chiefs in their
own right and were accepted as such by their African dependents.

Because the *prazos* siphoned resources while producing
only what was necessary for their own needs, they had a generally

depressing long-term effect on the economy. It was their military function that was most important, the *prazeros* providing the leadership and organization for the slave armies that were Portugal's only means of protecting its interests in the interior and fulfilling its obligations to the Munhumutapa. The Chikunda, as the warrior slaves of the *prazos* were known, were a hereditary caste who guarded the estates and mines, patrolled the trade routes, and were employed as elephant hunters and slave raiders, as well as in the military formations that the *prazeros* kept at their disposal. Continual warfare in the region ensured a constant flow of prisoners as new recruits, while others were donated to the *prazeros* as gifts or were collected in payment for litigation. Much of the servitude for the Chikunda was voluntary, however, as Africans put themselves under the protection of the *prazeros*, especially in times of famine or invasion or to escape capture by slave raiders. In return for their loyalty, they were guaranteed a livelihood and special status. Although bound to servitude, the Chikunda were not a subservient class, and they could pose a threat to any *prazero* who abused his position.

The Portuguese crown had not been able to realize the original purpose for creating the *prazos*, i.e., to enable it to exert influence in the interior of Mozambique without having to expend its own resources. The Portuguese crown had no means of influencing the *prazeros*, who controlled the only credible military forces in the region. They took sides in the conflicts of the African chiefs to whom they were allied or had become related, as well as in the local rivalries of the areas that they had settled. Deeply involved in African politics and increasingly Africanized in their cultural and social outlook, the *prazeros* also entered into the African economy in competition with distinctly Portuguese interests. To support their retinues, for instance, they resorted to raiding for livestock and slaves. In some areas these raids so depleted the African population that too few remained to carry on gold-mining operations.

In 1677 the Portuguese crown acted to curtail the growing independence of the *prazeros*. An edict issued that year ordered the breakup of the large *prazos* and limited the size of new leaseholds to a maximum of approximately 15 square kilometers. Its intent was not only to check the power of the *prazeros* but also to open up more land for additional Portuguese settlement in Mozambique. Presumably the crown would be better able to impose control over a large number of relatively small *prazos*. To avoid the further Africanization of *prazero* families, males, who it was conceded would take African wives, were categorically excluded from succession to the leasehold. Borrowing from a system already practiced in Portuguese India, property was to pass thereafter only through the female line for three lifetimes on the condition that the heiress apparent married a white born in Portugal. Among other conditions for leasehold, the *prazeros* were required to reside permanently on their estates and to put the land into cultivation. The edict also demanded that they remit a quitrent in gold dust in recognition that the crown held title to the *prazos*.

The conditions of the edict were largely disregarded, although female succession did become the established rule in *prazero* families. Prospective husbands were difficult to find in Portugal, even when they were sought there, and the life expectancy of those who did come to Mozambique was usually short. The *donas* (mistresses) of the *prazos* generally married Goans or men from other *prazero* families. Through intermarriage among the *prazeros*, leaseholds were consolidated, and particular families were able to retain sizeable estates. Because there were no markets for surplus goods in Mozambique, the *prazos* continued to produce only what was necessary for their inhabitants, earning income from participation in internal trade, commerce in slaves, and the profits of war. Also contrary to the intent of the edict and subsequent attempts at reform, the *prazos* remained an essentially African institution.

### Challenges to the Portuguese Presence in East Africa

Portuguese political influence north of Cape Delgado was exerted through allies, such as the sultan of Malindi, but resentment against their commercial monopoly continued to fester in Mombasa and other Muslim towns. In 1592 the sultan captured Mombasa and invited the Portuguese to install a garrison there. For close to four decades thereafter, Portuguese dominance was undisputed. From the 1630s, however, their position along the entire northern coast was challenged by the growing power of the imam of Oman. After the Portuguese surrendered the harbor fortress at Mombasa to the Omanis in 1699, European influence north of Cape Delgado was nonexistent for the next century until the start of British antislaving activities in East Africa.

South of Cape Delgado, the challenge to the Portuguese presence in the coastal settlements came from rival European powers. In 1580 the Portuguese crown passed to Phillip II of Spain. Because of the dynastic union, Portugal was drawn into the European wars in which the Habsburg monarchs were deeply committed, and its colonies and trade were exposed to attack by Spain's enemies—England, France, and the Netherlands.

The Dutch pounced on Portuguese holdings throughout the East and destroyed their naval supremacy in the Indian Ocean. Ceylon, Malacca, and the East Indies fell to the Dutch, as did the Portuguese depots in Angola and a large part of Brazil. Dutch expeditions attacked the settlement on Ilha de Moçambique in 1604 and again in succeeding years. These were the first battles between Europeans to be fought on southern African soil, and a Dutch victory would have forced Portuguese withdrawal from the Zambezi and transferred control of the gold trade to the Dutch East India Company. Although the settlement on the Ilha de Moçambique was repeatedly burned in these attacks and the countryside ravaged, the fortress of São Sebastião and its small garrison each time withstood the Dutch siege.

In 1640 the nobility in Portugal abjured their allegiance to Habsburg king Phillip IV and elevated their leader, the duke of Bragança, to the Portuguese throne as João IV. It was believed that breaking the Spanish connection would mean peace with Spain's enemies and save the Portuguese empire from destruction at their hands. In fact, the Dutch took still more territory and demanded concessions in return for support against Spain. Although they failed to dislodge the Portuguese from East Africa, the Dutch offensive at sea deprived Portugal of its trade monopoly in the Indian Ocean, lost Portugal its most valuable commercial outlets, and irreparably damaged its shipping.

Portugal's most serious reverse in the seventeenth century came at the hands of an African opponent, the Changamire *mambo*, Dombo. Reputedly a wizard whose touch could kill, he ruled the Shona as much through fear as by force. His formidable army was composed of a warrior elite called the Rozvi (literally, destroyers), who considered themselves a separate and superior breed of men among other Shona.

From his base in Guruhuswa (southeastern Zimbabwe), Dombo began to encroach on the Dande region, where, in a series of battles, the Rozvi defeated the Munhumutapa forces. The Changamire saw an opportunity to exact tribute from newly conquered chiefs and to wrest control of trade on the upper Zambezi, but Dombo also had very complex political motives for attacking the lands of the neighboring dynasty. The Munhumutapa's subservience to the Portuguese had fostered conspiracies by rivals within the royal clan, and the Changamire had exploited these differences by backing the anti-Portuguese factions. When the reigning Munhumutapa, Siri Kazurukumusapa, tried to turn away from his alliance with the Portuguese and succeeded, as a consequence of this, in bringing several former tributary rulers back to their allegiance, Dombo felt compelled to take pre-emptive action before his political influence grew too strong.

When Kazurukumusapa died in 1692, his uncle, Nyakunembire, called on Dombo to support his claim against the Portuguese candidate for the position of Munhumutapa. At the head of 2,000 Rozvi warriors, whose arsenal included firearms, Dombo invaded the Munhumutapa heartland, overran the market settlements on the Zimbabwe plateau, and forced the Portuguese to flee to locations down the Zambezi for protection. It was only Dombo's death in 1695 that spared the lower river basin from invasion.

The Munhumutapa was reduced to the status of a tributary of the Changamire. Tributary chiefs of the Munhumutapa either switched their allegiance to the Changamire, asserted their independence, or, in some cases, sought protection from the Portuguese. For some time, the Portuguese and the Changamire regularly backed rival candidates for the enfeebled office of the Munhumutapa. Eventually, the Munhumutapa transferred their kingdom to the lower Zambezi, where without significant influence they ruled over a small area under Portuguese protection.

### Mozambique in the Eighteenth Century

Portuguese interests in Mozambique had entered into a sharp decline by 1700. Direct administrative control by Portuguese officials was restricted to the Ilha de Moçambique. Tete, and portions of the Quiteve triangle (the territory, including the Zambezi delta, that lay within lines drawn from Sena coastward to Quelimane and Sofala). Portugal could extract gold more economically in Brazil, and the spice trade, which the Portuguese had financed with gold and ivory shipped from Mozambique, had fallen into Dutch hands. Large external markets had not yet been developed for slaves from southeast Africa, and Portuguese attention to the Atlantic slave trade was fixed in Angola. Agriculture could not be exploited without more settlers and capital, neither of which were forthcoming from Portugal.

Although the Changamire had destroyed the fairs in Mashonaland, Dombo's successors greatly valued continued trade links with the Portuguese—but on their terms. It was a primary point of Changamire policy to keep the Portuguese at a distance and to isolate the kingdom from foreign influence. When a new fair was founded at Zumbo in 1714 to exchange goods with the Portuguese, it operated under Changamire patronage. An alternate trade route to Sena and Tete was opened through Manicaland, and traffic over it was guarded by the Rozvi. Repeatedly during the early eighteenth century, Rozvi warriors were sent to protect Portuguese traders at the fairs and in 1743 were dispatched by the Changamire to defend Tete from attack.

The Changamire actions were dictated by enlightened self-interest. Although the Portuguese were prohibited from mining in their kingdom, gold from the Zimbabwean mines, as well as ivory, wax, rock crystal, and skins, were traded at the fairs in exchange for cloth, beads, firearms, gunpowder, distilled liquor, and luxury items for the Changamire court. The Portuguese recognized the benefit of a relationship that allowed them to trade in relative security. A governor of the period reported that the Changamire compelled his subjects to "love the Portuguese" and went on to describe the reigning *mambo* as "a man without many defects, except for his color and paganism."

The Portuguese expanded into the area north of the Zambezi after gold strikes were reported in Maravi territory. The course of that expansion closely paralleled events south of the river in the seventeenth century. A trading system based on fairs was set up, followed by the founding of small settlements by *sertanejos*. Resistance by African chiefs gave an excuse for further Portuguese penetration and eventual extension of their influence on the north bank as far as Cahora Bassa by the end of the century.

Attempts to attract settlers from Portugal, however, met with failure. Many of those did come to Mozambique were soon struck down by disease. The church had obtained grants to a number of *prazos*, particularly in the Quelimane area, diminishing the land available for settlers. Of those settlers who did arrive in Mozambique, a large proportion were Goans who often arrived as soldiers and stayed to carve out land for their own *prazos* or married into established *prazero* families.

The *prazeros* participated in two worlds. Although thoroughly mixed racially by the eighteenth century, they had full status as Portuguese and were accepted socially by colonial authorities on that basis. On their estates, however, their day-to-day activities and relationships reflected their acculturation to an African way of life. The *prazeros* were proud of their Portuguese family names, were at least nominally Roman Catholic, and as reserve officers commanded African troops in Portuguese service. But they were also known by familiar African names and bore African titles, participated in—and, indeed, officiated at—African rites that were incompatible with their Roman Catholicism, and fought private wars as African chiefs leading slave armies. Past the middle of the eighteenth century, their situation still presented an example of cultural duality rather than a merging of cultures. The closing of the Jesuit school at Sena after the expulsion of the order from Portuguese territory in 1759, however, deprived the *prazeros* families of their last formal link with Portuguese culture and accelerated the process of Africanization among them.

Numerous attempts were made by the Portuguese crown to enforce decrees regulating the *prazos* and to establish its authority over the *prazeros*. These all failed, essentially because Portugal needed the *prazo* system to maintain its presence in southeast Africa more than the *prazeros* required that presence to retain their land and privileged position among the Africans. It was the propensity of the *prazeros* for fighting among themselves that did more to limit their power than anything Lisbon could have done. Some of the most important families lost their land and positions as a result of this warfare, and by 1730 many of the great estates built up during the previous century were in decay or had been abandoned. This development, combined with the cumulative effects of Lisbon's attempts to bring more settlers into the area, yielded a greater number of smaller *prazos* after mid-century. Other great families, however, not only survived the wars but also profited from them, and these exercised even greater independence than before. In general, the weak disappeared and the strong grew stronger.

Mozambique's administrative subordination to Goa was ended in 1752 when a governor and captain general responsible directly to Lisbon for both civil and military affairs in the colony was appointed. Portugal also reached an agreement with the imam of Oman that confirmed his control of settlements north of Cape Delgado and the Rovuma River and acknowledged Portuguese hegemony to the south of those points as far as Delagoa Bay. The Portuguese had occupied Inhambane in 1731 to take up the trade that had earlier been carried to Sofala. Using Inhambane as a base, the Portuguese had blocked further expansion by the Tsonga and thereby prevented them from totally absorbing the southern Tonga.

The agreement with Oman did not, of course, deter European powers from making claims in the region. The Dutch East Indian Company established a trading station at Delagoa Bay in 1721 from which it took out slaves, ivory, and copper, but the Dutch left nine years later when they were unable to tap into the gold trade from that location. Portuguese traders tried to reopen their lost markets there, but colonial authorities levied such heavy duties on their ships that they could not compete with British traders who had also become active in Delagoa Bay. The Portuguese attempted to establish a settlement on the left bank of the estuary of Espírito Santo at the present-day site of Maputo (formerly Lourenço Marques) in 1776, but the next year an Austrian company expelled them and built a fortress there. The Portuguese returned to the settlement (which was named in honor of Lourenço Marques, the sixteenth-century navigator who had first charted Delagoa Bay) after the company ceased operations in 1781. During the Napoleonic wars the French attacked the Portuguese coastal settlements and for a time occupied Lourenço Marques.

### Portuguese Administration in the Early Nineteenth Century

Mozambique offered no more incentives for European settlement in the nineteenth century than it had in the sixteenth. Most of those who did come from Portugal were convicts—either political prisoners, often of genteel background and ill fitted for life in tropical Africa, or condemned criminals. Despite the large number of landless peasants in Portugal, it was difficult under the circumstances to lure colonists, even with the promise of land. Other members of the small European community included administrative and military officers on long assignments, merchants, clergy, and retired officials who often had married in Mozambique and chose to remain there. The Portuguese in Mozambique numbered no more than a few thousand, even including Goans and *mestiços* (see Glossary) who had been accepted as Portuguese.

After Brazil became independent in 1822, the Portuguese government made a conscious attempt to improve administration in the African colonies, but the colonial question and, particularly, deeper financial involvement in Africa became enmeshed in issues of party politics. Criticism of government policy, the size of military expenditures, deficits in colonial budgets, profiteering on the part of corrupt colonial administrators, and the continuation of the slave trade was frequently heard from political opponents of the liberal oligarchy that dominated Portuguese politics throughout most of the nineteenth century. Portugal lacked the domestic capital to support an ambitious colonial policy, but up to 80 percent of the country's trade involved re-export of colonial goods. Hence, Portugal in the mid-nineteenth century could neither afford to improve its situation in Africa nor let the colonies slip from its grasp. Economic considerations, therefore, combined with Portugal's concern for its prestige as a colonial power, dictated that the Portuguese remain in Africa—but with minimal profile.

The liberal Portuguese constitution of 1822, which was initially conceived as encompassing Brazil, defined the "Portuguese nation" as embracing inhabitants of all Portuguese territories, but each territory was to be governed by special laws according to its needs. To upgrade the colony's status, Mozambique in 1837 was put under a governor general, who was responsible to the overseas section of the Naval Secretariat in Lisbon. The subordinate regional administrations—Quelimane, Lourenço Marques, Cape Delgado, Sofala, Inhambane, and the Rivers of Sena—were governed with relative independence by military officers holding the rank of lieutenant general (*tenente general*) of the region. In the Rivers of Sena region, this office was usually assigned to a member of a prominent *prazero* family. The colonial civil service was small, and the five military outposts maintained in Mozambique were garrisoned by only a few hundred soldiers, mostly conscripted convicts and African auxiliaries. Public works other than harbor facilities were almost nonexistent, and little was accomplished to encourage economic or social development. Administrators were unable—and often unwilling—to carry out well-intentioned decrees from Lisbon.

### The Slave Trade

Although the internal slave market flourished in Mozambique, before the 1780s the external, i.e., overseas, trade had seldom amounted to more than a few hundred slaves shipped annually from Portuguese-controlled ports. When the demand for new sources of slaves grew in Brazil, Madagascar, and on the French Indian Ocean islands of Réunion and Mauritius in the late eighteenth century, however, the *prazeros* answered it by expanding their slaving operations, first through the established network in the interior but soon after by stepping up raids on neighboring districts and later by selling off their own slaves and free tenants. By 1790 approximately 9,000 slaves were being exported each year from Mozambique. This figure represented only a small portion of the overall Atlantic trade but at one point accounted for about 40 percent of all slaves brought to the Río de la Plata for sale. Serious depopulation occurred, particularly in the coastal areas that were scoured first and most thoroughly by slave traders. The tribal wars along the Zambezi intensified as a result of movements by large groups of Africans trying to escape the slave raids and thereby augmented the number of slaves taken as prisoners that were available to the traders.

The blockade imposed by British antislaving patrols off the West African coast early in the nineteenth century caused slave traders supplying markets in the Americas to shift more of their operations to southeastern Africa. As the risk involved in evading

British patrols became greater, so did the profit from a successful passage, and as a result the volume of the Atlantic slave trade actually increased. The 1820s and 1830s were the peak years of Mozambique's participation, annual exports reaching 15,000 Africans, or an estimated 10 percent of the Atlantic trade during that period. Brazil absorbed the largest number, almost all of whom were transported in Portuguese vessels. In addition, the *prazeros* sold slaves to Yao traders, who resold them to Swahili traders for shipment to Indian Ocean markets. The slave trade became Mozambique's most important business—so important that when official attempts were made to curb it, traders there as well as in Angola considered following the example of Brazil in declaring independence from Portugal.

Under strong pressure from Britain, Portugal agreed to a treaty in 1815 that prohibited its ships from engaging in the slave trade at ports north of the equator. The trade was subsequently banned altogether in 1836. Lacking the means of coercion and the full cooperation of colonial authorities, however, the Portuguese government could not enforce the law in Mozambique. The best the governor general of the day could do was to triple the head tax on slaves being exported from ports where the government could monitor the loading of ships. The tax did not significantly affect the volume of traffic, but it did divert a portion of the profit to the pockets of colonial authorities, giving them all the more reason to ignore directives from Lisbon.

The British patrols had not interfered with Portuguese flag vessels out of respect for Portugal's sovereignty in its colonies' coastal waters. In 1844, however, an Anglo-Portuguese treaty was concluded authorizing the Royal Navy to board Portuguese ships suspected of carrying slaves. This ended the overt trade, but large-scale smuggling of slave cargoes continued. A lucrative illegal trade with Cuba, for instance, developed in the 1850s. The prosperity of the Muslim ports in the north also revived as a result of trade taken over from the Portuguese. Initially, the Portuguese were reluctant to intervene, but fears in Lisbon that Britain would act unilaterally to stop the commerce in areas claimed by Portugal led to naval cooperation between the two powers in the 1860s and closure of the Muslim ports to the slave trade.

Once again in response to British protests—this time following the publication of reports by the missionary-explorer David Livingstone on conditions in Mozambique—Portugal began to abolish slavery by stages, concluding with a decree of total abolition in 1878. It took many more years, however, to suppress the practice in all Portuguese-controlled areas of Mozambique.

**The Ngoni Migrations**

A major consideration in the history of Mozambique in the nineteenth century was the migrations that were set off by a convulsion among the Nguni-speaking peoples of southern Africa. These movements, which coursed through Mozambique and Zimbabwe between the 1820s and 1850s, severely tested the Portuguese presence in southern Mozambique and profoundly altered the balance of power in the Zambezi basin.

In the first years of the century, Dingiswayo had imposed his rule over a confederacy of Nguni-speaking groups in Natal. When Shaka, his general and the chief of the small Zulu clan, became leader of the confederacy, he undertook a campaign of conquest that reshuffled the ethnic map of southern Africa, as defeated tribes were absorbed or displaced and as others sought to escape subjugation in a historical episode known as the *mfecane* (literally, the crushing). One such group, the Ngoni (a variant of Nguni), crossed in parties with their chiefs into southern Mozambique in about 1820. The Gaza Ngoni, later called the Shangaan after their leader, Soshangana Nxumalo, occupied the area in the Limpopo basin inhabited by the Tsonga that became known as Gazaland. Another Ngoni chief, Zwangendaba Jere, continued with his followers across the Limpopo and in 1835 sacked Great Zimbabwe, shattering the Changamire kingdom. Zwangendaba's Ngoni moved northward to form a kingdom on the shores of Lake Nyasa, but some segments remained in the Zambezi to raid the *prazos*.

The dissidents who broke away from Shaka's empire survived by raiding. Ngoni warriors carried off the women, as well as the livestock, of those groups whom they encountered on their march and perpetuated their ranks by recruiting the young males. In the process, while Soshangana imposed a hierarchical and thoroughly militarized social structure on his adopted followers, the Gaza Ngoni within a generation had become largely Tsonga in ethnic composition.

Initially, the appearance of the Gaza Ngoni was considered fortuitous by the Portuguese because the large amount of ivory received by Soshangana as tribute from conquered tribes was traded through the ports of Lourenço Marques and Inhambane. Later, however, Soshangana found this trade to be so profitable that he began to intrude on Portuguese-held territory on the coast. Conflict with the Portuguese escalated, and in 1843 his warriors overwhelmed the garrison at Inhambane. In 1833 a Zulu war party led by Shaka's brother Dingane had captured the fort at Lourenço Marques and massacred the garrison because the Portuguese governor general had refused to supply them with the firearms and ammunition they had demanded. The Zulu would remain in control of the southern shore of Delagoa Bay until their defeat by the British in Natal in 1879. In the intervening years the potential threat posed by the Gaza Ngoni and the Zulu to Portugal's already tenuous position in southern Mozambique left the region vulnerable to penetration by both Britain and the Afrikaner republics.

Soshangana had his own problems with Ngoni rebels. One such group had migrated north, had overcome the tribes along the Save River, and had become a major power in the hinterland of Sofala. In 1836 the rebels attacked the Portuguese at Sofala but two years later were subdued by Soshangana, who annexed their conquests to his own domain. Together with Zwangendaba's Ngoni, who had crossed the Zambezi upstream from Tete in 1835, they devastated the Maravi chiefdoms in their paths and fed the Swahili slave markets with their captives. When Zwangendaba died, many of the Ngoni who had followed him split up, some dispersing to form new kingdoms farther north. After 1850 the Portuguese moved to fill the vacuum left in the Tete region and in northern Mozambique by the passage of the Ngoni. In the meantime, Soshangana had consolidated his hold as overlord of the Tsonga people in the interior between the Zambezi and Incomati rivers, collecting tribute from African subjects and Portuguese alike and raiding the Zambezi *prazos* at will.

### The Downfall of the Prazeros

The *prazeros* had been weakened by attacks from the Barue, Maravi, and Quiteve during uprisings in the 1820s and 1830s, and about 80 percent of the *prazos* had suffered damage as a result of raids by the Ngoni. Many had also been destroyed or deserted by the Chikunda, who revolted when their masters had attempted to sell them during the heyday of the external slave trade. The stronger *prazeros* survived, in part, by building a system of *aringas*, large stockades—some more than a kilometer in circumference—that were supplied to withstand long sieges. In the aftermath of the Ngoni intrusion, the Portuguese had managed to take over the smaller *prazos* around Quelimane, but in the interior many small and abandoned estates had been absorbed by the great *prazeros* into so-called successor states.

The relationship of the *prazeros* to Portugal had grown even more ambiguous in this period than it had been earlier. On the one hand, even as Portuguese authorities were acting to revoke the tenure of the *prazeros*, colonial authorities had conferred royal commissions on the *prazeros* to seize territory from rebel chiefs and incorporate areas left in disarray by the Ngoni migrations. It was assumed that land taken in this manner would be claimed for the Portuguese crown and then rented back to the *prazeros*. On the other hand, the *prazeros* were completely independent of any Portuguese control, although the influence they exercised was identified with the Portuguese presence, and they resisted—with force when necessary—any encroachment by colonial authorities. The settlers of one generation, extending Portuguese influence in Mozambique, usually became the leaders of resistance to Portuguese authority in the next.

By the mid-nineteenth century, a few families controlled most of the Zambezi region. These included the Pereiras of Macanga, the Vaz dos Anjos of Massingire, the da Cruz of Massangano, and the de Sousas. The estates of the first two families were located north of the Zambezi, the Pereiras in the Tete region west of the Revúboè River and the Vaz dos Anjos east of Macanga up to the Shire River. The da Cruz and the de Sousas held property south of the river, where the latter had married into the royal house of the Makombe of the Barue (see fig. 4). They ruled their estates as princes in their own principalities, intimately involved in the politics of neighboring African groups and engaged in intense rivalries with other *prazero* families.

None of these families could trace their origins directly to Portugal. The da Cruz were descended from a soldier of fortune from Southeast Asia, and the others were of Goan ancestry. They had arrived in Mozambique in the eighteenth century, and much of their land had been taken in conquest from Africans and was not held under the *prazo* tenure system. All were thoroughly Africanized, and some of their members had reportedly lost the use of Portuguese.

The da Cruz power grew under António Vicente, the family's head, who was usually called by his Bantu name, Bonga (Wildcat). An infamous river pirate, Bonga demonstrated the extent of his power by extorting a tax from all vessels passing through the long stretch of the Zambezi that he commanded and closing the fair at Zumbo to all but his trade. In 1853 the lieutenant general of the new Tete province undertook an expedition, with the help of Bonga's rivals, the Pereiras, to capture Bonga's *aringa* at Massangano. Although Bonga turned back the assault, in which troops brought from Portugal participated, Zumbo was reopened under Portuguese control in 1862. Four more campaigns were organized against the da Cruz in the 1860s, and each in turn was defeated; but the constant pressure applied by the Portuguese persuaded Bonga to agree to a peace treaty in 1875, according to

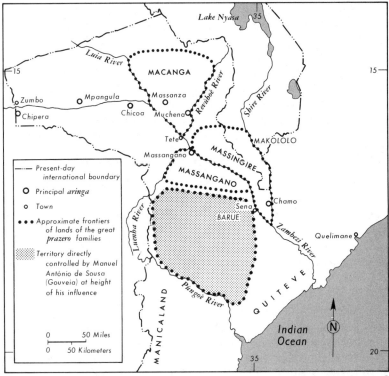

*Figure 4. Lands of the Great Prazero Families, Nineteenth Century*

the terms of which he received a pardon in return for his recognition of Portuguese sovereignty in the Tete area.

Around 1850 Manuel António de Sousa (called Gouveia) had come from Goa to manage his family's estates on the lower Zambezi. An adventurer and opportunist of the first order, he soon became the largest private landowner in Mozambique. In recognition of his abilities, Gouveia was appointed captain major of Manicaland to defend the area against the Ngoni and to bolster Portuguese claims there. Later, he was named to serve as regent for his kinsman, the Makombe, and in 1880 took advantage of a dispute in the royal house to seize the territory of the Barue.

During the 1850s and 1860s many Africans from different groups, who were fleeing before the Portuguese advance north of the Zambezi, had sought the protection of the Vaz dos Anjos. Frightened by the arrival in the region of the Makolo—a group who had been introduced from the upper Zambezi by

31

Livingstone as bearers on one of his treks—the Massingire people turned on their patrons, overthrew them, and ceded the territory to the Portuguese. Heavily taxed by colonial authorities, they soon revolted again and brought terror to settlers in the area between Sena and Quelimane. The Portuguese turned for assistance to Gouveia, who used his private army to scatter the rebels in 1884 and capture their leaders. In 1886 Gouveia collaborated with Joaquim de Andrada, a Portuguese army officer and agent of the Mozambique Company, to stake a claim in Mashonaland ahead of Cecil Rhodes' British South Africa Company (BSAC). The expedition failed to reach its objective, however, and Gouveia joined Portuguese forces marching on the da Cruz *aringa* at Massangano. The stockade, which had resisted previous sieges, was reduced by artillery and captured, leaving 6,000 defenders dead. Its fall in 1888 marked the end of an era and left Gouveia as the last remaining *prazero* able to exercise an independent influence in Mozambique.

## The Modern Colonial Era

Portugal had regarded the 1815 Anglo-Portuguese treaty regulating the slave trade as recognition of its sphere of influence in the area extending from Cape Delagoa Bay, but the territorial limits of Portuguese sovereignty were not demarcated in any international agreement. In the early 1820s the Royal Navy surveyed the coastline of southern Mozambique, and the British made trade agreements with African chiefs there in competition with the Portuguese at Lourenço Marques. In 1843 Britain annexed Natal as a colony, claiming jurisdiction up to the Black Umbuluzi River. In the conflict over zones of influence, Portugal cited rights based on explorations dating from the early sixteenth century, whereas Britain stressed the absence of effective Portguese occupation.

After the founding of the Afrikaner republics in the 1840s, the port of Lourenço Marques received an increasingly large volume of goods for shipment inland to the Transvaal Republic and the Orange Free State. The discovery of diamonds in 1867 and the gold strike in the Witwatersrand 20 years later made access to the port invaluable to the Afrikaners.

Two events in 1869 brought the Anglo-Portuguese controversy in the region to a head. The first was a treaty concluded between Portugal and the Transvaal Republic in which the Portuguese allowed the latter favorable access to Delagoa Bay in return for recognition of Portuguese sovereignty there. The second was a British attempt to establish legal claim to the disputed territory in southern Mozambique. The matter was submitted to French arbitration, and in 1875 the Portuguese claims were upheld without exception, awarding borders roughly corresponding to Mozambique's present-day southern frontiers. The decision was ratified in subsequent treaties with the Orange Free State and the Transvaal Republic, the latter also approving construction of a railroad line from Pretoria to Lourenço Marques. British interests nonetheless continued to maintain considerable influence in the area.

### Portugal and the European Scramble for Africa

As a rule, African colonies had been regarded as expensive liabilities by the great European powers, especially where trading concessions could be exercised without resorting to annexation. Attitudes changed toward the end of the nineteenth century, however, as rival industrial powers—Britain, Germany, France, and Belgium—scurried to find and develop overseas markets for their goods. In 1885 the Berlin Conference was convened to resolve conflicts of interest in Africa by allotting areas of exclusive exploitation to the participating colonial powers. The conferees enunciated the principle that "effective occupation" was a precondition to legitimate title to colonial possessions. What followed was the so-called scramble for Africa in which the colonial powers sought to establish their respective claims.

Despite expansion at the expense of the *prazeros*, Portuguese authority in the early 1880s was still restricted in Mozambique to the central coast and lower Zambezi basin and to the Lourenço Marques and Inhambane enclaves in the south. The northern region was claimed but not occupied. At the Berlin Conference the Portuguese sphere of influence was recognized by France and Germany on the basis of historic claims but not by Britain. Based on several cross-continental expeditions by Portuguese explorers, the Portuguese foreign ministry in 1886 published the so-called rose-colored map (*mapa côr de rosa*), which showed a continuous strip of Portuguese territory through south-central Africa, connecting the two coasts (see fig. 5). France and Germany acknowledged its validity, but Britain again contested the claim on the grounds that Portugal had not demonstrated its effective occupation of the territory. If upheld, Portugal's claim would have blocked designs to bring a Cape-to-Cairo railroad through African territory under the British flag.

For several years a small-scale undeclared war was waged in

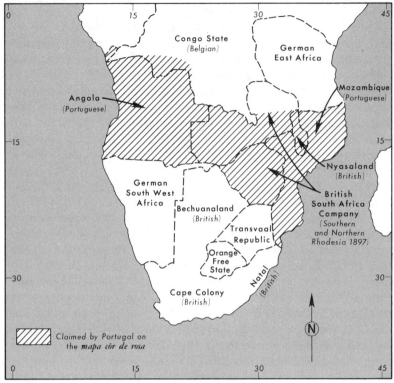

*Figure 5. Southern Africa about 1890*

the interior between Portuguese and British agents vying to conclude treaties with local chiefs. A more serious confrontation occurred when Africans, claiming British protection, attacked Portuguese outposts on the Shire River. A gunboat was sent to overawe the insurgents, who were forced to submit to Portuguese jurisdiction. Britain seized on the incident, however, to present Portugal with an ultimatum demanding a settlement of their differences. The resulting Anglo-Portuguese convention, imposed by the British government and signed in London in January 1891, defined the two countries' spheres of influence to Britain's advantage. Portugal reluctantly conceded the BSAC's position in Mashonaland, where the first British settlers had arrived the previous year, and agreed to the partition of Manicaland, where the Portuguese had claimed exclusive rights. The convention also guaranteed rail access from the new Mashonaland settlements to the port of Beira and free navigation of the Zambezi.

The agreement, dictated by Britain, was extremely unpopular in Portugal, and the government fell when the Portuguese parliament refused to ratify it. In the meantime, the BSAC had contacted the chief of the Shangaan (formerly referred to as Gaza Ngoni) with a proposal to open a new outlet to the sea through Gazaland, and its agents had also made a treaty with the Mutasa of Manica, Portugal's traditional ally, granting the company mineral rights in his territory. Persuaded by these developments and diplomatic pressure from Britain, the new Portuguese government acquiesced to a modified convention, approved in Lisbon in June.

Meanwhile, Gouveia and Andrada had been arrested in Manicaland by BSAC police while they were on a mission to the Mutasa for the Mozambique Company, and they were taken in custody to Cape Colony. Gouveiva was soon released and returned to Mozambique, but in his absence the personal empire he had built between the Zambezi and Save rivers had fallen apart. In an attempt to recover his holdings, he was killed by supporters of a rival member of the royal house of the Makombe, and the Barue people came under a new ruler hostile to the Portuguese.

Between 1885 and 1902 Portuguese forces, composed mainly of African levies, were engaged in no fewer than 15 military campaigns to win effective control of the interior. The most fiercely contested was against the Barue and required the use of 20,000 troops to suppress them and their allies. These campaigns ended the independence of many other old chieftaincies in the Zambezi region, including that of the Munhumutapa. Many different African groups were involved in separate uprisings against the Portuguese during this period. Although they entered into alliances of expediency, no lasting pattern of multiethnic resistance emerged, and the Portuguese were still able to win African allies in the campaigns by exploiting historic animosities.

### Gungunhana

The Shangaan raiding parties, which had disrupted trade and threatened the Portuguese settlements and dependent African groups, were a constant source of concern for colonial authorities, who lacked the resources to counter them. A break came for the Portuguese when Soshangana's two sons, Mahueva and Muzila, fell out over the succession after his death in 1858. Muzila pledged loyalty to Portugal in return for help in suppressing his brother.

Muzila was succeeded as chief of the Shangaan in 1885 by Gungunhana, who recognized Portuguese sovereignty but at the same time continued Muzila's practices of taking tribute from groups under Portuguese protection and permitting raiding parties to attack Portuguese settlements. Gungunhana's position was so strong that Europeans seeking trade in his region were obliged to deal with him and to give him tribute or military supplies. His *kraal* (enclosure) was on the edge of the Zimbabwe plateau between the Portuguese and the British. Outwardly loyal to the Portuguese, he repeatedly made deals with the British.

Gungunhana had a strong sense of his Ngoni heritage. He knew the extent of his traditional lands and regarded the raiding system as part of his inheritance. His desire to regain lands held by his grandfather caused him to lead a number of his people, variously estimated at between 40,000 and 100,000, into the lower Limpopo River valley in 1889. This move would have enabled Gungunhana to dominate the tribes in the area, but it brought him uncomfortably close to Portuguese coastal settlements.

Gungunhana's dealings with the British and the disruption caused by his raids and devastation of the countryside during the Shangaan migration motivated the Portuguese to move against him. He in turn was pressured by his generals, who, having achieved some success against other Africans, had grown increasingly belligerent and were convinced that they could defeat the Portuguese. The Portuguese, for their part, habitually overestimated the strength of the Shangaan.

Gungunhana's fate was sealed by the Anglo-Portuguese border settlements, which made it no longer necessary for the Portuguese to stay on good terms with Gungunhana to prevent him from going over to the British. The Portuguese seized an opportunity to attack Gungunhana in 1894, launching a series of actions that lasted more than a year. In November 1895 the Portuguese won a decisive battle against the Shangaan at Coolela. Gungunhana was captured and spent the rest of his life in exile in the Azores. The last Shangaan resistance was stamped out in 1897, leaving all of southern Mozambique under Portuguese control.

### Portuguese Penetration of the Northern Interior

Even after the expeditions to suppress the slave trade there, Portuguese influence on the northern coast was limited by the strength of the Swahili shaykhs who had close relations with the sultan of Zanzibar. Beginning in 1896 the Portuguese established coastal forts, and in 1910 they defeated the shaykh of Angoche and forced him to submit to Portuguese authority.

The Portuguese effectively occupied the area included in the present-day Cabo Delgado and Niassa provinces between 1899 and 1912. Their first concerted action was taken against the Yao. Originally organized in small and autonomous units tending toward fragmentation, Yao groups consolidated in the nineteenth century as they began handling a greater volume of slave trade over longer distances. As that commerce became more lucrative, the best traders began to attract a following that sought to share the wealth, and the size of political units grew dramatically. After 1890, in reaction to the pressure from the Portuguese to end the slave trade, the majority of the Yao converted to Islam in order to identify their interests with those of the coastal shaykhs. The Yao offered stiff resistance to the British, Portuguese, and Germans alike, aided by their strong strategic position in the highlands around Lake Nyasa and by supply lines to the coast through territory that the Portuguese could not control.

Finally, the raids of one Yao chief, Mataka Cisonga, in Nyasaland (present-day Malawi) drew British complaints that moved the Portuguese to take military action that drove Mataka across the Rovuma River into German East Africa (present-day Tanzania). In 1909-10 they subdued the Macua and Maconde who stood between them and the Yao further west. By 1912, after a major expedition against the Yao, the Portuguese successfully established a string of posts in their territory and made good their claim to effective occupation of northern Mozambique.

### The Chartered Companies

The Portuguese had originally sanctioned the *prazos* in the hope that they would bring administrative control to the Zambezi without the accompanying expense. After the *prazos* were shattered, the Portuguese turned to another expedient. Copying the British example, companies were charted by the Portuguese government and granted concessionary rights to develop land and natural resources. Of the three major companies that operated in Mozambique, the only profitable one was the Zambezia Company. Chartered in 1892, the company held the concession in the present-day Tete and Zambezia provinces. By 1904 the company completed its first task, that of taking over a number of *prazo* holdings. It then used its capital to establish civil and military posts and to develop agriculture wherever possible. Numerous mineral and agricultural concessions were sublet.

Less successful financially but more notorious were the Mozambique Company and the Nyassa Company. In 1891 the Portuguese government initially granted the Mozambique Company a charter in an attempt to compete with Rhodes' BSAC in Manicaland and Mashonaland. The government recognized that success depended on attracting foreign capital; for example, even before it was chartered, more than 40 percent of the Mozambique Company's shares were controlled by British investors. Under the charter the company was given sovereign rights in the present-day Manica and Sofala provinces. In return it was charged with constructing railroads, roads, and ports, settling Portuguese families, building schools and hospitals, and generally developing the area. Disregarding the terms of the charter, the company carried out only the construction necessary for its commercial operations. One of the few contributions the company made was the construction of a railroad linking Southern Rhodesia (present-day Zimbabwe) with the port of Beira. The line made the company's most important business the transit of goods to and from the interior. As late as 1910 its only other important economic activity was the operation of a few sugar plantations.

One of the most damaging long-term effects of company activity was its labor policy. The Portuguese attitude had always been dictated by the need for a dependable supply of cheap labor, obtained earlier by slavery and later by forced labor for pay. The Native Labor Code, enacted in 1878 shortly after the formal abolition of slavery, made a gesture toward the improvement of labor conditions by enabling Africans to decide whether they wanted to work for Europeans. The only people who could be compelled to work were those judged to be vagrants under the terms of the Portuguese penal code. The Native Labor Code was circumvented, however, by interpreting the vagrancy clause to include all Africans engaged in their traditional work instead of making themselves available to Europeans.

After the financial crisis of the 1890s the Portuguese decided that a radical revision of their economic policy, particularly concerning the colonies, was necessary. In 1898 a committee to study the labor situation in Portuguese Africa decided that forced labor was required for economic development and for the cultural and moral development of the Africans. The principles set forth by the committee were adopted in a decree that remained substantially unchanged for almost 30 years.

The Mozambique Company prohibited labor recruitment for work outside its territory. The manpower of the area was thereby reserved for the exclusive use of the company. The company required male Africans to work on local sugar plantations and on such public works as were carried out. Men caught trying to leave had to perform 20 months of forced labor without pay. Women were made to grow cotton and other cash crops for sale to the company, resulting in a lack of food crops to sustain the local population. As an extra measure, the company set the hut taxes so high that African inhabitants had to work for extremely long periods just to pay them.

Conditions were even more cruel in the lands managed by the Nyassa Company. Because its vast territory across the northernmost part of Mozambique was the least developed land of the colony and the most remote, the Nyassa Company predictably attracted less capital. Lacking prospects for development, the company earned income by exporting labor from its territory to other parts of Africa and by severely taxing those who remained. The company's local officials were paid next to nothing but were allowed to keep a percentage of the taxes they collected, a policy that led to enormous abuses.

Families had been broken up when males were exported to work in other areas, and most of the remaining population was made up of women and children. In this situation rape was so common that it was accepted without surprise, and murder was considered a slight indiscretion. Work was also compelled by withholding food, and there were some reports of crucifixions. The Africans resisted when they could, but more often they fled to British Nyasaland and German East Africa. In less than 30 years more than 100,000 left for Nyasaland alone. Between the exportation of labor and the flight to neighboring colonies, the area suffered a massive depopulation.

In addition to abusing the African population, the chartered companies retarded the development of Mozambique. Although they rejuvenated the commerce of older coastal towns and—particularly in the territory of the Zambezia Company—established new towns, and although the transit trade did expand Mozambique's economy, the companies failed to bring substantial development capital into the country. Because they were dominated by foreigners, the companies effectively removed large portions of Mozambique from Portuguese control. The Mozambique Company belonged to British interests, and in 1914 Germans bought the Nyassa Company. Portugal itself was too far in debt to Britain to complain and, after the Portuguese sold the confiscated German-owned Nyassa Company to Britain during World War I, Mozambique, from an economic standpoint, became more a British than a Portuguese colony.

### The Colonial Regime

The colonial administration of Mozambique was reorganized in 1907, introducing a system that remained virtually intact until independence was achieved in 1975. In response to complaints that little could be accomplished as long as the colonial administration was directly dependent on apathetic officials in Lisbon, the governor general, resident in Lourenço Marques (to which the seat of government had been moved in 1898), was given greater autonomy to act in the interests of the province, but ultimate financial responsibility remained with the central government. Provision was made for a provincial council, which possessed limited legislative powers, and for subdivision of the province into districts and rural jurisdictions (see fig. 6). The district governors, replacing the old lieutenant generals, were essentially responsible for implementing the policies of the governor general and for overseeing both African and European local governments that functioned at the next level. The constitution of 1911, written a year after the establishment of the Portuguese Republic, reaffirmed the principal that administration of colonial possessions should be decentralized.

Direct management of African affairs came under the administrator of the rural jurisdictions, each of which was composed of several subordinate units, called posts, headed by a chief of post who might exercise authority over as many as 40,000 people. The chief of post was in turn assisted by African magistrates, usually traditional chiefs who were put in charge of collecting taxes, recruiting labor, and imposing punishment for infractions in an assigned cluster of villages. Magistrates also commanded uniformed African police. The underpaid and poorly trained Portuguese officials developed a reputation for incompetence, cruelty, and corruption. Because of their frequent use of coercive measures to effect policy and enforce the law, the whip and the cudgel became the recognized symbols of Portuguese authority among the great mass of rural Africans. Rural parishes, organized as civil jurisdictions in areas where Europeans had settled, and urban municipalities were separately administered and enjoyed a degree of self government.

In 1920 a high commissioner replaced the governor general as the chief official in Mozambique. This change was intended to lessen Lisbon's control of the colony because the high commissioners had financial autonomy. In fact very little changed, and the financial burden of the colony may have increased as each successive high commissioner abandoned his predecessor's programs and launched new ones of his own. Reforms did nothing to decrease corruption, which was present at all levels of the colonial government. The Portuguese government and the colonial administration were eager to grant offices and land concessions to friends and political favorites. Frequent changes of government in Lisbon meant a rapid turnover in colonial personnel. There were tax scandals and incidents involving officials in extortion and counterfeiting. The Banco Nacional Ultramarino (National Over-

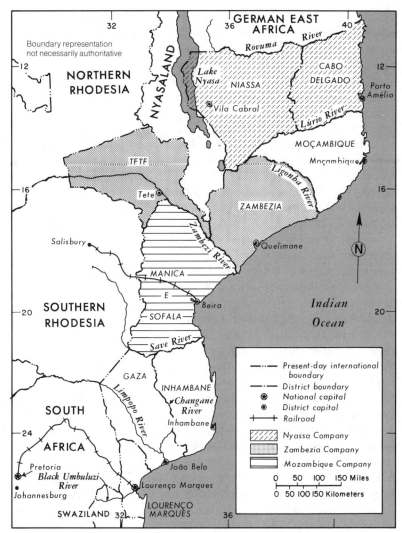

*Figure 6. Portuguese Mozambique, 1907*

seas Bank), the official bank for Angola and Mozambique, paid off officials in the colonial administration. Corruption and the bank's policies caused high inflation and a rapidly depreciating currency, which prevented Mozambique from becoming commercially competitive with other colonies producing the same products.

Migration for employment in South Africa had been a practice since the discovery of gold in the Witwatersrand region of the Transvaal in 1886. Informal migration was regulated by a 1909 con-

41

vention that provided for an exchange of labor from Mozambique in return for the transit trade from the Transvaal. A subsequent agreement in 1928 regulated the number of workers to be employed in South Africa, as well as working conditions, repatriation arrangements, and the amount of transit guaranteed Mozambique. This exchange of labor and trade resulted in direct revenue and foreign exchange for Mozambique and also reflected the dominance of British and South African interests in the province.

Anticlerical governments in Lisbon had in various ways discouraged Roman Catholic missionary activities since the 1830s. International agreements reached in the late nineteenth century, however, allowed Protestant missionaries sent from Britain and Germany to enter Mozambique and contributed to a relaxing of restrictions on expanding existing Roman Catholic missions. The number of Portuguese missionaries, particularly the Jesuits, was increased substantially as a result. The missions introduced some medical care and education for Africans in the interior and improved facilities for both Europeans and Africans in the towns.

### World War I and the Zambezi Rebellions

Portugal entered World War I on the side of the Allies in 1916, its government arguing that a German victory would mean the loss of the African colonies even if the country remained neutral. A largely African-recruited Portuguese army joined British Empire forces in East Africa in pursuit of German general Paul von Lettow-Vorbeck's elusive colonial army.

Some areas in Mozambique had never been completely pacified, and banditry, peasant revolts, and resistance to forced labor were all reminders of continuing opposition to colonial rule. African workers were forcibly recruited for a major roadbuilding project begun in 1914, and the number of those inducted for construction work and as bearers (sometimes taken by government raiding parties) increased sharply after Portugal's entry into the war. In 1916 colonial authorities were told to provide 5,000 additional African recruits for military service. When efforts to attract volunteers failed, they resorted to conscription. Chiefs who were reluctant to cooperate were replaced by collaborators.

Conscription and the forced labor policy provoked bloody uprisings in the Zambezi region in the spring of 1917. The Barue—by virtue of their tradition of resistance—assumed leadership and sent emissaries to other groups to revive the alliances that had been crushed by the Portuguese in 1902. The Zambezi rebellions, directed as much against African allies of the Portuguese as against the colonial regime itself, came as Lettow-

Vorbeck had crossed with his army into northern Mozambique and was thought to be marching toward the Zambezi. The Portuguese were obliged to abandon Zumbo to the insurgents, and Sena and Tete were threatened. More than 20,000 troops, most of them African levies, were brought in to break the back of the rebellion with their superior firepower. Retribution was brutal; villages suspected of supporting the rebellion were burned along with their fields, cattle were confiscated, and hostages were taken to prevent a recurrence of the uprisings. The rebellion was a short-lived but fierce affair, and isolated guerrilla attacks continued until 1920. Further pacification was required in the region as late as 1930.

Despite the protest against conscription in the Zambezi region, the Portuguese managed to field over 100,000 armed Africans during World War I. Under the accords of the Treaty of Versailles, Germany paid Portugal reparations for 130,000 African soldiers and laborers reported dead from all causes as a result of the war in East Africa.

### Salazar and the Colonial Statute of 1930

A right-wing officers' coup overthrew Portugal's unstable parliamentary regime in 1926. Two years later a civilian economist, António de Oliveira Salazar, was brought into the predominantly military government as finance minister with a mandate to balance the budget and reduce the external debt. In a few years Salazar succeeded in bringing about a solvent currency, a favorable balance of trade, and surpluses both in foreign reserves and in the national budget. He achieved this in great measure by radically altering Portugal's colonial policy. Priority was given to colonial development, Salazar insisting that the overseas territories be made to pay for themselves and also provide the trade surpluses required by Portugal to import the essentials it could not produce itself. In essence he updated Portuguese mercantilist policy. By increasing production and improving the marketing of colonial goods, it was also expected that the overseas possessions would become self-supporting, alleviating the drain on the Portuguese treasury for defense and maintenance.

These aims were reflected in the Colonial Statute of 1930, which tightened Lisbon's control over the colonies and removed the discretionary powers that had formerly been exercised by colonial authorities. The statute declared that metropolitan Portugal and the overseas territories were interdependent entities, although it was clear from the context that the interests of Portugal took precedence over those of the separate colonies.

Mozambique, along with the other overseas territories, technically became a political and juridicial unit of a "Greater Portugal," bound together in what the statute called the "spiritual unity of those within it of all races who accepted the Portuguese language and culture as their own."

Bringing development to Mozambique meant breaking up the special interests. The Banco Nacional Ultramarino was too strong to be attacked head-on, but Salazar designed a number of measures to limit what it could do independently. The most important was the requirement that government appointees be included among the bank's directors. When the Nyassa Company's charter came up for renewal in 1928, Salazar refused to approve it. Because the Mozambique Company showed some inclination to work with Salazar, it was permitted to operate until its once renewed charter expired in 1941. To reduce further the influence of the chartered companies, the military government withdrew their right to use forced labor. The Native Labor Code of 1928 detailed the obligations of workers, employers, and government in labor relations and forbade the use of forced labor by private persons or enterprises. Colonial authorities retained the right, however, to enlist the labor of any African who did not fulfill certain critieria for self-sufficiency and economic contribution to the society. Africans were obliged to carry work passes in which their employment histories were recorded. A labor inspectorate was formed to ensure compliance with the code, but it was understaffed, inadequately financed, and ineffective.

### The New State

In 1932 Salazar became prime minister and introduced a civilian government in Lisbon. The period of transition to an authoritarian republic promised after the military coup concluded with the adoption of the 1933 constitution that created the corporatist New State (Estado Novo). Referring to the Colonial Statute, the document reiterated that Portugal and the overseas territories were "one and indivisible."

Once again the Portuguese government tried to encourage emigration to Mozambique. Several projects failed, but by the 1950s Portuguese farmers had been successfully settled in southern Mozambique, either in cooperatives or in modest family holdings. By the mid-1950s, however, the European population was still only about 50,000 and was concentrated in coastal cities and in towns along the Zambezi, but the number of permanent residents engaged in business, the trades, and the service sector had surpassed the number of government functionaries who would return to Portugal at the end of their tours.

After World War II the Portuguese state was sufficiently solvent and its colonies sufficiently secure that some of the restrictive tariffs on goods and raw materials were eased. Lines of transportation and communication were built to connect many previously isolated centers, and the metropolitan government began to make plans for further development. The First Six-Year National Development Plan (1953) laid down a schedule of priorities for economic development of the African province that included railroad construction, development of ports, and hydroelectric projects. As a result of these initiatives, white-owned and operated commercial enterprises, farms, and light industry prospered, and the interior was brought into closer contact with the coast.

According to colonial theory, Africans were encouraged to become Portuguese and accept Portugal as their motherland, but those who wanted to obtain equal rights and status would have to give up their African identity and become "civilized" by accepting Portuguese standards and values. Beginning in 1927 Africans who were able to speak Portuguese, had abandoned their traditional way of life, and earned income from an occupation in commerce or industry, could apply for legal recognition as *assimilados* (assimilated ones). They were thereby classified as full Portuguese citizens and were freed from control measures imposed on other Africans. Africans who could not or did not apply to meet these qualifications were defined as *indígenas* (indigenous people). Europeans, Asians, and *assimilados*, on the one hand, and *indígenas*, on the other, came under separate legal codes. The *indígenas* were subject to curfews and conscriptive labor contracts and were obliged to carry passbooks. African farmers were allowed to plant only those crops directed by the authorities. The basic distinction remained one of race, however, and blacks—regardless of legal status—were consigned to live in a segregated society.

During the 1950s Portugal began to introduce reforms in the African colonies in response to growing criticism in the international community, but reforms were counterbalanced by increased restrictions on individuals. The Organic Law of 1955, for example, gave African areas of Mozambique their own local councils, and some attempts were made to eliminate abuses in the labor system that had driven so many Africans from the colony. But no changes were made in the labor law. After 1954 the government tightened regulations for qualifying as an *assimilado*, excluding many Africans who by previous standards would have been considered assimilated. Applicants, for instance, were thereafter required to speak "proper" Portuguese. Africans were controlled by a colonial administration that reached into every village. In 1958 an official in Lourenço Marques stated that it was "practically impossible for a native . . . to avoid the vigilance and supervision of the authorities." Salazar also introduced Portugal's secret police apparatus into the country to tighten surveillance over both whites and Africans. While political dissidents were being subjected to beatings, jail and torture, the government attributed Mozambique's public order, which was observed and remarked upon by visitors, to its enlightened policies and racial tolerance, constrasting the apparent tranquillity there with the turmoil evident elsewhere in Africa. But the regime's repressive policies increased the flight of Africans to neighboring countries.

In the early 1960s the government in Lisbon, faced with a serious rebellion in Angola, was forced to make some changes in the status of the overseas provinces and in the regulations affecting their inhabitants. It gave greater powers to the organs of local administration and made legal provisions for greater participation by the African population in government and in the social and educational systems. Expenditures on rural development, health, sanitation, and education were increased, and the legal distinction between *indígenas* and the rest of the population was abolished. Henceforth, all persons born Portuguese nationals were to be granted the full rights of citizenship. Legislation was also enacted abolishing forced cultivation of commercial crops, and the Native Labor Code of 1928 was finally repealed.

## The Rise of African Nationalism

Opposition to Portuguese rule by Africans under traditional rulers had persisted well into the twentieth century, reflecting in part the belated efforts of Portugal to establish an effective administration over the country's hinterlands and in part the harshness of life for the Africans under company management and colonial administration. Living conditions led to the continued flight of many Africans to South Africa and the neighboring British colonies after World War I. The major cause of discontent was the harshness of regulations, chiefly in the form of forced labor laws, imposed by the Portuguese.

If Africans had the opportunity, they sought employment on European farms in their home regions. If not, they faced three choices: six months of annual labor at little or no pay under police supervision on public works; fleeing the country entirely to seek an easier life in the surrounding British territories; or accepting employment as contract laborers in South Africa. Those two forms of emigration, one permanent, the other temporary, had a number of effects on Mozambique. From the immediate Portuguese point of view the most important of these was that remittances from workers in South Africa provided Portugal with large amounts of foreign exchange.

Within Mozambique government control through the police and censorship kept to a minimum any demonstrations of political or economic unrest and knowledge of such unrest as did occur. These included dockers' strikes, unrest in Lourenço Marques in 1948, and protests in Inhambane and other towns to protest labor conditions, inadequate pay, or poor food supplies. Many were killed in the riots, and others who took part were imprisoned or suffered reprisals.

Two other classes of Mozambicans were sources of opposition to Portuguese rule: the small number of educated Africans and persons of mixed ancestry and the up to 500,000 people who had left Mozambique to make a living in neighboring countries. Mozambique's indigenous elite was composed of *mestiços* and Africans recognized as *assimilados*, but according to the 1955 census, these two groups numbered only 30,000 and 4,500, respectively. To them could be added an estimated 250,000 Africans who had achieved a degree of education or entered the modern economy in the cities.

Those who left for political reasons or to obtain schooling that was not available to them in Mozambique joined the multitude of ethnically diverse Mozambican workers who had lived abroad for years in the British colonies. This group of educated expatriates helped to encourage a political orientation in some of the existing social organizations—student associations and regional mutual aid societies, for example—for Mozambicans in those countries. Greatly influenced by the ideas and successes of nationalist parties in their host countries and eager to improve conditions in Mozambique, the leaders of these organizations concluded that independence from Portugal was essential.

Once it became clear that these organizations had taken a political turn, the strong hand of the Portuguese police kept them from forming any overt branches within Mozambique. Because there were few connections between the Mozambicans in the different neighboring states, each country of refuge provided its own group of refugee political organizations. In East Africa the major political group was the Mozambique African National Union (MANU) founded in 1960. The adopted English name was a deliberlate attempt on the part of the Mozambican liberation movement to make common cause with the Tanganyikan and Kenyan political parties, TANU and KANU. Its leaders including Mathew Mwole and Lawrence Millinga, were longtime residents of Tanganyika and Kenya and had been active in their host countries' independence movements. In Southern Rhodesia refugees joined the National Democratic Union of Mozambique (União Democratica Nacional de Moçambique—UDENAMO), founded in 1959 by Adelino Gwembe. In Nyasaland the National African Union of Independent Mozambique (União Nacional Africana de Moçambique Independente—UNAMI) was led by Baltazar Changona.

### Founding of the Front for the Liberation of Mozambique

In June 1962 representatives of the three groups—MANU, UDENAMO, and UNAMI—met in a conference at Dar es Salaam under the sponsorship of Tanganyikan leader Julius K. Nyerere. The result was the formation of a new organization, the Front for the Liberation of Mozambique (Frente de Libertação de Moçambique—FRELIMO). Chosen as its president was Eduardo Chivambu Mondlane, a southern Mozambican educated in South Africa, Portugal, and the United States. Mondlane had spent several years on the United Nations Secretariat staff and in 1960 had traveled through Mozambique on a United Nations (UN) passport, which gave him a rare opportunity to observe his own country without governmental interference. When FRELIMO was founded, he resigned a faculty position at Syracuse University to organize the party's headquarters in Dar es Salaam. Other FRELIMO leaders were chosen from the three former organizations and included Uria Simango, a Protestant minister who became vice president, and Marcelino dos Santos, a Marxist ideologue. Party leadership was officially vested in a grand council composed of these three and from seven to 12 others. FRELIMO held its First Party Congress in September 1962. The congress adopted a platform aimed at mobilizing forces to attain self-government and independence for Mozambique.

The merger of the three parties to form FRELIMO did not result, however, in a unified independence movement. Between 1962 and 1964 major splits among the leaders resulted in the resurgence of UDENAMO with a modified name, the National Democratic Union of Munhumutapa. In 1965 the Revolutionary Committee of Mozambique (Comitê Revolucionnario de Moçambique—COREMO), a coalition of five parties, was formed in Kampala, Uganda. Its leaders, Paulo José and Illomulo Chitofo Gwambe, had been members of FRELIMO at its inception, but they had opposed Mondlane's appointment and criticized the exiled leadership for not being sufficiently active inside Mozambique. Support for COREMO inside Mozambique was strongest in Tete District (after independence districts were designated as provinces), where between 1965 and 1968 it was responsible for guerrilla actions against the Portuguese conducted from bases in Zambia. Nevertheless, in 1965 when Mondlane described the other parties as "office organizations" led by people who were disappointed in power struggles within FRELIMO, he was probably giving an honest evaluation of the situation. FRELIMO was clearly the dominant organization of the liberation movement; alone among the contending groups it had established a bureaucratic structure, a program of political action within Mozambique, and a military wing. It had gained the recognition of the Organization of African Unity (OAU) as the legitimate representative of the Mozambican people and, more important, the active support of the Tanzanian government.

**War of Liberation: The Initial Phase**

The armed guerrilla struggle against Portuguese colonialism began in earnest in September 1964 under FRELIMO's direction. The Portuguese forces, having experience with a similar insurgency in Angola, were prepared, however, and had 30,000 troops deployed in Mozambique. The level of success of the nationalists in the first three years of the war of liberation was to prove a point of considerable debate. On the one hand, FRELIMO announced more than 7,000 Portuguese casualites, the downing of 16 aircraft, and the capture of most if not all of two districts, while condemning members of the North Atlantic Treaty Organization (NATO) for arming the Portuguese forces. On the other hand, the Portuguese at first said FRELIMO was responsible only for a "few acts of banditry." By 1967 they were admitting limited casualites and some loss of territory to rebels, while protesting that the insurgency had been instigated by the Soviet Union.

That same year the Portuguese established a "no man's land" inside the northern frontier, abandoning to the rebels the remote and thinly populated regions along the border with Tanzania. Below the no man's land they concentrated the population in a series of *aldeamentos* (fortified village complexes), where the Portuguese forces could both provide security for Africans and isolate them from contacts with FRELIMO forces. The bringing together of larger numbers at central locations also gave the Portuguese the opportunity to provide Africans with social services, many for the first time, in an effort to win their support for the Portuguese cause. Gradually FRELIMO spread westward, however, heavily infiltrating parts of the Niassa District.

By 1968 the name of Samora Moises Machel appeared in the uppermost ranks of FRELIMO as commander of its military wing. Machel, like Mondlane from southern Mozambique, replaced a northerner as head of an army composed largely of northerners, especially members of the Maconde group, whose homeland straddled the border between Mozambique and Tanzania and was a natural recruiting ground for FRELIMO. The Maconde plateau was protected by steep escarpments and dense forests that were ideal for insurgent operations. Though capable of forcing their way into the area, the Portuguese drew their defense perimeter beyond its edges and established the line of *aldeamentos* further south and east among the Macua-Lomue ethnic group, segments of which had been historically in conflict with the Maconde.

The role of the Maconde and other northern ethnic groups created problems for FRELIMO in the late 1960s as it sought to extend its area of operations to the south, far from the homelands of most of its soldiers. This stirred up another internal problem, namely, the divisions among those competing for leadership within the party who sought backing along ethnic and ideological lines. Between 1966 and 1970 a number of FRELIMO leaders were assassinated by rival factions within the party, by Portuguese security units, or by right-wing political groups active within Mozambique's European community. The assassinations further heightened tensions within the party and caused a number of party leaders to defect to the Portuguese. The attacks reached their peak in February 1969 when a series of bombs were sent through the mail, one of them killing Mondlane. Despite intensive investigation by international organizations, the identify of his assassins remained a mystery, although accusations ranged from the Portuguese secret police to communist elements within FRELIMO. Mondlane, it was noted, had come under attack from the Soviet Union and China because he had sought to limit the degree of communist involvement in order to win greater support in Western countries.

Most of the foreign assistance on which FRELIMO depended in its first five years of the war of liberation was provided by African sources. Much of the nonmilitary aid came from Western sources, including the United States. As the military effort increased, however, so did the insurgents' need for arms. The communist states in Europe and Asia provided scholarships,

*FRELIMO soldiers during the war of liberation reflected the need for foreign assistance. Courtesy AIM, Maputo*

military training for officers, diplomatic support at the UN, and funds as well as arms. By 1971 FRELIMO recruits were receiving indoctrination in Marxism along with their military training.

Nevertheless, FRELIMO's most important foreign support came from the government of Tanzania, a country whose ruling philosophy was socialist but clearly non-Marxist. Tanzania provided a headquarters for FRELIMO, refugee settlements and educational opportunities for its members, training for its soldiers, and safe supply routes and rear-echelon bases for its forces. The Portuguese contemplated punitive military action against Tanzania but were reluctant to stir up world opinion further against its colonial policies. A few Portuguese attacks against targets in Tanzania close to the border did occur, but these were isolated incidents. Tanzania was compelled to enlarge its army at considerable cost to defend the remote border, but Nyerere's support for the Mozambican liberation movement never faltered.

After Mondlane's death, Simango assumed the presidency temporarily, but at the next meeting of FRELIMO's Central Committee his request to remain in office was rejected in favor of a three-man presidential council consisting of Simango, dos Santos, and Machel. Six months later Simango broke with the other two, accusing them of inciting tribalism and calling them responsible for the assassinations and defections that had taken place. Although Tanzanian president Nyerere and the OAU tried to reconcile the leaders, the executive committee suspended Simango from his post. The following spring he and several lesser figures were expelled from FRELIMO, and the Central Committee named Machel the new president and dos Santos vice president.

### The Cahora Bassa Project

After the death of Mondlane, Portuguese authorities hoped that FRELIMO might founder without his leadership. Instead its military activity increased. Early in 1969 FRELIMO forces began to infiltrate Tete District, intending in one step to bypass the relatively successful Portuguese containment effort in the north, to open a new front to divide the Portuguese military forces, and to present a threat to Portugal's major hope for improvement in the Mozambican economy—the huge Cahora Bassa hydroelectric project.

Portugal's determination to hold onto Mozambique, despite rising military costs, stemmed partly from exaggerated notions of its "civilizing mission" in Africa and partly from the belief that Mozambique had great economic potential. Although commercially exploitable mineral deposits existed, the economy continued to be narrowly based. Its pillars were the export of a few primary agricultural products, remittances from Mozambican laborers in South Africa, and the role of the country's ports and railroads in the trade of South Africa and Southern Rhodesia. The construction of a huge hydroelectric project in Tete District at Cahora Bassa, a narrow defile in the upper Zambezi valley 120 kilometers from the Zambian border, had long been considered. A major change in Portugal's laws in 1962, which encouraged investment by foreign companies in the overseas provinces, made the financing of the project a possibility for the first time. The site provided a location that would allow the construction of a mammoth dam at relatively low cost and would impound one of the world's largest man-made lakes and create one of the five largest electric sources in the world. Power generated by the dam could be sold profitably to South Africa and would also provide cheap energy on which new industrial and mining production might eventually be based in Mozambique. The Salazar government also laid heavy emphasis on plans for placing up to 1 million settlers—white and African—on 2 million hectares of new farmland that the waters of the lake would irrigate. Salazar intended the project as a clear statement of his country's intention to remain permanently in Africa.

FRELIMO also recognized the dam as a symbol of Portuguese determination to remain in Mozambique and reacted particularly against the colonial government's proposal to bring more European settlers into the country. Blocking the construction of the dam became its primary objective in the late 1960s. Opposition to the construction of the Cahora Bassa project was organized on an international scale. Sympathetic groups in Western countries were solicited to pressure their governments to block private participation in the project on the grounds that such involvement would contribute to the maintenance of white minority rule in southern Africa. American, Swedish, Italian, and other bidders withdrew their tenders as a result of such pressures, but the project went ahead primarily with Portuguese and South African support and private French and West German involvement.

Although supporters of FRELIMO abroad continued to oppose the construction of the Cahora Bassa dam, the insurgents altered their views as time went on. The Portuguese government did not have the success it anticipated in inducing European emigrants to settle in Mozambique. More important, as FRELIMO came to control territory surrounding the dam, they began to see it as a significant asset to an independent Mozambique. By 1972 FRELIMO was concentrating on slowing its construction and raising its costs but has given up plans to do material damage to the project.

**Final Phase of the Liberation War**

In 1970 the Portuguese commander, General Kaulza Oliveira de Arriaga, launched the largest military operation of the pervasive Mozambican war in an effort to crush the 10,000 FRELIMO guerrillas. Penetrating the northern areas of Cabo Delgado and Niassa districts long left to FRELIMO, Arriaga demonstrated the ability of the Portuguese troops to inflict tactical defeats on any FRELIMO force anywhere in the country. Nevertheless, the campaign and its aftermath clearly pointed up Portugal's actual strategic military weakness, i.e., the inability of colonial forces to maintain control over a combat zone of nearly 400,000 square kilometers. By 1972 the regular Portuguese army troops in Mozambique numbered 60,000 men, of whom 40,000 were Africans serving in racially mixed units. Most of the officers were white or *assimilados*. Elite, all-black units were employed, however, to lead sweeps against suspected enemy concentrations. Although major blows could be struck at the insurgents, most of their forces were too widely dispersed for the Portuguese to locate and engage.

The insurgents depended almost entirely on units of platoon size or smaller, although on rare occasions they were able to combine them into joint attacks involving as many as 400 men. The units engaged primarily in mining roads and paths, intimidating scattered villages, and ambushing small Portuguese patrols or pro-Portuguese African self-defense units. When large Soviet rockets became available, the guerrillas launched them at Portuguese bases and towns.

Marcello Caetano succeeded Salazar as prime minister of Portugal in 1968. He was considered a moderate within the regime and spoke of "evolution within continuity." Caetano advocated an expansionist economic policy in Africa, took steps to return a measure of control over local affairs to the colonies, and worked to reduce racial discrimination. These reforms, however, were very limited in scope. The major one, the Organic Law of 1972, made Mozambique a constituent state in a Portuguese union, instead of simply a province of "Greater Portugal." A 50-member legislative assembly was created, 30 of its members to be chosen by interest groups, the other 20 elected. Although the franchise was extended to all literate Mozambicans, only a small percentage of the population took part in elections. Opposition to Caetano's policy of liberalization from right-wing elements in the regime and the threat of an army coup subsequently led the prime minister to take a harder line on Africa.

During 1972 and 1973 FRELIMO was able to improve its military position substantially despite continued counteroffensives by the Portuguese forces. FRELIMO's major growth occurred in Tete District. Zambia's president, Kenneth Kaunda, who had earlier backed COREMO, was persuaded by Nyerere to throw his support to FRELIMO, whose insurgents could thereafter enter Mozambique across the remote and unmarked Zambian border. Although unsuccessful in their efforts to slow construction of the Cahora Bassa dam, the FRELIMO troops were able to disrupt road and rail traffic on a regular basis and won control of sizable areas of Tete District along the Zambian frontier.

Malawi, long open to accusations of being the only friend of the white minority regimes in Black Africa, was a poor country dependent on Portuguese Mozambique for access to the sea. In 1970 a new rail link had been completed, carrying Malawi's trade more efficiently through the Mozambican port of Nacala and for the first time allowing for the interconnection (through Southern Rhodesia and Malawi) of all three Mozambican rail systems.

Strong economic ties of this kind had prevented overt Malawian support for Mozambican nationalists, but by 1973 Malawi was providing important strategic assistance to FRELIMO, allowing it to use that country as a transportation route and sanctuary. The proximity of the Malawi frontier allowed FRELIMO forces to attack the railroad to Tete, which ran parallel to the border, and to attack Zambezia District, an area that the Portuguese had previously been able to leave unguarded.

South Africa and Southern Rhodesia gave increasing support to the Portuguese. South African assistance was limited to economic cooperation, including substantial involvement in the Cahora Bassa project. Southern Rhodesian assistance was military, its troops aiding the Portuguese in raids against the insurgents from both countries who were operating in Tete District in the area along the Rhodesian frontier.

Although the Portuguese forces were able to prevent direct attacks on Cahora Bassa and the routes leading to it, the steady movement of insurgents to the south put them under increasing pressure. By early 1974 attacks occurred regularly in Vila Pery District (present-day Manica Province), directly affecting white settlers south of the Zambezi and bringing the war within striking distance of Beira and other major population centers. FRELIMO's terror tactics and the inability of the thinly spread Portuguese forces to stop the infiltration added greatly to the alarm of Portuguese settlers and pro-Portuguese Africans, who in turn pressured the government to take firmer measures against the insurgents. The result was an overreaction by Portuguese troops. Africans were forcibly removed from their villages, many of which were destroyed, and taken to *aldeamentos*. This action contributed to an appreciable growth of African support for FRELIMO in areas that had earlier been indifferent to the liberation movement (see fig. 7).

## Independent Mozambique

By 1974 there were signs of widespread disenchantment in Portugal with the government's colonial policies. Although the army seemed technically capable of sustaining military activities against African insurgents for an indefinite period, confidence within the armed forces had been shaken by the apparent success of FRELIMO's offensive campaign. More than 80 percent of Portugal's available forces had been committed to the three colonial wars being fought simultaneously in Africa. The increased length

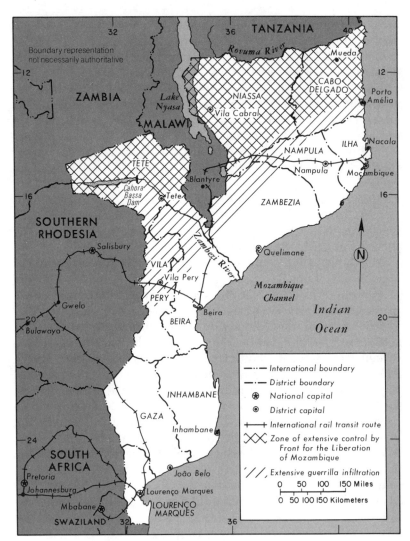

*Figure 7. Mozambique, 1974-75*

of military service demanded of conscripts to meet manpower requirements and severe economic strains in the early 1970s added to the climate of dissatisfaction. More significantly, long tours of duty in indecisive colonial wars and other professional grievances, coupled with exposure to their opponents' revolutionary ideology and a growing awareness of Portugal's social, political, and economic stagnation, contributed to the perception among many in the officer corps that changes were needed at home as well as in the colonies.

On April 25, 1974, officers belonging to the Armed Forces Movement (Movimento da Forças Armadas—MFA) overthrew the Caetano regime in a bloodless coup. The new government that they sponsored saw as its first objective the effective end of the wars in Africa by granting self-determination in the overseas territories. General António de Spínola, the provisional president, intended that this should be achieved within a Lusitanian (Portuguese-speaking) confederation in which the former colonies would maintain close economic and political links with metropolitan Portugal.

In Mozambique the government set a cease-fire with FRELIMO as its immediate objective, to be followed by a popular referendum, within one year to determine the country's future. The Spínola government offered the people of the territory three choices: total integration in a greater Portuguese state, self-government within a Lusitanian confederation, or complete independence. In the meantime, FRELIMO was invited to participate openly in the democratic process in competition with other groups.

FRELIMO, however, refused to agree to a cease-fire until Portugal had accepted its terms in full. These were the immediate granting of complete independence without a referendum, the recognition of FRELIMO as the sole legitimate representative of all the peoples of Mozambique, and an agreement to transfer all powers of government directly into FRELIMO's hands. Spínola refused FRELIMO's demands on the grounds that there was no evidence that FRELIMO represented the majority of Mozambique's people, and he ordered a resumption of hostilities. Escalation of the conflict met with growing refusal by Portuguese troops, black and white, to continue to fight for what now seemed a lost cause. Widespread strikes over economic issues by African and European workers, newly released from decades of police control, erupted in the cities.

The deteriorating security situation and the left-wing orientation of the MFA and the civilian leaders that it chose to participate in the government not only alarmed the European community and pro-Portuguese Africans in Mozambique but also rapidly eroded Spínola's ability to control events in Lisbon. In May representatives of the Portuguese government approached FRELIMO to hold talks despite the gap that existed between the positions of the two sides. Discussions began in Lusaka, Zambia, in June between Machel and the Portuguese foreign minister, Mário Soares.

In an attempt to force FRELIMO to accept less than it had

originally demanded, additional Portuguese forces were brought into the country, and settlers were issued arms. But FRELIMO had also augmented its ranks, as many Africans who had not taken sides in the struggle previously were inspired by the prospects of an early victory to support its efforts. By the end of July the local commanders on both sides had begun to reach cease-fire agreements of their own in much of the country.

In the civilian sector widespread strikes for higher wages in the cities were matched by unrest on the Portuguese-owned farms and plantations, much of it to protest low wages and poor working conditions. In areas now deprived of effective security, would-be guerrillas turned to looting and banditry, driving Portuguese farmers into the cities or out of the country. By August the two military forces were cooperating in efforts to stop banditry and civil disturbance.

Secret negotiations had continued in Lusaka, but while FRELIMO remained adamant, the resolve of the Portuguese government weakened. In July Spínola conceded his government's willingness to recognize the right of the colonies to independence without referenda. On September 6 Machel and Soares announced that an agreement was being signed granting Mozambique its independence as of June 25, 1975, the thirteenth anniversary of the founding of FRELIMO. The Lusaka agreement was a complete triumph for FRELIMO, effectively meeting all of its demands. A cease-fire was ordered, and security until independence became the joint responsibility of FRELIMO and Portuguese forces. A transitional government was to be established in which the prime minister and three cabinet ministers were to be appointed by the Portuguese and six other ministers were to be named by FRELIMO.

The transitional government took office in late September under Joaquim Alberto Chissano as prime minister. Chissano was one of three central figures in FRELIMO and had been its secretary of defense and security. Machel and dos Santos, the party's vice president and chief political theoretician, stayed outside the government. Machel also stayed out of the country, remaining aloof from the compromises that had to be made during the transition. A Portuguese officer remained as high commissioner and as commander in chief of the joint security forces. Soon after the transitional government took office, efforts were made to Africanize the top administrative positions.

The agreement came as a blow to the white community and to the plethora of African, white, and integrated political groups that had come into being after the Portuguese coup. A small, liberal, multiracial political organization that had been formed shortly before the coup—the United Group of Mozambique (Grupo Unido de Moçambique—GUMO) attracted large and enthusiastic crowds of whites and Africans to rallies in May with its call for gradual movement toward self-government—but only because the rallies were the first free public manifestations of the sentiment for an end to colonialism. Even then it had begun to be clear that the support of most of the Africans, even in Lourenço Marques, a city far removed from FRELIMO's strongholds, was going to FRELIMO.

GUMO soon fell apart. It was succeeded by the National Coalition Party (Partido da Coligação Nacional—PCN), which brought several anti-FRELIMO black groups under one umbrella. Most of its leaders had previously been leaders of COREMO or were FRELIMO leaders who had been forced out of the party. Notable among the last were Simango, once FRE-LIMO's acting president, and Lazaro Kavandame, chief of the Maconde people, who made up the majority of FRELIMO's army during the war. The PCN favored a referendum and opposed negotiations with FRELIMO on the grounds that other political groups had not been included in the discussions.

Several political organizations opposed to FRELIMO had sprung up within the white minority was well. The most signifi-cant of these was Fico (Portuguese for "I stay"), which demanded that arms be issued to European civilians to defend themselves against FRELIMO. Right-wing terrorist groups were responsible for the bombings of a number of offices associated with pro-FRELIMO interests. Others in the white community were widely believed to be forming secret military units backed by mercenaries, in the hope of seizing control of the country before Portugal could grant it independence.

The efforts of anti-FRELIMO elements culminated pre-maturely in a disorganized attempt to seize power in September 1974. The attempted coup, supported by whites in Lourenço Marques and Beira as well as by the PCN, was set in motion by the announcement of the independence agreement between Machel and Soares. An organization calling itself the Free Mozambique Movement seized strategic points in the two cities without interference from the army. But when rioting began in the black suburbs, reportedly after armed attacks on blacks by white youth groups, Portuguese and FRELIMO security forces intervened to crush the riots and the coup.

Although a similar incident occurred in late October, the col-lapse of the Free Mozambique Movement's effort marked the effective end of organized opposition to FRELIMO rule by either blacks or whites. It also signaled the beginning of the exodus of whites from the country. Most of them went back to Portugal, emigrated to Brazil, or sought to settle in South Africa or Southern Rhodesia. By June 1975 the country's white population had declined from about 200,000 to an estimated 40,000. The leaders of the PCN and FRELIMO's other black opponents had few places to flee, and by the end of 1974 most had been arrested and imprisoned by FRELIMO.

### The Transitional Government

Before the end of 1974 FRELIMO appointees, in addition to their ministerial posts, held the governorships of half the country's districts and had replaced most of the mayors. Two of the country's six newspapers were handed over to FRELIMO. With the help of the remaining Portuguese forces the transitional government put a lid on public demonstrations of opposition or discontent. Strikes over economic issues were brought rapidly to an end, and it was made plain that no political activity outside FRELIMO's direct control would be tolerated. The government made few moves to take control of the economy, however, and sought to avoid measures that might further hasten the flight of white managers and technicians, who were recognized as valuable to the country's economy. The flight of whites continued unabated, however. Their departure was a major cause of the country's economic problems as independence approached. Equally important causes were the damage and dislocation resulting from the war and the attitudes displayed by many African workers who had expected an immediate improvement in their incomes.

The few whites who chose to stay in Mozambique fell into two categories: civil servants on contract to the new government and the small number of leftists who sympathized with FRELIMO's announced aims of improving the living standards through socialism. Their numbers declined as the extent of Machel's adherence to Marxism-Leninism became clearer. By early 1977 only 30,000 Portuguese remained in Mozambique; most were temporary residents working on contract. Whites continued, however, to occupy positions of importance in the FRELIMO regime.

FRELIMO was also concerned about the approximately 30,000 African troops in the Portuguese army as a potential source of opposition, particularly the members of the all-black elite combat units. Demobilized gradually over the nine-month transition period, all were apparently reabsorbed without conflict into the

*Mozambicans at a political rally in the capital city
celebrating national independence; an early version
of the country's flag was a featured attraction.
Courtesy United Nations/Bob Van Lierop*

society, perhaps because FRELIMO was in firm control of the
government by the time they were discharged. Only a few
appeared to have participated in the anti-FRELIMO movements. Later FRELIMO denunciations of "reactionary" elements
in the society included blacks accused of having been pro-
Portuguese. About 3,000 purported opponents were arrested in
raids by the newly formed security police in October 1975. Most
of them were sent to reeducation camps for ideological training

rather than to prisons.

## Independence

As the date for independence approached, it appeared to outside observers that FRELIMO would gain complete control over the country without significant political threat to its radical program for restructuring the society along Marxist lines. The liberation movement did, however, clearly face two major problems: a rapidly declining economy crippled by a lack of skilled managers and technicians and an approaching confrontation with its white neighbors.

Machel entered the country via Mueda in the north exactly one month before independence. He spent the interval making a triumphal tour of the country, arriving in the capital just before the June 25 independence ceremony and his subsequent elevation to the presidency. The first Council of Ministers (cabinet) was selected by Machel and sworn in on July 1, 1975.

The immediate objectives of the government were set forth in the new president's inaugural message. All land was nationalized, as were all abandoned houses and businesses. Private schools, including those operated by missionaries, were taken over by the state. The private practice of medicine and law was made illegal, and later all privately owned rental properties would be nationalized. The army was to be redirected to the task of ensuring a radical transformation of society.

During August and September several conferences were held to discuss and decide on policies in particular areas. The decisions reached at these sessions were indicative of the direction to be taken by the regime. Regarding agriculture, for instance, it was announced that the organization of communal villages, state farms, collective farms, and production and sales cooperatives would be the first major objectives. In addition, the *aldeamentos* were to be retained and expanded to serve as one major base for collectivization of the rural economy and society.

## The FRELIMO Regime

The People's Republic of Mozambique—as the newly independent nation was formally named—was from its inception a one-party state in which FRELIMO permitted no legitimate internal opposition to its rule. But in 1975 the victorious liberation movement had no party organization outside the districts where FRELIMO had been strong during the liberation war— Niassa, Cabo Delgado, and Tete. Everywhere else in the country, party infrastructure had to be built virtually from scratch.

Rather than recruit a mass following through local party organizations, the task was assigned to members of hastily formed dynamizing groups (*grupos dinamizadores*—GDs), who were assigned to convey the party's message to the masses and to mobilize their economic efforts (see Party Structure, ch. 4). Machel guided the party and, through it, the Mozambican government, but he and the narrow circle of colleagues that sat on the Political Bureau did little at first to enlarge FRELIMO's membership beyond the 8,000 or so militants who had served in the guerrilla army or whose ideological commitment was beyond question. Frequent purges of party ranks prevented the rise of rivals to challenge their leadership. Potentially influential mass groups, such as FRELIMO's youth and women's organizations were closely controlled by the Central Committee. No popular participation in the decision-making process was allowed, and few party conferences were held where policies might be discussed outside the Central Committee. A political commissariat was created to maintain ideological discipline within the army (see Front for the Liberation of Mozambique, ch. 4).

FRELIMO's Third Party Congress (the second had been held in 1968) was convened in February 1977 in Maputo (as Lourenço Marques had been officially renamed a year earlier) amid mounting economic difficulties and differencies on the policymaking level over the role of the party and the direction in which it was to lead the country. Formally declaring adherence to Marxism-Leninism, FRELIMO officially became a "vanguard party," modeled closely on the Soviet communist party. Centralized decisionmaking, already the rule in FRELIMO, was reconfirmed. The congress stated that the aims of the party were the destruction of capitalism and the construction of a material base for socialism, anticipating that a powerful working class, organized by FRELIMO, would assume the leadership of society as Mozambique moved toward socialism. The importance of agriculture was acknowledged, but the congress identified the growth of an industrial sector as the decisive factor in the country's future economic development (see Ideology and Program, ch. 4).

From the first, the FRELIMO government had stressed the need for social and economic development to overcome the disparities created by the colonial exploitation of the country's people and resources. A massive literacy campaign was inaugurated among a population that was more than 85 percent illiterate at the time of independence, and teacher training and classroom building programs were approved. Plans were also made to extend and improve medical care.

Initially, nationalization applied only to small businesses that were converted into state-operated retail outlets. In 1977, however, as the regime became more outspoken in its ideological commitment, larger enterprises, including insurance companies, the Portuguese-owned oil refinery at Beira, and petroleum distributorships, were also seized. At the same time, the government lifted the ban on repatriation of profits imposed by the Portuguese and invited foreign investment that could be channeled into areas of development to which it had given priority.

Economic development projects were costly and depended on both foreign assistance and reliable markets for success. The surplus from exports that once went directly to Portugal now stayed in Mozambique, but independence coincided with a drop in commodity prices owing to the world recession and a rise in energy costs. Agricultural and industrial production dropped about 50 percent in the first three years after independence. The cashew industry, which produced Mozambique's main export crop, was impaired by the collapse of the collection system. Drought and floods in turn damaged production on the cooperatives and communal farms set up by the state. Severe food shortages occurred in many parts of the country.

The government attributed Mozambique's economic difficulties to the disruption caused by the war, the conflict in Southern Rhodesia, and to sabotage by Portuguese leaving the country. Production goals were also set back, as the government noted, by slack work habits and walkouts by workers (strikes being illegal). At one point, Machel accused workers of "anti-white racism" for refusing to cooperate with expatriate Portuguese managers and technicians. The economy's poor performance could be attributed not only to the loss of most of the country's trained and experienced personnel and other causes cited by the government but also to mismanagement of state-run enterprises by its own officials. As an emergency measure to halt the critical outflow of foreign exchange, the government imposed a tough and extremely unpopular austerity program that limited imports, thereby removing many consumer items from the market. Wage increases were restricted, prices were allowed to rise, and greater demands were made on workers and farmers.

Despite the emphasis placed on building a strong industrial sector where almost none had existed, agricultural development remained a matter of particular importance for both economic and political reasons in what was essentially an agrarian society. FRELIMO was committed to promoting communal farms based on village communities, some adapted from the *aldeamentos*, as the fulcrum for development in the countryside. But no policy was consistently implemented to give them priority, and their production was insignificant compared with that of private family small holdings. In practice, however, greater confidence was placed on the collectivized state farms to raise agricultural output rapidly. These mechanized and highly bureaucratized units, converted from former Portuguese holdings, soon demonstrated their inefficiency.

A major shake-up in the cabinet in April 1978 was linked to the disarray in agriculture. The minister of agriculture, Joaquim Ribiero de Carvalho, was dropped for having overemphasized the technological approach on state farms while blocking development of communal farms and disregarding the potential for family farm production. To these charges were added those of moral corruption and violation of FRELIMO's "revolutionary ideology." Further dismissals of ministers for incompetence in office occurred over the next several months.

Opponents of the regime outside Mozambique ranged from the Portuguese who had resettled across the border to the disillusioned members of FRELIMO who had escaped the party purges. Their interest converged in several small groups claiming to be pro-Western and anticommunist that were organized with South African and Rhodesian support. They had in common a hostility for Machel and the methods employed by a regime that had increasingly revealted its dictatorial nature. Reports of the hardships caused by the austerity program won them some backing in the Mozambican communities abroad, but their strength lay almost entirely outside Mozambique. After 1977 some of the external opposition groups merged as the Mozambican National Resistance (Resistência Nacional Moçambicana—RNM, sometimes referred to as RENAMO) and operated from bases inside South Africa and Southern Rhodesia.

The repeated purges of party officials and crackdowns on malcontents showed the difficulty of building a disciplined monolithic party in Mozambique. During the late 1970s as many as 10,000 persons were believed to have been detained at any given time in so-called reeducation camps located in different parts of the country. These numbers apparently included those considered politically unreliable by the regime but also many who were accused of corruption and other criminal acts. Large but undetermined numbers of Goans and *mestiços* were expelled from Mozambique during the same period, and travel by others outside the country was banned.

Local elections, the first of any kind since independence,

were held in September 1977. The national People's Assembly was constituted in a process involving "election" by district and provincial assemblies of people nominated by the party. The national assembly was to convene twice each year to approve actions determined in advance by the party and government leadership.

### Foreign Relations

Mozambique regarded itself as nonaligned in its foreign relations. Although it associated with the Soviet Union and other communist countries on most international issues, in practice Mozambique attempted to maintain good relations with any country willing to assist in its development. At independence its warmest ties outside Africa were with China, followed by the Soviet Union, Cuba, and other communist states that had supported FRELIMO during the War of Liberation. In 1977 Mozambique entered into a 20-year treaty of friendship and cooperation with the Soviet Union. Moscow supplied Mozambique with most of its military equipment in the late 1970s.

Aid and diplomatic support were generously forthcoming from Western Europe, especially from Sweden and other Scandinavian countries that had given nonmilitary aid to FRELIMO during the liberation war. Mozambique also cultivated good relations with Portugal and Brazil after independence. Contacts with the United States were at first cool, owing to the perception in Maputo that Washington had aided the Portuguese through their NATO contacts during the liberation war.

In Africa Mozambique's closest relations were with neighboring Tanzania and Zambia. Its most crucial—and ambiguous—relations, however, were with the white-minority regimes in South Africa and Southern Rhodesia. Machel, who had pledged that Mozambique would be a "revolutionary base against imperialism and colonialism in Africa," provided a sanctuary in his country for both the South African black nationalist African National Congress (ANC) and the Zimbabwean liberation movements. South Africa's white-minority government warned that it would not tolerate insurgent bases across its borders. Although it supported the Mozambican dissidents, the most damaging weapons that South Africa used against FRELIMO were economic. South African gold, which had formerly gone to Lisbon as remittances, went to Mozambique after independence. In 1975 Mozambique earned the equivalent of US$175 million in foreign exchange, about one-third of its total earnings, from this source. The number of Mozambican mine workers in South Africa

*President Samora Moises Machel, a key figure in FRELIMO's effort to perpetuate independent Mozambique's popular revolution*
*Courtesy AIM, Maputo*

was cut from about 120,000 in that year to under 40,000 in 1978, causing Mozambique a substantial loss of anticipated revenue. Economic cooperation was important, however, for both countries. At independence Mozambique's ports and rail system handled nearly 20 percent of South Africa's imports and exports, transit charges accounting for another one-third of the country's foreign exchange earnings. South Africa, therefore, continued to invest money and technical assistance to maintain Mozambique's rail and port facilities. Despite the hostility that existed between the governments, deliveries of hydroelectric power from Cahora Bassa to South Africa began in 1977.

The histories of the people of Mozambique and Zimbabwe (formerly known as Southern Rhodesia until 1980) had been intertwined for centuries. After independence Mozambique allowed bases to be set up by Zimbabwean liberation fighters and accepted 200,000 refugees. This made its territory a target for raids by the armed forces of Southern Rhodesia, against which Mozambique was incapable of defending itself. Rhodesian forces moved troops and launched air strikes against nationalist bases and refugee camps and frequently crossed the border in hot pursuit of insurgents. In one such raid on a camp in August 1976, some 600 were killed; 1,200 were left dead in a massive assault in November 1977.

In retaliation for Mozambique's backing of Zimbabwean guerrillas, the Rhodesians provided base facilities for the RNM to carry out raids across the border. In addition to attacks from Southern Rhodesia, Mozambican authorities became involved in disputes between rival Zimbabwean liberation movements that were fought on their soil. Many Zimbabwean insurgents were arrested and confined in the process of restoring order.

As one of the so-called front-line states (see Glossary) opposing the white-minority regimes in southern Africa, Mozambique joined the mandatory embargo imposed against Southern Rhodesia by the UN at great cost to its own economy. Mozambique estimated that it lost the equivalent of more than US$550 million in transit revenues and remittances from Southern Rhodesia between 1976 and 1980. Rail lines, bridges, and oil storage facilities destroyed during the fighting were valued at about US$50 million. A total of more than 1,300 Mozambican civilianis lost their lives as a result of the hostilities, and 700 more were missing and presumed kidnapped.

Mozambique supported a negotiated settlement between the nationalists and the white-dominated government. Understandably it welcomed the end of sanctions, and it established good relations with Zimbabwe when that country became independent under a black-majority government in 1980.

### A Change of Direction

At the Third Party Congress in 1977, FRELIMO launched itself into a new phase of Marxism-Leninism that leaned more heavily on the Soviet model, stressing leadership by a vanguard of party elites rather than a mass movement and insisting on the need for class struggle as part of the popular revolution. Machel took pains to demonstrate that FRELIMO's ideology blended orthodox Marxist theory with the unique national experience of Mozambique.

Ideological factors notwithstanding, inefficiency and inertia had had a paralyzing effect on the Mozambican economy. Corruption was evident in the running of the state-owned retail shops, housing construction, transportation, and port operations. The nationalized agricultural estates were failing because of incompetent management. Inexperienced civil servants at the middle level lacked initiative. Planning at the top level bore little relation to the reality of an economy that was grinding to a halt. The country's economic malaise recommended to Machel a reevaluation of the ideologically motivated policies that had been imposed by the party. It also persuaded Machel to moderate his reliance on the Soviet Union and other communist countries in order to improve relations with the West and to obtain its economic assistance.

Machel charted a new course for his government's economic policy in a speech delivered on March 18, 1980, in which he criticized the performance of the state-run enterprises and blamed excessive bureaucratic interference in the economy for its inefficiency. Small businesses, he announced, would be returned to private hands, and state enterprises would be expected thereafter to make themselves profitable. Machel denounced the "ultra-leftism" of officials whose ideological commitment seemed to take precedence over their responsibility to the government, and he paved the way for another round of purges aimed this time at combating inefficiency rather than punishing political deviation. In the weeks that followed Machel's speech, a number of officials were removed from their posts, and some were detained on charges of corruption or embezzlement. A reorganization of the cabinet was also carried out.

The direction pointed to in Machel's March 1980 speech was in no way intended as a departure from socialism. An effort was made, however, to separate party and government responsibilities. The speech also signaled a more pragmatic and flexible approach to domestic policies, a more balanced foreign policy, and less emphasis on ideology in the overall conduct of the affairs of the people's republic.

\* \* \*

A concise survey of Mozambique's history to independence is found in Thomas H. Henriksen's *Mozambique: A History.* Two important studies of the *prazos* and Portuguese penetration of the interior are M.D.D. Newitt's *Portuguese Settlement on the Zambezi* and Allan F. Isaacman's *Mozambique—The Africanization of a European Institution. Capitalism and Colonialism in Mozambique: A Study on the Quelimane District* by Leroy Vail and Landeg White offers a detailed social and economic history of the nineteenth and twentieth centuries that has implications beyond the region selected by the authors for study. Especially recommended for its treatment of the rise of the nationalist movement and the international aspects of the liberation war is *Mozambique in the Twentieth Century* by Luís B. Serapião and Mohamed A. El-Khawas. Keith Middlemas' *Cabora Bassa: Engineering and Politics in Southern Africa* examines both the project and the political events that surrounded it during the period 1968-74. Tony Hodges' essay, "Mozambique: The Politics of Liberation," provides a balanced treatment of Mozambique from independence to 1978. (For further information and complete citations, see Bibliography.)

# Chapter 2.   The Society and Its Environment

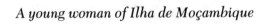

*A young woman of Ilha de Moçambique*

LIKE MOST AFRICAN STATES, Mozambique has the task of integrating an ethnically and linguistically diverse population and of minimzing conflict phrased in ethnic terms. Portuguese rule succeeded neither in integrating regions and groups nor in significantly exacerbating such ethnic differences as there might have been. After independence in 1975 there were indications of tensions framed in regional and occasionally in ethnic terms, but they did not pervade the political and social atmosphere as they seemed to do in some other African countries. This may have been in part a consequence of the fact that none of Mozambique's ethnic categories—and certainly not its largest ones (Macua-Lomue and Tsonga)—were themselved unified entities that had at any point acted as a single group.

Perhaps a greater problem from the perspective of the ruling party, the Front for the Liberation of Mozambique, were the tensions generated by the presence in high posts in the party and government of white Portuguese and *mestiços* (persons of mixed European and African ancestry) and by the extensive use of Europeans in significant economic and technical bureaucratic roles. That the extraordinary inadequacies of the colonial educational system made that necessary may not have been an acceptable explanation for Africans who expected national independence to provide opportunities for their own rise to status and power. The party has nonetheless strenuously resisted what it considers the racism of blacks who criticize the power of whites.

The postindependence regime attempted to institute rapid changes in the way of life and the social structures of Mozambique's peoples. The pervasiveness of such change, however, and the degree to which new practices and relations have become firmly rooted in the nine years since 1975 have been difficult to assess. Because of its potential impact on the 90 percent of the population that was still rural in the early 1980s, the most significant attempt at change was the institution of communal villages. These villages were intended to gather typically dispersed peasants into larger communities where the educational and health services so desperately needed by rural Africans could be efficiently distributed. But the communal villages were also to be linked to collective farming and to social changes guided by party cells and branches of the Mozambique Women's Organization.

Except in a few places, the formation of communal villages did not proceed as rapidly as the party had hoped. The establishment of collectives took place at an even slower rate, and by the early 1980s it was acknowledged that family farms would continue to be the dominant form of rural economic organization. The effort to abolish marriage payments, initiation rites, and child marriage and actions intended to raise the status of women and encourage their participation in public affairs have had some success in the communal villages; these actions have not been as effective among the great majority of rural people outside the villages.

Local institutions of the colonial era, particularly chieftainship, which was in turn based on elements of the precolonial systems, have been formally abolished. There have been indications, however, that chiefs still have influence in many places and that groups based on kinship and descent control the loyalties and behavior of many, if not most, Mozambicans.

The new elite consists of the leading members of the ruling political organization, which was proclaimed a vanguard Marxist-Leninist party in the late 1970s. The party showed many signs of conversion from the relative egalitarianism that had characterized it in its earlier incarnation as a liberation movement. Rank was clearly established and given due recognition. Those in power were entitled to certain perquisites. The extent to which party members were granted respect and deference, however, was another matter. In the early and mid-1980s, Mozambique's economy had not been rewarding for most of the country's people. Moreover, the regime may have attempted to change social institutions too rapidly for the taste of most Mozambicans. In these circumstances it is possible that the prestige accorded party leaders has not been very high.

## Physical Setting

Mozambique's 799,380 square kilometers (an area about twice that of California) are marked by a terrain that rises from the Indian Ocean littoral and its hinterland to plateaus and highlands in the west. Mozambique's great north-to-south extension, its location between the Indian Ocean and the great Central African plateau, and its varied topography contribute to marked differences in rainfall and temperature, sometimes in areas only a short distance from one another. Mozambique's rivers flow from west to east, all draining ultimately into the Indian Ocean. The river valleys have generally served as overland routes for population movements between the Central African plains, highlands and the coast, but the marshes that are characteristic of parts of these valleys, particularly near the coast, have hindered movement. The great Zambezi River has also been an obstacle to easy movement between north and south.

### Terrain and Drainage

Topographically, the Zambezi valley divides the country into northern and southern halves (see fig. 8). North of the valley and to the east of the Malawi (formerly Nyasaland) border, a narrow littoral, in most places less than 30 kilometers wide, gives way to hills and low plateaus to the west, eventually rising to extensions of the Central African highlands, as does the westernmost part of all Mozambique. High points generally take the form of isolated peaks situated on plateaus or of sharply rising systems of hills, escarpments, and plateaus. North of the Zambezi valley the highest and most rugged features are found in three unconnected highlands, the Livingstone-Nyassa highland, the Namuli highlands, and the Angonia highlands. The Maconde plateau, situated in the far northeast near the Tanzanian border, is of lower elevation. North of the river at the head of the Mozambican section of the Zambezi valley are the Tete highlands.

South of the Zambezi valley the littoral extends farther and farther inland until, south of the Save River, it takes up almost the entire width of the country—about 300 kilometers—with the exception of the small, isolated Gorongosa highlands and the eastward extension of the Central African highlands, known in Mozambique as the Manica escarpment. In that area stands Mount Binga, at more than 2,400 meters the highest point in Mozambique. In the far southwest lies the narrow strip of the Lebombo Mountains.

Many low areas are marshy, particularly along the coast. Among the land so characterized is that around the mouth of the Zambezi River and the lower reaches of the Púngoè River, at the mouth of which the important port of Beira is sited. There are also marshes between the lower reaches of the Limpopo River and the Incomati River, which has its outlet to the Indian Ocean just north of Maputo.

About 44 percent of Mozambique's terrain consists of littoral lowland and marshes. Low plateaus and hills at altitudes between 185 and 615 meters constitute 17 percent of the land area. High plateaus and hills at elevations between 650 and 1,000 meters make up another 26 percent of the area. The remaining 13 percent of the land consists of mountains higher than 1,000 meters.

Five major basins and several smaller ones, all flowing to the

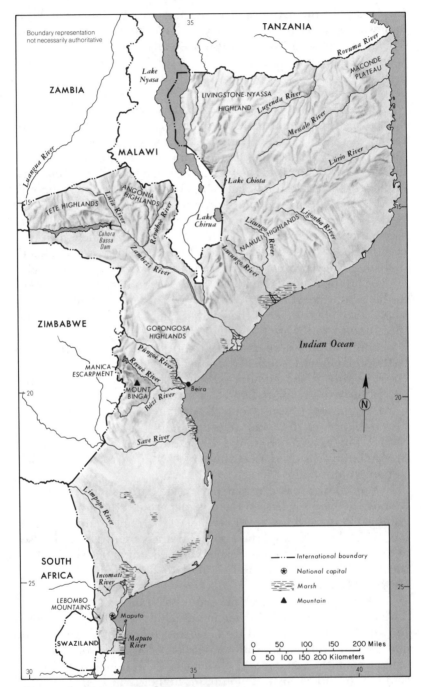

*Figure 8. Terrain and Drainage*

Indian Ocean, drain the country. Several have major catchment areas as far away as eastern Angola. Flow tends to fluctuate, owing to the alternation of the wet and dry seasons. The greatest flow takes place between January and March, the least between June and August.

The largest and most important basin is that of the Zambezi River. From the town of Tete downstream, the valley is low-lying and of a very gentle slope. Tete having an elevation of only a little more than 150 meters. Farther upstream, the river enters a narrow gorge, which prompted the construction of the Cahora Bassa dam— one of the largest in the world in power-generating potential—near Songo. The lake created by the construction of the dam extends roughly 240 kilometers to the west, approaching the point at which Mozambique borders both Zambia and Zimbabwe (formerly Northern Rhodesia and South Rhodesia, respectively) and it covers, respectively an area of more than 1,500 square kilometers.

Other major basins from north to south include those of the Rovuma, the Lúrio, the Save, and the Limpopo rivers. The Limpopo, largest of these streams, fed principally by the Changane River, is sluggish other than at flood tide, prompting Rudyard Kipling to describe it as "the great gray-green greasy, Limpopo River, all set about with fever-trees."

Except for the lake newly formed by the Cahora Bassa dam, Mozambique has access only to one other large body of fresh water—Lake Nyasa, which it shares with Malawi and Tanzania. A very small portion of Lake Chirua lies in Mozambique; most of it lies in Malawi, where it is known as Lake Chirwa. Another small lake (Lake Chiota) also straddles the Mozambique-Malawi border near the headwaters of the Lugenda River, a major tributary of the Rovuma. None of these bodies of water have been exploited by Mozambique.

## Climate

Each year is marked by a wet and a dry season; 80 percent or more of the annual rainfall occurs during the wet season, which lasts in most of the country from October to April. In many parts of Mozambique only traces of rain occur during the dry season, which lasts from April through September. Fluctuations in annual precipitation are marked, and drought is not uncommon, particularly in the south. Mozambique had suffered acutely in the great pan-African drought of 1974, and famine threatened much of the country in 1983 and early 1984 as a consequence of the drought that began in mid-1982, lasted through 1983, and was followed in the south by a cyclone and flooding in 1984.

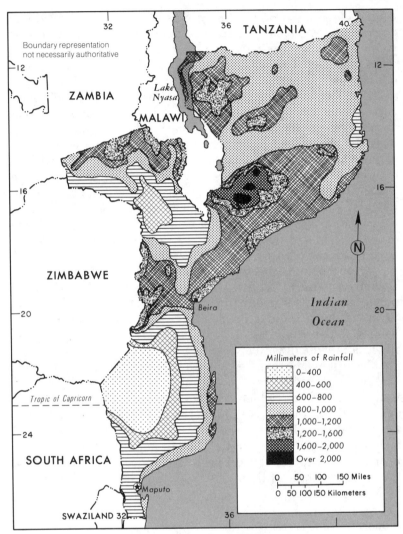

*Figure 9. Distribution of Annual Rainfall*

Only in a small part of Mozambique—in parts of the Namuli highlands—does annual rainfall exceed 2,000 millimeters (see fig. 9). Annual rainfall between 1,200 and 2,000 millimeters is more widespread, occurring also in the Namuli highlands, on the central coast, and in a few other places. Very low annual rainfall—less than 400 millimeters—occurs mainly in the southwest between the Save and Limpopo rivers. The arid zone in the southwest is fringed by another fairly large area in which annual rainfall ranges between 400 and 600 millimeters. It is this area, encompassing most of Gaza Province and part of Inhambane Province and marked by average annual rainfall of less than 600 millimeters, that has been most subject to periodic drought.

Broadly, temperatures and humidity are higher than average in the rainy season and lower in the dry season. The coast, affected by the warm Mozambique current flowing south from near the equator, tends to have higher temperatures and humidity than inland areas. Coastal temperatures moderate, however, in southerly latitudes, e.g., around Maputo. Inland, temperatures are affected by altitude and the presence of natural features, such as Lake Nyasa.

## Demography

The 1980 census—the first held after independence—yielded a total population of 12.1 million, nearly 48 percent larger than the 8.2 million enumerated 10 years earlier during Portuguese rule (see table 2, Appendix). Based on these totals, the average annual rate of growth in the intercensal period was 4 percent, a very high figure. It has been suggested, however, that migration across international borders, the inaccessibility of some areas, and other problems generated by the war for independence led to an undercount of roughly 10 percent in the 1970 census. An adjustment of the 1970 total yields a population of 9 million at that time and an annual intercensal growth rate of 3 percent. The 1980 total, however, reflects not only natural growth in the preceding 10 years but the return of Africans who had been outside the country in 1970 and the departure of the great bulk of the 170,000 Portuguese who formed part of the enumerated population at that time (see Ethnicity, this ch.). It is probable that the Africans returning exceeded the non-Africans departing, but a precise figure is not available.

Using a 2.7-percent annual rate of growth, various sources estimated the mid-1983 Mozambican population to be about 13.1 million. If that rate were to persist, the population would double in 26 years, but the rate may go higher before it drops. From its inception, the Mozambican regime has stressed a program of preventive medicine which, if effective, should have an impact on the infant mortality rate. In the early 1980s that rate was estimated between 114 and 120 per 1,000 live births, at the low end of the range for most Sub-Saharan African countries but still quite high. Further, the drought of 1982-83 had led to increases in malnutrition and child mortality. Nevertheless, if the infant mortality rate should be lowered substantially in the 1980s and early 1990s, Mozambique's natural rate of growth may hover around 4 percent.

**Age and Sex Structure**

Pending the publication of data showing age and sex cohorts at yearly or five-year intervals, only the most general outlines of the age and sex structure of the population in 1980 may be shown. Given the relatively high rate of natural growth, a substantial proportion of the population in 1980—42.5 percent—was under 15 years of age. Nearly as large a segment—42.2 percent—was between 15 and 44 years of age. The proportion of the population between ages 45 and 64 was 11.9 percent; that over 65 was 3.4 percent. The relatively small proportion of the population over 45 years of age was consistent with an estimated life expectancy at birth of 47 years in 1980.

The segment of the population between 15 and 64 years of age is commonly reckoned to constitute a country's labor pool; the segment under 15 and above 65 is construed as the dependent population. In Mozambique 54.1 percent of the population made up the labor pool in 1980; 45.9 percent constituted the dependent segment.

The ratio of women to men in the total population in 1980 was 105 to 100, females exceeding males in all categories except that of children under 15 years of age, in which males very slightly exceeded females. The sex ratios in urban and rural areas were markedly different, however. In Maputo there were 100 men for every 87 women, and it is likely that publication of detailed census results will show the ratio of men to women to be similar in other urban areas. Conversely, women outnumber men in the rural areas by a ratio higher than that for the population as a whole. In the province of Maputo, almost entirely rural, there were nearly 109 women for every 100 men. Except for the capital city of Maputo (which has provincial status), all provinces except one show a surplus of women. The exception is Sofala Province, of which Mozambique's second largest city, Beira, is the capital.

**Densities and Rural-Urban Distribution**

Mozambique's average population density of 15.2 persons per square kilometer in 1980 was fairly low but fell within the range of variation characteristic of neighboring states in southeast and central Africa. The range of densities within Mozambique was relatively narrow, however. Density data for 1980, available only at the provincial level, showed the highest densities to be in Nampula (between 29 and 30 persons per square kilometer) and

*Central business district of Maputo,
Mozambique's capital city
Courtesy Mozambique Information Office, London*

*Central business district of the major port city of Beira
Courtesy Mozambique Information Office, London*

Zambezia (between 23 and 24) and the lowest to be in Niassa (about four persons per square kilometer)' and Tete (between eight and nine). The capital city had a density between 1,200 and 1,300 persons per square kilometer.

If densities for small units such as districts were available, they would probably show a slightly wider range of variation. Data acquired in 1970 show that some districts in westernmost Tete, northernmost Niassa, and western Gaza provinces had fewer than two persons per square kilometer. Conversely, a few districts that incorporated some of Mozambique's coastal towns and their rural hinterlands had densities of more than 50 persons per square kilometer. By the mid-1980s the minimum and maximum rural densities had probably risen, but not substantially, and were a long way from approaching the much higher rural densities of parts of neighboring countries, such as Tanzania, Zambia, and Zimbabwe, let alone very densely settled Malawi.

The 1980 census showed 9 percent of the population to be urban. Roughly two-thirds (755,300 persons) of that urban population was found in the capital city of Maputo. Beira, the second largest city, was less than one-half Maputo's size. The urban population may have risen above 10 percent of the total by 1983, when Maputo's population was said to be nearly 1 million.

The comparatively low level of urbanization of the African population was, in part, a consequence of labor policy and practice in the colonial era. In colonial Mozambique many white- and blue-collar jobs filled elsewhere by Africans were reserved for Portuguese. Most Mozambican Africans who worked at non-agricultural jobs did so outside the country, mainly in South African mines. Consequently, at independence the African component of Mozambique's urban population was a very small portion of the country's total African population.

The postindependence departure of most Portuguese depleted urban population by 20 percent or more, but large numbers of Africans—more often males than females—soon arrived to replace them. Most of them lacked the training or skills sought by the new regime, but they came nevertheless. Among the new arrivals were males accustomed to earning wages in South Africa; after independence the mining companies recruited only about one-third of the Mozambicans they had employed annually in the early and mid-1970s. Under these circumstances many former mineworkers (or young men who would have turned to mine work) ventured to the towns.

The rush to the towns in the 1980s reflected the effects of very real hardships in the countryside generated by a long-lasting drought and by the activities of the Mozambican National Resistance (Resistência Nacional Moçambicana—RNM, sometimes referred to as RENAMO). The drought, which lasted through the 1981–82 and 1982–83 growing seasons (and was followed by destructive floods in some places), made cultivation so difficult that people, regardless of their lack of skills, left their rural homes to seek a livelihood in the towns. The RNM apparently followed a policy of raiding selected rural targets, especially collective farms and transport links, that made farm life untenable in some areas and forced families off the land into the towns (see The Mozambican National Resistance, ch. 5).

By May 1983 the presence in urban areas of many who lacked what the regime considered useful jobs or skills led the president to announce "Operation Production," which was intended to get 100,000 persons out of the cities. President Samora Moises Machel and others were angered by the fact that some Mozambicans were making a living through black market activities and other techniques distasteful to the regime. Efforts to get volunteers to resettle in the rural areas were unsuccessful. By July identification brigades were rounding up numbers of the presumably unemployed and engaging in nighttime raids, seeking "unproductive" persons. These roundups and raids were based in part on information provided by neighborhood residents who were urged to submit the names of hoarders and other "antisocial" persons. By September 1983, after some 50,000 persons were thought to have been removed from the cities, it was acknowledged that personal dislike had motivated many of the accusations and that many of those evicted from the cities had been dumped, without support or jobs, in rural areas. The People's Assembly, meeting in late April 1984, appeared to recognize the validity of the complaints lodged against Operation Production and urged that these complaints be dealt with. The deputies nonetheless considered the operation "the correct means of guiding a surplus of residents from the urban centers to take up productive activities in the rural areas . . . ."

## Ethnicity

Portuguese officials and ethnographers have divided Mozambique's peoples into 10 ethnic groups based on supposed commonalities of language, culture, and history. In the absence of more thorough and adequately conceptualized descriptions, these ethnic categories have been accepted by students of

Mozambique as first approximations for the classification of the country's peoples. Of these categories, only two—the Macua-Lomue in the northeast and the Tsonga in the south—include populations of substantial size. These two categories and others, however, represent entities that have been historically marked by political or social cohesion in only a few cases. Even the few groups that had achieved a degree of political cohesion inclusive of much of their membership had lost that cohesion by the mid-nineteenth century.

Ethnic identities have played some part in the way Africans have perceived and acted toward one another, but the kind of ethnic association that was so significant in politics and social life elsewhere in Africa, although present during the colonial period, was not important to Mozambique. Since independence, ethnicity as a basis for social and political relations had been strenuously discouraged by the regime. The not infrequent denunciations of "tribalism" by government spokesmen suggest that ethnic considerations still affected the behavior of many Mozambicans in the early and mid-1980s; it is also possible that the regime's references to tribalism are ways of attributing blame for problems, stresses, and strains that those in power have not been able to cope with. In any case, there have been no studies of the nature of ethnicity, its patterning, or its impact.

### Language

Language differences have been used as indicators of ethnic differences, and commonality of language has been a sign of other cultural commonalities, although not necessarily of actual or potential ethnic cohesion. Broadly, the link between linguistic and cultural similarity holds in Mozambique, but there are a few cases in which a complex history of movement and mixture had led to breaks in the linkage, i.e., some groups speaking dialects of the same language are otherwise different and perceive themselves as such.

All of Mozambique's indigenous peoples speak languages of the very widespread Bantu branch of the great Niger-Congo language family. Several subdivisions—clusters of presumably closely related tongues—of this branch are represented in Mozambique. The Mozambican versions of the languages in some of these clusters have not been well studied, but it is not always clear whether a given tongue belongs to a specific cluster or whether it is an independent language or dialect of a language. The exact number of independent languages spoken in Mozambique is therefore not established, but there are at least nine, and

it is likely that there are more. Only one of these languages—
Macua-Lomue, which may in fact be a cluster of languages—is
spoken by more than one-third of the population. In these circumstances, and given the political difficulties of assigning
national status to the language of any one group, the government
very quickly established that Portuguese was to be the national
language. In the mid-1980s, however, only a minority spoke and
understood Portuguese.

Of the several subdivisions of the Bantu branch, Southeast
Bantu includes the languages spoken by all of the peoples in the
southern third of Mozambique (south of the Save River) as well as
those spoken by the black populations of South Africa, Swaziland,
Lesotho, and Botswana and by some of the peoples of Zimbabwe.
Of the Southeast Bantu tongues used in Mozambique, the most
important (comprising several dialects) commonly called Tsonga,
is spoken by nearly one-fourth of the people and by a substantial
number in South Africa. Rjonga, a dialect of Tsonga spoken by the
people who live in the immediate vicinity of Maputo, has become
the lingua franca of Africans living in the city and its suburbs.
Nguni (the people are Ngoni), a group of tongues sufficiently close
to be considered dialects of one language, includes among its
speakers the Zulu, the Xhosa, and the Swazi peoples of South
Africa and Swaziland. In Mozambique, however, Nguni speakers
are few and are to be found mainly in the area near Maputo and
the border with Swaziland. A third Southeast Bantu tongue is
spoken by the Chopi and the Tonga living along the coast between
Xai-Xai and Inhambane (see figure 10). Because the Chopi and
the Tonga think of themselves as separate ethnic groups, the
dialects they speak have sometimes (incorrectly) been considered
separate langauges.

Yao and Maconde—spoken in Mozambique's far north, in
southern Tanzania, and, in the case of Yao, in Malawi—have been
grouped by linguist Derek Nurse with other Tanzanian tongues
into the Ruvuma (Tanzanian spelling of Rovuma) cluster. A
related language, Tanzanian Nguni, appears to include the language (or languages) spoken by the Ngoni (in Portuguese, Angoni)
of northern Mozambique. The term "Ngoni" is a variant of
"Nguni," and the Ngoni have their origins among the Nguni-
speaking peoples, particularly the Zulu of South Africa. Although
the Ngoni retain a number of Nguni terms, they have adopted a
language akin to those of the people among whom they live. The
languages of the Ruvuma cluster and the Ngoni are spoken by no
more than 4 percent of Mozambique's population.

The status of Macua-Lomue is unclear, as is the nature of

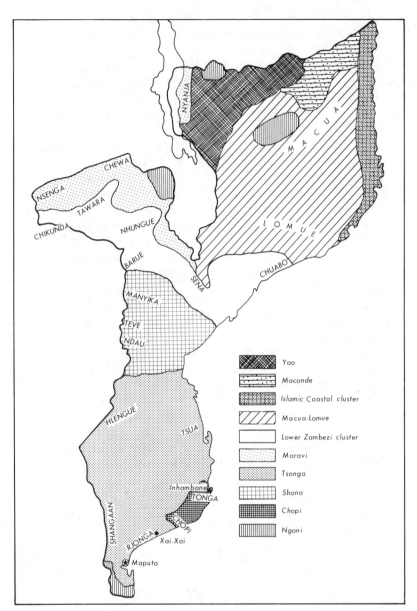

*Figure 10. Peoples of Mozambique*

dialect differentiation within the language. Some of the tongues considered dialects of Macua-Lomue may be independent languages. Some groups of Macua origin living along the coast speak a form of Swahili as a mother tongue, and the Chuabo, ordinarily placed in the Lower Zambezi cluster, speak a dialect of Macua.

Most of the groups between the Save and Zambezi rivers, a few south of the Save, and the great bulk of the population of neighboring Zimbabwe speak languages of the Greater Shona language group. Work by linguists Christopher Ehret and Margaret Kinsman indicates that Greater Shona includes at least four independent languages, of which three are represented in Mozambique. Once again the Mozambican languages are the least well known, and the precise status of the speech of some communities is therefore uncertain. Core Shona, the most important of these independent languages, is geographically the most widespread and is spoken by almost all Shona speakers in Zimbabwe and by most of those in Mozambique. It includes a number of tongues that are treated as dialects of a single language, but some of these may in fact be independent languages. The Core Shona dialects (or languages) in Mozambique are Shanga, Ndau-Garwe, and Plateau Shona. Plateau Shona consists of a large number of dialects, including most of those spoken in Zimbabwe and several also spoken in Mozambique. Among the latter are Manyika, Teve, and Unyama, of which the first is the most important.

On either side of the Zambezi River in Mozambique (and in part of Malawi and Zambia) is a cluster (or clusters) of languages whose boundaries have not been clearly determined. Several of these tongues—Chewa, Nyanja, and Manganja—are clearly part of the Chewa-Nyanja cluster and appear to be dialects of one language. The Sena-Nsenga group consists of a number of lesser known tongues that are considered to be independent languages, pending further study. Some linguists have joined the Chewa-Nyanja and Sena-Nsenga groups in a tentative larger language group.

Chewa and the closely related Nyanja are the languages of most of the Africans classified as Maravi by the Portuguese, but Nsenga is the language of some Maravi communities. Most of the communities in the hodgepodge, referred to as the Lower Zambezi cluster by colonial officials and ethnologists, speak languages of the Sena-Nsenga cluster; but some may speak Chewa, and a few speak tongues with other affinities.

## Ethnic Groups

With very few exceptions the ethnic categories recognized or established by the colonial authorities and the ethnologists who served them include groups that have emerged as the result of the biological and cultural mixing of several populations. The ancestors of some of the elements that entered into the contemporary populations were present in the area early in the first millennium A.D. Others arrived gradually, their migrations continuing into the nineteenth century (see Precolonial History; The Ngoni Migrations, ch. 1). In addition to the processes of ethnic formation initiated and carried forward by African peoples and on the coast and elsewhere by Arabs and other Muslim peoples, the Portuguese also contributed to the formation and transformation of African groups, particularly in the Zambezi valley and along the coast.

Because of this history of mixture and of the adaptation of different sections of a people to varying environments, communities in any ethnic category may be culturally similar, but they are never uniform and sometimes may differ radically from one another. Occasionally a centralized political order can impose a degree of uniformity and leave a residual sense of unity even after the political order has been fragmented or has decayed under outside pressures. Some of Mozambique's peoples were involved in centralized political systems for periods of time, but the scale of such systems was not large nor did they last long enough to mark the communities they included with a sense of loyalty to a larger whole.

Mozambicans have not been directly queried or enumerated with respect to ethnic affiliation since 1950 (the colonial authorities declared all to be Portuguese in 1961). In 1973, however, António Rita-Ferreira, a government official who had functioned for some time as a colonial ethnologist, provided estimates of the numbers of Mozambicans in several ethnic categories. He based his figures on the populations of specific districts, making the assumption that those districts were inhabited by persons of a specific ethnic group. Ethnic self-identification played no part in defining the categories or assigning individuals to them. The estimates for the early 1980s are extrapolations of Rita-Ferreira's estimates based on the 1970 census (see table B). The 1980 census takers did not gather data directly relevant to the enumeration of ethnic groups.

The largest of the commonly recognized ethnic clusters— and the least known—is the Macua-Lomue. The Macua section of the category, living for the most part north of the Ligonha River and along the coast, had a population nearly three times that of the Lomue, most of whom live to the south of the Ligonha and in the interior. The terms *Macua* and *Lomue* acquired a certain currency as ethnic names in the twentieth century, having been used by the Portuguese, eventually by the people themselves, and occasionally by representatives of the postindependence govern-

## Table B. Ethnic Categories, 1980

| Cluster Subgroup | Selected Alternative Names or Spellings | Percentage of Population |
|---|---|---|
| Macua-Lomue | Makwa-Lomwe | 37 |
| Macua | Makwa | (27) |
| Lomue | Lomwe | (10) |
| Tsonga | Thonga, Thonga-Shangane | 23 |
| Rjonga | Ronga | |
| Shangaan | Shangana, Changane | |
| Tsua | Tswa | |
| Hlengue | Hlengwe, Lhengwe | |
| Lower Zambezi | n.a. | 11 |
| Sena | n.a. | |
| Podzo | Marromeu, Chipango | |
| Tonga | n.a. | |
| Nhungue | Nyunwe, Nhungwe | |
| Chikunda | Chicunda | |
| Chuabo | Maganja | |
| Shona | Karanga | 9 |
| Manyika | Manika, Manica | |
| Ndau | Búzi | |
| Tawara | Tavara | |
| Barue | Bargwe | |
| Islamic Coastal | Suahaili, Swahili | 6 |
| Swahili | Suahaili | |
| Maca | Maka | |
| Mvani | n.a. | |
| Chopi | Chope, Chopi-Bitonga | 6 |
| Maravi | Marave, Malawi | 3 |
| Nsenga | Senga | |
| Zimba | n.a. | |
| Chewa | Cheua | |
| Pimbe | n.a. | |
| Nyanja | Nianja, Niassa | |
| Yao | Ajaua, Iao | 2 |
| Maconde | Makonde | 2 |
| Ngoni | Nguni, Angoni | 1 |
| TOTAL | | 100 |

n.a.—not available

Source: Based on information from Thomas H. Henriksen, *Mozambique: A History*, London, 1978, 247; and Irving Kaplan, et al., *Area Handbook for Mozambique*, Washington, 1977, Table 2.

ment, but they did not originate among the people to whom they are applied. Both words have been used pejoratively in some situations, e.g., people of Macua communities may apply the term *Lomue* in such a way to signify "barbarian."

Beginning as early as the sixteenth century and for periods of varying duration, portions of the Macua (more rarely the Lomue) were involved in confederations of chiefdoms, but these were rarely long lasting or firmly institutionalized. They did not become and remain the focuses of the loyalties and identities of their constituent communities. Loyalty and identity tended to be limited to the small-scale chiefdoms (clusters of villages) characteristic of these people, and armed conflict between Macua (or Lomue) chiefdoms was not uncommon. Other historical experience introduced other cultural and social distinctions within each of the sections. Among the Macua a difference developed between coastal communities that were converted to Islam (or heavily influenced by it) and those that resisted such conversion. In the case of the Lomue, those communities that had been forced to move in the direction of Malawai came under the substantial influence of the Nyanja-speaking peoples who lived along Lake Nyasa.

In the period preceding Mozambican independence, some politicians of Macua origin sought to find a power base among the Macua-Lomue and to that end attempted to play upon a putative Macua or Macua-Lomue ethnic identity or to develop such an identity. The attempts did not appear to be successful. Because overpoliticization of ethnic identity has been strongly discouraged by the regime and because there has been no published research dealing with the question of ethnic solidarity among the Macua-Lomue or either section separately, the extent and political significance of such solidarity in the mid-1980s could not be determined.

The Tsonga cluster is the second largest of the major ethnic categories. The name was applied by the expanding Nguni-speakers (Ngoni) to the peoples of a number of chiefdoms occupying most of the area south of the Save River and some of the land just north of it. Because the name was initially used by the conquering Ngoni in the nineteenth century and has a pejorative connotation, it has been rejected by the Rjonga, one of several sections into which the Tsonga are divided. The Rjonga who live in the vicinity of Maputo were able to resist or elude the Ngoni conquerors, and they have tended to deny identification with other Tsonga who were conquered or otherwise influenced by the Ngoni. One of these groups, the Shangaan, carries a name derived from that of an early leader of the Ngoni group that conquered them in the early nineteenth century. A third section, the Hlengue, occupies the largest area, having expanded northward before the nine teenth century and absorbed a group called the Tonga (not to be confused with the Tsonga). Closer to the coast is a fourth section called the Tsua. These sections are essentially dialect groupings rather than sociopolitical ones. In the precolonial era each was divided into a number of chiefdoms. The Shangaan are descendants of those Tsonga groups that came directly under the domination of the Ngoni who established the Gaza kingdom in the nineteenth century (see The Ngoni Migrations; Gungunhana, ch. 1). Portions of the Shangaan live in South Africa. A small number of Hlengue live in Zimbabwe. Although heavily influenced politically by the Ngoni, the Tsonga in effect absorbed their conquerors, who adopted the Tsonga language and other features of their culture.

Tsonga males have long been accustomed to migrating to South Africa as mineworkers. The Rjonga, who live close to Maputo, have been much affected by their proximity to Mozambique's capital city. The effect on Tsonga society of the varied experience of the male population and the absence of substantial numbers of males from the local community at any one time has been commented on but not satisfactorily analyzed.

The other ethnic groups in southern Mozambique—the Chopi and the Tonga—are much smaller. Some observers have placed them in the same ethnic category because they speak dialects of the same language, but they are otherwise different and think of themselves as separate groups. The Tonga appear to be the remnants of a once more widespread people, most of whom were absorbed by the expanding Tsonga. The Chopi emerged in the early eighteenth century, having developed out of a mixture of peoples and cultures over several centuries. The Tonga were one ingredient, as were Shona-speaking peoples and, later, the Tsonga. Despite the cultural and biological significance of the Shona and the Tsonga, the language of the Tonga prevailed (see Early Population Movements, ch. 1). Like the Tsonga, Chopi men (and to a lesser degree those of the Tonga) were deeply involved in migrant labor in the South African mines.

The Shona-speaking groups of Mozambique are the easternmost extention of a people who stretch to the western border of Zimbabwe. Many of the groups in Zimbabwe and most of those in Mozambique were parts of the Munhumutapa and/or Changamire empires (see The Shona Dynasties, ch. 1). One of the sections of these people, the Karanga (in the modern era located entirely in Zimbabwe), dominated these larger states, and the Portuguese who first encountered them called all Shona speakers

Karanga, a usage that persisted for some time. In Mozambique several sections, i.e., groups of chiefdoms the members of which speak a given dialect or closely related dialects, have been recognized; the most important of them are the Manyika and the Ndau (both also found in Zimbabwe). Other groups, e.g., the Tawara, the Teve, and the Dande, are more remotely connected to the Core Shona, who constitute nearly three-fourths of Zimbabwe's population. Prominent (because of their leadership of resistance to the Portuguese in the nineteenth century) but small in number, the Barue sometimes have been included with the Shona because of their association with the empire of the Munhumutapa, but they speak a Sena-Nsenga tongue akin to that of peoples of the lower Zambezi valley.

The term *Shona* was initially used by others—its origin is unknown—and was taken up by Europeans in Southern Rhodesia in the nineteenth century as a cover term for the people in that territory who spoke dialects of the same language and were characterized by broad similarities of culture. The name has been widely accepted by the people in Zimbabwe, and it conveniently designates Mozambican Shona speakers. But it is not clear that Mozambicans have a significant Shona consciousness as opposed to an awareness of themselves as, e.g., Manyika, Ndau, or Teve.

The Lower Zambezi cluster, a catchall category, brings together the quite varied peoples of both the lower Zambezi valley and a substantial part of the coastal area on either side of the mouth of the Zambezi River and particularly to the north of it. The Zambezi valley has been a highway for African peoples from central Africa to the Indian Ocean and for Arabs, Portuguese, and the Portuguese-sponsored Goans to move from the coast to the interior. It was in this area that the *prazos* (see Glossary) were established in the seventeenth and eighteenth centuries; some of these emerged in the nineteenth century as virtually independent states under Afro-Portuguese rulers called *prazeros* (see The Rise of the Prazos; The Modern Colonial Era, ch. 1). In addition to the people who had already been in place, others were brought in as slave soldiers for their private armies. It was in this area, too, that armed African resistance to the Portuguese erupted in the late nineteenth and early twentieth centuries.

By the twentieth century, therefore, there had emerged a variety of groups marked by experience—sometimes friendly, sometimes hostile—with each other and with Afro-Goan or Afro-Portuguese rulers. Some of these peoples, e.g., the Sena and the Tonga, had probably been in the area a very long time but had undergone substantial cultural change in the course of centuries of turmoil. Others, such as the Chikunda and probably the Nhungue, actually came into existence in the eighteenth and nineteenth centuries on the *prazos*, developing a special culture as a consequence of their peculiar roles as slave soldiers and hunters. More than half of the Chikunda appear to have had their origin among the Chewa-speaking and related peoples that constituted the Maravi states to the north and west of the Mozambican portion of the Zambezi valley. A number of other groups, among them the Lomue, were also represented in the Chikunda amalgam. But the language used on the *prazos* and by the Chikunda after they left was Chewa.

The origin of the Nhungue is less certain. They may also have emerged from the slaves of the *prazos*, but it has been suggested that they may have been Shona-speaking Tawara who developed a different culture and political orientation owing to sustained contact with Portuguese over a long period. The language they speak has been classified with the Chewa-Nyanja group rather than with the Shona group.

The peoples of the Maravi cluster constitute one of the smaller groupings in Mozambique, but they are an extension of a category heavily represented in Malawi and Zambia. No section or community in this cluster calls itself Maravi. The present-day use of the term generally denotes those communities that are the remnants of a political confederation founded by Undi, a chief who belonged to the Chewa, one of the components of the cluster. The other main components are the Nyanja and the Nsenga. Chewa and Nyanja are essentially dialects of the same language; Nsenga is a related but quite different language. In Mozambique the Nyanja (sometimes called Niassa) are found in the provinces of Niassa and Zambezia along the border with Malawi and the shores of Lake Nyasa. The Nyanja in this remote northern portion of Mozambique have been among the few groups influenced by the Anglican church and, in the colonial era at least, were more likely to know English than Portuguese. Chewa groups are found in the Tete highlands, and the Nsenga are also in Tete Province, mainly north of the Zambezi River. Although the Chewa-Nyanja peoples in Malawi and Zambia have been well studied, little is known of the Mozambican components of these peoples or of the Nsenga, and there is no indication that the involvement of their ancestors in the Maravi confederacy has left a residue of significant ethnic identity.

The Yao were principal intermediaries in trade between the coast and the interior, and during the eighteenth and nineteenth centuries they dominated the ivory and later, the slave trade with the Arabs. In part as a consequence of their sustained contact with

Arabs and other coastal Muslims, they were influenced by East African Islamic (Swahili) culture, and in the late nineteenth century the Yao converted en masse to Islam, the only group in the interior to do so. Arab and Swahili influence and the conversion to Islam notwithstanding, the Yao retained much of their indigenous religious practice. Up to the mid-nineteenth century the flow of trade—particularly the Yao involvement in slave hunting and trading—led to large concentrations of Yao population under the political and military leadership of chiefs who had demonstrated their military and commercial capacities. After the mid-nineteenth century the formal end of the slave trade and the migration of many Yao to what were to become Tanganyika and Nyasaland led to the disintegration of these larger political groupings.

Because the Maconde area in the north was early and deeply involved in the activities of the Front for the Liberation of Mozambique (Frente de Libertação de Moçambique—FRELIMO) and because Maconde made up a significant proportion of FRELIMO forces in 1970 when the census was taken, estimates of their number varied. Based on earlier censuses, it is likely that their number in the early 1980s was roughly equivalent to that of the Yao. The Maconde have demonstrated a substantial degree of cultural homogeneity and resistance to influence or domination by other groups, including the East African Muslims who controlled the coast east of the Maconde plateau. Their cultural homogeneity and their resistance to outside influence notwithstanding, the Maconde were not characterized by a centralized political order.

The relatively small groups making up the Ngoni cluster are usually considered together only because of their ultimate common origin among the Nguni-speaking peoples of South Africa and their eruption into Mozambique (and other areas in southeast and central Africa) in the first half of the nineteenth century (see The Ngoni Migrations, ch. 1). These remnants, however, are otherwise quite different. Only in the far southeast do they retain their language and something approximating their original culture. During the colonial era Ngoni exercised a degree of local dominance and commanded some deference in the Angonia highlands, where the largest concentration of Ngoni was found, and in Niassa, where they had intermingled with the Yao. Despite that intermingling and their use of non-Nguni language as mother tongues, the Ngoni, particularly those of chiefly lineage, tended to retain a clear sense of their identity and their presumed superiority. Whether that has persisted into the independence period is not clear. In any case, the small numbers and wide dispersion of the Ngoni limit their significance as a potential ethnic force on the national level.

Along the coast between the mouth of the Ligonha River and the Tanzanian border lived an estimated one-half million Muslims in 1970, between 6 and 7 percent of the population (see Religion, this ch.). That proportion has probably remained stable as of early 1984. Although sometimes known collectively as the Swahili group, only those in the far northern part of the coast are Swahili, that is, related to the coastal peoples of Tanzania and Kenya. Most of the remainder are derived from local peoples and others brought to the coast in the long history of the slave trade. In the case of these coastal peoples, their religious affiliation is decisive for their ethnic identity, i.e., they are coastal Muslims regardless of their remoter ethnic origins.

On the eve of independence in 1975, roughly 250,000 Portuguese were permanent residents of Mozambique. (There were also a few thousand British, Germans, white South Africans, and others.) Despite Portugal's long involvement with Mozambique, most Portuguese in the territory were relative newcomers, and two-thirds of them had been born in Portugal. In the period beginning after World War II and continuing into the 1960s, the influx of Portuguese of all kinds—particularly poor ones—had led to a stratified white society ranging from administrators at the highest levels and some very wealthy businessmen to semiskilled workers and rural shopkeepers. Some of the latter were in fact mixed Euro-Africans (*mestiços*). Beginning with the institution of the transition government in 1974, Portuguese left the country for a variety of reasons. By the late 1970s there were only about 15,000 of them in Mozambique, and most of them were not permanent residents but expatriates—the "cooperants" who performed tasks that black Mozambicans had not yet been trained to do (see Independent Mozambique, ch. 1).

In the mid-1970s there were also in Mozambique an estimated 20,000 Asians, i.e., descendants of persons originating in the Indian subcontinent. Of these, perhaps one-third were Hindus, and two-thirds were Muslims (the latter category may have included persons from Mauritius and the Comoro Islands). In addition to these were the Goans—some of part-Portuguese ancestry and all of them Christians—who had played a considerable role in the economy and administration of Mozambique since the seventeenth century. Unlike other Asians, the Goans often identified themselves with the Portuguese. There were also about 3,000 Chinese in Mozambique just before national independence. Asians, including Goans and to a lesser extent

Chinese, were engaged in wholesale and retail trade in the urban and the rural areas. Assuming that their businesses would be taken over by the new regime, many of them left. Even so, according to one source, the Asians, defined as the Indo-Pakistani community, still controlled about three-fourths of private commerce in Mozambique in the early 1980s. In 1983 an Asian Muslim businessman was secretly tried by the military revolutionary tribunal of Maputo for black market and other fraudulent activity and was shot despite the protests of the Asian Islamic community. Several hundred Asian businessmen in Beira and elsewhere were reported to have left the country or were preparing to leave.

### Interethnic Relations

Ethnic heterogeneity does not necessarily imply ethnic conflict. Both before and since Mozambican independence, there has been a good deal of assertion and counterassertion concerning ethnic relations but very little description and analysis of the kind that would permit an assessment of the potential for conflict. During the 1960s and early 1970s assertions that one group did not like another were generated in the course of the armed struggle and the propaganda war waged between the Portuguese and FRELIMO. The Portuguese sought to claim the loyalty of groups such as the Macua-Lomue or at least to argue that they ought not to support FRELIMO because it was fundamentally a Maconde movement led by people from the far south, i.e., persons belonging to one or another Tsonga subgroup. In particular, the Portuguese sought to play on the notion that the Macua-Lomue and the Maconde were traditional enemies. Before Eduardo Chivambu Mondlane's murder in February 1969, conflicts among the FRELIMO elite were sometimes couched in terms of ethnic (tribal), regional, or racial differences. After Mondlane's death, however, the surviving leaders argued that those who stressed ethnic or racial issues were governed by "petty bourgeois considerations." In short, ethnic matters could not legitimately be raised.

Historically, armed conflict between groups of different languages and culture was not uncommon. One group established short- or long-term domination over another; raiding parties of one people captured and sold as slaves persons of another. Rarely, however, did all the members of one ethnic category engage in conflict with or consider as enemies all members of another category. Strife usually occurred on quite a different scale; for example, a Macua chiefdom against a Maconde community. Moreover, intraethnic conflict—raiding or other forms of conflict between chiefdoms of similar language and culture—was also frequent. In general, interethnic hostility was not particularly deep-seated, long-lasting, or inclusive of entire peoples in the era before the Portuguese established firm control over the whole of present-day Mozambique.

It was only in the twentieth century, then, that some ethnic elements in Mozambique got to know others well enough to develop stereotypes of them. That was certainly the case for the groups living north and south of the Zambezi River, which marked a major cultural as well as a geographical division. Further, the duration, nature, and intensity of the Portuguese impact varied from region to region (and therefore from one ethnic group to another). An ethnic category location also affected the extent to which its members had employment opportunities in adjacent countries.

Although Portuguese colonialism did not establish itself in the south until the late nineteenth century, it had a more significant impact on ethnolinguistic groups living near the capital (Lourenço Marques, in 1976 the name was changed to Maputo) than it did on remoter groups. Men from these southern groups also worked for wages in South Africa and Southern Rhodesia where, whatever the hardships they may have undergone, they became more familiar with Western or modern ways than did peoples of the north. By far the greatest proportion of Portuguese, Asians, Chinese, and persons of mixed origin—*mestiços*—lived in the southern portion of the country, and virtually all of the partly or wholly urbanized African population in and around the capital originated in ethnic groups living south of the Save River, i.e., among the Tsonga, Chopi, and Inhambane Tonga. In the north, by contrast, the major external influence had been that of Islam. Between the north and the south lay the Shona-speaking peoples and the socially and culturally mixed peoples of the lower Zambezi cluster. The Shona speakers and the peoples of the Zambezi had been more affected by non-Africans that those of the north, but the impact of non-Africans had been less pervasive (and less Portuguese) than it had been in the south.

Out of this differential impact emerged a set of perceptions noted by political scientist Walter C. Opello, Jr.: "Groups from the north . . . such as the Makonde and Yao are considered by southerners as 'backward,' 'primitive,' and 'traditional,' while groups in the south like the [Tsonga] are considered by northerners to be 'aggressive,' 'domineering,' and 'corrupt.' Ethnolinguistic differences are thus simplified into a perception of regional differentiation . . . In some cases, notably among the Islamic Yao and Macua-Lomue, religious differences exacerbate a sense of separation." It is also possible to note among some people of the central region (of Shona origin) a sense that southerners have been included to be excessively deferential to Portuguese culture, even as some of them led the rebellion against Portuguese political domination.

These stereotypes and attitudes notwithstanding, the characterization of conflict within FRELIMO during the struggle for independence (and afterward as conflict between African ethnic groups) may not be an accurate depiction of the situation. Opello argues that in the competition for a limited number of positions of status and power, some leaders who lost out claimed that the ethnic group to which they belonged had been thereby ill-treated. But their efforts to mobilize the groups from which they stemmed in support of their perspective failed for the most part; in short, they did not represent ethnic groups but sought to manipulate them.

Perhaps more significantly was the feeling of some northerners and people from the central areas that whites, *mestiços*, and *assimilados* (those who qualified by virtue of literacy in Portuguese and way of life for Portuguese citizenship) played an overwhelming role in FRELIMO's leadership. Strictly speaking, *assimilado* status did not constitute a legal category after 1961, but it persisted as a de facto social and cultural status into the 1970s. Before its abolition as a legal category, only a small proportion—perhaps 3 percent—of the 250,000 black Africans eligible for *assimilado* status had actually been granted it. Of those eligible, whether or not granted the status, a disproportionate number were southerners, however. Most of the black Africans in FRELIMO's leadership, particularly after Mondlane's death, have been southerners who would have been eligible for *assimilado* status had it still existed. The others were *mestiços* or Portuguese with whom the southern *assimilados* were more comfortable than were Africans from other regions.

After independence the availability of political and administrative status at high levels should have permitted sufficiently wide distribution of rewards to mitigate the effects of ethnic, regional, or social competition. In fact, this appears not to have happened. At the very highest levels of party and government, two considerations appeared to determine the allocation of power and authority and therefore of status between independence in 1975 and mid–1984: reliability in a party of doctrinal sense and/or technical competence. The important figures in FRELIMO were, with few exceptions, those who were important before independence; they remained the same mixture of southern

*A broad ethnic mixture of Mozambicans celebrating*
*May Day 1983 in Maputo*
*Courtesy AIM/Ander Nilsson*

*assimilados, mestiços*, whites, and Asians. The important figures
in the government were either those at the highest levels of the
party or non-Africans chosen for their professional capacities (see
Government Institutions and the Party, ch. 4). Further, at intermediate levels in the bureaucracy and the economy, the lack of
trained black Mozambicans had led the regime to employ numbers of whites—mainly Portuguese—to whom they were compelled to furnish monetary and other incentives.

In these circumstances it is possible that resentment at
what appears from a regional or ethnic point of view to be a
torted distribution of rewards could lead to a mobilization of
regional or ethnic groups. From time to time Machel or an
essayist in a newspaper or magazine has deplored any manifesta-
tion of "tribalism," but it was not possible on the basis of available
information to argue that ethnic or regional conflict was a major
issue at the onset of the mid-1980s. Resentment of the racial composition of the political, administrative, and technical elites may
be another matter.

Some observers of the Mozambican scene have taken the
continuing significance of non-Africans—particularly of whites—

at the highest reaches of party and government as indicative of racial tolerance or at least of indifference to the question of race on the part of ordinary black Mozambicans. In September 1982, however, editorial commentary by Machado da Graça in *Notícias*, entitled "Racism Is Not Dead," while reiterating the FRELIMO position against reverse racism, offered what was probably a more realistic appraisal of the situation:

> [Racism] is not dead . . . far from it . . . It surfaces at meetings in companies, cooperatives and communal farms. It surfaces in the way this or that person is criticized with a vehemence disproportionate to the error he has committed; it appears in the way the hall enthusiastically applauds criticism against a member of another race; it appears in the way disagreements between two individuals are transformed into conflicts between two races. These demonstrations of racism often rest on a visible base. We frequently find members of the white race, either nationals or foreign cooperants, directing a wide variety of companies or government sectors. In these instances, the relationship of chief to subordinate, normally sensitive in itself, is aggravated by the race difference and the memory of a still recent colonialism in which white colonialists dominated all the positions of leadership . . . These problems, in which racism is associated with other types of disagreements in work places, are complicated by aspects of social comradeship, which appear to confirm, a racist division in our society.

The reference to social comradeship apparently refers to the lack of ordinary sociability outside the work place among persons of difference races. It is not clear whether this social remoteness pertains even at the highest levels of party and government where such persons of different races have been working together for as long as two decades.

## The Social Order

Because blacks were excluded almost entirely from the middle and upper strata of the colonial society and economy and made up only a very small part of the stable and comparatively well-paid class of manual workers, there did exist a firmly established urban middle class in a position to play an important social and political role in postindependence Mozambique. The minuscule group of *assimilados* and the segment of *mestiços* who had been part of the colonial middle class (economically if not socially)—and who had skills required by the new regime under FRELIMO—were used in the bureaucracy and the economy but were closely watched because they were politically suspect. In the rural areas a degree of social differentiation existed based on varying combinations of traditional status, for example, membership in a lineage of chiefs, control over land and cattle, remunerative wage labor, and participation in small-scale commerce. In the colonial era, however, even small-scale trading by blacks was rare, most of it being in the hands of Asians, poor Portuguese, or *mestiços*. Although differentiation among rural blacks had not reached the level that occurred in other African colonial territories before independence, there was enough of it in some areas to be a major factor impeding the achievement of the egalitarian communal villages that were among FRELIMO's principal goals.

## Local Rural Structures

Rural social structures in place at independence in each community or group of communities were the consequences of patterns rooted in the past but affected in varying ways by the direct impact of Portuguese rule. By the time the Portuguese had firmly established control over all of Mozambique, i.e., well into the twentieth century, large-scale chieftaincies marked by a hierarchy of greater and lesser chiefs and headman were a thing of the past. At best there might be two levels of chiefs and headmen of lineages. The most obvious effect of colonial rule was the conversion of these chiefs into dependents and agents of the colonial authorities. The power of chiefs had varied from one ethnic group to another and even within ethnic groups, but they had been in a significant sense responsible to and for their people. Under the Portuguese they became functionaries of the colonial regime. In some instances they were appointed by the colonial authorities as a reward for previous service, e.g., in the army, but most succeeded to office as brothers, sons, or sisters' sons of preceding chiefs; in a few instances they were elected, if that had been the mode of succession. In all cases, however, they were subject to the continuing approval of Portuguese administrators. A chief who chose to confront the colonial authorities on behalf of his people was not likely to last long. Many chiefs were encouraged in their conservatism by the opportunities they were given to have relatively large quantities of land cultivated for them through the labor of their people.

Historian Thomas H. Hendriksen makes the point that the chiefs "incurred the enmity and opposition of the nationalists in the 1960s and 1970s for their exploitation and collaboration." On coming to power, FRELIMO ended the formal political role of the chiefs, turning authority at local level over to assemblies of the locality (*localidade*) and to local FRELIMO cells. But local communities did not in all cases share the antipathy of FRELIMO for chiefs, particularly in those areas where the chiefs had not taken advantage of their position under the Portuguese to exploit their own people. Moreover, in some communities chiefs were among the few who had a smattering of education, an acquaintance with the ways of bureaucracy, and enough self-confidence to deal with local party people and centrally appointed administrators. In any case, there were reports in Mozambican publications that members of local councils (or candidates for them) had served the colonial authorities (see Local Government, ch. 4). The suggestion that significant influence, if not formal authority, in many rural areas still lies in the hands of traditional leaders implies that these leaders retain a good deal of prestige and that they may also control local sources of wealth, such as land and cattle. Information on these matters, however, is limited to occasional references to and denunciations of the continuing significance of "feudal leaders." Systematic studies of the power and status structure of local communities, whether of the kind characteristic of various ethnic categories before independence or of the communal villages that have been formed since 1975, are almost nonexistent.

Studies of the Chopi in the late 1960s and early 1970s and of a Tsonga communal village and cooperative on the Limpopo River in 1978 suggest that men other than chiefs could acquire substantial power or control an economically significant enterprise in the latter part of the preindependence era. In these southern ethnic communities, Africans who became "big men" locally had extensive experience with wage labor. They were able to combine the proceeds of such labor with cash cropping or some other form of entrepreneurship to distinguish themselves from others in the same community and to become patrons of a number of dependents. In part because of the significance of migratory labor in this part of Mozambique, there were also a number of women in the ethnic groups who had learned how to cope with a variety of problems while the men were away for long periods. It was these women, for example, who in the absence of their husbands made the decision to form communal villages when their homes and plots were inundated by the Limpopo floods of 1977. In general, then, many southern communities had a pool of people who were ready to take over from chiefs once the support of the government was withdrawn from the latter. Elsewhere, especially north of the Zambezi River among the Macua-Lomue, it may take some time before a sufficient number of rural people have acquired the educational and other experience to encourage them to offer themselves as alternatives to the chiefs.

It has long been known that the ethnic communities south of the Zambezi valley, i.e., the Tsonga, the Chopi, the Inhambane Tonga, and the Shona-speaking peoples, reckon descent, succession, and inheritance patrilineally. The peoples north of the Zambezi River, i.e., the Macua-Lomue, the Chewa and other groups of the Maravi cluster, the Maconde, and the Yao do so matrilineally. The Yao appear to have retained much of their matrilineal orientation and organization despite the influence of Islam, and that is probably also true of the Maca and other segments of the Islamic Coastal cluster. In the Zambezi valley and among those communities directly affected by Ngoni conquerors and incorporated in Ngoni-dominated social systems, limited inquiry suggests transitional or mixed systems.

Unilineal descent generates kin-based groups that have political, social, economic, and religious functions. A clan consists of persons who claim but cannot trace descent from a remote common ancestor. If descent is assumed to have occurred from a male ancestor through males, the clans in a system are patrilineal; if descent is assumed to have occurred from a female through females, then the clans are matrilineal. Typically, in either system, clans were dispersed and did not have political or economic functions, but they were likely to control marriage to the extent that men and women were expected to marry outside the clans to which they belonged. At times, clans also had ritual functions.

Each clan consists of a number of lineages. Whether the lineage is matrilineal or patrilineal, the ancestor may be quite remote, and the lineage is therefore genealogically deep and usually quite large. But if the common ancestor is only three to five generations from the youngest living adult generation, his or her descendants may be few enough for form the core of an extended family household or of a hamlet. These shallower (three- to five-generation) lineages were typically the most important groups in Mozambican society through the late colonial era, despite changes of various kinds. To the extent that land had not become privately held, lineages had control over its allocation. The lineage ancestor was an important religious figure. In disputes of various kinds, lineages were expected to support their own and to have a degree of responsibility for their behavior.

Partly out of ideology, partly out of experience in the north (particularly in Cabo Delgado Province) during the fight for independence, and partly out of necessity generated by the departure of the Portuguese who abandoned their farms, the FRELIMO regime sought to establish a new social and economic order in the rural areas (see the FRELIMO Regime, ch. 1). The elements of this new order were to be communal villages, state farms, and collectives. Ideally, collective farming was to be the material foundation for most communal villages, i.e., members of a village were to raise and market crops collectively, although it was expected that they would also cultivate family plots, at least in the foreseeable future. The income from collective farming was, in theory, to permit the acquisition of necessities and amenities for the village. Participation in a collective was not made mandatory, however, and most members of communal villages remained exclusively family farmers. Moreover, the failure of the state to deliver promised inputs and to provide technical help led many who had joined a collective to drop out. State farms were established mainly on the holdings of Portuguese who had left. In a few cases it was expected that the social organization of the labor force on such farms would take the form of communal villages, but this was rare. In any case, by the mid-1980s the lack of success of such state farms had led to the dismantling or restructuring of many of them (see Agriculture, ch. 3).

Communal villages were intended to accomplish two ends: first, in a country in which homesteads were either dispersed or people lived in small villages, communal villages permitted the clustering of enough families in one place to allow services, such as health and education, to be efficiently delivered and administered; second, these villages were expected to provide a milieu for the transformation of the social and political orders and the values of rural Mozambicans. In some areas conditions were conducive to the formation of large communal villages. In Cabo Delgado Province, where FRELIMO had been most active and successful in the struggle for independence, the Portuguese had constructed *aldeamentos* (large fortified villages) to isolate the local people from FRELIMO. These villages provided a ready-made physical base for the social and political apparatus of the communal villages. Moreover, in the area controlled by FRELIMO before independence, social and political forms and processes foreshadowing those planned for the communal villages had already been instituted, and a portion of the population was accustomed to them. In addition to these predisposing conditions, many northerners had been outside the country during the late 1960s and early 1970s, and it was easy to settle them directly to the newly established communal villages when they returned after independence.

In Gaza and Maputo provinces in the south, the floods of 1977 forced many people to leave their low-lying dispersed homesteads for the neighboring ridges; there, they responded to very strong government urging to form communal villages on high ground. Elsewhere in the north (Niassa and Tete provinces), where *aldeamentos* had been built, they too were converted into communal villages. In other provinces where neither ready-made villages nor natural disaster helped the establishment of communal villages, communities were apparently built and settled in response to promises of a range of benefits. Now and then some residents of communal villages have stated that they were responding to the notion of collective living, and it has been suggested that Mozambican peasants found the idea of communal living attractive.

Historian Allen Isaacman and attorney Barbara Isaacman have claimed that "those not opposed [to communal villages] were relatively privileged members of rural society, such as chiefs and African capitalist farmers who, through collaboration with the colonial regime, had acquired substantial holdings and exploited African labor." According to the Isaacmans, African farmers in the coastal regions opposed the formation of communal villages because they owned cashew and coconut trees and feared that they would lose their income from them. There are indications, however, that some farmers, well-off in the preindependent era, have become members of communal villages and the cooperatives linked to them if they see such adaptation as the best way to maintain their advantages.

It has been suggested that the constraints imposed on men by the features of some matrilineal systems have pushed them toward membership in communal villages. For example, among the Macua of Nampula Province, men have customarily gone to live with the families of their wives after marriage and thereby have come under the control of their wives' matrilineages. In order to escape that control, men have gone to live in communal villages, according to some accounts. It is not reported how their wives are persuaded to go with them, or why their wives' matrilineages are ready to relinquish control over the women. The quite different patrilineal system—that of the Chopi—may also have pressed young men in the direction of membership in a communal village, where inheritance and succession to chiefly office passed from older to younger brother before descending to sons. Unless a young man did very well as a migrant mineworker and could retain some of his earnings free of the control of lineage elders, it would be years before he had a degree of real independence. It is possible that from the point of view of such young men, membership in a communal village was a form of independence, but the observations necessary to explore that possibility have not been made.

It has been argued that some peasants were attracted to communal villages on ideological grounds and that others objected to them because they were advertised as the locus of efforts to overcome what were termed reactionary ideas and values, particularly those making for the inequality of women. The significance of ideological attraction to the idea of the communal village or repulsion from it cannot, however, be easily measured. Whatever the importance of ideological and material interests in recruitment to communal villages, the fact remains that as the establishment of these villages reached a plateau in the early 1980s, the great bulk of them were located in the area where specific events and physical availability of villages made their early institution feasible. In 1982, of 1,352 communal villages, 543 (40 percent) were in Cabo Delgado Province. The next highest number of communal villages, 260 (a little more than 19 percent of the total), lay in Nampula Province, where the establishment of such communities had not been affected by preexisting fortified villages or by the return of refugees. Gaza Province was home to the third largest number of communal villages, 139 (a little more than 10 percent of the total).

Of the three provinces having the greatest number of communal villages, only two—Cabo Delgado and Gaza—had substantial proportions of the provincial populations living in them. Cabo Delgado's communal villages incorporated 45 percent of the 1.8 million people living in such villages and 87 percent of the province's rural population. It should be noted, however, that many of Cabo Delgado's complexes were communal villages in name only in 1980. Neither the educational and health benefits nor the political mobilization theoretically characteristic of communal villages had been securely instituted. In Gaza's communal villages were nearly 17 percent of the people living in communal settlements and more than 30 percent of the province's rural population. By contrast, Nampula's communal villages provided homes for less than 9 percent of the people living under communal conditions and only a little more than 6 percent of the province's rural population.

Some observers have suggested that communal villages have

been quite successful in changing social relations. According to these observers, peasants in communal villages have begun to acknowledge their right and duty to participate in the election of communal village authorities and of representatives (deputies) to the provincial people's assemblies and the selection of new party members. The fact remains that in 1982 less than 40 percent of the communal villages had party cells; moreover, it was not clear that the debates over party members were necessarily indicative of political rather than personal concerns.

It has been argued further that communal villages have made the greatest efforts to end initiation rites, child marriage, polygyny, and bride-price (marriage payments) and to involve women as equals in all phases of the political process at the local level. The success of these efforts has been variable, and there has been no attempt to specify the conditions that make for success as against those that are conducive to failure.

Despite the lack of detailed description and analysis of the actual power and status relationships of members of communal villages, the Isaacmans' observations (and those of Barbara Isaacman and June Stephen focusing on the ideology, law, and practice pertaining to the status of women) suggest that changes have taken place in the communal villages. These changes reflect the presence of the Mozambique Women's Organization (Organização das Mulheres de Moçambique—OMM) in these villages or of local, less ubiquitous cells of FRELIMO (see MAss Associations, ch. 4). For example, in many communal villages the party cells and the OMM have insisted that the age of prospective spouses be publicized and that the authorities grant approval for marriage only if those to be married are old enough. This practice was in force even before the formal institution in late 1982 of portions of a new family code requiring that a girl be at least 16 years old and a boy 18 if they were to be married in a church or a registrar's office. Most Mozambican marriages, including those of communal village members, involve traditional procedures and rites or, in urban areas, are common-law marriages. It is likely, however, that OMM members in communal villages will insist on the marriage ages called for in the code.

In conformity with FRELIMO doctrine (and with the very strong support of local representatives of the OMM), communal villages have also tried to eliminate or at least to curtail polygyny among their members. A polygynous family could enter a communal village if that family existed at the time the village was formed, but polygynous marriages thereafter were strongly discouraged.

The extent to which members of communal villages shared the drive to change social relations and abolish traditional social practices has remained uncertain. Most rural Mozambicans did not live in communal villages, however, and the tenor of most comments in the press and radio-broadcasts suggests that less has changed in rural Mozambique than the accounts of the Isaacmans and their colleagues indicate. But these accounts, whatever their limitations, constitute the only extended treatments of the first five to six years of the Mozambican experience.

By late 1983 resistance to change in social practice had apparently led FRELIMO and the OMM to reconsider its policies. A radio-broadcast noted that citizens who discussed traditional social practices at a meeting in a suburb of Maputo were told that they would have "an opportunity to correct mistakes made by the FRELIMO party in formulating national social policy after independence." A member of the OMM told those at the meeting that OMM's call for the abolition of certain practices, such as brideprice, initiation rites, and polygyny, without going to the people had been a mistake and that meetings throughout the country were to be held in 1984 to discover what the people wished to do about such traditional customs.

### Urban and National Structures

In the late 1960s and early 1970s, Portuguese observers distinguished three strata of urban Africans on the basis of occupation and their degree of Europeanization. The very small and heterogeneous upper stratum consisted of civil servants, a few prosperous merchants, nurses, and others whose jobs required literacy and perhaps some other training. Most of the Africans of southern Mozambique who were active outside the country in FRELIMO would have been part of this very small stratum had they not rebelled. Largely because of the location of the largest city and because most Portuguese were in the south, the members of the African upper stratum were disproportionately southerners. This upper stratum had adopted European standards of dress and behavior and tended to reject—overtly, at least—traditional forms. Needed because they were literate and skilled, these people and others like them—particularly those who had been in the civil service—were suspect because they had not made a commitment to FRELIMO in the preindependence period or because they seemed insufficiently ready to accept FRELIMO leadership in all matters. Many were put to work, after public confession, in the first few years of independence; some were sent to reeducation camps (see The Legal System, ch. 4). Such relatively well-educated, skilled persons would ordinarily have reasonably high status in a society like Mozambique's, but that status may be ambiguous because they do not have the right political credentials.

The middle urban stratum in the colonial period consisted of manual workers and artisans, many self-employed, whose jobs did not necessarily require literacy. Although likely to speak Portuguese and to have at least a rudimentary literacy, they had not made a significant effort to assimilate Portuguese culture. These people and others like them who have come into the cities since independence were, unlike members of the higher stratum, not politically suspect, although those who had been self-employed might have been regarded by FRELIMO cadres as petty bourgeoisie. It may well be that much of the next generation of party members will come from the children of members of this stratum. Their parents will probably see to it that the children receive an education and, to the extent that the parents are considered "working class," their children are likely to be perceived as proper candidates for recruitment into the party. In the colonial era, however, the people in this stratum were much more African than European in their outlook, and it is probable that they would have been uncomfortable with the world view of party cadres.

By far the largest stratum of urban Africans in the colonial period was unskilled workers—stevedores, construction workers, canners, and the like. Illiterate, these Africans were for the most part oriented to their places of origin. After independence they were augmented by the influx from the hinterland of large numbers of young people whose flooding of the urban centers led to the government's drive to evict "nonproductive" persons from the cities.

Responding to the utter ineffectiveness of the retail distribution system in early 1980, the regime returned small business to private hands. Retail business had been taken over by government in the first instance not so much because doctrine demanded it but because Portuguese and Asian small business men had fled the country. The new small businessmen, therefore, were to be mainly Africans. In effect, the formation of a new class was being made possible. Whether within that new class significant differentiation would be permitted to take place so that wealthy businessmen could flourish could not be determined in early 1984. Economic conditions in the early and mid-1980s were so bad that retail businesses had very little to offer in the legitimate market and risked dire penalties if they were caught engaging in black market activity. Further, although small business was to be permitted, it was not at all clear that successful entrepreneurs were necessarily given an honorable position in the society.

The new upper class is constituted in one sense by the core of FRELIMO. The preindependence orientation of the movement had been, in principle, egalitarian. When in early 1977 the Third Party Congress of FRELIMO declared itself a Marxist-Leninist vanguard party, FRELIMO also demonstrated a considerable consciousness of rank within the party, according to some observers. By late 1979 Machel explicitly condemned "ultra-leftism," i.e., excessive egalitarianism. As a long-time observer, journalist Jean-Pierre Langellier, noted, Machel called for "a sense of discipline, appropriate dress, and respect for leadership." The widespread use of the term *comrade* was to end, and the term was to be restricted to use by party members engaged in party business. In short, it had become a sign of special status rather than a sign of the equality of all working in a common cause. In the context of economic activity, where much had been made of the notion of worker control under socialism, the point was made that such control did not mean that the director of a factory lacked the power to make decisions. In 1980 the group that had avoided the institution of ranks and grades as a guerrilla force became the army of Mozambique, and ranks and grades were duly established (see Place in the National Life, ch. 5). Thereafter, the awarding of high ranks within the armed forces and medals to civilian leaders without significant military experience was used as a way of indicating status within the party.

The recognition of status and power within a party or economic context is one thing; the conferring of certain preogatives on party leaders because of rank is another matter, although it has been common practice wherever Marxist-Leninist parties hold power. In 1979 Machel made the point that it was not right that leaders "line up for meat and bread," and observers have noted that the declaration did not necessarily meet with popular approval. By early 1984, after several years of severe drought and economic difficulty, privileges accorded the party hierarchy may be appreciated even less by ordinary Mozambicans.

FRELIMO (largely through the OMM, the senior party-sponsored mass organization) has carried on a propaganda drive for the equality of women, having been more active in this respect than many newly installed ruling parties in Africa. Although there has been only one woman at cabinet level through early 1984 (Graça Machel, minister of education and culture and wife of the president), women were comparatively active in public life in communal villages and in some urban areas and work places, particularly if the point of reference was the situation in the preindependence era. The OMM has played a major role in the attack on certain customary practices that they have perceived as demeaning to women. Although a reevaluation of the meaning and value of these practices seemed to be in the offing in early 1984 and the attack on these practices may become less vehement than it has been, the drive for improving the status of women was solidly founded, and the organization leading the drive appeared able to recruit members.

## Religion

Mozambique's Constitution affirms the secularity of the state, insists on the "absolute separation between the state and religious organizations," and asserts that the "state guarantees citizens the freedom to practice or not to practice a religion." The wording seems to reflect not so much an emphasis on religious liberty as an animosity toward religion. In the case of FRELIMO's leaders—self-proclaimed Marxist-Leninists—that animosity may be part and parcel of their ideological orientation. But it also flows from their sense that the Roman Catholic church (identified with Portuguese prelates and priests) was a bulwark of the colonial regime.

The relations between party and state on the one hand and religious groups—particularly the Roman Catholic church—on the other have been difficult and were likely to continue to be so despite occasional efforts at accommodation. The nature of these relations makes it hard to assess the meaning of religious affiliation in the postindependence period and of the data pertaining to it. The meaning of affiliation before independence was also problematic. At that time there may have been a perceived advantage to affiliation with, or the profession of, Christianity, particularly Roman Catholicism. In that earlier era, the *World Christian Encyclopedia* notes, many Africans professed to be Christians (mainly Catholics), "thus forming part of a sizable nominal fringe. After 1975 this fringe rapidly decreased in size." This suggests that those who have retained their Catholic faith in the post-independence period, even if they do not flaunt it, are committed.

### Religious Affiliation

In 1970, when the census enumerated a population of 8.2 million, 60 to 65 percent of the African population was estimated to adhere to indigenous (tribal) religions. That estimate did not take into account the many professing, formally affiliated, and fairly active Christians and Muslims who, to one degree or another, continued to perceive the world in terms of indigenous religious notions and to participate in rituals related to those notions. Tribal religionists made up 70 percent or more of most ethnic groups north of the Save River. The exceptions were the Yao (80 percent or more were professed Muslims), the coastal Swahili-speaking peoples, and up to 20 to 25 percent of the Macua, who were also Muslims. (A smaller proportion of the Macua were Christians.) The *World Christian Encyclopedia* states that about 43 percent of the Maconde were Muslims, but this seems to contradict sources that stress Maconde resistance to both Muslim and Christian missionary endeavors.

In the same census year of 1970, about 19 percent of the total population was affiliated with the Roman Catholic church. The proportion of affiliated Catholics in the African population at that time was estimated very roughly at about 17 percent. A little more than 5 percent of the African population was affiliated with non-Catholic Christian denominations, most of which were evangelical Protestant missions, such as the Pentecostal Assemblies of God and Baptists of several varieties. Also represented were a few Anglicans, mainstream Protestant groups, such as Presbyterians and United Methodists, and marginal groups, such as Jehovah's Witnesses. African independent churches, i.e., those run by Africans and detached from all missionary control, were of considerable significance in what was then Southern Rhodesia, in South Africa (where many of them first emerged), and elsewhere in southern and eastern Africa. But they had been harshly dealt with by the Portuguese colonial authorities, who saw them as potentially political. In the immediate preindependence era the relatively small number of Mozambican Africans who belonged to these indigenous churches were divided among 100 or more groups. Fragmentation of this kind has been typical of indigenous churches, regardless of the political climate in which they functioned. In addition to the 22 to 23 percent of Africans who belonged to Christian churches, another 5 to 6 percent professed to be Christians but did not claim organizational affiliation.

About 12 percent of the African population were professed Muslims in 1970, according to the *World Christian Encyclopedia*. Of these, all seemed to be adherents of Sunni Islam and of the Shafii school of Islamic law. A Muslim source claimed that Muslims constituted as much as 45 percent of the population in 1979, a figure arrived at by assuming that virtually all the Macua-Lomue were Muslims.

Roman Catholics were distributed throughout Mozambique, although there seemed to have been more of them in proportion to population south of the Zambezi River. Non-Catholic Christians were found mainly south of the Zambezi River and predominantly south of the Save River, i.e., among the various Tsonga sections, the Chopi, and the Inhambane Tonga. Some Protestant groups had missions among the Shona and the Sena. Exceptions included Anglicans among the Nyanja and the Yao along Lake Nyasa and Seventh-Day Adventists among the Chuabo in the Quelimane region. Almost all of the Muslims lived north of the Zambezi and, with few exceptions, north of the Ligonha River.

In good part because the regime has been hostile to religion in general and to the Roman Catholic church in particular, there have been obstacles to the growth of religious affiliation and church activity since independence (see Religion, the Party, and the State, this ch.). It may be noted, however, that growth of membership in the Roman Catholic church in the years before independence may have reflected an African accommodation to what was perceived as the church of the colonial power rather than conversion out of wholly religious considerations. Thus, before independence church schools attracted Africans, but because all schools have been taken over by the state since independence, one of the church's attractions is no longer available (see Education, this ch.).

As of early 1984 only the *Catholic Almanac*, an American publication, provided some indications of the numbers adhering to that faith. The data, published in 1983, probably cover the 1981-82 period. At that time there were 1.6 million Catholics (children included), or about 100,000 more than there had been a decade earlier. But more than 200,000 Portuguese, most of them Catholics, had left in the interim. It may therefore be estimated that the number of affiliated Catholics in the African population (well over 99 percent of the total) had increased by about 250,000. Even so, the proportion of Roman Catholics in that population had declined from about 17 percent to a little more than 13 percent.

### Religion, the Party, and the State

The Constitution's formal assertion of the "freedom to practice or not to practice a religion" may be said to reflect a grudging acceptance of the existing religious affiliations or commitments of Mozambicans at the time of independence. It may also have reflected recognition of the difficulties of a direct assault on religious faith, whether Christian, Muslim, or indigenous. But a FRELIMO document published in the *Guardian* of London on

December 19, 1975, and reported in *Keesing's Contemporary Archives* in 1976, says something about the fundamental attitudes of the Constitution's drafters. The document states that "the masses will be protected against any pressure . . . to attend . . . services, practice religion, or organize associations dependent upon any religious group. Once religion is no more a duty . . . it will be slowly forgotten . . . and religion will be no more than an episode . . . worthy of mention in the history of the world communist movement." In this document the Roman Catholic church is singled out as a "reactionary organization which gives rise to counterrevolutionary activities . . . so that . . . it is necessary . . . to put an end to the influence of this church. . . . When the political struggle and the forces of production reach a high level, we can destroy it."

FRELIMO's particular antipathy for the Roman Catholic church arose in part from the history and actions of its Portuguese bishops and clergy during the colonial era and specifically in the period beginning in the 1940s. A concordat and a missionary accord between the Portuguese government and the Vatican, signed in 1941, guaranteed that the bishops in Mozambique would be of Portuguese nationality and would be appointed by the Vatican, subject to the approval of the Portuguese authorities. Although the Portuguese did not always get bishops who supported the colonial order, most bishops and priests did. Among the exceptions were the Portuguese bishops of Nampula and Beira. Further, non-Portuguese missionary priests, such as those belonging to the White Fathers (of varied national background) and the Burgos Fathers (a Spanish order), refused to follow the lead of most of the Portuguese hierarchy in supporting the colonial regime. The White Fathers, in direct conflict with the hierarchy over the cooperation due the colonial authorities, left Mozambique in 1971. From the perspective of FRELIMO's leadership, the existence of some Catholic clergy sympathetic to African independence was not significant compared with the salience of unsympathetic Portuguese bishops. Most FRELIMO leaders hailed from the south, where Portuguese priests were most in evidence and non-Portuguese clergy were scarce. The archbishop of Lourenço Marques, who had ecclesiastical authority over most of the region, strongly supported the colonial regime. In the south, moreover, Protestant missions, which were looked at askance by the Portuguese authorities, offered a contrast to the Portuguese Roman Catholics, although the Protestants were not militantly anticolonial. Certainly Machel has from time to time compared the behavior of the Protestant missions and the Roman Catholics to the detriment of the latter.

All religious organizations had a difficult time in the 1970s and early 1980s. Among other things, the clergy could not move freely, permission to build or rebuild churches was withheld, services outside churches were forbidden, and local officials were permitted, if not encouraged, to harass congregations in various ways, such as scheduling ball games immediately outside a church at the time of service. In late 1982, however, FRELIMO leaders, including Machel, met over an extended period with leaders of Christian and Muslim organizations in an attempt to deal with the differences between them. It is not clear why FRELIMO was ready to make that move, but given the environmental and economic problems it had been facing and the presence within Mozambique's borders of opposition movements, rapprochement with, rather than hostility to, religious groups may have seemed in order.

Reports on the meeting, published in early 1983, suggest that the results were mixed. Joe Hanlon in the *Guardian* indicated that Muslims, Hindus, and traditional Protestant churches, e.g., Methodists and Presbyterians, "expressed strong support for FRELIMO [and] said they were freer to practice their religions under FRELIMO than under the Portuguese." In the course of its presentation, the Mozambican Christian Council, encompassing most of the mainstream Protestant groups, did note that "Marxist-Leninist ideology and religions diverge on certain basic points." The *Guardian* reported that the "newer evangelical churches" are in a separate association and that some of them in the Maputo suburbs "have confronted FRELIMO directly by scheduling services at the same time as FRELIMO has called a public meeting." These churches, according to the report, had been growing rapidly in the Maputo area. The composition of the evangelical category is not made clear, but reference to the South African links of some of them suggests that the category may include the independent African churches that had led a semiclandestine life under the Portuguese. Such churches, wherever they exist, have rarely been explicitly political in the sense that they ask their members to act in opposition to the government. At the same time, governments typically find it difficult to use these independent churches to mobilize their members for the goals of a specific regime.

The Roman Catholic hierarchy and FRELIMO had begun a rapprochement of sorts in 1981, when the church, which by the late 1970s had an entirely African hierarchy, seemed to be ready to lend its support to Mozambican development under FRE-

LIMO's rule. Later that year, however, Mozambique's bishops met with Pope John Paul II in Rome and seemed thereafter to be more critical of the regime. At the meeting between the churches and FRELIMO in late 1982, however, tension between church and state heightened. The position of the Roman Catholic church was less conciliatory than that of the others, according to several observers. For example, they asked for compensation for nationalized schools and hospitals, and they argued that restrictions on the mobility of the clergy violated the constitutional guarantee of freedom to practice a religion. In fact, the restrictions on the movement of the clergy concerned the other churches as well, but they had simply asked that the restrictions be lifted, whereas the Catholics insisted on their rights. The bishop's justification for the demand for compensation was that the church had made substantial contributions to education. Machel's response was quick and direct—he accused the hierarchy of provoking confrontation. Its claim of discrimination, he stated, was merely a reaction of the Roman Catholic Church being treated like other churches. Further, Machel charged that the church in the colonial era was not interested in the health and education of the people for their own sake but rather in "civilizing the natives" to serve the state.

Machel was particularly vehement in his response to the suggestion by Jaime Goncalves, bishop of Beira, that FRELIMO should negotiate with the Mozambican National Resistance (Resistência Nacional Moçambicana—RNM) and that Goncalves might serve as mediator. Machel stopped short of accusing Goncalves of ties to the RNM, but some of his comments suggested such ties. In any event, of the religious organizations represented at the 1982 meeting, the change in atmosphere seemed to affect least the relations between the Roman Catholics and the regime's leaders.

Mozambique's African Muslims have not played a significant role in FRELIMO, but some Muslims constituted part of the colonial military establishment, and there have been indications that FRELIMO may regard Islam as a barrier to development. African Muslims appear to have come to some accommodation with the regime, however. Apparently on the assumption that their relations with the government would be smoother if they were organized, Muslims formed the Mozambican Islamic Council in early 1983 and announced that a national conference would be held. On the occasion of the announcement of the creation of the council, its leaders presented a check to the minister of justice to support FRELIMO's Fourth Party Congress in April.

The long-range outcome of the 1982 meeting is uncertain. It

was expected that the clergy would be allowed greater mobility, that the arbitrary closing of churches would be stopped, and that some rebuilding and reopening of religious structures would be permitted. These expectations have either been met or were on the verge of being met. According to the United States Department of State's *Country Reports on Human Rights Practices for 1983*, the government continued to monitor religious activities closely, and the regime insisted that religious groups exhibit a Mozambican character rather than represent foreign entities. It was in part on the grounds that the Roman Catholic church is responsible primarily to the Vatican and also that it has continued to be critical of the government that the regime in Maputo has subjected the Catholics to tighter controls than other religious groups.

Luís B. Serapião, a Mozambican who had attended a Roman Catholic seminary in the early 1960s and has written critically of the colonial church, thinks that the leaders of FRELIMO have kept a tight rein on the church because the hierarchy and even the ordinary African priests are among the few well-educated Africans in Mozambique who are able to articulate a point of view different from that of the ruling party. Serapião, trained in the United States and having taught there, thinks the clergy is respected for its educational status by many Mozambicans who are not Catholics, and that this is understood by FRELIMO leaders as a challenge.

At the 1982 meeting, Machel stated that control over health and education, which was taken from the Roman Catholic church immediately after independence, would never be returned to religious organizations. It remained government policy eventually to nationalize all schools and hospitals. The United States Department of State's human rights report for 1983 asserts that nationalization policy was not being actively implemented in 1983. That, however, probably reflected a lack of financial wherewithal and skilled personnel on the part of the government rather than change in policy (see Education; Health, this ch.).

Although the practice of indigenous religions has been criticized and sometimes ridiculed, the regime has not taken steps against it. The ridicule arises in part from the emphasis of African belief and ritual on the effects in this world of the actions of ancestral spirits, other spirits, witches, and sorcerers. In this sense, tribal religions offer explanations of and remedies for the afflictions and events of life that fly directly in the face of scientific materialism that FRELIMO's leaders claim to abide by. The organization and ritual activity of indigenous religions usually pertain to members of kin groups or local communities, however, and are not likely to pose a threat at the political level.

There are exceptions to this highly local and kin-based character of indigenous religion, particularly among the Shona-speaking peoples and those influenced by them, e.g., the Barue and other peoples of the Zambezi valley. Among these peoples, community tutelary spirits, typically ancestors of the chiefly lineage but sometimes representatives of a former ruling group in the area, are significant. Their jurisdiction is territorial rather than kin-based. Some among these communal guardian spirits become lion spirits, possessing first a lion and then a medium. The term for lion, *mhondoro* is often used for both the spirit and the medium, although the usual term for medium is *svikiro*. Lion spirit mediums played a considerable role in early Shona opposition to British rule in Southern Rhodesia and to Portguese rule in Mozambique in the late nineteenth and early twentieth centuries. Such mediums have not always been believed by their people, especially if they seem to counsel action that is objectionable. But if they articulate a sense of wrong that is strongly felt by the people, they can become leaders of political movements. Although there has been no documented instance of a lion spirit medium having played a political role in the postindependence era, it has been suggested by some observers that FRELIMO has been opposed to their religious function as "reactionary," and that mediums have therefore been receptive to RNM appeals.

## Education

When FRELIMO began governing the country in 1975, the population was largely illiterate, and the numbers of Africans educated to a secondary or higher level was much smaller than that of neighboring territories at independence. The new regime, therefore, sought to establish an educational system that would increase Mozambique's literacy rate as quickly as possible and that would, in the not too distant future, furnish at least part of the required skilled labor force. From the point of view of the political leaders, if not necessarily of the people themselves, the schools had the additional task of indoctrinating the young and of helping to alter the social order by giving girls the same opportunities for education as boys.

Education for Africans had been so inadequate under the Portuguese that the development of the system under the new regime started from a very low level. It was possible to expand vastly the number of children in the four elementary grades by making schooling free and encouraging parents to send their daughters to school. But the lack of teachers trained to a reasonable level and the shortage of appropriate textbooks and other equipment were impediments to the achievement of the regime's educational goals. In 1981, therefore, when the goal of seven years of universal and compulsory primary education was established, it was not assumed that it would be achieved at once.

In the words of historian Thomas Henriksen, "a separate and vastly unequal educational system emerged before World War II, and the period afterwards brought scant departure from the inequalities." The government's *Economic Report* of 1984 notes that the Portuguese made last-minute efforts (in the early 1970s) to speed up the training of Africans, but these efforts accomplished little.

In the colonial period the Portuguese—usually through the Roman Catholic church—provided a form of schooling (called rudimentary education after 1956) intended to bring African children to the level of Portuguese or *assimilado* children entering primary school, i.e., capable of speaking and understanding Portuguese. After three years of rudimentary schooling, few African children passed the examination that would make them eligible for entrance into a regular four-year primary school because teaching was exclusively in Portuguese. If they did pass after several attempts, they might be considered too old to enter such a school. Moreover, admission fees to primary schools were high for most African families. Under these conditions few entered primary school, fewer completed four years, and even fewer finished the fifth year of primary school—rarely available in rural areas—deemed necessary for entrance to secondary school. If after overcoming these obstacles the child (usually the son) of a rural African family was ready to go to a secondary school, he found few openings in academic institutions. Vocational training was deemed more suitable and desirable for Africans.

It was only in 1962 that higher education became available in Mozambique, when the University of Lourenço Marques was opened, but the ratio of white to black students began at 60 to one and did not improve in the years before independence. Over the years very few blacks were sent to Portugal for higher education. A number of black Mozambicans acquired secondary and higher educations in Southern Rhodesia and South Africa, however.

In 1970 only about 5,000 black Mozambicans were being educated beyond four years of primary schooling. No great change in these numbers occurred in the ensuing four or five years. Owing in part to a late drive to enroll African children in primary schools in the early 1970s and during the transitional period, 672,000 were recorded as registered in such schools in 1975. In the same year 23,000 students were enrolled in secondary education—a seven-year program—and the bulk of those were probably in the first cycle, i.e., the first two years of that program:

Reliable statistical series for the years from the mid-1970s to the early 1980s were not available, but a general pattern was discernible. Elementary education was made available to all children free of charge, and a special effort was launched to encourage girls to go to school. Within two or three years the number of children in primary schools was more than double that in 1975, i.e., between 1.3 and 1.4 million. By 1979 the number had reached nearly 1.5 million and by 1980 nearly 2 million. The figures for 1982 indicated a drop to between 1.3 and 1.4 million. In this period girls constituted between 40 and 45 percent of primary-school pupils. In principle, the children eligible for primary grades were those between six and nine years of age. In fact, many who had not gone to school in the colonial period and were beyond six years of age (and in many instances beyond nine) started primary school in the first few years of the independence era. The apparent decline in numbers in 1982 may have reflected the fact that the pool for primary-school students had by then shrunk to the six-to-nine age cohort. It may also reflect the drought that affected almost all provinces beginning in 1981 and made normal schooling as well as other activities so difficult.

The number of students in secondary schools also grew substantially through 1981 and appeared to have dropped in 1982. The secondary-school system comprised three cycles. The first two years—through classes five and six—sometimes were referred to as presecondary or intermediate. The second cycle—classes seven through nine—constituted secondary school proper. The third cycle consisted of classes 10 and 11. In addition, there were technical schools at three levels: elementary, basic, and middle. In 1980 roughly 150,000 students were enrolled in the first cycle of secondary school; presumably, most were young people who had passed through the four years of primary school since independence. Only about one-fifth as many—slightly more than 30,000 students—were in the second cycle, and far fewer—only about 1,200 students—were in the third cycle. The steep decline from the first to the second cycle, and especially from the second to the third, reflected the fact that second-cycle and particularly third-cycle students would have had to begin their primary schooling well before independence to be ready for advanced secondary education by 1980. The decline also reflected the relative unavailability of facilities and teachers for these higher levels in the late 1970s and 1980s.

Young women were not going to secondary school at nearly

*A primary school classroom in rural Mozambique*
*Courtesy Mozambique Information Office, London*

*A secondary school classroom in Maputo*
*Courtesy Mozambique Information Office, London*

the rate they went to primary school. The decline began in the first cycle; in 1980 girls constituted only about 25 percent of those in the first two years of secondary school. They made up about 22 percent of the total in the second cycle. It had been difficult enough to persuade parents to allow girls to go to primary schools that were near their homes. To persuade parents to allow them to leave home for secondary school, particularly after the girls reached puberty and were thus eligible for marriage, has been much harder. Interestingly, the proportion of young women in the third cycle increased slightly—to 29 percent. If they were not withdrawn from the educational stream for reasons associated with marriage, the chance of their continuing to higher levels began to approach that of young men, although in the early 1980s there was still a considerable gap between them.

In addition to the general (or academic) secondary schools, there were technical schools at several levels. It appeared that the level referred to as technical-elementary was at the primary level. It apparently drew only 1,000 students in 1980, more than 75 percent of them boys. The level referred to as technical-basic drew more than 9,000 students, and the technical-middle drew slightly more than 1,400 students. At these higher levels the proportion of males was even greater—between 80 and 85 percent—although an effort had been made to open these schools to young women, particularly for those courses that did not deal solely with commercial skills. Although the need for people with industrial and commercial skills has been great and compensation adequate, Mozambican Africans have been likely to prefer a more academic education, if only because they had been shunted to vocational training by the Portuguese. Because Mozambique's own schools have not been in a position to train as many students at the secondary, technical, and higher levels as the country needs, several thousand students, most of them of secondary-school age, have been sent to communist countries for schooling. The greatest numbers have gone to the German Democratic Republic (East Germany) and Cuba (see Communist Countries, ch. 4). A few have been sent to West European countries.

In 1984 there was only one institution of higher education in Mozambique, the Eduardo Mondlane University (formerly the University of Lourenço Marques, renamed in 1976). It was financed by the state and governed by a council consisting of a rector, academic and administrative directors, and representatives of the ruling party.

The university included facilities (departments or schools) of agriculture, civil engineering, veterinary medicine, natural sciences, medicine, law, and economics. A training center for secondary teachers was also part of the university, as were centers for African studies, ecology, the development of natural resources, and studies in communications. Most subjects required three years of university study, at the end of which a *bacharelato* was awarded. Two years of further study led to the *licenciatura*.

Detailed information on the educational and national background of the teaching and research staff was not readily available, but, given the lack of black Mozambicans with higher education, most of the faculty was probably Portuguese. The language of instruction was Portuguese.

Access to the university required a secondary-school-leaving certificate (after a total of 11 years of primary and secondary schooling) and passing an entrance examination. In the early 1980s there were comparatively few who met the formal requirements for admission to the university. A special commission was therefore established to assess applications for equivalents to the secondary-school-leaving certificate.

Because so vast a proportion of its population—estimated as high as 95 percent—was illiterate at independence and, because very few had the skills required by the modern sector of the economy, a good deal of emphasis has been placed on a literacy campaign among adults and on making courses available at the work place and during evenings. Particular priority has been given to people in nationalized industries, state farms, cooperatives, and communal villages, although opportunities have also been made available to the majority who were still outside the socialized or quasi-socialized sector of the economy. In any case, it was estimated that by the early 1980s the rate of illiteracy had been reduced to 75 percent. Most affected by the drive for literacy were the young and the males. Those between ages 10 and 24 either had been formally educated in the schools or had quickly taken advantage of the literacy campaigns. The illiteracy rate among Mozambicans between 15 and 24 years old had dropped to 57 percent and among those between ages 10 and 14 to 60 percent. The rate of those between ages five and nine was 93 percent, reflecting in part the fact that literacy does not take hold immediately among those in school but also that Mozambican children do not begin their schooling at age six. The illiteracy rate among women (over 86 percent) was more than 20 points higher than that for men (63 percent). Among the older portions of the population, only a few women would have attended school during the colonial era, and there was still a considerable gap between men and women with respect to literacy after independence, if only because there were more men working in places where literacy instruction was readily available.

## Health

The approach of independence and FRELIMO's explicit intention to end the private practice of medicine brought the departure of most of the 550 physicians who had been in Mozambique in 1973; by 1975 fewer than 90 remained. In the next three or four years, physicians from a number of countries arrived, either directly under contract to the government in Maputo or provided for by various foreign governments or other sources of aid. The influx of foreign physicians, however, was a stop-gap measure. The new regime's leaders intended a different approach to health care. During the colonial era almost all private practitioners had emphasized curative medicine for the white, largely urban, population. After independence medical personnel, as employees of the state, were to provide free health care to the entire population, the great bulk of which lived in the rural areas. The use of physicians as primary health care providers and the continuing stress on curative medicine would have required thousands of physicians. These circumstances in effect forced FRELIMO to take the view that a program of preventive medicine emphasizing inoculation, hygiene, and nutrition would have far greater impact on the health of most Mozambicans than a traditionally oriented curative program. Further, it was assumed that the tasks of inoculation and education in hygiene and nutrition could be accomplished by persons who had a good deal less training than physicians or even nurses. Such persons could also perform a limited range of curative practice, such as dispensing pills and making referrals.

Preindependence data on the illnesses suffered by Africans were fragmentary, but these data suggest that malaria, tuberculosis, bacterial and amoebic dysentery and other gastrointestinal infections, pneumonia, measles, and infectious hepatitis were among the most common diseases. Outbreaks of cholera were intermittent. Information for the late 1970s, which presumably covered the illnesses of rural Africans more fully than colonial statistics, indicates that in addition to these medical problems, meningitis and leprosy were of some importance and that there had been an outbreak of cholera in 1979. Cholera also broke out in a slum of Beira in 1981. Tetanus occurred with some frequency in the late 1970s. Not reported, perhaps because of inadequate data gathering, was schistosomiasis (snail fever), common in tropical Africa, and sleeping sickness, which occurs in regions affected by the tsetse fly. A good part of northern Mozambique is so affected.

Most of these illnesses may be controlled, if not wholly eradicated, by immunization or by achieving and maintaining reasonable conditions of sanitation in and around human settlement, particularly with respect to water supplies. Almost immediately after independence two comprehensive campaigns were launched, one for mass immunization against measles, diphtheria, tetanus, typhus, poliomyelitis, tuberculosis, and smallpox, and the other for the building of latrines everywhere in the country. The use of latrines was regarded as essential in maintaining community sanitation and in breaking the cycle by which gastrointestinal diseases and hepatitis were transmitted. These campaigns were initially successful, but there were problems in follow-up. As of 1983 a considerable number of people had yet to be reached by the inoculation program, and only about one-half of all households had access to latrines. Both programs were proceeding in the mid-1980s, although there were still difficulties in getting enough staff to do all the jobs in preventive and curative health care.

There have been no systematic studies of the incidence of malnutrition in Mozambique, but it has not been uncommon, particularly among children and especially in drought years. Malnutrition has been an underlying problem in African countries that have been better-off than Mozambique, rendering children susceptible to a wide range of infectious diseases. Newspaper reports in 1982 and 1983 indicated that lack of food was a major problem in much of Mozambique south of the Zambezi River owing to the devastating drought of those years and also to hostile action by the antiregime RNM.

Lacking adequate numbers of physicians and other health care personnel and aware that such numbers would not be available for decades to come, the authorities turned to the notion of using *agentes polivalentes elementarios* (basic healthworkers), roughly equivalent to China's "barefoot doctors." These healthworkers were to be chosen by their own communities to acquire basic preventive and therapeutic techniques at regional schools and to return to villages as educators and practitioners. Those chosen were expected to be literate, preferably to have completed four years of primary schooling. In fact, such persons were not to be found in some communities, and the demand for literates to fill other roles made it necessary to choose someone who first would have to undergo literacy training. Basic healthworkers were to be provided with housing, food, and other material support but were not to be paid a salary. In the late 1970s most of these basic healthworkers were chosen by the residents of communal villages or state farms and presumably recieved other payments to eke out a livelihood from the group of which they were members. It is not clear how such a system would work in those communities—by far the greatest number—that were neither communal nor state farms.

Health care personnel trained by the Portuguese or in schools for paramedics since independence have played an important role in rural health care. At the next level beyond the *agentes polivalentes elementarios* are the *agentes sanitarios* (sanitation workers), each of whom is expected to provide back-up service and advice to the basic health workers of several communities. It appears, however, that there are not enough *agentes sanitarios* or other health care providers at higher levels. Gill Walt of the London School of Hygiene and Tropical Medicine noted in 1981 that "one of the problems that affected all paramedical personnel . . . was the difficulty of providing sufficient supervision and structural support. For the village health workers in remote areas, it was often a day's journey to the next level health center. In the rainy season accessibility was further reduced." Such problems were inevitable in the early years when health personnel of all kinds were scarce, communications and transportation infrastructure were limited, and matters were further comlicated by drought and the activities of the RNM. Some of these problems have been overcome, and the agreement between South Africa and Mozambique in 1984 to refrain from helping insurgents may have consequences for Mozambican health care, particularly in the realm of nutrition.

In 1980 the government, with the aid of United Nations advisers, put together a program intended to improve the health of mothers and young children and to provide instruction and materials for family planning. Family planning as a mode of population control has not had priority in Mozambique; the growth rate, estimated at under 3 percent annually, was not yet that high in the mid-1980s, and the country was considered big enough to absorb a substantially larger population. Family planning, therefore, was thought of as a way of spacing births and, coupled with mother and child health care, of diminishing very high maternal and infant disease and death rates. The chief agents for accomplishing these goals were to be 750 nurse-midwives, each of whom was to have six years of schooling (presumably four years of primary and the first cycle of secondary) followed by three years of technical training. The first group of 150 trainees began their

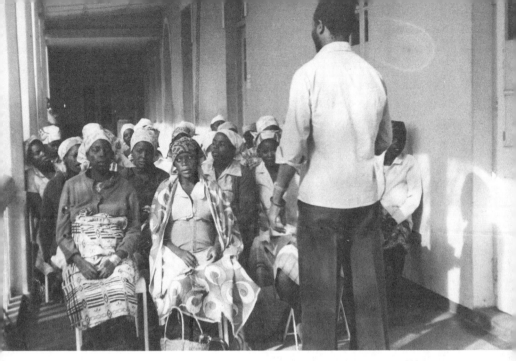

*Mozambican healthworker giving instruction to*
*pregnant women at a prenatal clinic in a district hospital*
*Courtesy Mozambique Information Office, London*

*Health care facility at the Center for Workers'*
*Accelerated Education in Lugela, Zambezia Province*
*Courtesy AIM/Lois Browne*

technical courses in 1981, and the first maternal and health care centers were to be established at the end of 1984.

\* \* \*

There has been no description and analysis of the national social order or the structure of local communities, rural or urban, since Mozambique's independence. D.J. Webster's article, "The Origins of Migrant Labour, Colonialism, and the Underdevelopment of Southern Mozambique," deals with some of the factors affecting social relations among the Chopi not long before independence; Laurence Harris, writing from a Marxist perspective, indicates the persistence and significance of differences between wealthier and poorer peasants in a Tsonga communal village and cooperative in the mid- to late-1970s. Two papers by Luís B. Serapião on the Roman Catholic church before and immediately after independence help to account for the situation of the church under the FRELIMO regime.

Of the many works dealing with postindependence Mozambique prepared by Allen and/or Barbara Isaacman, two attempts to describe social developments over a period of five years or more contain much useful detail. Both, however, have a sentimental affinity for the FRELIMO regime and lack a necessary objective detachment. The first book, by Allen and Barbara Isaacman, is *Mozambique: From Colonialism to Revolution, 1900-1982;* the second volume, by Barbara Isaacman and June Stephen, is *Mozambique: Women, the Law, and Agrarian Reform.* (For further information and complete citations, see Bibliography.)

# Chapter 3.  The Economy

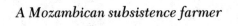
*A Mozambican subsistence farmer*

THE NEW GOVERNMENT at independence in 1975 took over an economy in which agricultural land of varying fertility and adequacy of water was the principal natural endowment. Forest resources were still substantial; there was a large, partially developed hydroelectric potential; and some economically important minerals had been discovered. There was also an industrial infrastructure of moderate proportions that was large in comparison with many other Sub-Saharan countries. The industrial establishment, however, had been developed mainly to supply the needs of Portuguese settlers and export markets. Overall, readily exploitable resources to provide the impetus for economic development of the new state were not present. Food production regularly fell short of requirements. The main transportation routes were oriented to serve neighboring countries rather than development of a unified Mozambican economy; in 1984 no rail line or through road as yet connected the northern and southern parts of the country. The human resources base consisted of a large number of individuals in subsistence farming, a small industrial and agricultural wage-labor force, and a limited number of Portuguese and other non-Africans who had elected to remain in Mozambique after national independence. In 1984 economic viability rested precariously on receipts from agricultural (including fisheries) export commodities, income from rail and port services provided to neighboring countries, and earnings by migrant labor outside Mozambique's borders.

When the Front for the Liberation of Mozambique assumed power, its leadership had as a general objective the ultimate imposition of a socialized economic system founded on classic Marxist-Leninist doctrine. Exactly how this was to be done, however, had not yet been clearly defined. As stated by President Samora Moises Machel in *A Nossa Luta*, the notion of what was wanted and how to get it was still vague. Ideological concepts—later expressed in concrete terms in guidelines issued by the front's Third Party Congress in 1977—played a significant part in the economic pattern that emerged. But necessary immediate measures and continuing difficulties, accentuated by natural disasters, resulted in gradually increasing pragmatism and the evolution and acceptance of a mixed economy composed of state, collective, and private sectors. All land of any kind is regarded as inalienable property by the state, which manages it for the whole people. A number of events have given the public sector a domin-

ant position. When the Portuguese abandoned industrial properties, plantations, agricultural estates, and commercial farms after
the liberation war, the new Mozambican governmment took them
over as a matter of operational necessity. The state also assumed
control of the former Portuguese national and provincial holdings
in the country, and financial institutions and various private operations were nationalized. Collectives, notably in the agricultural
sector but also found in industries, occupied a lesser position. The
agricultural collective was eventually to form the backbone of the
rural economy. In 1984, however, most of the rural population
still operated private family farms to which they held only
usufructuary rights but still by law were endowed with the right
to pass the land on to heirs.

In the initial period after national independence, the liberation front's attitude toward private commercial enterprise
appears to have been generally noncommittal, although there was
a tacit recognition of its value that included encouragement of
departed entrepreneurs to return and put their plants back into
operation. Nationalization of some functioning private enterprises did occur, but for reasons considered valid by the government. Continuing unfavorable economic conditions led finally to
adoption of a positive policy toward the private sector. Expressed
in a declaration by Machel in 1980, it stated that private enterprise had an important part to play in bettering the Mozambican
economy and that the state would establish favorable conditions
for operations by private entrepreneurs, commercial farmers,
shopkeepers, and traders. Participation by Western multinational corporations was included. They were viewed as posing
no risk to Mozambique; the party and the government in any
dealings knew what was wanted and how they wanted it done. All
private activities, however, would have to be conducted in line
with the state's socialist objectives and the state plan. The value of
the profit motive was recognized; it would result in mutual
benefit. Concrete examples of this policy in 1984 were the opera-
tive contracts with major international companies to search for
and develop petroleum and natural gas in Mozambique. Re-
affirmation of the importance of the private sector and support for
it were given by Machel at the Fourth Party Congress in 1983,
when he placed particular emphasis on the role played by the
private sector in agricultural production.

In early 1984 information on the economy was extremely limited
and marked by a dearth of detailed statistical data. There was, in
addition, the question of reliability of the figures available. The
departure of the Portuguese in the mid-1970s had decimated the

staffs engaged in the collection and collation of data. The government had reported the acquisition of computer equipment that was expected to improve the economic data base for planning purposes, but it was unknown when such data would be publicly obtainable.

## Economic Overview

The economy in 1975 contained several major structural weaknesses. Included was the institutionalization of an African sector largely engaged in subsistence agriculture and a commercialized sector operated exclusively by Portuguese, Asians (of Indian, Pakistani, and Goan origin) who dominated retail trade, foreign entrepreneurs, and a small number of African *assimilados* (those who qualified by virtue of literacy in Portuguese and way of life for Portuguese citizenship during the colonial era). The African population was involved in monetized transactions through cash cropping and was used as wage labor by the commercial sector, but it participated only negligibly in the management activities of that sector. The distinction between these parallel economies had been established during colonial times through the institution of such practices as compulsory labor by Africans, forced cash cropping, and the prohibition of commercial operations by Africans. The distinction was further emphasized by the concentration of official development funds in the commercialized sector, although it appears that one reason for this was the reported long-standing assumption by many Portuguese colonial authorities that the African economy in general could take care of itself.

The inherent danger in the economy's dualism came sharply into focus after 1974, when the vast majority of individuals running the commercial sector departed from the country. Included were those involved in urban-oriented food and export crop production, industry, transportation, the distribution system, and other activities; by 1977 about 90 percent of an estimated 200,000 people had left. The acute lack of managers, technicians, skilled and semi-skilled workers, and effective rural marketing services resulted in severe disruptions and major declines in output in all sectors.

Statistics from the period are imprecise and only fragmentary, but some suggestions of the impact on the economy is seen in the decline in cement production from 611,000 tons in 1973 to less than 216,000 tons in 1978. In the 1974-77 period marketed cashews dropped from 196,000 tons to 76,000; seed cotton declined from 144,000 tons in 1974 to 45,000 tons in 1978. In the case of cashews, the departure of the rural store operators, who bought the crop harvested by subsistence farmers, played the major role in the decline, although after independence a lack of purchasable consumer goods in rural areas was also significant. The drop in cotton output was related in part to the same factors, but an aversion to growing cotton appears to have arisen as a reaction to coercive cultivation measures and low prices during the colonial period, and many African farmers simply discontinued production after independence. The Portuguese exodus left the economy in a precarious position, but their withdrawal, it has been pointed out, also allowed the unopposed introduction of such major structural changes as the communal village cooperative system and state farms.

A serious weakness also existed in the heavy reliance on receipts from the transit trade from the Transvaal in South Africa, which passed through the port of Maputo, and similar trade with Southern Rhodesia (present-day Zimbabwe) and Zambia, which used both Beira and Maputo (see Railroads, this ch.). Earnings from this traffic and the use of port facilities had, during the decade before independence, offset most of Mozambique's large, perennial, merchandise trade deficits. The government in Maputo has charged that after it imposed sanctions against Southern Rhodesia in early 1976, in conformity with existing resolutions of the United Nations (UN) and the Organization of African Unity (OAU), South Africa gradually reduced its trade through Maputo. Figures cited for 1978 indicated that only about 60 percent of the 1973 volume passed through the port; in 1982 the amount was 32.5 percent. The government also has stated that a diversion of higher tariff cargo to South African ports had occurred. Nonetheless, there was considerable evidence that in the postindependence period the South African authorities have urged shippers in the Transvaal to continue to use Maputo. During 1983 discussions were carried on by Mozambique and South Africa concerning an increase in transit traffic. A factor that may have had an important bearing on South African traffic volume through Maputo was the opening of the new South African deepwater port at Richards Bay on the coast of Natal Province in 1976. This highly modern port, one at Durban, and the port of Maputo were roughly equidistant from Transvaal centers.

The transit trade with Southern Rhodesia handled by the Beira and Maputo ports declined after it became evident in 1974 that Mozambique would soon come under an independent government of the Front for the Liberation of Mozambique (Frente de Libertação de Moçambique—FRELIMO). A crash program was carried out that year by Southern Rhodesia to construct a direct connection between the Rhodesian and South African railroad systems. Purportedly, the new line was insurance against the cutting off of traffic by a potentially hostile Mozambican government. An estimated 80 percent of Rhodesian exports and imports had transited Mozambique, and a large number of tourists had also used the rail lines. By early 1976, when Mozambique enforced sanctions, the proportion had already dropped to between 20 and 40 percent, and the tourist trade had virtually ceased. The trade was resumed after the UN lifted sanctions in late 1979. The first cargo moved through Maputo in 1980 after restoration of the damaged rail line to the port; repairs to the Beira line were completed in 1981. Figures on the amount of this transit trade were unavailable in early 1984. Mozambique has estimated the loss in revenue during the sanctions period, together with damage resulting from Rhodesian military actions inside Mozambique, at about US$556 million.

The economy at independence was also heavily dependent on foreign exchange earnings from migrant laborers working in South Africa. African wage labor had been furnished under contract to that country since the late 1800s for work principally in coal and gold mines. In the early 1970s there was an average of over 100,000 Mozambicans in South Africa annually, and official figures for 1975 indicated about 118,000 that year. By agreement with the government in Pretoria, 60 percent of a mine worker's wages were withheld until the individual returned to Mozambique. In the colonial period the withheld amount was remitted to the Portuguese government in gold, the foreign exchange was credited to Mozambique, and the worker received the equivalent in Mozambican currency. Beginning in 1968 the market price for gold increased, but South African remittances continued at the official price, and the colonial authorities gave the returned laborer the amount due in local currency, also at the official rate. The gold was sold on the open market by Portugal at a growing profit as world gold prices advanced. This windfall was finally credited to Mozambique by Portugal at independence.

The gold arrangement with South Africa continued in effect with the government of FRELIMO until April 1978, when changes in International Monetary Fund (IMF—see Glossary) rules removed controls from official international gold dealings. South Africa subsequently transferred wage withholdings in gold values at the open rate. Mozambique benefited from the foreign exchange but no longer was able to realize a profit on gold sales. A second setback occurred when South Africa greatly reduced the number of Mozambican workers to an annual total between 1977

135

and 1982 of some 41,000 to 46,000. A variety of political and economic factors appear to have played a part in the drop, including a tendency among South African mine operators to reduce their dependency on foreign migrant labor. The Mozambican government had calculated that by 1982 the total receipts lost from the decline in migrant labor was the equivalent of US$568. The decline in migrant labor recruitment also had a direct impact on unemployment and on the livelihood of a large number of subsistence families for whom migrant wages were a significant supplementary source of income.

The adverse effects of these developments, the internal structural changes, and the losses from sanctions against Southern Rhodesia that the economy experienced after independence were compounded from 1977 through early 1984 by a series of natural calamities of major proportions. In February 1977 devastating floods in the major food-producing Incomati and Limpopo river valleys left several hundred thousand peasants homeless and resulted in the loss of large quantities of food crops grown mainly to feed the urban population. Irrigation works, granaries, housing, road infrastructure, transport equipment, and the rail line through the region were also destroyed or suffered damage. Extensive flooding occurred a year later in the Zambezi river valley, causing major losses of export and food crops and cattle, as well as further damage to the transport infrastructure, housing, schools, and social service facilities. According to government estimates, the two floods had cost the economy the equivalent of about US$100 million.

The most devastating natural disaster was the drought that began in December 1981, when the rains ceased halfway through the normal October-April rainy season and did not return generally in adequate quantity until November-December 1983. The drought affected the central provinces of Tete and Zambezia but was most severe in Manica, Sofala, Inhambane, and Gaza provinces in the south. Rainfall in the 1982-83 season averaged only 37 to 61 percent of the normal amount. In some places the usual total was received, but in an irregular pattern that damaged crops. Low-water flow in the Incomati and Limpopo rivers prevented full use of irrigation. In the lower parts of the rivers the decreased levels allowed saltwater to enter, damaging irrigation works. In the southern provinces an estimated 238,000 tons of cereals and some 190,000 head of cattle were lost. Seed was eaten by a hungry population, but new stocks had been obtained through foreign-aid sources to permit planting of crops for the 1983-84 season. Relief agency workers reported in late 1983 that

*Withered maize in a field near Moamba (Maputo Province) in 1983 shows the effects of the severe drought.*
*Courtesy AIM/Anders Nilsson*

*Members of the diplomatic corps in the national capital visit a drought zone near Moamba in March 1983.*
*Courtesy AIM/Anders Nilsson*

roughly 600,000 people in Gaza and Inhambane provinces alone were facing starvation. Large numbers in Manica and Sofala provinces were also in need of food, and shortages were also reported elsewhere. The government estimated that losses in crops, cattle, other livestock, and seed amounted to about US$75 million. About the same amount was needed to restore food stocks, obtain seed supplies, and otherwise bring conditions back to normal in the agricultural sector.

Mozambique's problems and need for assistance since independence have been addressed by substantial aid in the form of grants and loans from the West, the centrally planned economies, Third World states, and international organizations. After Mozambique's imposition of sanctions against Southern Rhodesia, help was furnished by UN members, partially offsetting economic losses. A large amount of foreign aid was also provided in the 1976–83 period in response to appeals by the Mozambican government for disaster relief. The government reported to the UN that in 1979 the equivalent of about US$113 million had been received and, in 1980, an additional US$55 million. Through September 1983 the United States had provided close to US$75 million, of which about three-quarters was in the form of grants consisting mostly of commodities through the Food for Peace Program (Public Law 480). As of that date the equivalent of US$100 million had also been made available by international organizations, including the United Nations Development Programme, other UN agencies, and the African Development Bank (ADB). Bilateral aid has been received from members of the European Economic Community, the Scandinavian countries, Japan, Brazil, India, Algeria, the Soviet Union, East European states, China, the Democratic People's Republic of Korea (North Korea), and others. Portugal has also become an important donor (official and private sources) since the rapprochement with FRELIMO that occurred in 1981 (see Portugal, ch. 4). Overall bilateral aid, already provided and projected under agreements, totaled in the hundreds of millions in United States dollar equivalents.

## Agriculture

In the early 1980s some 80 to 90 percent of the population was dependent on agriculture for all or a substantial part of their livelihood, and about two-thirds of the country's overall work force between the ages of 15 and 64 was estimated to be actually engaged in agricultural pursuits, including forestry and fisheries.

The sector's contribution to the gross domestic product (GDP—see Glossary) was estimated at about 44 to 45 percent in the late 1970s (the latest figures available). In the years preceding independence, domestic food output had regularly failed to meet internal demands, and large imports—especially of wheat—had been made annually. The departure of thousands of Portuguese farmers had greatly increased the shortage. Agricultural commodities had also accounted for most of Mozambique's merchandise export earnings; production had been similarly affected adversely by the Portuguese exodus.

Until independence the sector had been sharply divided into traditional and commercial elements based on land tenure (see Land Tenure, this ch.). At the beginning of the 1970s, the traditional economy consisted of about 1.6 million households that had possession of about 2.5 million hectares of land. Over three-quarters had two or fewer hectares, and 90 percent had holdings of three hectares or fewer. Although classified as traditional, a large number of the households also produced surpluses for sale. The commercial sector, which operated under Portuguese civil law, comprised at the time some 4,600 farms whose landholdings covered almost 2.4 million hectares, but only about one-third of the total appears to have been in use at any time. Over four-fifths of these farms were owned by individuals and were worked mainly by family members. Their output was intended primarily for the domestic market. The remaining commercial farms consisted of plantations and larger scale operations. The former, financed mainly by foreign capital, produced for export using paid labor. The latter's production was carried on mostly by African farmers who cultivated cash crops—the sale of which was handled by the Portuguese proprietors of the farms—mainly to the domestic market.

The patterns and degree of subsistence and commercial sector contributions in agricultural production differed at independence in the northern, central, and southern parts of the country. In the central area encompassing essentially the Zambezi River valley, subsistence farmers accounted for about 70 percent of total crop output. Somewhat more than one-half was for their own use, and the remainder went to the commercial market, constituting about 20 percent of the latter. Plantations growing sugarcane, coconuts (for copra), and tea produced close to 60 percent of commercialized crops; white settler farms and some larger ones accounted for the remainder. In the north some 60 percent of crops were cultivated for subsistence by the African population. African farmers also accounted for two-thirds of the commercial production, partly in the form of surplus food but mainly cotton raised as a cash crop and cashews collected for sale from trees that were part of the natural vegetation. White settler farms and a few plantations produced the remaining one-third. In the south, subsistence and commercial production each accounted for about half of the total agricultural output. Settler and large commercial farms, however, produced three-quarters of marketed crops, a small amount was supplied by plantations, and the remaining one-fifth was grown by subsistence farmers.

In early 1984 there appeared to have been few changes in the central area since independence, the basic difference being shifts in control of most plantations from private ownership to state enterprises. In the north an increase in large-scale operations had taken place through the establishment of newly developed state farms. A substantial drop in cotton cash-crop cultivation by subsistence farmers had occurred. In the early 1980s the government and the ruling political party, FRELIMO, were making efforts to revive interest in this crop. The amount of participation by the subsistence population in commercial agriculture had been markedly reduced by a sharp decline in cashew collection, and steps to reinterest farmers in this occupation were also being pursued by the government. In the south, effects of the postindependence changes in the agricultural sector were unclear.

Restructuring of the agricultural sector was a basic aim of FRELIMO. The envisioned pattern consisted of a system of collective farming carried out by communal villages that would produce both subsistence crops and, depending on conditions, surplus food and commercial cash crops. This system was to be supplemented by state farms, which would concentrate mainly on export crops and, especially in the south, food crops for the domestic urban population.

During the revolutionary period, FRELIMO had found that cooperative cultivation by the communal villages in its controlled areas had produced substantially larger crops than had farmers individually. In the postindependence food crisis, expansion throughout Mozambique of this system, termed the "basis of socialist rural development," was considered essential to increase food production, and efforts to establish communal villages were promoted through massive educational programs, mainly using local dynamizing groups (*gruppos dinamizadores*—GDs; see Glossary). In 1983 there were reportedly about 1,350 villages having a total of some 1.8 million inhabitants, or roughly one-fifth of the rural population. Formation of a large number of the villages appears to have been the result of voluntary association

*Subsistence cultivation on land farmed by smallholders*
*Courtesy Mozambique Information Office, London*

stemming from party and government promotion activities. A considerable number, however, originated differently. Some were started by refugee groups, particularly in the north, and others were based on the *aldeamentos* fortified villages established by the Portuguese). Groups of farmers were organized into villages in the Limpopo River valley after the disastrous floods of 1977 that destroyed the dwellings of tens of thousands of small cultivators. Other villages were formed in the Zambezi River valley the following year after similar floods. In areas of activity by the Mozambican National Resistance (Resistência Nacional Moçambicana—RNM), sometimes referred to as RENAMO), strong pressures were used to get local peoples into villages. An important consideration in the latter case was to isolate them from RNM influence.

The formation of agricultural cooperatives—"the economic base of the communal village"—proceeded much more slowly. Their production also proved in general to be well below expectations. In mid-1982 they reportedly numbered only 273. The slow growth has been attributed to a variety of causes. There was a basic hesitancy on the part of farmers to try collective production, a system with which the Africans were unfamiliar, as against known possibilities for individual farming. A disincentive was that most operational collectives did not make significant profits from their collectively farmed fields—one of the selling points to get farmers to join. Moreover, a farmer could join a communal village and gain the social benefits associated with it without having to participate in collective production. Also responsible for lack of interest in the collective was the government's failure to provide promised inputs and technical help. It was widely apparent that in many cooperatives famers actually spent more time cultivating their own plots than in tending the common fields. Perhaps the principal factor in this situation, as pointed out by government sources, was the absence of the positive leadership that had been a major element in the success of the early FRELIMO villages. This conclusion appeared to be borne out by reports of highly successful results attained by a number of cooperatives that were characterized by such leadership.

FRELIMO's initial emphasis in the socialization of agriculture was on the communal villages and cooperatives. But by the opening of the Third Party Congress in early 1977, the developing food crisis had brought the state farm to the fore as the apparently fastest was to improve the country's food output. This was to be accomplished by using to advantage the large size of the state farm, modern farm machinery, and more highly organized production methods. Mechanization and increases in cultivated areas of state farms were projected, and in 1977 substantial foreign exchange was used to import such items as combines, tractors, and cultivators. A considerable number of irrigation pumps was also procured.

Most of the state farms were formed from consolidation of small farms, estates, and plantations that had been abandoned by the Portuguese, although some, as in the case of state cotton farms in Nampula Province, were started from scratch. In 1982 the total state farm areas was approximately 130,000 hectares. Many of the farms produced specialized crops (cotton, sisal, sugarcane, tea, citrus fruits, and coconuts) that were grown mainly for export. Although producing a variety of crops, the largest single farm, the Limpopo Agro-Industrial Complex (Complexo Agro-Industrial Limpopo—CAIL) in the Limpopo River valley, concentrated principally on rice. CAIL, developed by the nationalization of some 1,500 holdings in an abandoned Portuguese settlement

*Combines imported in the late 1970s for use on state farms*
*Courtesy Mozambique Information Office, London*

scheme, covered an area of about 15,000 hectares. It employed between 2,500 and 3,000 regular workers and up to 10,000 seasonal laborers.

The size of the operation created management problems that were worsened by the lack of adequately trained staff. The machinery secured for the farm also proved in part to be ofd the wrong kind, and there were an insufficient number of skilled operators and mechanics to handle it properly and keep it fully operational. Within a short time a substantial amount of machinery was out of service. Dissatisfaction with the situation at CAIL led reportedly to plans for its dissolution in 1983, the establishment of five separate smaller state farms and peasant cultivators. The same lack of trained personnel and of spare parts had resulted also in large amounts of equipment becoming unusable on state sugarcane farms. In 1981 the Ministry of Agriculture contracted with a foreign-franchise distributor of machinery in Mozambique to rehabilitate equipment within the purview of its franchise; this equipment made up almost half of the total in the country. By mid-1983 more than 2,000 pieces of machinery, mostly used in farming, had been returned to oiperation. The contract was to run to mid-1985, and the franchisee was expected to double the number restored by them, assuming adequate foreign exchange for spare parts. The distributor also undertook to provide training for maintenance and service personnel and had established training centers in several parts of the country.

The state farms were almost entirely monocultural and produced only one crop each year. They required varying numbers of seasonal laborers to supplement regular workers at harvest time. By the late 1970s serious problems of recruitment had developed for most farms. Various reasons for the labor shortage have been advanced. In the case of CAIL the area's small family farmers were said to have attained a relatively secure livelihood from their own production and no longer were willing to sell their labor for the few weeks of harvest. Moreover, private farms reportedly paid better wages to those wanting to work. In the case of cotton, which was grown in the northern part of the country, the family farm members were busy harvesting their own cotton and other crops. For those wanted wage labor, some of the state farms were also unattractive because of their remoteness. In the 1981 harvest period in Nampula Province, for instance, it was necessary to use members of the armed forces to help save the crop. In 1984 there appeared to be no easy solution to the shortage of manpower (obtained in the colonial period largely through coercion) other than through an economically prohibitive increase in the number of permanent workers.

### Land Resources and Use

Estimates of land usable for agriculture (including livestock raising) vary, but there is general agreement that a large part of Mozambique is suitable for agricultural purposes. Official Portuguese data published in 1973 indicate that, theoretically, as much as 70 percent of the country's land area could be put to use for crop cultivation and livestock. In 1973, however, only about 4.4 percent was believed actually cultivated; the change by 1984 would be small. A somewhat larger amount (5.4 percent) was in temporary tree fallow, essentially for use on a rotational basis, and another 8 percent was used as pasture. A large amount of potentially cultivable ground, totalling about 53 percent of the country's land surface, was still occupied mainly by forests and woodlands (see table C, p. 180; Forestry, this ch.).

The country's soils are rather easily workable but are characterized generally by some degree of nitrogen deficiency. Various areas also exhibit deficiencies of certain minerals. Numerous local variations occur, but most soils can be classified in three broad groups based on origin. The greater part of the country is covered by soils that formed on crystalline-base rock of the Precambrian period. The soils along the northeastern coast support large numbers of coconut trees and, in a coastal zone somewhat farther inland, cashew trees, estimated to number in the millions. Depending on the adequacy of rainfall, in various parts of the north they are also important in staple food production and tea and tobacco cultivation.

Sandy soils formed on unconsolidated sediments occupy a considerable area along the coast in southern Mozambique. They are relatively intensively cultivated to produce the major crops of maize, cassava, sorghum, and peanuts. Perhaps the most important soils are the alluviums, both of fluvial and lacustrine origin, that stretch far upstream from the estuaries of the main rivers, notably the Incomati and the Limpopo. A large area of these soils also occupies the lower basin of the Zambezi River. Such soils are used for growing sisal and cotton and a variety of food crops, such as rice, maize, sugarcane, and bananas.

### Land Tenure

Until national independence, land tenure was governed by two separate systems: one based on African customary law, the other on Portuguese law. Under the traditional African system, land was regarded as belonging to the community, consisting of clan or chiefdom. Land laws were linked to the social and economic structure of the community and differed in detail among ethnic groups. But it was universally accepted that any household that belonged to the community was entitled to use of land for cultivation. The power to allocate land was held by a lineage (see Glossary), clan, village chief, or elders, from whom the household received the usufructuary rights to a specific area. These rights included continuous possession, full retention of the crops raised, and the right to bequeath the land to heirs. The rights remained contingent, however, on the cultivator's use of the land and acceptance by the group. Traditionally, there was no conception of land as a marketable commodity; it was used and passed on to heirs for their use in conformity with local customary law, or it reverted to the community. But the increasing commercialization of agriculture in some ethnic clusters in Mozambique and the significance of land possession in densely populated agricultural regions had by the 1960s resulted in a shift toward, and recognition of, the idea of private ownership of land.

Agricultural land held under the provisions of Portuguese law was limited to the Portuguese, aliens, and those Africans classified as *assimilados*, who came under the Portuguese civil code. Outright ownership of land was by registered title. There were also concessions, for which the occupier paid an annual rent, that provided for the granting of a formal title giving full property rights after a stipulated period of time if certain conditions had been fulfilled. Land could also be held under long-term lease—up to 50 years—that was granted mainly for livestock development. The law also provided for Africans to hold land as individuals through registration under a special title. But in such cases the rights granted were usufructuary only.

The Mozambique Constitution, effective at independence in 1975, nationalized all land. Land was declared to be the property of the state, which would determine the conditions for its use and exploitation. After passage by the People's Assembly on September 25, 1979, the General Land Law went into effect, establishing the direction and organization of land use and exploitation. The underlying precept was that land must not be used for the exploitation of man by man. The use and exploitation of land by the state and cooperative sectors was to be free and without limitation. Similar rights were given to the basic, largely subsistence, family farms that constituted the vast majority of agricultural holdings. Private title to land for economic exploitation was also authorized, but such land had to be used in conformity with the country's overall development plan. Payment of rent was required, and the title was valid for a stipulated period only. In the case of joint state-private enterprises, the use of the land and benefits from it were guaranteed by the former for the life of the undertaking.

Land belonging to all categories of usage was included in the State Land Fund. The General Land Law directed the creation of the National Land Register, which was to obtain and make available a variety of statistical data as a basis for solving planning problems and facilitating the distribution of the country's resources. All transactions dealing with land had to be registered. Certain administrative bodies were assigned responsibility for land matters in cities and urban areas, but rural land was not covered. Reportedly, the controls and powers exercised by local tribal authorities had been ended, but there was no information on the extent to which this had actually occurred. Concerning the large family farming sector, the law stated that the goal of such farms was to meet the needs of the family household; no use could be made of paid workers. At the same time, an important restriction was placed on the taking over of new land by a family household, the requirement being that land currently held must be worked for a minimum of three consecutive years before a move could be made.

**Agricultural Crops and Production**

Variations in Mozambique's topography and climate make possible the cultivation of both tropical and temperate crops. Several, including cashews (mostly from natural growth), cotton, sisal, sugar (from sugarcane), and tea, were important foreign exchange earners in the preindependence period. With the exception of sisal, they remained the leading commodity exports in 1984. Cultivated also for export of their products were coconut trees (copra and coconut oil) and oilseeds, especially those of sunflowers. Crops grown primarily for domestic consumption included cassava, maize, millet, rice, sorghum, beans, peanuts, potatoes, citrus fruits, bananas, and tobacco. Beans, bananas, citrus fruits, and tobacco were also exported but were of secondary importance in foreign trade.

Data on crop cultivation and production since independence were meager in early 1984 (see table 3, Appendix). The available information indicated that a substantial decline in the output of both domestic food crops and export commodities (except tea) had occurred since 1973, a date that has generally been used as the base production year. The decline was attributed to a number of causes, among which were floods in the 1976–77 and 1977–78 growing seasons, as well as in early 1984, and drought—particularly the prolonged period from late 1981 to late 1983 that affected large areas of southern and central Mozambique. In 1982–83 the lack of precipitation for rain-fed crops was compounded by the low flow of the rivers that were the source of water for major irrigation complexes. Production in some places was also reported to have been disrupted seriously by the activities of the RNM. The departure of Portuguese farmers and managers also had a major impact on production, as did the withdrawal of rural traders. The lack of consumer goods in the countryside, a condition that persisted into 1984, was a significant disincentive to small-farmer crop production.

Cashew trees, whose products (nuts and oil) have been Mozambique's largest foreign exchange earner, were introduced from the Western Hemisphere by the Portuguese in the sixteenth century. Commercial exploitation began in the 1920s, when India began importing the unhulled cashew, which was then processed and exported as Indian cashew nuts. High world prices in the 1960s led to the start of local processing, and by the early 1970s over two-thirds of Mozambique exports were in the form of shelled nuts. At independence there were eight processing enterprises that controlled the export market. In 1976 control of marketing was taken over by a government department. Subsequently, the state-owned National Cashew Enterprise (Empresa Nacional de Caju—ENC) was established to handle marketing and development. The ENC has also taken over a number of processing facilities that were abandoned by their former owners.

Most of the cashew harvest is carried out by small farmers who collect the nuts from numerous trees (one estimate placed the total at about 96 million) that grow wild. Some farmers had started to cultivate trees along with their regular crops. But the practice was not widespread because of the five- to six-year period after planting before nuts were borne and the some 12 years before maximum production began. In the preindependence period non-Africans also grew cashews on small- to medium-sized farms; the status of these holdings was unknown in 1984. In the early 1970s Mozambique and Tanzania were the top two producers of cashews. Mozambique held first place in 1972 and 1973, when its officially reported commercial production was 186,000 and 196,000 tons, respectively. Production dropped precipitously in 1976 (90,000 to 95,000 tons), apparently largely as the result of damage from natural causes, but also attributable to the virtual collapse of the local marketing outlets. Production continued to decline thereafter, in part for the same reason. But in the early 1980s the principal explanation for the failure of farmers to harvest the crop was the lack of goods available for purchase with their earnings; low prices paid for the fruit appear to have played a part as well. Officially reported marketed production figures for 1980 were only 17,600 tons and for 1981, some 16,900 tons.

Sugar, the second largest earner of foreign exchange in the preindependence period and third in the early 1980s, was produced before 1974 primarily for the Portuguese market, which secured about one-half of its total requirement from Mozambique. From 1974, by agreement with Portugal, Mozambique was also able to sell sugar on the world market. In the early 1970s sugar production had been over 300,000 tons a year. Output dropped substantially after independence, and production for 1980 and 1981 was reported at 170,000 tons and 177,700 tons, respectively. Six sugar enterprises were reported in operation in 1982. A major problem in production was the shortage of manpower in the cane-cutting season, and thousands of tons of cane were not harvested; at one enterprise the estimated amount left in the fields in the 1981 season was 50,000 tons. This same problem had existed also in the colonial period but had been resolved through forced labor and, after the practice was outlawed, through various labor recruitment procedures involving collusion with the colonial authorities. Other important factors in the decline of production were shortages of spare parts for equipment, transportation, technical personnel, fuel, and others.

In contrast to other export commodities, tea has recorded substantial increases in production. In the harvest year that ended June 30, 1982, output was 23,000 tons; it had totaled 18,800 tons in 1973, which had been the highest amount produced in the colonial period. The growing of tea in Mozambique began in the mid-1920s; by the mid-1950s it had become a major export item. Varieties are similar to those in India, and most exports have been to India and Sri Lanka for blending with more expensive teas produced in those countries. The growing areas are in the highlands of Zambezia Province, where more than one-half are located in Gurué District. Before independence about 90 percent of all production was by large, privately owned plantations. The total area devoted to tea was close to 16,000 hectares. The Portuguese operators of the estates, as well as smaller Portuguese producers, abandoned their holdings in the exodus of the mid-1970s, and they were taken over by the new government. In the early 1980s they were managed by the state-owned Mozambique Tea Enterprise (Empresa Moçambicana de Chá— EMOCHA), which had 12 processing factories. Two additional new plants were to be constructed with financial assistance from the ADB.

Cotton is the fourth largest agricultural export commodity by value. Nampula Province is the largest producer (in 1981 about 50 percent of total output); Cabo Delgado and Zambezia provinces account for a substantial proportion of the remainder. Although a few commercial farms had grown cotton during the colonial period, cultivation was overwhelmingly by small family farms that devoted part of their holding to it and part to subsistence crops. Beginning in 1926 Africans were strongly encouraged and—after 1938—required to grow cotton because of the colonial government's attempt to ensure adequate supplies for Portugal's textile industry. The cotton was sold at an extremely low price to government-authorized regional concessionaires, who in turn made it available to Portugal at well below world market prices. Strong external criticisms arose over the practice, and finally in 1961 compulsory cultivation was abolished. The concession system was ended in 1966. Production from the late 1960s to 1974 averaged about 138,000 tons of seed cotton a year.

In 1984 information on cotton production after independence was scanty. There appears to have been a substantial decline that has been attributed to marketing problems and weather conditions. A report on Cabo Delgado Province pointed out that in 1978 most of the crop had not been marketed, and the small family farmer, who produced about 75 percent of the cotton crop, lost interest. In 1979 production in the province reached the lowest level ever reported. A turnaround occurred in 1980, when the government took steps to correct this situation, and further improvement in output was registered in 1981. State farms had also entered into cotton production after independence, particularly in Nampula Province. Serious shortages of labor were experienced in the harvest period and had to be met by using members of the armed forces. In 1983 mechanical harvesters bought in the Soviet Union were used for the first time on two state farms in the province. In 1980 and 1981 state farms accounted for 20 and 22 percent of the crop, respectively; private commercial and family cash crop operations produced the remainder. The amount recorded by the cooperatives was relatively negligible. Production throughout Mozambique was reported officially at 63,900 tons in 1980 and 73,600 tons in 1981.

Among the food crops cassava has been the most important main staple for a large part of the population. It is cultivated throughout the country—virtually entirely for subsistence purposes—but about one-half the annual production is concentrated in Nampula Province. Maize, second to cassava as a staple, is also grown throughout Mozambique, mainly in white varities. It is cultivated principally for subsistence, but surpluses are marketed. In the preindependence period some 1,400 commercial farms, some of large size, also planted maize, producing roughly 7 to 8 percent of the total crop. In the 1980s an unknown amount continued to be produced commercially by large private enterprises. Rice had been largely a subsistence crop grown in Zambezi and other river valleys and in swamps along the southern coast. Early on, the Portuguese government encouraged increased production of rice through a system of concessions, many in the Limpopo River vally, to Portugese entrepreneurs, who were given a monopoly on purchases of rice in stipulated areas from African farmers. Output had increased, but uncontrollable amounts of rice were consumed by the growers themselves, and the concession system was given up in 1961 as not sufficiently profitable. Before independence some Portuguese had also set up large farms that had begun using mechanical reapers.

More than one-half of the annual rice production before 1975 had come from fewer than 2,000 of the Portuguese commercial operations. The rest was produced by a large number of small farms, of which about half were abandoned in the mid-1970s.

They were taken over by the government, which consolidated many into the CAIL state-farm complex. The Portuguese government had also encouraged settlers to grow wheat; cultivation was mainly in areas south of the Save River. Most of the crop was consumed in the urban areas. Production was usually far short of demand, and substantial quantities were imported. In the early 1980s the government was looking into the possibility of increasing wheat cultivation. A program to test various types of wheat for different climatic conditions in Mozambique had been started, financed by the UN's Food and Agricultural Organization (FAO).

**Livestock**

All principal large livestock animals used for food—cattle, goats, hogs, and sheep—are raised in Mozambique. Near the end of the colonial administration, official statistics showed between 1.4 and 1.5 million cattle, 214,000 hogs, 500,000 goats, and 131,000 sheep. In addition there were about 19,000 horses, mules, and donkeys. The Portuguese exodus of the mid-1970s was accompanied by a decline in the number of cattle. Animals were sold off and slaughtered, resulting in a surplus of meat in the market in contrast to the usual situation—still prevalent in 1984— in which demand outstripped supply. Considerable numbers were also driven by emigrating Portuguese farmers across the border into South Africa. In 1976 there were probably about 1.3 million cattle. This number rose gradually to well over 1.4 million head in 1981. The serious drought that affected the cattle-raising area in southern Mozambique from December 1981 to November 1983 was reported by the government to have resulted in the loss of some 190,000 head of cattle through starvation or slaughtering caused by a lack of forage.

Because of tsetse fly infestation, cattle raising is restricted largely to the southern third of the country, including lower Manica and Sofala provinces, a substantial part of Gaza Province, and part of Inhambane Province. The FRELIMO government has continued a colonial program of controlling the infestation, but in Gaza Province, the principal cattle area, serious damage to the main disease-control station from RNM raids had set the program back and reinfestations were reported in the early 1980s. Important assistance for the cattle industry was received in 1982 from the ADB, which provided a loan equivalent to US$4 million for a campaign against foot-and-mouth disease.

Goats, hogs, and sheep, which are not affected by the tsetse fly, are found on farms throughout the country. Goats, estimated by number about 340,000 in 1981, are raised for milk and meat—both important protein sources in the diet. Sheep, of which there were some 108,000 in 1981, are raised for meat rather than wool. The hog population was reduced in the late 1970s in the central part of the country by an outbreak of African swine fever. There were an estimated 115,000 hogs in 1979. The government made breeding stock available to private- and family-farm hog raisers during 1980 in Manica and Sofala provinces in an effort to reestablish production. This was part of a broader program to increase local output of short production-cycle meat to supply regional urban centers. During 1983 hog and poultry raisers were also organized into district-sized associations in Maputo for the same purpose.

Chickens are raised throughout the country; most farms keep small flocks for eggs and meat. Around urban centers farms also produce broilers and eggs for town markets. At Maputo a substantial part of the supply in mid-1984 appeared to be provided by a state poultry enterprise. The government had also encouraged the raising of ducks in suitable environments. Estimates of poultry in 1981 indicated about 17.5 million chickens and 570,000 ducks.

### Fisheries

The continental shelf, extending a considerable distance from shore along much of Mozambique's 2,470-kilometer coastline, constitutes a rich—but in 1984 still not fully surveyed—fishing area. Until the mid-1960s domestic fishing had been either a subsistence occupation or a small-scale commercial enterprise that supplied the local markets. In 1964 the total recorded catch was some 4,400 tons, of which about 3,500 tons were fish, 364 tons were shrimp, and about 550 tons were other marine animals. Mechanical trawling was prohibited in territorial waters, and fishing practices were relatively primitive. Fishing restrictions were eased after the mid-1960s, and the shrimp catch, for which a foreign market had developed, had risen to 850 tons in 1968. Most of the fishing off the coast beyond the then three-nautical-mile limit was carried out by foreign vessels. This activity increased in the early 1970s and included operations by ships from France, Japan, South Africa, the Soviet Union, and Spain. In August 1976 the FRELIMO government passed legislation designed to protect its inshore fishing grounds and to bring unrestricted offshore fishing under its control. The new law established a 12-nautical-mile zone along the coast that was designated as territorial waters and a second economic zone of "sovereign waters" whose normal outer limit was 200 nautical miles from shore. Fishing in these zones required a license from the government.

Private Portuguese commercial fishing operations in Mozambique had increased in the early 1970s, for both fresh fish and shrimp, the latter primarily for export. In 1974 the commercial and marketed small-scale fish catch totaled over 9,000 tons. Additionally, almost 5,900 tons of shrimp and some 600 tons of other marine animals were caught; shrimp exports in 1974 were equivalent to almost 80 percent of the catch. The FRELIMO victory in 1974 was followed by abandonment of equipment by various private operations. These companies were taken over by the government and placed under the management of so-called administrative commissions. In September 1977 control of about 10 of these companies was given to a newly established state enterprise, the Mozambican Fishing Company (Empresa Moçambicana de Pescas—EMO-PESCA), which had development of the fisheries industry as a main goal. Operations appear to have been satisfactory, and in April 1980, in conjunction with a shake-up of EMOPESCA's administration, the managed private companies were nationalized along with several private fishing operations whose activities were declared not in the best interest of the Mozambique ecomony.

Information on the fishing industry in the early 1980s was meager. In 1981 about 30,000 tons of commercial fish were reported taken. Official sources indicated that commercial operations carried out by three state enterprises and a few fishery cooperatives accounted for 13 percent of the catch, three joint government-foreign firms for another 33 percent of the catch, and artisanal producers for about 50 percent. Private companies accounted for about 5 percent. The joint enterprises had been formed by the Mozambican government in conjunction with private interests in Japan and Spain and with a Soviet government agency. The Mozambican-Japanese company was based in Quelimane. Its fleet in 1981 consisted of 12 medium-draft shrimp boats and two deep-draft craft. In mid-1982 two additional shrimp boats were obtained.

The joint Mozambican-Soviet fishing company was established in 1979 with the principal aim of providing fresh fish for the local domestic market. Shrimp were also to be caught for export. A further aim was to train Mozambican crews for the fisheries industry. Mozambique held a 51-percent share in the venture. In October 1983 the company had eight boats; four were used to catch fish and four for shrimp. An additional vessel arrived in January 1984, and two more were scheduled to be added to the fleet in 1985. Each of these latter craft will have shellfish-catching capacities of 1,500 to 2,000 tons a year; the catch will be exported. In 1980, its first year of operation, the company caught 5,772 tons of fish (against a goal of 6,000 tons). The shrimp take, however, was only some 30 tons compared with a projected catch of about 800 tons. The low catch was attributed in considerable part to the extremely late arrival of four vessels from the Soviet Union. In 1983 the fleet had caught more than 5,000 tons of fish and 200 tons of shrimp by the end of October. The shrimp tonnage was reportedly below expectation because of the effects of the severe drought on water conditions in the fishing areas.

The joint Mozambican-Spanish operation (in which Spanish participation was 49 percent) was established in late 1979 and early 1980 to catch shrimp for export to Spain. Headquartered in Beira, the company had 14 vessels operating in Mozambique's territorial waters in 1983; the number was being increased in 1984. It reportedly caught 3,280 tons of shrimp in 1981 (later figures were unavailable). Food fish caught during shrimping operations were turned over to one of the state enterprises for domestic distribution. In 1982 Mozambique had also discussed the formation of a joint company with Portuguese interests. Reports indicated, however, that agreement had been reached for Portuguese craft to fish for shrimp up to a limit of 700 tons a year in Mozambique territorial waters. In return the Portuguese government was to provide training and technicians for Mozambican government fishing operations.

In the early 1980s shrimp had become the country's second largest earner of foreign exchange (after cashews). In 1981, when 8,680 tons were caught, exports produced the equivalent of about US$55 million, some 18 to 19 percent of total merchandise export receipts, according to government figures. Roughly 15,000 tons were believed harvestable annually from Mozambique waters on a naturally sustainable basis.

### Forestry

Based on satellite data (from 1972 and 1973), aerial photographs, calculations of losses from deforestation and overexploitation, and ground observations in 1979 and 1980, FAO experts have estimated that at the beginning of 1981 nearly three-quarters of Mozambique's land area, or about 576,000 square kilometers, had some trees. Tree cover ranged from comparatively small areas of closed high forest, found at higher elevations and in gallery forests along rivers and streams, to more open forest and woodlands and low-tree savanna. The latter is characteristic of much of the country's vegetation.

About one-half of the area having trees (somewhat more than 286,000 square kilometers) was classified as forest and woodland. Over 116,000 square kilometers of this total were considered to be generally unusable for commercial timber exploitation because of unfavorable terrain features, low density of desirable

*Fishing boats at the port of Beira*
*Courtesy Mozambique Information Office, London*

tree species, or other reasons. Another 132,000 square kilometers was in forest fallow—land ordinarily used for agricultural purposes but temporarily being rested and whose tree cover was secondary growth. Exploitable productive forests comprised about 38,000 square kilometers. The remaining half of wooded land (about 290,000 square kilometers) consisted mostly of tree savanna, or parkland, having scattered low trees mainly between five and seven meters in height.

The colonial administration had sought to protect certain forest areas through the designation of reserves, but actual management of the latter appears to have been relatively negligible. Other forest areas were set aside in national parks. Afforestation projects were also undertaken, the earliest plantings occurring in about 1929 or 1930. These first plantations were designed to fix moving sand dunes at the mouth of the Limpopo River. Later, so-called industrial plantations to provide timber and wood for commercial puposes were established in Gaza, Maputo, Niassa, Manica, and Sofala provinces. Conifers (mainly pines) predominated in the more northerly plantations, whereas various hardwoods, including eucalyptus, were planted in the southern part of the country.

Before national independence about 13,000 hectares (130

square kilometers) of industrial plantations had been established. It was estimated that another 8,000 hectares, including private stands, were to have been established for general purposes, including firewood. Data available were tentative, but it has been estimated that by 1980 up to 3,000 hectares of industrial plantings and 1,500 hectares of other kinds had been established.

During the colonial period commercial exploitation of the forests was comparatively small compared with the potential. Average annual production of sawlogs and logs for veneer averaged some 400,000 cubic meters in the early to mid-1960s. In the latter half of the decade, the total declined to 360,000 cubic meters and dropped further in the early 1970s; it was 283,000 cubic meters in 1973, including 5,000 cubic meters that were exported. The Third Party Congress in early 1977 established general lines of development for the forest industry, but only limited information was available on its progress. (In a report to the Fourth Party Congress in April 1983, Party Chairman Machel stated that 30 percent of the budgetary allocations to the agricultural sector were devoted to forestry.) A further decline in the production of sawlogs and veneer logs occurred in the post-independence period. About 180,000 cubic meters were produced in 1979; exports, however, increased to 20,000 cubic meters. In 1980 aid was received from Sweden for the construction of a major forestry complex in Manica Province. Designed to use timber from government forestry plantations in the area, the complex consists of a sawmill having an annual capacity reported at 26,000 to 39,000 cubic meters and a plywood plant. Both installations were reported in operation in mid-1983.

Information on deforestation through cutting, clearing for agricultural use, and fire damage in wooded savanna areas was incomplete. But it was estimated that at the beginning of the 1980s there was a reduction of as much as 115,000 hectares of forest and woodland annually, mainly through conversion to agriculture. About two-thirds of this total consisted of unproductive forest and woodland. A near-term shortage of firewood supplies and poles for general use was not indicated except in certain larger urban areas. In 1978 the government established eucalyptus plantations around Maputo to help meet the local demand. A similar project was started in the area of Beira in 1981, and another was to be carried out at Nampula.

## Mining

The mining sector played a relatively small role in the

*Workers loading logs at the government's Penhalonga
forestry plantation in Manica Province
Courtesy AIM/Paul Fauvet*

economy in the early 1980s. Mozambique, however, possesses an
estimated 1 percent of the world's coal reserves, 2 percent of the
beryllium reserves, and 10 percent of the tantalite reserves.
Beryllium and columbo-tantalite ores were mined, but the most
significant mineral products were coal, limestone (for the cement
industry), salt (produced by solar evaporation), and quarried
sand, gravel, and stone. Other exploited minerals were asbestos,
clay (including kaolin and bentonite), copper, precious and
semiprecious stones, gold, and mica. Deposits—estimated to be
generally large—of apatite, bauxite, flourite, graphite, and
magnetite have also been reported. Natural gas has been found,
and there is a good possibility that petroleum deposits exist (see
Petroleum, this ch.). Since 1975 a number of major mineral surveys using various techniques including aeromagnetic mapping,
gamma-ray spectrometry, Landsat imagery, and surface exploration have been undertaken in a search for new deposits.
Geologists and technicians involved in these efforts have come
from Britain, Czechosovakia, France, Italy, the Soviet Union,
and Yugoslavia. Exploration for petroleum by foreign (including
American) firms was also under way in 1984.

In 1984 bituminous coal was the most valuable mineral

product. Deposits are located in Manica, Tete, Niassa, and Cabo Delgado provinces, but the most important ones occur in three coal-bearing basins over a stretch of almost 350 kilometers along the Zambezi River. In the early 1980s the estimated potential reserves in these three basins appeared to be well over 7 billion tons, according to surveys carried out since 1975 by geologists from the German Democratic Republic (East Germany), Finland, and Sweden. In early 1984 exploitable reserves in the Moatize area, east of the provincial capital of Tete, were estimated at almost 600 million tons; this was the only area of significant commercial mining at the time. A second area to the west reportedly had confirmed reserves of 450 million tons lying within 200 meters of the surface, and a total estimated potential of about 3 billion tons. The third basin in western Tete Province contained reserves estimated at over 3.5 billion tons. The size of the deposits in the other provinces had not yet been determined.

Some coal had been mined in the Moatize area as early as the mid-1800s, but the first major effort to exploit deposits there was undertaken in the mid-1920s by a multinational corporation largely financed by Belgian interests. The corporation's concession ended in 1948, and a new venture, the Mozambique Coal Company (Companhia Carbonífera de Moçambique—CARBOMOC), was established. The Mozambique government held 10 percent of the shares, private Mozambican (Portuguese) sources had 41 percent, and the South African Iron and Steel Corporation, a South African government-owned enterprise, held the remaining 49 percent. In May 1978 the FRELIMO government announced that, because of accidents at the mines—a major underground explosion in 1976 had killed some workers—and mishandling of operations, the company was being nationalized; compensation would be given under certain circumstances. A new state enterprise, the Mozambique National Coal Company (Empresa Nacional de Carvão de Moçambique, which has continued to use the CARBOMOC acronym), was established to take over operations.

Four mines, all underground, were developed at Moatize. Mining had remained on a relatively small scale until 1949, when a railroad connection to the Beira line was opened (see Railroads, this ch.). Production in the first half of the 1960s averaged about 275,000 tons a year. Output rose to about 300,000 tons at the beginning of the 1970s and increased to an average of about 400,000 tons through 1975. Since independence, efforts have been made to increase output, and almost 535,000 tons were reported mined in 1981. But production appears to have declined thereafter, reportedly in large part because of transportation problems and shortages of mining equipment. CARBOMOC has announced plans for four new mines at Moatize, and work on one was started in 1981. This mine and two others will be underground operations having a projected annual production capacity of 200,000 tons. The fourth mine is being constructed as an openpit mine. This is essentially a pilot undertaking to develop techniques and train personnel for large-scale strip mining later in the decade.

In 1984 virtually all salt produced in Mozambique was obtained by solar evaporation of seawater in salt ponds located at a number of spots along the coast. Production in the early 1970s had been reported at about 28,000 to 31,000 tons a year. In the mid-1970s some operations were abandoned by their Portuguese owners and eventually taken over by the new Mozambican government. The Third Party Congress in 1977 called for increased exploitation of salt potentials in anticipation of increased domestic consumption. A drying pan in the Pemba Bay region was reported to have been constructed in 1980 by a government salt-producing enterprise. Its ultimate annual production capacity has been rated at 5,000 tons of salt. In the late 1970s a specialist team from North Korea began construction of a large salt pan at Nova Mambone in Inhambane Province. In 1981, its first year, the pan produced over 1,000 tons of salt and by 1984 was expected to produce 7,500 tons annually. Extension of facilities was also undertaken in Maputo Province, a major producing area, by both government and private operators. A nationwide total of 75,100 tons of salt was produced in 1980 and 86,300 tons in 1981.

## Manufacturing

A limited amount of manufacturing was under way in Mozambique by the 1920s. The major effect was on processing primary products for export to Portugal, mainly sugar and sisal. By the end of the decade, however, several import-substitution industries had been set up to cater to the needs of a growing number of Portuguese settlers. Products included cement, beer, mineral water, maize flour, pasta, cigarettes, and soap. During the 1930s the production of bricks, butter, ceramics, and cordials had been added. Some expansion in production for the domestic market occurred after World War II, when maize mills were constructed, together with cotton- and jute-spinning and weaving plants. Foreign capital was largely excluded from investing in the colony, and Mozambique remained basically a captive market for Portuguese-supplied raw materials, intermediate goods, and manufacturers—a situation that was perpetuated by extensive controls and regulations established by Portugal to protect its home industries.

A revolt in colonial Angola in 1961 led to Lisbon's modification of economic policies toward the overseas territories that was designed to create a more viable economic relationship. By 1965 a number of the limitations on local industrial activities had been removed, and the long-standing restrictions on non-Portuguese investment eased. The expansion was largely along export substitution lines and was accompanied by increased imports of raw materials and parts for assembly. Large arrears and delays in payment accumulated, especially with Portugal. In 1971, as a means to correct this situation, Portugal imposed restrictions on the use of foreign exchange. One result was an important new stimulus to investment in domestic manufacturing to replace curtailed imports.

The number of industrial establishments of all sizes, which had stood at about 2,000 in 1970, almost doubled by 1973. In the latter year approximately two-thirds of total industrial production, as measured by gross value, was for the domestic market. But many of the firms producing for this market were dependent on imported raw material and parts. The colonial government in Mozambique had planned to give greater encouragement to the establishment of enterprises based on local materials, but little progress was made. There were also plans to encourage location of new plants throughout the country; almost 50 percent of existing manufacturing facilities were situated in the Maputo area, and another 16 percent were around Beira.

The manufacturing industry in the early 1980s covered a diverse range of goods. Major facilities processing agricultural products for exports included several sugar mills, cashew decortication plants, tea factories, and vegetable-oil mills. Consumer goods industries included wheat and cassava flour mills, pasta plants, and facilities for prepared seafood and dairy and meat products. According to reports, three breweries produced high-quality beer. The textile industry, centered in Manica Province, had greatly expanded after the mid-1960s, when laws protecting the Mozambican market for Portuguese textile manufacturers were altered. Among the more significant chemical manufacturers were paints, varnishes, perfumes, cosmetics, and (on a smaller scale) insecticides, fertilizers, and matches. Other industries included those that manufactured glass and wood products

*Mozambican workers at the government-owned steel
rolling mill in Maputo
Courtesy AIM/Paul Fauvet*

*Assembling railroad cars
at an industrial plant
in Maputo
Courtesy AIM, Maputo*

and simple metal items, such as aluminum-ware, nails, screws, and electric cables. There was a bicycle factory, and railroad cars were also assembled; some parts were manufactured in Mozambique. Three cement plants, a petroleum refinery, and a small iron foundry having a capacity of 80,000 tons constituted the main part of an incipient heavy industry.

The Portuguese exodus between 1974 and 1977 had a devastating effect on manufacturing, depriving it of the major part of the skilled and semiskilled technical personnel who had run the factories and mills, as well as the supporting infrastructure. There was also substantial damage and destruction of plant equipment and other facilities by departing owners and workers. As an early countermeasure to keep industries operating, the government appointed administrative commissions to manage the abandoned factories. The situation was further complicated because of the attitude of African employees, who at first frequently refused to work under the remaining whites. Others, in what has been described as a mistaken belief that independence freed them from supervision, rejected any management. Productivity dropped, and absenteeism became rampant. Between 1975 and 1977 the share of manufacturing in GDP dropped from 9.3 percent to 7.1 percent.

In 1977 the government directed the establishment of production councils in all plants, i.e., those already owned and operated by the state, those taken over by the administrative commissions, and private establishments. The production councils, consisting of workers from the plant or enterprise, were to participate actively in resolving production problems. As time passed, the councils in effect became embryonic elements of a national union organization. The latter finally emerged officially in late 1983 in the Organization of Mozambican Workers (Organização dos Trabalhadores de Moçambique—OTM). Improvement in production was reported in various factories, although the councils for a variety of reasons were not universally successful (see Mass Associations, ch. 4). The National Planning Commission, in an early 1984 report, stated that an increase in gross industrial production of 13.7 percent had been attained between 1977 and 1981 and that an important part of the gain was the result of improvement in labor discipline. The gains, however, were erratic, and some industries revealed decreases. An overall decline of 4.4 percent occurred in 1982 in gross industrial production. A major problem after 1981 was the shortage of raw materials and parts for assembly caused by the lack of foreign exchange. The commission's report noted, moreover, that machinery and equipment had not been adequately maintained after the Portuguese left and that there had been a lack of investment to replace worn out equipment.

## Energy Sources

Data available in early 1984 on the commercial production, overall supply, and consumption of energy were limited, and published figures varied, sometimes considerably. Mozambique had large domestic energy resources in its extensive forests and woodlands, comparatively vast coal deposits, and large hydroelectric potential. Natural gas deposits—one of which had been of substantial size—had been found but had not yet been exploited. The country's geology also indicated the possibility of petroleum—to the extent that several major international oil companies were actively engaged in exploration. Figures for 1980 showed the consumption of commercial energy in comparable values to have been derived roughly 20 percent from solid fuels, 55 percent from liquid fuels, and 25 percent from electricity. Liquid fuels (petroleum and petroleum products) accounted that year for more than 80 percent of gross energy imports.

### Wood and Coal

Firewood and charcoal were the principal energy sources for the rural population and also constituted major sources of energy for urban residents. Wood fuel was also of some importance to commercial operations, such as bakeries. The large sugar mill on the Búzi River in Sofala Province depended on wood fuel to fire its boilers. The FAO estimated that in 1978 total fuelwood and charcoal production amounted to 9.9 million cubic meters. By comparison, the total commercial production of sawlogs in 1979 was only about 180,000 cubic meters. Coal was used as a fuel for railroad steam locomotives, thermal power-generating stations, and various manufacturing plants, including cement and iron and steel factories, some sugar mills, and others. A considerable part of the domestic coal output was exported mainly to surrounding countries. Exports were, however, partially offset by imports from South Africa for use in southern Mozambique.

### Electric Power

The country's some 60 rivers have been estimated to have a hydroelectric potential of roughly 11,800 megawatts. A detailed inventory of these resources, funded by the Norwegian government's overseas development agency, was in progress in 1984.

The principal developed site was at Cahora Bassa, a deep gorge on the Zambezi River northwest of the town of Tete. Initial investigations of the dam site began in 1956. Envisioned in the project was the production of an enormous quantity of electricity that would permit the exploitation of mineral deposits, the development of large irrigated agricultural areas in the Tete region, and the furnishing of power to surrounding countries, primarily South Africa. Work on the dam began in 1969. Portuguese resources were inadequate to finance the undertaking, and a large part of the funding was provided by an international consortium in which South Africa played the leading part. South Africa also contracted to purchase some 1,400 megawatts of power annually at—even for that time—a very low price. The lake behind the dam, extending approximately 240 kilometers to the Zambian border and up to 30 kilometers at its widest point, began forming in December 1974. Power from the first of five planned 425-megawatt generators was produced in April 1975; the last generator was installed in 1979.

Initially, FRELIMO strongly opposed the Cahora Bassa project, and the rail line connecting the Tete area with Beira was mined and traffic disrupted frequently. During the early 1970s, however, the FRELIMO leadership appeared to have concluded that the dam and power station would be a major asset to an independent Mozambique, and from that point work to complete the project proceeded with little hindrance. After independence a new corporation, Cahora Bassa Hydroelectric (Hidroeléctrica de Cahora Bassa—HCB), was formed by Mozambique and Portugal—the latter holding about 80 percent of the stock—to operate the Cahora Bassa facility. Under the agreement a gradual transfer of shares was to occur whereby Mozambique would acquire full ownership in the year 2005.

Virtually all the power produced at the Cahora Bassa facility was sold to South Africa. Beginning in 1980, however, major interruptions in power occurred that were attributed to sabotage of the transmission line (about 1,000 kilometers in length inside Mozambique) by forces of the RNM. In April 1981 several towers were destroyed, and in mid-1981 the mutual agreement with South Africa on the required amount of electricity to be sent was suspended. No further transmission of power appears to have occurred. In early 1984, however, it was reported that South African power company officials were expecting transmission to be resumed soon. In April a tripartite agreement between Mozambique, Portugal, and South Africa provided for a maximum of 1,450 megawatts of power to be supplied to South Africa, which was to furnish from its own system up to 90 megawatts to south-

*South Africa is the major consumer for power provided by hydroelectric facilities at Mozambique's Cahora Bassa dam on the Zambezi River.*
*Courtesy AIM/Paul Fauvet*

ern Mozambique. South Africa had long been the principal source of power for that section of the country. The agreement also provided for payment by South Africa of a higher price for power, which would enable HCB to operate profitably.

The production and distribution of electricity for domestic use was comparatively limited in the preindependence period. In 1973 there were 783 power-generating facilities (many quite small units) throughout the country, having a total installed capacity of 383 megawatts. More than 80 percent of the plants were privately operated, serving small localities, manufacturing plants, and the like. The publicly owned plants, which were not interconnected, produced about 648 million killowatt-hours (some 85 percent of total kilowatt-hours generated) in 1973. The FRELIMO government has embarked on a program to expand power services with the aid of several foreign countries, including France, Italy, the Netherlands, Norway, and Sweden. By 1983 almost 1,000 kilometers of new power lines were reported to have been constructed in the central and northern parts of the country to use power from Cahora Bassa. The new power supply permitted elimination of local state-owned diesel plants. The government had also built several small power plants, including facilities at Lichinga in Niassa Province and Nacala in Nampula Province, and power lines had been extended into various rural areas. The 1984 agreement on Cahora Bassa reserved 200 megawatts of power for Mozambican domestic use. In anticipation of further general expansion of the use of power throughout Mozambique, plans were under way for construction of a second generating plant at the dam that would raise power-output capacity to an eventual 4,000 megawatts (effective capacity, 3,600 megawatts).

### Petroleum

All of the country's petroleum requirements in 1984 were satisfied by imports, which included both refined products and crude oil. The latter was processed by the refinery of the state-owned Mozambique National Petroleum Company (Empresa Nacional de Petróleos de Moçambique—PETROMOC), located in Matola, a suburb of Maputo. The refinery was constructed in the early 1960s, financed by private Portuguese interests (76 percent) and a French company. In May 1977 the enterprise was nationalized along with associated distribution facilities. (The nationalization decree mentioned compensation, but subsequent details were not available.) The refinery's initial crude oil throughput capacity was about 600,000 tons, from which distillate and residual fuel oils, gasoline, and kerosine were produced. In the mid-1960s facilities were expanded to produce liquid petroleum gas for household use and asphalt. Some of the refinery's products were in excess of domestic requirements and were exported (see Foreign Trade and Balance of Payments, this ch.).

In the preindependence period crude oil was obtained from Iraq. The latter continued to supply oil that, at least in the late 1970s, was furnished at a special price. This flow ceased after the outbreak of the Iran-Iraq war in September 1980, and Mozambique then secured oil from Saudi Arabia. In 1982 an agreement was concluded for Libya to furnish oil at a price below world market levels. Mozambique also bought certain petroleum products—diesel oil and jet fuel—that were produced in inadequate amounts by the refinery. Some were obtained on the spot market and some from the Soviet Union. In the early 1980s government sources indicated that crude—and refined-oil imports by value accounted for roughly 25 percent of all merchandise imports. Of greater significance, the cost of petroleum imports equaled some 70 percent of all merchandise export earnings. Shortages of foreign exchange had resulted on occasion in inadequate crude oil supplies for PETROMOC; the refinery had been forced to suspend operations twice during 1983. In April 1981 a ration system for liquid fuels had been established by the People's Assembly.

Sporadic onshore exploration for petroleum in Mozambique's coastal area started in the early 1900s. No significant discoveries were made until 1961, when a large natural gas field was located at Pande in Inhambane Province. Recoverable gas was estimated at 18 billion cubic meters, and an additional 60 billion cubic meters were considered potentially recoverable; exploitation had not been undertaken, however. In early 1984 Mozambique was seeking financing by foreign investors for development of the field. Further explorations located small fields at Búzi and Temane in Sofala Province; neither was of economically viable size. Offshore drilling for oil began in 1969, but only limited indications of gas were reported. Most of the oil companies had relinquished their concessions by 1972, and the last concessionaire withdrew in 1974 as the political situation in the country deteriorated.

In October 1981 the FRELIMO government, in a move to encourage renewed oil exploration in offshore waters, passed legislation containing features attractive to Western firms. The latter were to provide, at their own risk, the necessary capital for exploration and development of any discoveries, but provisions of the law permitted them to export a part of the oil found, to recover expenses, and to make a profit. A new state enterprise, the Mozambique National Hydrocarbon Company (Empresa Nacional de Hidrocarbonetos de Moçambique—ENH), was established and given control of all oil exploration and production. Interested foreign companies were required to set up subsidiary companies in Mozambique that would then enter into agreements with the ENH on the scope of their activities. The State Secretariat for Coal and Hydrocarbons, under which the ENH operated, signed agreements in 1981 with an American company and a Norwegian firm to obtain offshore seismic, magnetic, and gravity information in areas extending from the South African frontier to the Tanzanian border. Earlier, an aeromagnetic onshore survey of the Rovuma basin in northern Mozambique was carried out by a French company. These results and data from the pre-1974 period have been made available to any interested company. In 1983 subsidiaries of two American oil companies, Exxon and Shell, signed contracts covering onshore areas in the Rovuma basin. The entire offshore zone was divided into 17 blocks for leasing. By late 1983 more than 20 companies had purchased bid-submission documents for offshore leases; the closing date for the bids was March 31, 1984. Reportedly, a model contract that had been prepared by the government appeared to have been favorably received by prospective foreign investors.

# Transportation

In 1984 the transportation system was inadequate for the integrated development of the economy projected by the FRELIMO government. A substantial amount of railroad trackage existed but did not comprise a single net (see fig. 11). As a result the movement of goods between the southern, central, and northern parts of the country had to be made either by a greatly underdeveloped road system or by coastal shipping. Mozambique has undertaken, with foreign assistance, a major program of road improvement and construction to link the three regions with paved roads, but completion was not anticipated until after the mid-1980s. The secondary and feeder roads to provide access by the rural population to local and urban market centers were also inadequate, and during the rainy season existing roads-tracks were largely unusuable in many parts of the country.

The railroads and ports were of major importance to the implementation of regional plans by neighboring landlocked Black African states of the Southern African Development Coordination Conference (SADCC) to bypass the South African transportation system. Beyond this political motive, however, was the economic fact that routes through Mozambique's ports were substantially shorter.

## Railroads

In 1984 Mozambique's railroad system had a total route length of some 3,100 kilometers. Almost all track was of 1.067-meter gauge, the width common throughout southern Africa. State owned, the system was run by the Mozambique Railroad Company (Companhia Ferroviária de Moçambique—CFM), which was responsible to the National Directorate of Ports and Railroads. The national rail net was divided into four separate systems. They included CFM-South, which was based in Maputo and consisted of 1,036 kilometers; CFM-Central, totaling 950 kilometers and based in Beira; and CFM-North, having a route length of 920 kilometers and its terminus in Nacala. The fourth system, the Zambezia, consisted of a single line that ran inland from the minor port of Quelimane for a distance of 146 kilometers. There was no direct connection between any of these systems within Mozambique. This drawback was the result of the original purpose for the construction of the three major systems (not including the Zambezia Line)—the provision of outlets for goods from neighboring South Africa, Zimbabwe, and Malawi.

The southern system, based in Maputo, consisted of six main lines and three branch lines. It included the country's first rail

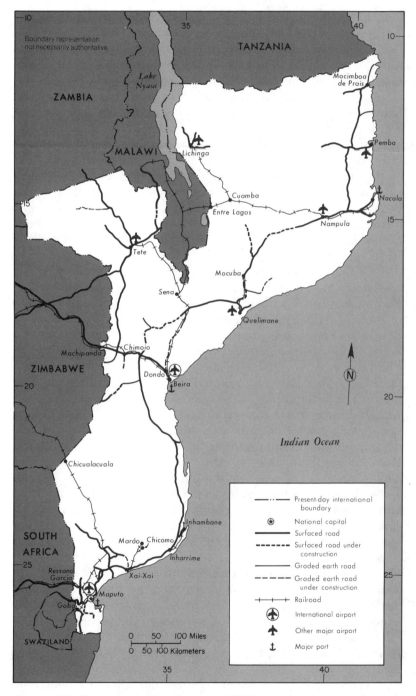

*Figure 11. Transportation System, 1984*

line, officially opened in 1890, which ran from Maputo to the South African border at Komatipoort, where it connected with a line leading to the mineral-rich and highly industrialized Witwatersrand region centered in Johannesburg. Known as the Ressano Garcia Line and 88 kilometers long, it was built as the result of an agreement with Portugal made by President Paul Kruger of present-day Transvaal Province (then officially the South African Republic) to open a route to the ocean for Witwatersrand that would be outside the control of British finanicial interests. Subsequent Portuguese agreements with a unified South Africa included a guarantee by the latter that over 40 percent of the Witwatersrand traffic would be handled by the Ressano Garcia Line. Lower freight rates than for shipment through southern South African ports were also agreed to. These provisions were reaffirmed in a new agreement with the FRELIMO government in 1979.

Of the remaining southern main lines, the most important one was from Maputo to Chicualacuala on the Zimbabwe border. Having a route length of 538 kilometers, this Limpopo Line opened for service in 1955, providing, through the then Southern Rhodesian rail system, outlets also for traffic from Zambia and Zaïre. After Mozambique closed its border with Southern Rhodesia in early 1976, the line was closed to external freight until December 1979 and completion of repairs to the connecting line in the latter country. Occasional traffic interruptions were reported through 1983 as a result of RNM actions. The line had been an important element in plans by the SADCC to reduce dependence on rail routes through South Africa (see Neighboring Black African States, ch. 4). Also important was the Goba Line, which branched off from the Ressano Garcia Line west of Maputo and ran 64 kilometers to the Swazi border. It had reached the latter area in 1912, providing access to an iron ore mining operation inside Swaziland. The connection to the main Swazi system was not made, however, until 1964. The line was not only of great importance as an economical route for Swazi foreign trade, but it also carried raw materials for a cement plant near Maputo. The southern system also included two isolated lines. One in the coastal region based in Xai-Xai carried agricultural products for export—this line was of 0.75-meter gauge; the second was a 92-kilometer railroad from Inharrime to the minor port of Inhambane. Port facilities at the latter were reportedly in deteriorated condition in 1984.

The central system included three main lines for which the port of Beira was the outlet. One ran from Beira to Machipanda on the Zimbabwe border; one ran from Sena, branching from the Beira line at Dondo northwest of the port and proceeding to the Malawi frontier; and the other (the Tete Line) that extended from the Sena Line to Moatize, center of the coal mining industry in Tete Province. The Beira Line was built in the 1890s to provide a reliable means of transport for goods and supplies to settlers in territory in Southern Rhodesia belonging to the British South Africa Company. It reached Umtali (present-day Mutare) on the border in 1898. The railroad attained increasing importance as the rail system developed in central Africa for exports of tobacco, maize, and copper. Use of the line was curtailed after imposition of UN sanctions against Southern Rhodesia in 1965 and the subsequent blocking of Beira by the British to prevent shipments of commodities and oil to Southern Rhodesia. Traffic came to a halt in 1976, when Mozambique began enforcing the sanctions. Freight movement was renewed in late 1981 after repairs to the line, but traffic appears to have continued in the early 1980s at a low level relative to capacity because of unsuitable port conditions at Beira.

The Sena Line, 335 kilometers long, was Malawi's only rail route to the Indian Ocean until 1970, when a new Mozambican railroad opened the northern port of Nacala to Malawian traffic. The Sena Line reached a point on the southern bank of the Zambezi River south of Malawi in 1922. Until 1935, when a bridge connected the two, freight from the latter was ferried across the river from a rail line extended earlier to the northern bank by Malawi. The Tete Line (254 kilometers long) ran northwest from that point to Moatize. It was opened in 1949 and permitted expansion of coal production in the Tete area for export. The line proved of great value in transporting supplies and equipment for the construction of the Cahora Bassa dam and power station over the 10-year period from 1969 to 1979.

The northern system, based in the port of Nacala, consisted of two main lines and one short spur. The Mozambique Line ran from Nacala to Lichinga, capital of Niassa Province, some 800 kilometers from the port. This line, opened in December 1969, handled agricultural products, supplies, and the like. The Cuamba Line (78 kilometers), opened in mid-1970, branched from the Mozambique line in western Niassa Province and proceeded to the Malawian border at Entre Lagos, where it connected with the Malawian system. Much of Malawi's freight, as well as some from Zambia, was expected to be handled through Nacala; but substantial deterioration of the rail line occurred during the 1970s, and it operated under great handicaps in the early

1980s. A plan for complete renovation has been developed and will be financed largely with aid from Canada, France, and Portugal. The initial work was expected to get under way in 1984.

### Roads

According to government figures, the road system of national and regional roads totaled about 26,460 kilometers at the beginning of 1975; an additional 2,775 kilometers were under construction. At that time some 3,900 kilometers were asphalted, and 22,560 kilometers consisted of graded earth. There were also an estimated 12,500 kilometers of unimproved dirt roads. By 1982 the primary system of roads had grown at about 27,200 kilometers. The total of surfaced roads had risen to almost 4,600 kilometers; a considerable part of the increase was attributable to new construction.

A paved road ran from Maputo to the South African border and another from Beira to Machipanda on the Zimbabwean frontier. In 1984 it was possible to travel from Maputo to Tete by asphalted roads, but in 1984 there still was no direct paved connection between the southern part of the country and the northeast. In 1972 the colonial government had begun work on the Central-Northeast Highway to link the two areas, but work was abandoned by the contractor after Mozambique's independence. The project was continued by the FRELIMO government. By late 1983 workers had completed a substantial part of the section north of the Zambezi River to an already existing paved road in upper Cabo Delgado Province. The remaining part was expected to be finished during 1985. No schedule for completion of the highway below the Zambezi River, which will connect with a paved road to Maputo, had been announced as of late 1983.

### Ports

There were three major ports serving oceangoing traffic, located roughly equidistant along the coast at Maputo in the south, Beira in the center, and Nacala in the north. In addition there were a dozen small ports that handled mostly coastal shipping; only about one-half of them were in working condition in 1984. Maputo and Beira were developed in the late 1800s as adjuncts to the railroads running inland to South Africa and present-day Zimbabwe. In 1984 they continued to be main foreign trade handlers for those countries and for Malawi, Zambia, and Swaziland. Nacala, originally a minor coastal port, was developed in the late 1960s as the terminus for the railroad built to provide a route for outward movement of agricultural products from northern Mozambique and to profit from transit

*Quayside in the harbor at Beira*
*Courtesy Mozambique Information Office, London*

traffic with Malawi.

In 1984 Maputo had modern cargo handling facilities. A deep-water port, its alongside berthing locations could accommodate 17 vessels at one time. Rail lines on the main wharf allowed direct loading and unloading of cargo into and from ships. It also had a large amount of covered storage space. A large cold storage plant for fruit was positioned to permit direct loading. In addition, the port had a plant for freezing fish. Special facilities included mechanical coal-handling equipment, a complex for bulk sugar, and facilities for bulk grains. A container wharf, in operation since mid-1971, was being newly equipped with cranes capable of handling containers of up to 40 tons. In late 1980 Mozambique contracted with the Soviet Union for a floating dry dock for the port, allowing it to take vessels up to 4,500 tons. The dry dock arrived in late 1981. Payment was to be in the form of repairs to Soviet ships. In addition to Maputo's facilities, nearby Matola possessed a wharf for unloading bulk petroleum and other liquid fuels. A second wharf handled bulk ores.

Natural conditions at Beira were less satisfactory than at Maputo. Among the port's problems were the shallow coastal and harbor waters that made it necessary for ships to approach the port through a channel some 20 kilometers long. The depth of the channel placed a limit of about 25,000 deadweight tons on ships using it. There was also a steady problem with silting, and dredging was required regularly to allow vessels to tie up at wharves at low tide. The port, a main outlet for exports from Zimbabwe, Malawi, and Zambia, was a key element in the SADCC program for the region. In mid-1982 the Netherlands government agreed to a long-term, low-interest loan for rehabilitation of the port under the SADCC plan. The initial undertaking included dredging the docking area; a dredge acquired from the Netherlands for this purpose arrived at Beira in June 1983. The main facilities at Beira included 10 wharf berths for general cargo and containers, one for fishing craft, facilities for bulk coal, and bulk-oil facilities that serviced the pipeline to Zimbabwe (see Pipelines, this ch.).

Nacala is a natural deep-water port. In 1984 it had two wharves that included four general cargo berths. Substantial container traffic reportedly went through the port from Malawi, and a new crane to facilitate container handling was installed in 1982. Use of the port has been affected by the poor condition of the railroad to the hinterland and Malawi.

### Civil Aviation

In 1984 domestic services were furnished by two state-owned airlines, Mozambique Air Lines (Linhas Aéreas de Moçambique—LAM) and the National Air Transport and Services Company (Empresa Nacional de Transporte e Trabalho Aéreo—TTA). Air service was first introduced in Mozambique in 1936. At national independence regular domestic and international flights were provided by the government-owned Directorate of Air Transport Exploitation (Direcçao de Exploração dos Transportes Aéreos—DETA). DETA's domestic flights were supplemented by feeder services operated by private air-transportation companies, which furnished air-taxi connections between secondary towns. Helicopter services by a private company had started in 1966. After independence DETA's operations deteriorated, and in May 1980 the company was replaced by LAM. In 1983 LAM had regular domestic flights between Maputo, Beira, Quelimane, Tete, Lichinga, Nampula, and Pemba. Maputo and Beira had international airports. The provincial capitals and about 20 other towns had airfields with paved runways. A large number of small airstrips were scattered throughout the country. LAM also offered regional and international flights; the latter included service to East Berlin, Lisbon, Paris, and Sofia. Among foreign carriers serving Maputo were Brazil's Varig, East Germany's Interflug, and the Soviet Union's Aeroflot; a flight connection also existed with Cuba. In 1982 LAM reportedly was operating five aircraft (Boeing 737s and Fokker F27s); a new Douglas DC-10 was added in 1983.

TTA was established in 1980 to restore domestic service that used light airplanes and helicopters. This service had collapsed after independence, creating serious communications problems; at the time of the TTA takeover, only eight airplanes and three helicopters owned by existing companies were operational. In 1981 TTA rehabilitated 37 additional airplanes and in November began scheduled flights between provincial and district capitals. The service was of special importance in the central and northern parts of the country because of the dearth of communications, which worsened during the rainy seasson when roads became practically impassable. TTA also assumed the crop-dusting and agricultural-spraying activities of the companies. In 1982–83 new airplanes for passenger and freight traffic and for agricultural service were added to the fleet. In 1981 TTA carried about 30,000 passengers, and the number increased to 47,000 in 1982, when regular flights were made to some 30 cities and towns throughout the country.

### Pipelines

In 1984 a pipeline carrying mainly gasoline and diesel fuel connected the port of Beira to the Zimbabwean town of Mutare 288 kilometers inland. Constructed by the Britain-based multinational conglomerate, Lonhro, the line originally began operations in 1964, providing petroleum to a refinery near Mutare that shut down in 1966, when UN sanctions cut off supplies. After Zimbabwean independence in 1980, the line was rehabilitated, including the main pumping stations. It was ready to move petroleum products commercially by the end of 1981, but the first shipments were not made until July 1982. The delay occurred until agreement on royalties on products was reached between Mozambique and Zimbabwe and with Lonhro's Mozambican subsidiary on charges for use of the line. Subsequently, minor damage to the line was inflicted on various occasions by RNM insurgents, but this was quickly repaired. A major halting of the flow occurred in December 1982, however, when fuel storage tanks in Beira were set afire; a spokesman for the RNM claimed responsibility for the act. In mid-January 1983 the flow was resumed when petroleum products were fed directly into the line from tankers offshore. The line normally supplied about three-quarters of Zimbabwe's requirements.

## Foreign Trade and Balance of Payments

A few agricultural commodities (mainly cashews, cotton, sugar, and tea, along with timber and—from the late 1970s—shrimp) have accounted for an average of about 60 percent of the foreign exchange earned annually through trade. In the late 1970s, as the result of increased world prices and greater production by the PETROMOC refinery, certain petroleum products, largely in excess of domestic requirements, also became major foreign exchange earners (see table 4, Appendix). The government has attempted to diversify exports, with an emphasis on increasing the export of manufactured goods. In the latter case, a major success resulted from the construction of a new tire and tube factory whose tire exports became a significant source of exchange in 1982.

Some change in the composition of imports has occurred since national independence. In 1975 imports in the category of consumer goods, food, and other commodities constituted (by value) about 29 percent of total imports. Equipment and spare parts formed another 29 percent. All other imports, grouped as raw (including semiprocessed) materials, made up the remaining 42 percent. In 1975 crude petroleum and petroleum products accounted for about one-third of the raw materials total (see table 5, Appendix). By 1979 this proportion had grown markedly to almost 56 percent, reflecting increases in world oil prices and, to some extent, growing demand. Equipment and spare parts imports had also grown (to about 35 percent in 1982) as industrial plants and other operations were rehabilitated and new projects were started. Faced by a shortage of foreign exchange, however, the government had cut back in the late 1970s on the amount of nonpetroleum raw-material imports. The consequence was a reduction in the production of goods for both the domestic and the export markets by the largely import-substitution industrial sector. The cut also adversely affected the quantity of certain items needed in agriculture.

In the final year before independence, Portugal had been the principal destination for exports, taking 33 percent of the total (see table 6, Appendix). The United States was second with 10.5 percent and South Africa third with 9.3 percent. The combined purchases of the European Economic Community (EEC) accounted for 15.6 percent, and exports to countries in Black Africa totaled another 9.5 percent. Export destination statistics for the period since independence were available primarily from Mozambique's trade partners. According to these, the United

*Oil tanker pumping diesel fuel into the pipeline that runs
from Beira in Mozambique to Mutare in Zimbabwe
Courtesy AIM/Carlkos Cardoso*

States (with 16.9 percent) was the largest purchaser of Mozambican goods in 1982; the main commodity was cashew nuts. Portugal bought only 4.1 percent of the total, and the EEC share was 19.9 percent. The government has sought to diversify trade sources, and among other significant importers in 1982 were Japan, Singapore, and the oil-exporting countries. Figures for South Africa were unavailable, but trade with that southern neighbor remained important to the Mozambican economy.

The EEC had supplied over 33 percent of Mozambique's imports in 1974, of which well over one-half came from the Federal Republic of Germany (West Germany) and Britain, but South Africa (with 19.6 percent) was the largest single source (see table 7, Appendix). Portugal provided 16.6 percent, and the United States supplied 4.8 percent. Petroleum from the oil-exporting countries accounted for 7.8 percent of Mozambique's import costs in 1974, but by 1982 rising oil prices had increased the proportion to 13.9 percent of the total. Petroleum came largely from the United Arab Emirates. Portugal's share in exports to Mozambique in 1982 were only half of the 1974 total. An increase in imports from African countries had occurred; Kenya and Zimbabwe were the largest suppliers by value. The EEC provided

24.7 percent of total imports, and France was the largest supplier.

Trade with communist countries increased markedly in the late 1970s after the conclusion of agreements on cooperation with the Soviet Union and several other states that had centrally planned economies (see Communist Countries, ch. 4). As of 1978 such trade had been comparatively slight, but a sharp rise occurred in 1979, when communist countries accounted for 15 percent of Mozambique's foreign trade. This trade continued to increase thereafter, and in 1982 more than 31 percent of all imports originated in the communist states. The value of Mozambican exports to those countries, however, was only about one-sixth of that for imports, and the trade deficit constituted over 27 percent of the country's overall trade deficit. Official Mozambican sources have stated that there were certain advantages in dealing with the communist countries, particularly with respect to credit arrangements. The latter have permitted Mozambique to purchase a variety of foreign goods needed for its economy on the basis of future deliveries of commodities and services. The arrangement constituted, in effect, a one-way barter system.

Mozambique's trade during the colonial period customarily showed a deficit. This deficit increased in the final years of Portuguese rule, and in 1973 the colony's earnings from exports covered only about one-half of the cost of its imports. The deficit was directly related to the markedly skewed trade with Portugal. Mozambican trade with other countries was also perennially in deficit, but receipts from services and other invisibles (primarily rail and harbor services furnished to South Africa and Southern Rhodesia and income from Mozambican migrant labor in those countries) more than offset the negative visible trade balance. The surplus was applied to the overall trade deficit but, on the average, covered only about three-fourths of the latter from the late 1960s to 1974. During that period net capital transactions were usually negative, and the overall balance of payments (the summary in money terms of transactions with the rest of the world) was in deficit, except in 1972.

After 1976 the balance of payments deteriorated sharply, in considerable part because of greatly reduced earnings from services that resulted from enforcement of UN sanctions against Southern Rhodesia and the cutback by South Africa in the number of Mozambican migrant workers. A drastic drop in the world price for sugar that lasted from late 1976 to late 1979 also played a part, as did rising import costs affected by world inflationary trends. Some relief from the rising cost of petroleum imports was provided for a time by several oil-producing states that furnished their products at subsidized rates. Comprehensive data on Mozambique's balance of payments position have not been published by the government, and the situation could not be assessed accurately in early 1984. But a limited amount of summary material was available, and an economic report by the National Planning Commission provided summary figures for the 1980-83 period (see table 8, Appendix).

To meet foreign exchange requirements the government has been forced to use its reserves, which were reported at a high of about US$250 million in 1977. But these have been inadequate, and shortages have been covered in part through foreign-aid grants and loans and in part through foreign borrowing. Foreign sources estimated that the external public debt in 1980 was about US$523 million, not including debts of the state enterprises. According to the National Planning Commission's 1984 report, the debt in mid-April 1983 was the equivalent of roughly US $1.8 billion. The total included the debt to international organizations, other governments, and banks; it did not include the debt to communist countries. In 1983 the government expressed its interest in joining the International Monetary Fund (IMF), whose various credit facilities could provide some relief to the critical debt situation. As of early 1984, however, Mozambique had not yet become a member. In February it had been reported as seeking a rescheduling of the external debt.

\* \* \*

In early 1984 the broadest source of information on the economy was *Mozambique: From Colonialism to Revolution, 1900–1982*, by Allen and Barbara Isaacman. The authors have field experience in Mozambique, but in dealing with various aspects of the economy they have been limited by data available. Of substantial value is the *Economic Report*, published by Mozambique's National Planning Commission in January 1984.

Other works that provide useful data are Jens Erik Torp's *Industrial Planning and Development in Mozambique;* "The Mechanization of Present-Day Mozambican Agriculture," by Marc Wuyts; *Mozambique Land Law*, published by Harvard University; and Keith Middlemas' *Cabora Bassa*, a historical description of the giant Cahora Bassa power project from planning stage through the start-up of production. A worthwhile view of Mozambique's economic needs is contained in the United Nations Security Council's series of annual reports on special economic and disaster relief assistance. A wide range of miscellaneous current economic detail and occasional analyses are contained in the economic series of the *Africa Research Bulletin* and in the *Sub-Saharan Africa Report* of the Joint Publications Service. The latter carries translations from Mozambican sources. (For further information and complete citations, see Bibliography.)

*Table C.   Land Use, 1973*

| Land Use | Area | Percentage |
|---|---|---|
| Cultivated ......................... | 2,509 | 3.2 |
| Land under permanent crops ............. | 953 | 1.2 |
| Land in tree fallow .................... | 4,239 | 5.4 |
| Pasture ........................... | 6,299 | 8.0 |
| Wild Forest ....................... | 25 | --- |
| Forest concessions ................... | 870 | 1.1 |
| Nature reserves .................... | 2,780 | 3.6 |
| Game parks ....................... | 7,270 | 9.3 |
| Communication routes, urban areas, and other | | |
| man-made features ................. | 2,000 | 2.5 |
| Uncultivable ........................ | 10,000 | 12.7 |
| Cultivable[1] ........................ | 41,551 | 52.9 |
| TOTAL ........................... | 78,496 | 100.0[2] |

---means negligible.
[1] Covered mainly by forest and woodland.
[2] Total as published.

Source:  Based on information from Mozambique, Secretaria Provincial de Economia, *A Economia de Moçambique em números*, Lourenço Marques, 1973, 22.

# Chapter 4.   Government and Politics

*Official symbol of FRELIMO, Mozambique's sole political party.
The hammer and hoe symbolize the worker-peasant alliance
under the star of internationalism.*

UPON COMING TO POWER in 1975, Mozambique's independent government assumed authority over a nation that had a modern veneer but that in reality was among the poorest and least developed in Africa. The mass of its people were illiterate, lacking modern skills and a sense of national unity. Its new leaders, most of whom had spent the previous decade in armed struggle against Portuguese colonial forces, committed themselves to forging a new society free of ethnic and racial discord. They expected to form the vanguard of a movement that would mobilize all of its citizens in pursuit of ambitious political and economic goals. Their chosen ideology, an orthodox form of Marxism-Leninism, seemed, however, singularly inappropriate to an agricultural population for which the concepts of class struggle, dictatorship of the proletariat, and leadership by the industrial workers had little meaning.

In spite of its poverty and backwardness, Mozambique embarked on its independence with certain advantages. It contained a limited number of trained cadres and administrators and a small entrepreneurial class, although most were Portuguese expatriates and Asians. It derived revenues from its considerable transit trade and was the recipient of offers of help from countries of both the West and the East. However, the turbulence of the transitional period and the application of the new government's Marxist policies brought about an exodus of most of the skilled personnel and businessmen, gravely impairing the modern economic sector. Conflicts with its relatively powerful neighbors, the white regimes of South Africa and Southern Rhodesia (later Zimbabwe), and a series of natural disasters compounded the disarray.

By the early 1980s President Samora Moises Machel was obliged to admit that the country's difficulties had reached a critical stage. The food supply had broken down in some areas, production continued to decline, and local administrative bodies coped ineffectually with their responsibilities. Nevertheless, the monopoly of power by the single party, the Front for the Liberation of Mozambique, still seemed secure. The governing clique remained the same guerrilla fighters and revolutionaries who had thrown off Portuguese rule a decade earlier. The two political milestones of this period were the party congresses of 1977 and 1983. The first had marked the transformation of the national liberation movement into a vanguard communist party on the Soviet model. It had also brought about a semblance of representative institutions of government, including people's assemblies at district, provincial, and national levels, their members chosen by a system of direct and indirect election of candidates having the endorsement of the ruling party.

The 1983 party congress came at a time when the authorities were having to contend with further economic reverses, the demoralizing effects of sabotage and terrorism by antigovernment insurgents in the countryside, and institutional and human failures of the Marxist system. The congress ordained the reform of agricultural policies to reduce the emphasis on state farming and the cooperative sector in favor of individual family farms. Scope for private entrepreneurship in retail trade and small industry was promised, and foreign investment was to be encouraged. Leading officials of the party were detached to the provinces to stem administrative confusion and inertia.

The newly adopted pragmatism in domestic policies corresponded to increasing flexibility in foreign relations. Without renouncing its alignments with the Soviet Union and other communist countries, Mozambique sought a more balanced orientation. Contacts with Western Europe were intensified in 1982–84 in the search for aid. In addition to welcoming a flow of skilled technicians from the former colonial power, Mozambique appealed to Portugal for military training and equipment, for which it had previously relied entirely on the communist countries. Political doubts over formal association with the European Economic Community were overcome. A more positive attitude was adopted toward the United States. An event of vital importance to Mozambique's security was the negotiation of an agreement with South Africa in early 1984—The Nkomati accord—pledging both sides to prevent their territories from becoming a base for subversion or aggression against the other.

Even if security could be restored in rural areas, critical problems of economic viability and development remained. Existing institutions of government were fragile, and the country's revolutionary philosophy had not shown that it was capable of producing solutions. It was too soon to conclude that Machel's growing flexibility in both domestic and foreign affairs was not simply tactical but represented a retreat from its commitment to Marxism-Leninism. Nonetheless, the greater realism of his policies seemed to offer fresh promise for a turn in Mozambique's fortunes.

## Government Institutions and the Party

The government system of Mozambique can be visualized as

two parallel structures extending from the national level down through the regional and local bodies. The first consists of the party organization, the Front for the Liberation of Mozambique (Frente de Libertação de Moçambique—FRELIMO), and the second is composed of the traditional organs of government for the exercise of executive and legislative functions. At the apex of the party is its president, Machel, who presides over a small committee of ranking political figures, the Political Bureau, to chart the overall policies of the country. The day-to-day affairs of the party are supervised by the Secretariat of the Central Committee headed by key members of the Political Bureau and a permanent staff organized into departments. In theory, a party congress brings togther FRELIMO adherents from all parts of the country every four years to discharge supreme party authority. It elects the Central Committee of 130 members to represent it during the intervening period. The corresponding government bodies are the national People's Assembly, whose 226 members meet semi-annually to give perfunctory approval to legislative acts by its own Permanent Commission of 14 members, and the Council of Ministers, which oversees the administration of the state, its instructions being conveyed through the ministries and other government agencies (see fig. 12).

Involvement in party affairs is available only to the carefully screened adherents of FRELIMO who have shown their unquestioning allegiance to its Marxist-Leninist doctrines. The party's purpose is to establish the broad lines of national development, to give overall direction to society, and to identify major tasks and priorities. In principle, free discussion of alternatives takes place within the hierarchies of the party starting at its provincial and district committees; once policies and courses of action are agreed on, however, all members must unite behind them and work loyally for their fulfillment.

The state instrumentalities have the role of exercising political and administrative authority, subject to the guidance and supervision flowing from party bodies at appropriate levels. The boundary between state and party structures is often of little more than formal significance. Machel is president of both, and members of the Political Bureau generally hold senior government posts. Conversely, not all members of the Council of Ministers are high party functionaries; some hold office because of special professional qualifications and competence. The distinction between the legislative and executive branches of government is also of limited consequence. Ministers are ex officio members of the national People's Assembly. The assembly's Permanent Com-

185

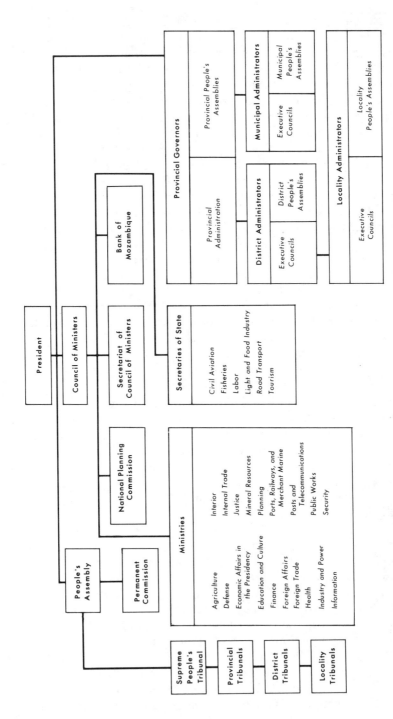

*Figure 12. The Mozambique Government, 1984*

mission is controlled by leading officials of the party and the executive branch.

The interlocking nature of party and government operations is an integral feature of political life. Combined sessions of the Central Committee and the Permanent Commission are not unusual. At provincial and district levels little effort is made to maintain hard and fast separation between administrative and party units. Governors of provinces are also provincial party heads, following the pattern at the national level.

In contrast to the party organization, which is controlled and staffed by a limited number of FRELIMO party elites, the state structure ostensibly provides an opportunity for all citizens to exercise a role in government. In practice, the participation permitted for nonparty members is strictly circumscribed. Although not all deputies of the national People's Assembly are in the party, their nomination by FRELIMO is tantamount to election. Associations open to women, youth, labor, and other groups among the general public are intended to act as channels for dissemination of party policies and for imposing party control over society rather than as a means for ordinary citizens to voice their interests.

### The Constitution

The Constitution of the People's Republic of Mozambique was written and approved by the Central Committee of FRELIMO to take effect at national independence on June 25, 1975. The Constitution was revised and expanded in 1978, its most significant changes being found in the sections dealing with the operations of the state organs—the People's Assembly, the presidency, the Council of Ministers, provincial and local governments, and the judicial system. The enlarged text was given pro forma approval by the People's Assembly on August 14, 1978.

The blurring of the distinction between the party and the state is fully demonstrated by the language of the Constitution, which declares that the people's republic is guided by the political line of FRELIMO as the leading force of the state and society. FRELIMO is further enjoined to direct and supervise the work of state organs to ensure that state policy is in conformity with the people's interests.

Among the fundamental national objectives set forth in the Constitution are the building of people's democracy and the construction of the material and ideological foundations of a socialist society. The state sector is defined as the leading and driving factor in the national economy. Encouragement is given to peasants and workers to organize themselves in collective forms of production. Although personal property is recognized and guaranteed, it is not to be used to the detriment of the national interest. Foreign capital is explicitly authorized to operate—but within the framework of state economic policy.

The Constitution entitles all citizens over 18 years of age to vote and to be elected to office, except for those legally deprived of this right. Women and men enjoy the same rights and duties; this principal is to be followed in all legislation and administrative matters of the state. Guarantees of freedom of opinion, assembly, and association are extended to all citizens with the qualification that they are to be exercised in fulfilling the objectives of the Constitution. The inviolability of the home is protected, as is the secrecy of correspondence, although limits may be imposed on these rights in circumstances especially provided for by law. Active participation in defense of the country and the revolution is declared to be the right and highest duty of all citizens, both men and women. The freedom to practice or not to practice religion is guaranteed.

The rights of every citizen to work and to be educated are prescribed by the Constitution, as is the right of disabled and elderly persons to assistance. No one can be arrested or tried without legal justification, and the right of a legal defense for accused persons is guaranteed. In practice, however, defendants may be denied counsel when the court rules a case to be of insufficient significance. Freedom of movement is not guaranteed by the Constitution. In 1984 a travel pass was required for travel outside one's administrative area.

Although the fundamental freedoms elaborated in the Constitution are broad in scope, in reality little respect is shown for personal rights under Mozambique's authoritarian system. The Constitution specifically forbids acts construed as jeopardizing social harmony or contrary to FRELIMO's objectives and civil order. The "misuse" of rights and freedoms in a manner judged to be prejudicial to the people's interest is also punishable. The effect of these qualifying conditions can be interpreted to proscribe all forms of behavior not deemed to be supportive of the existing regime and under control of the FRELIMO party.

A nationality law that went into effect at the same time as the Constitution extended citizenship to all Portuguese—regardless of past attitudes or actions—born in Mozambique or whose parents were born there. Those wishing to renounce Mozambican nationality were given 90 days after independence to do so. Dual nationality was not recognized. Renunciation of Mozambican citizenship was widespread, in part because persons opting to retain their status as Portuguese were permitted to transfer a portion of their salaries to bank accounts abroad. In 1977, however, expulsion was ordered for all such individuals. In 1982 the nationality law was amended to pardon those who had "committed the serious error" of renouncing their nationality and allowing them to return and become Mozambican citizens once they had offered political and moral guarantees of their reintegration into Mozambican society.

### The President and the Council of Ministers

According to the Constitution, the president of Mozambique is also the president of the FRELIMO party. No provision is made for the periodic election of the president. In the event of the incumbent's death, resignation, or permanent incapacity, the functions of the office are assumed by the FRELIMO Central Committee, which must name a new president in the shortest possible time.

As the head of state the president is invested with broad governmental authority and appointive powers to create ministries and commissions; direct the activities of the Council of Ministers; promulgate laws, decrees, and resolutions; conclude treaties; and proclaim a state of mobilization. The president's power to declare a war or conclude a peace is based on prior approval by the Central Committee of FRELIMO. The president appoints and dismisses ministers and vice ministers, provincial governors, the governor and vice governor of the central bank (Bank of Mozambique), the president and vice president of the Supreme People's Tribunal, the procurator (prosecutor) of the republic, and the secretaries of state. The head of state presides over the Council of Ministers, the People's Assembly, and the Permanent Commission of the People's Assembly when the legislature is not in session.

The Council of Ministers, in effect, is the accredited governing body of Mozambique, exercising authority and control over the domestic and external affairs of the country. Under the Constitution it is accountable to the People's Assembly for its actions. In 1984 its membership of 22 individuals included, in addition to Machel, the heads of the 19 ministries, the governor of the central bank, and the vice minister of defense, who is also chief of the general staff of the army (see table 9, Appendix). Its formal composition may not be strictly adhered to when the most important matters are addressed. The security talks with South Africa were reviewed by an enlarged meeting of the Council of Ministers consisting of the regular council members joined by the Political Bureau of FRELIMO, the Secretariat of the Central Committee, the Permanent Commission of the People's Assembly, secretaries of state, and senior cadres of the armed forces.

The functions of the Council of Ministers include submitting legislation and decrees for approval by the People's Assembly, drawing up the state plan and budget, and implementing them after they have been approved by the assembly. The council also directs and coordinates the functioning of the ministries and other subordinate organs of the national government. It established the structure and operating rules of local government bodies. The council is responsible for public order and social discipline and for guaranteeing civil rights.

The Secretariat of the Council of Ministers was created in 1981 as an organ of support for the president and the council in executing their functions. The secretariat was divided into departments concerned with economic and social affairs, governmental organization, local government bodies, the justice system, personnel and training, and government investigations.

Seven of the individual ministers were assisted by vice ministers; in some instances their duties were formally specified, such as the vice minister for agriculture, who was responsible for the cooperative and family sector. The secretaries of state (17 as of 1983) had responsibilities corresponding to those of the vice ministers, often for priority sectors of the economy, such as fisheries, cashew nuts, and irrigation. As part of a major reorganization in 1983, Machel announced that certain key sectors were to be separated from ministries and made directly responsible to the Council of Ministers. Headed by secretaries of state, these sectors included road transport, civil aviation, light industry and food processing, labor, and tourism.

The individual ministries are not intended to have policy-making functions, being regarded as administrative bodies acting in response to the national plan and budget adopted by the Council of Ministers and to the policy line of FRELIMO. Several of the economic ministries are, however, responsible for various industrial sectors and large state production units. As a consequence, they are directly involved with industrial and agricultural output and growth. Thus, a number of agricultural complexes are directly subordinate to the Ministry of Agriculture, including the Maputo and Manica citrus plantations, the Lioma and Angonia agricultural and cattle-raising complexes, and the sugar mills of Luabo and Mafambisse. The secretary of state for light industry and food processing has under his direction several textile and food enterprises and a blanket factory.

A pronounced linkage could be found between FRELIMO

*President Samora Moises Machel (center) and members of the
Permanent Commission of the People's Assembly, 1977
Courtesy AIM, Maputo*

leadership and the senior cabinet posts on the Council of Ministers. Nine of the 11 members of the FRELIMO Political Bureau
were simultaneously members of the Council of Ministers in
1984. Nevertheless, the fact that eight of the 22 members of the
council were not on the 130-member Central Committee of the
party could denote a trend toward separation of party and state
functions. Relatively fewer of the vice ministers and secretaries of
state were members of the Central Committee.

Ten of the members of the Council of Ministers were black,
seven were white, and the remaining five were Asians, Goans, or
*mestiços* (see Glossary). The higher reaches of the civil service,
which have suffered a chronic shortage of skilled and experienced
officials, were described as still dominated by nonblacks,
although confirmatory data were unavailable. The conspicuous
number of nonblacks in some of the highest government and
party posts has never been fully accepted by the general public. It
would not, however, be regarded as realistic for anyone other
than a black to aspire to the presidency of the state and party.

A majority among the senior leadership were believed to be

willing to accept a reasonable degree of ideologic flexibility. A smaller but still influential contingent was identified with a firmer commitment to orthodox Marxism. Among those in the second group were Marcelino dos Santos, second in the party hierarchy and resident minister to Sofala Province; Jorge Rebelo, ranked sixth on the Political Bureau list, who had been detached from the government to concentrate on party organization; Minister of Justice José Oscar Monteiro; and Sergio Vieira, a former head of the central bank who had also been detailed to supervise a province. The frequent shifts of government office among the top FRELIMO figures could not be easily explained in terms of contending power blocs or ideological divisions. Outwardly at least, Machel had succeeded in reconciling the views of senior party elements on major issues. Some transfers of personnel could be interpreted as allocating to those of proven capability the country's most taxing economic and security problems. Other appointees, like Monteiro, Vieira, and Jacinto Veloso (who was entrusted with negotiations with South Africa), appeared to be among those enjoying Machel's personal confidence.

Several cabinet members, most of them white or *mestiço*, were regarded as having earned high government posts chiefly for their professional experience and managerial qualities. They included Minister of Foreign Trade Joaquim Ribiero de Carvalho, Minister of Public Works Júlio Zamith Carrilho, and Minister of Finance Rui Baltazar dos Santos Alves. Although they did not figure among the ranking party personalities, some were members of the Central Committee.

### The People's Assembly

The independence Constitution provided for a national legislative body, the People's Assembly, which it defined as the supreme organ of state power. Until elections could be held, the assembly was to be an appointive body, embracing senior FRELIMO officials, representatives of the armed forces, party cadres, and mass organizations chosen by the Central Committee from each province. This appointive assembly was convened on September 1, 1977, to ratify an election law proposed by the Central Committee, setting the stage for local and national elections during the fall of that year. On conclusion of these elections, the national People's Assembly met for the first time on December 23, 1977.

Under the Constitution as revised in 1978, the People's Assembly is convened and presided over by the head of state. Its sessions, usually lasting for two days, are held twice a year, although this rule has been disregarded at times. In periods between sessions the Permanent Commission carries on the functions of the assembly.

The duties of the People's Assembly are to pass legislation; to approve the state plan and budget; to ratify acts of the Permanent Commission; to alter provincial, district, or municipal organizational structures; and to annul decisions of lower people's assemblies found to be contrary to the Constitution or legal rulings. The assembly must sanction the suspension of constitutional guarantees when a state of siege or emergency is declared by the president. It has authority to grant pardons and amnesties and to ratify treaties.

Decisions of the People's Assembly are taken by majority vote of the members present except for constitutional amendments, which must be approved by two-thirds of the full membership. Proposed legislation may be initiated by the Central Committee of FRELIMO, the Permanent Commission, the Council of Ministers, or commissions (committees) of the assembly.

As a matter of practice, legislation is generally enacted by the Permanent Commission, followed by perfunctory ratification by the full assembly during its brief semiannual sessions. In the course of the September 1982 session, for example, the reported main agenda item was a discussion of ways in which deputies of the national, provincial, and local assemblies could contribute to the preparations for the Fourth Party Congress of FRELIMO. The assembly also ratified nine statutes approved by the Permanent Commission since its previous session in December 1981. These ranged from laws on the reacquisition of Mozambican citizenship to formation of associations by private businessmen. The eleventh session in March 1983 approved a major law on the national system of education as well as the 1983 central economic plan and state budget. Laws concerning both the celebration of "Family Day" (Christmas) and more severe sentences for black marketeering and crimes disrupting social peace, already in effect after approval by the Permanent Commission, were ratified by the entire assembly. Notwithstanding the fact that this session took place at a time of acute financial distress and amid reports of famine conditions in parts of the country, official information shed no light on whether these urgent matters were debated or whether any questioning of the government's actions to deal with these emergencies was permitted. During the twelfth session in April 1984, Machel proposed a number of reforms intended to lend more weight to the deliberations of the People's Assembly. He declared that state agencies should be required to give accounts of their activities to the assembly and answer questions from the deputies and that assembly working committees should be established with defined tasks and programs over a specific span of time, to be followed by a submission of reports to the full assembly. Machel said that permanent committees on foreign relations and inspection should be set up as well.

At its first session in December 1977, the assembly elected the 14 members proposed by the Central Committee to act as its Permanent Commission. They included Machel and five other ministers, two governors, and the heads of the armed forces, the police, the production councils, and the universities, all of whom were members of the Political Bureau or Central Committee.

### Elections

Preparations got under way for the first elections open to all Mozambicans after the Third Party Congress of FRELIMO determined in 1977 that the time had come for democratic institutions to be introduced "directly by the masses and in the service of the masses." The elections were to be regarded as part of the process of normalizing the mechanisms of government by a gesture purporting to give representatives of the wider public a hand in nonparty institutions. The elections were also viewed as a school for political and ideological training, for infusing a greater sense of national unity, and for demonstrating that FRELIMO was backed by an overwhelming popular mandate.

The election law decreed that elections for local assemblies were to be held from September 25 to November 13, 1977, for district and municipal assemblies by November 27, and for the 10 provincial assemblies and the national People's Assembly by December 4. Direct popular elections were held only for the 894 local assemblies. From among their members these assemblies chose delegates to a district electoral conference that elected deputies to the 112 district assemblies and the 10 municipal bodies. These assemblies elected delegates to the provincial assemblies, which in turn approved a list of candidates for the People's Assembly that had been compiled by the Central Committee.

Lists of candidates at the local level were prepared by the neighborhood FRELIMO committee or by party-sponsored dynamizing groups (*grupos dinamizadores*—GDs) in areas where the party was not yet organized (see Party Structure, this ch.). No actual vote was taken; the candidates were simply presented at open meetings where the public had an opportunity to voice objections to individual nominees. It was announced that 22,230 deputies from the 894 localities had been elected. More than

1,500 candidates were rejected on the grounds of having served in the former colonial administration or affiliated groups or having been local functionaries or village chiefs during colonial times. More than 600 other candidates were rejected for improper behavior. At the district level 3,390 deputies were elected, and about 200 were rejected because of prior associations with the colonial regime. A further 26 were rejected as city assembly delegates. A total of 734 deputies were elected to the 10 provincial assemblies, and 11 were rejected.

Of 226 deputies elected to the national People's Assembly, 198 (87.6 percent) were men, and 28 (12.4 percent) were women. The social composition was given as 71 workers (31.4 percent), 65 peasants (28.8 percent), 25 government employees (11 percent), 35 members of the armed forces (15.5 percent), and 13 representatives of mass organizations (5.7 percent). (The remaining 7.6 percent was unspecified.) There was no indication of an effort to achieve balanced regional representation, such as allotting a certain number of seats to each province. Less than 20 percent of the deputies were party members at the time of election; the proportions may have risen as a result of the subsequent membership drive.

In *Mozambique: From Colonialism to Revolution, 1900–1982*, Allen and Barbara Isaacman argued that the constitutional right of universal suffrage had been respected in the elections and that the mass of Mozambicans were able for the first time to participate in political life by electing their own representatives, to discuss openly and without coercion the qualifications of candidates, and to reject those regarded as unfit. In contrast, however, other observers noted that the voters had little influence on the result, not having had the opportunity to choose between competing candidates or parties, and that the assemblies were all indirectly elected except at the lowest level. The composition of the national People's Assembly was in reality determined by the FRELIMO party.

National elections were supposed to be held every five years. The second election of deputies to the People's Assembly was not held in 1982 as scheduled but was postponed until September 1985 to form part of the country's tenth anniversary celebration.

### Local Government

The Constitution, as revised in 1978, allots the subordinate people's assemblies broad responsibility for promoting social progress, consolidating the power of the state, increasing production and productivity, and improving conditions of cultural and social life. A governor appointed by the president is the senior official at the provincial level; he has considerable authority in his province but is answerable to FRELIMO, the president, and the Council of Ministers. Wide latitude apparently has been granted the governors in dealing with administrative, developmental, and security problems. The governor is the presiding officer of the provincial assembly and generally is also secretary of the provincial party structure. Each assembly consists of about 75 deputies, including other members of the provincial party committee, officials of the mass organizations of women and youth, peasants (who were in most cases members of cooperatives or of party-sponsored bodies), district officers, provincial and district party functionaries, the provincial directors of health, agriculture, public works, and finance, other officeholders, and members of the armed forces.

The combined budgets of the 10 provinces plus the city of Maputo amounted to the equivalent of US$115 million in 1982, of which US$73 million was made available by the national government. A substantial increase in the central government subsidy was planned for 1983 (US$132 million of the total provincial budget of US$173 million) to finance the decentralization of services as mandated by the Fourth Party Congress. Revenue collections by the national government also outstripped those of the provinces, amounting to US$472 million and US$42 million, respectively, in 1982.

Each of the 112 districts is headed by a district administrator, who is assisted by other district leaders delegated to manage priority sectors of governmental activity at the district level. The administrator and district leaders compose the executive council. Its members are appointed by the provincial governor after consultation with the appropriate ministry in Maputo. Major functional areas of the district executive council include agriculture, communal villages and cooperatives, the supply of goods and marketing, local industry, upkeep of roads and airfields, literacy programs, preventive medicine, and law and order. The district administrator is expected to cooperate with the head of security in the district but does not exercise authority over him.

The 10 municipal assemblies and executive councils are organized similarly to the district councils, although with somewhat broader functions. These include supervision of administrative agencies, production units, schools, and health units. They are expected to deal with public sanitation, water and power supplies, local transportation, and street maintenance. They promote the organization of cooperatives and arrange for food production on the perimeter of cities, mobilizing the unemployed to work on these nearby plots. In 1983 the city of Maputo was divided into eight municipal councils.

Assemblies at the level of locality (of which there are 894), have 15 to 35 members and are presided over by the locality administrator. An executive council, the permanent executive organ of the assembly, consists of the administrator and two other deputies who have the confidence of the assembly. Both the assembly and the council are subject to the political direction of the local FRELIMO committee. Tasks assigned to the locality assemblies by the 1977 law defining their activities include creating and improving productivity of collective farms; regulating markets; promoting cultivation of vegetables and cotton; helping to harvest, process, and market the cashew crop; encouraging better sanitation in villages; organizing welfare for the ill and aged; and encouraging enlistment in the military and militia.

Serious deficiencies found among local government bodies have been recurrent topics in speeches by Mozambican leaders and in the press. In an evaluation of the Matola District government in 1980, it was found that the four working committees set up by the assembly—those responsible for schools, production cooperatives, housing, and communal villages—had been virtually inactive. Some committee members failed to participate at all. Others blamed the lack of resources and transport for their inability to carry out their programs. In the same year in Cabo Delgado, several locality assemblies had to be dismissed or elections postponed because members or candidates were found to be persons who had served the colonial regime and "traditional feudal society." In many cases it appeared that actual authority continued to be exercised by traditional leaders. In those areas little or no effort was made to respond to party or government directives.

The report to the Fourth Party Congress charged that locality assemblies were meeting only to fulfill legal requirements and had not assumed a real leadership role. In his address to the congress, Machel noted that the districts had been defined as the basic units of production planning because they were in the best position to assess human and material resources, but they had failed to carry out this function. Planning had been imposed from above. Local organs had not assumed their responsibility to mobilize labor and organize small-scale production but waited for orders from higher authorities. Machel focused blame mainly on the absence of qualified cadres and experts and the concentration of activity at the central level. He called for a strengthening of district and provincial structures by introducing experienced and strongly motivated officials and by instilling local organs with greater self-reliance and initiative. Machel later called for greater participation by deputies of the people's assemblies and more concrete discussion of local problems and issues. He announced that provincial assemblies would meet every four months, district assemblies every three months, and locality assemblies every two months.

### The Legal System

The chaotic conditions under which Mozambican independence was achieved severely impeded the introduction of an effective system of justice. After the hasty departure of the Portuguese, enforcement of law by FRELIMO troops and untrained police was capricious at best. Large numbers of people were rounded up as chronic criminals or vagrants or as collaborators with the former colonial power and shipped off without trial to remote "reeducation centers." Abuse of police power was widespread, and the breakdown of the court system resulted in long delays before charges against detained persons were heard. Nationalization of the practice of law in 1975 depleted the ranks of trained lawyers already thinned by the Portuguese exodus. Only a handful of people with legal backgrounds were available to act as judges.

The dearth of qualified persons hindered the formulation of new laws in harmony with the objectives of the revolutionary regime. Legal codes bequeathed by the Portuguese had to be retained for the time being, although automatic revocation was provided for former legislation considered contrary to the Constitution. As of 1983 old Portuguese codes, decrees by the Mozambican authorities, and new laws covering major criminal activity, dissidence, and insurgency were still being applied in a haphazard manner. Legislation adopted in 1982 as part of a new family code under preparation established minimum ages for marriage and regulated marriage procedures, augmenting efforts to discourage polygamy and to extend legal protection to common-law wives.

In 1984 many people were still believed to be held under austere conditions in reeducation centers, although instances of excessively cruel treatment have been checked after they were sharply denounced by Machel. Civilians were tried in military courts, without benefit of normal safeguards, for certain serious offenses, and the lower level court system was still rudimentary. Nonetheless, institutionalization of the justice system was proceeding gradually, and the practice of detention without respect for normal legal process had diminished.

The Constitution provides for a Supreme People's Tribunal

and other courts as determined by law, subordinate to the People's Assembly. Judges are to be independent in discharge of their duty and to be subject only to the law. In reality the government exerts strong influence over the judiciary. The Constitution also provides for a procurator of the republic (prosecutor) in charge of a hierarchically organized system of legal officers to represent the state and supervise the carrying out of laws and fulfillment of legal norms. The Law of Judicial Organization (1978) provides that in addition to the Supreme People's Tribunal, which has authority to ensure the uniform application of the law by all courts, there will be people's tribunals at the levels of provinces, districts, and localities.

Under the Mozambican system of justice, considerable discretion and power rest with the public prosecutor and the investigatory and trial judges. The main provincial courts are staffed by one qualified judge and four elected "jurors." Judgments are rendered by majority vote. Provincial courts can be composed of several sections; the one in Maputo Province is divided into three civil sections, five criminal sections, a children's section, and a police section to deal mainly with traffic accidents. About 200 courts established during the colonial period continue to sit in urban areas.

As of 1983 only 34 district courts had been constituted. These were staffed by a judge and two jurors. To be qualified as a district judge, a sixth-grade education was required plus participation in a legal course for six months. People's courts at the locality level had been formed in 535 communities. Judgments were rendered by persons with primary-school education and rudimentary exposure to legal precepts. They were instructed to apply good sense in deciding disputes and dealing with minor infractions. The locality tribunals reportedly met once a week, and in many communal villages all adults would attend. One such tribunal, for example, heard 26 cases over a six-month span—half involving divorce or polygamy, the others dealing with robbery, prostitution, and debt and property conflicts.

In trials for serious offenses at the provincial or district level, a defendant has the right to choose counsel or to have a court-assigned defender. A public defender is required to have the same qualifications as a district judge, although law students and qualified lawyers may also serve in this capacity. It has been charged that defenders are often not given an opportunity to gather facts for the defense, sometimes learning about a case only at the beginning of a trial. Western observers who attended criminal trials noted that a presumption of innocence prevailed, witnesses were vigorously questioned, and intense debates between the public defender and state prosecutor marked the proceedings.

Some of the shortcomings found in the exercise of justice could be traced to the illiteracy of the defendants and witnesses, misunderstandings arising from their limited comprehension of Portuguese, and anxieties of the parties springing from memories of the colonial justice system. In addition, the educational gap between the judge and jurors conferred excessive authority on the former. Dissatisfaction with the conduct of the courts was expressed by the Mozambican president in March 1983, when he announced the temporary suspension of the law faculty at Eduardo Mondlane University. Machel complained that lawyers and judges were little different from those of the colonial era, favoring the bourgeoisie and wealthier individuals and preoccupying themselves with legalisms. He said that the function of the public defender was to defend the people's interest, not to defend criminals in imitation of capitalist lawyers.

Officials have criticized the unconscionable periods of incarceration before accused persons were brought to trial, presumably as a consequence of the dearth of trained legal personnel. During a state inspection in 1982, it was found that no action had been taken for several years in the cases of 200 prisoners in Nampula awaiting trial on charges of murder, diversion of state funds, professional negligence, and other offenses.

The civil court system administered by the Ministry of Justice is relatively free of political influence and respects normal legal processes. The Ministry of Interior, operating independently, may detain persons deemed guilty of antisocial behavior, political dissent, or economic crimes. Both the justice and interior ministries may send to reeducation centers prisoners who are judged to be capable of rehabilitation, the difference being that those handled by the Ministry of Justice probably have access to at least some legal safeguards. Sentences are often indeterminate, and release follows an official finding that the individual is ready to be reintegrated into society. In many cases release has been conditional on settling in remote areas adjacent to the reeducation center. No data have been released on the number of people still in detention, although estimates have ranged up to 10,000 or more in 12 centers as of 1980. On two subsequent occasions the mass release of more than 1,000 detainees was announced. In 1981 Machel acknowledged that many prisoners were being held in violation of the law. Whether a subsequent investigation by the government's inspector general produced needed reforms was not made clear.

A third system of justice—the Revolutionary Military Tribunal—was invoked in March 1979. The tribunals are charged with hearing cases against both civilian and military personnel accused of crimes against the people and state security, the definition of which has been broadened to include such economic offenses as black marketeering. Sentences ranging from eight years to death are mandated. The tribunals' secret proceedings are conducted by military personnel, some of whom have legal training. Large numbers of civilians accused of collaboration with the former white regime in Southern Rhodesia (present-day Zimbabwe) were given long sentences by the tribunals; the death penalty has been administered to a number of persons, mainly on charges of terrorism in connection with membership in an insurgent group.

The rising tension linked to guerrilla attacks, an upsurge of disorder and criminal activity, and attempts to curb black marketeering, smuggling, hoarding, narcotics trafficking, and other offenses associated in part with the country's economic distress have led to the imposition of harsh new penalties. The law on the defense of the economy (1982) provides sentences of two to eight years for mismanagement or falsifying reports that result in serious economic losses and lesser sentences for abuse of power, corruption, speculation, hoarding, and illegal trading. Cases tried under the law on crimes against the people and the people's state, which are heard by the military tribunals, carry the death penalty. The law was extended in 1983 to encompass cases of aggravated hoarding and smuggling. In the same year public flogging, a practice abolished after national independence, was reintroduced for all forms of black marketeering, price gouging, currency and narcotics dealings, armed robbery, theft, and rape. For the more severe crimes floggings were mandatory and supplemented the normal sentence.

Standard legal safeguards were apparently not available to the 50,000 or more individuals evicted from major cities during 1983 under a program to ease overcrowding and to rid Maputo and other urban centers of "marginal elements" of unemployed and black marketeers (see Demography, ch. 2). Reactions to the attacks and atrocities by anti-FRELIMO insurgents have produced other cases of arbitrary legal conduct. On at least two occasions in 1983, alleged guerillas were "tried" under the direction of senior government officials before large, hostile crowds and executed on the spot after a sentence of death was pronounced.

## Front for the Liberation Of Mozambique

Under Mozambique's Marxist-Leninist system the normal policy, administration, and lawmaking functions of government cannot be clearly distinguished from the influence and activities of the FRELIMO ruling party. FRELIMO is recognized in the Constitution as the agency that prescribes the basic political orientation of the state and directs and supervises the work of state organs. At its founding congress held in newly independent Tanganyika in 1962, FRELIMO was not dominated by a single ideology. It was a coalition of three parties that had been formed by emigrants and exiles from Mozambique between 1960 and 1962, each with distinct ethnic or racial ties (see Founding of the Front for the Liberation of Mozambique, ch 1). FRELIMO's original program was a simple one of national independence and opposition to colonialism. It did not embrace any particular economic doctrine aside from its rejection of foreign economic domination.

Having proclaimed a state of general insurrection in 1964, FRELIMO embarked on extended guerrilla warfare, initially hit-and-run raids from Tanzanian territory, later expanded to attacks from liberated areas in the remote northern regions of the country. Supported with arms and training by both the Soviet Union and China, the thinking of the leadership under the front's president, Eduardo Chivambu Mondlane, gradually evolved in a Marxist direction. FRELIMO's political theories were first applied in the liberated zones of the north, where communal villages and cooperatives were formed, complete with local political committees, crop-growing schemes, and rudimentary health and literacy programs. At this stage the Chinese provided the main model, their history of guerrilla warfare and collectivized life in liberated rural areas being more akin to Mozambique's revolutionary experienice. At the Second Party Congress in 1968, its functioning and structure were consciously shaped in a communist mold. FRELIMO's radical program became more pronounced after the assassination of Mondlane in 1969 and the assumption of the presidency by Samora Moises Machel, commander of the guerrilla army, following the collapse of a brief triumvirate leadership.

The overthrow of the authoritarian right-wing regime in Portugal in April 1974 by a group of liberal and radical officers under General António de Spínola was followed by an offer of a cease-fire to FRELIMO as the forerunner of a referendum on future relations with Portugal (see Independent Mozambique, ch. 1). FRELIMO countered by demanding an immediate grant of national independence, recognition of FRELIMO as the sole legitimate representative of all the peoples of Mozambique, and the transfer of government powers' directly into FRELIMO's hands. A renewed FRELIMO offensive, combined with the reluctance of Portuguese troops to fight in spite of reinforcements, weakened the resolve of the government in Lisbon. In September 1974 a cease-fire was negotiated with Machel, and agreement was reached on full independence under a FRELIMO government after a nine-month transition period. FRELIMO's control was virtually complete well before the end of the transition phase. Efforts of other African, white, and mixed groups to organize against FRELIMO, which had made clear its intention to establish a one-party state, were frustrated after opposition forces of both the white and the black communities made separate but unsuccessful attempts to seize power in September 1974. Before the end of that year FRELIMO held 12 of the 15 ministerial posts, filled half of the provincial governorships, and had replaced most of the mayors. The front's monopoly of power was sealed by Machel's elevation to the presidency of the country on June 25, 1975, and the swearing-in of an all-FRELIMO cabinet a week later.

### Ideology and Program

Although launched as a front uniting various elements in the struggle to overthrow Portuguese colonialism, domination of the movement by FRELIMO's left-wing faction was evident by the time of the Second Party Congress. The communist orthodoxy of the revolutionary leaders set them apart from most other nationalist movements in Africa, although it was similar to that adopted by Angola, another former Portuguese territory in southern Africa. FRELIMO rejected the doctrine proclaimed in many other African countries of a specifically African socialism, i.e., the ideological adaptation of Marxism-Leninism to African conditions and the remodeling of African societies along socialist lines without completely repudiating traditional customs and practices. The Mozambican leaders emphasized the participation and mobilization of the masses in building a new society, as well as the concept of class struggle against all exploiters. The exploiters were defined as the colonial bourgeoisie (and a small number of individuals who aimed to occupy the places left vacant by them), the wartime collaborators of the Portuguese, and the lawless elements of the society.

At the preliminary stage of carrying its program into effect upon coming to power in 1975, FRELIMO announced the takeover of private schools, the abolition of private medical and legal practices, and the nationalization of land. A massive literacy campaign was launched, and a program of preventive medicine was initiated. Both efforts were designed to benefit primarily the rural population, which had been virtually ignored by the colonial regime. Initially, nationalization of industry was restricted to former Portuguese enterprises—sawmills, processing plants, plantations, and large farms—which in many cases had already been abandoned. Rental properties were taken over, housing vacated by returning Portuguese was assigned to homeless families, and rents were collected by the state. A program of communal villages and collectivized agriculture was introduced. A second wave of nationalization in 1977 affected private insurance companies, the Portuguese-owned oil refinery, and all but one of the private banks. Production enterprises were generally nationalized as a consequence of unprofitability, abandonment, or inefficiency rather than as a rigorous application of ideology.

The Third Party Congress, held in February 1977, marked the transition of FRELIMO from a rural-based revolutionary armed front to a nationwide party applying the concepts of "scientific socialism," thereby reemphasizing the ties with Marxism-Leninism rather than African or other derivative forms of socialism. FRELIMO's strategy was now declared to be the reordering of Mozambican society through the efforts of a small group of dedicated elites rather than through a mass movement. Democratic centralism was adopted as a fundamental concept of organization and work, embodying the principles of free internal party discussions, complete and loyal acceptance of decisions reached, continued analysis, and self-criticism. The hard core of the party was to be composed of industrial workers, some peasants being allowed to join if they had experience on collective farms. The masses of the people were to be organized through affiliated bodies obedient to the directives of the party.

The decisions of the Third Party Congress were widely interpreted as a shift in Mozambique's orientation closer to the Soviet organizational model of a small group of urban proletariat militants leading and mobilizing the masses. As explained by Machel, however, the decisions of the congress represented a synthesis of Mozambique's own experience with the basic principles of Marxism-Leninism. In their book *Afrocommunism*, journalists David and Marina Ottaway have questioned the argument used to justify the idea of a proletarian dictatorship in a predominantly rural and peasant-based society, especially when the peasants had provided the main support for FRELIMO during the liberation war and the working class in the cities have proved irrelevant. They concluded, moreover, that the stress on class struggle that dominated the congress could not easily be related to the real situation in the country.

The congress did acknowledge Mozambique's great reliance on agriculture, which had to form the base for further development. It declared that, as a short-term policy, agriculture would be encouraged to provide vitally needed food and serve as the means for organizing rural society along collective lines. In the second phase industry would be the propelling factor, and in the final, decisive stage heavy industry would be established. Only then would the industrial proletariat be sufficiently strong to bring about the transformation to a workers' society and the emergence of what Machel termed "New Man, Socialist Man," free from subservience and exploitation and displaying the values of the working class.

**Party Structure**

The formal source of authority within FRELIMO is the party congress, which by statute is to be convened every four years. In practice only two congresses have been held since independence— the Third Party Congress in 1977 and the Fourth Party Congress in 1983. A total of 667 delegates assembled for the Fourth Party Congress, making it far larger than the Third Party Congress, which was attended by 379 delegates. Elections by party committees of the 10 provinces determine the composition of the congress. Treated as a major political event, a party congress may be two years or more in preparation. Among the preliminary actions are the adoption of "theses" highlighting problems to be taken up at the congress, which are subject to extensive debates in lower level party organs during the months preceding the congress. In addition to the delegates, the congress is attended by large numbers of observers and official delegations. In the case of the Fourth Party Congress, 58 countries were represented, mostly from the ruling parties of communist nations but also from other leftist governments, communist parties of Western countries, and governing parties of neighboring African states.

The party congress, which extends over about five days, tends to be carefully structured. The delegates read prepared statements and unanimously approve policy changes that have been adopted in advance by the leadership or endorse strategies that have already been introduced. During the Fourth Party Congress, however, it was reported that lively discussions were permitted, numerous delegates from rural areas frankly charging that government and

*Participating in FRELIMO's Fourth Party Congress, April 1983,
are (left to right) Marcelino dos Santos, President Machel,
and Joaquim Alberto Chiassano.*

*Delegates voting at FRELIMO's Fourth Party Congress, April 1983*

Members of FRELIMO's new Political Bureau elected at the Fourth
Party Congress, April 1983, included (left to right) President Machel,
Marcelino dos Santos, Joaquim Alberto Chissano, General Alberto
Joaquim Chipande, Armando Emilio Guebuza, Jorge Rebelo, Mariano
de Araujo Matsinhe, General Sebastião Marcos Mabote, Jacinto Veloso,
Mário da Graça Machungo, and José Oscar Monteiro.

Introduction of FRELIMO's newly elected Central Committee (standing)
to delegates (seated in foreground) at the Fourth Party Congress, April
1983. The new Political Bureau is seated on the dais behind the Central
Committee; observers and official delegations from foreign countries are
seated in the background.

Photographs courtesy AIM/Anders Nilsson

party policies had contributed to the agricultural crisis.

Between sessions of the congress the responsibilities of policymaking and ensuring implementation of directives from this body are assumed by the Central Committee. In addition to the party president, the Central Committee consists of provincial representatives, heads of FRELIMO's permanent departments, and others elected by the congress. Before 1983 the Central Committee had been composed of 67 members, most of whom were party officials from the national level. The new Central Committee of 130 members elected at the final session of the Fourth Party Congress was drawn heavily from peasants and workers of the provincial and district party committees who had joined in the criticism of the party during the congress.

The Central Committee meets annually, although a number of extraordinary sessions have also been held. In addition to deliberating over party matters, the committee gives policy endorsement to government actions before ratification by the People's Assembly. Thus, at its eleventh regular session preceding the Fourth Party Congress, the Central Committee assembled for three days to review agricultural policy questions, party organization, foreign policy, and the enactment of a comprehensive education law. Guidelines for the central plan and the state budget were approved, as were preparations for the impending party congress.

At the apex of power and decisionmaking is the Political Bureau (formerly the Political Committee), comprising the highest echelon of the party. Remarkably stable in its composition, the Political Bureau consisted of the same 10 individuals from independence until 1983, when an eleventh member was added (see table 10, Appendix). Complete secrecy surrounds the policymaking process among these leaders, who may differ strongly with one another and engage in sharp debate over FRELIMO policies but maintain a united front in public. Machel has been clearly paramount, his public statements conveying a sense of personal authority and accountability. Announcements of personnel changes, new programs and policies, explanations of major government actions, and assignment of blame for failures almost invariably have emanated first from him. Although subordinate to Machel, the other members of the Political Bureau are veterans of the movement and his compatriots in the liberation war, and they are undoubtedly influential in high party deliberations.

The ongoing work of the Central Committee is entrusted to the six-member Secretariat, whose members also oversee the permanent administrative departments of the party. As of 1984 there were eight such departments: economy, defense, mass democatic organizations, training and documentation, information and propaganda, foreign relations, organization, and administration and finance.

Beneath the national level the party was organized into 10 provincial committees of 60 to 70 members each, 112 district committees, and hundreds of cells organized at work places and in the agricultural communes. Administrative functions at the provincial and district levels were handled by departments corresponding to those at the Central Committee level, although fewer in number (see fig. 13).

During the early postindependence period, when FRELIMO was not yet organized in all areas of the country, the task of political indoctrination of the masses was entrusted to the dynamizing groups (GDs). Selected at assemblies held in villages, towns, factories, and state farms on the initiative of local FRELIMO units, the GDs were intended to organize people in a locality or workplace and act as a means of communication between the party and the unorganized masses. The GDs were expected to form committees to deal with local problems—crime fighting, neighborhood cleanups, literacy classes, and day-care centers— and to help deal with local or national emergencies.

The experience with the GD system was only partially successful. In many cases the GDs were controlled by persons who were not in sympathy with the FRELIMO ideology. Frequent purges were directed against GD officials charged with being opportunists and reactionaries who had formerly opposed FRELIMO. The absence of established government institutions resulted in many instances of abuse of authority and dishonest practices. In businesses and factories the GDs sometimes acted more like grievance committees in demanding pay increases and improved conditions on behalf of the workers rather than as instruments to mobilize labor for greater production effort and discipline as intended by FRELIMO.

A new party organizing effort mounted after the Third Party Congress in 1977 resulted in a gradual shift from reliance on the GDs. Until then FRELIMO membership had been restricted to about 15,000 wartime adherents and to a few others considered wholeheartedly committed to its ideology. Now, striving to adopt a more orthodox party structure akin to the Soviet model, basic cell units were to be organized throughout the country in work places, farm cooperatives, communes, other communities, government offices, and military units. A vast recruitment drive was launched, but membership was still to be granted only to dedicated believers in the FRELIMO ideology who were also respected by their neighbors and co-workers. Aspiring members had to appear before assemblages of GD or party militants to undergo searching probes of their personal histories, after which those accepted provisionally by the party provincial committee were to have their behavior scrutinized for a year before final admission to FRELIMO's ranks. Initially, recruitment failed to meet its goals, although the number of party members and candidates was given at the Fourth Party Congress in 1983 at over 110,000. This was still less than one for every 100 citizens. It was claimed that 53.5 percent of the members were peasants and 18.9 percent were workers. Most of the remainder were presumably officials and military personnel.

It was stated at the time of the Third Party Congress that the hard core of the party was to be composed of factory workers who had experience with the cooperative requirements and discipline of organized labor. Inasmuch as 90 percent of the inhabitants lived in the countryside, this was not a viable objective. The peasants who were encouraged to join were those associated with cooperative or communal endeavors. The communal village movement, initially a major symbol of the Mozambican approach to organizing the rural sector, had, however, lost its momentum. At the time of the Fourth Party Congress, the movement appeared to be stabilized; 1,350 communal villages had been formed, and party cells could be found in 515 of these.

After the campaign to build party units throughout the country, the GDs were stripped of their political functions and eliminated in the countryside and work place. They continued to perform educational, liaison, and mobilization functions in urban areas. In spite of the effort since 1978 to introduce more effective party machinery, Machel conceded during the Fourth Party Congress that the party apparatus remained weak. It had not been possible, he said, to keep pace with the growing membership by providing enough qualified cadres to lead units at provincial, district, and locality levels. The cells at the grass roots had no work programs and reflected laziness on the part of the members. In the factories party organs had been isolated by management and were not involved in production decisions or compilation of annual plans. Machel said that in order to maintain party supervision the senior party cadres had been assigned to executive posts in government and industry. The result, however, was that the cadres had become absorbed in their job responsibilities to the detriment of their party duties. As a measure to activate at least some of the 4,200 existing cells, it was announced that 20 to

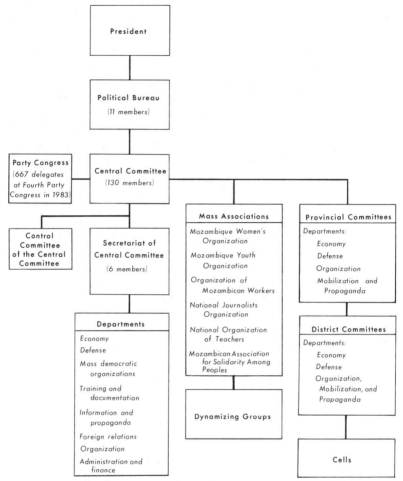

*Figure 13. Structure of the Front for the Liberation of Mozambique, 1984*

30 cells in each province—those situated in strategic areas or strategic enterprises—were to be made to function properly. These would then serve as models for other cells.

**Mass Associations**

In observance of Leninist precepts, FRELIMO has sponsored a number of "mass democratic organizations," which are intended as a means of mobilizing various interest groups in support of FRELIMO's objectives. The mass organizations are the sole mechanisms, aside from religious bodies, permitting non-

211

party members to act in combination with one another. Carefully supervised by the party, the mass organizations provide an opportunity for FRELIMO to indoctrinate the wider public in its ideology and function as instruments through which its political decisions are communicated to and imposed on society at large. The existence of other interest groups—even those having only social, professional, or charitable purposes—would not be countenanced unless brought under control of the party.

The range of such organizations in Mozambique has been comparable to, but not yet as wide in scope as, that in other countries with Marxist-Leninist systems. The three major groups are concerned with women, youth, and labor. In addition, the National Journalists Organization (Organização Nacional das Journalistas—ONJ) was formed in 1978, the Mozambican Association for Solidarity Among Peoples (Associação Moçambicana Amizade e Solidariedade com os Povos—AMASP) was founded in 1980, and the National Organization of Teachers (Organização Nacional dos Professores—ONP) was founded in 1981.

The senior mass organization is the Mozambique Women's Organization (Organização das Mulheres de Moçambique—OMM), which held its first conference in Tanzania in 1973. The OMM has as its objective the incorporation of large numbers of women in the political and economic life of the country and the emancipation of women from their subordinate place in society. The OMM has also been in the forefront of campaigns against traditional practices, such as bride-price, child marriage, and polygyny. The resistance to women casting off their traditional roles in society remained strong, although participation by women in political bodies has been rising. In the elections of 1977, women accounted for 12 percent of those elected to district assemblies. Women were reportedly active in communal villages, sometimes holding a majority of the elected positions.

The Mozambique Youth Organization (Organização da Juventude de Moçambique—OJM) was established in 1977 after a decision taken by the Central Committee and ratified by the Third Party Congress. The paramount task assigned to the OJM was to unite and mobilize Mozambican youth in the correct implementation of the FRELIMO program. It was also directed to involve itself in literacy and vocational training, in volunteer work by young people, and in organizing sports and recreational activity. The number of youth recruited by the OJM and its rate of growth have not been revealed, but the organization clearly failed to meet the expectations of the party leadership. In one case an entire provincial secretariat was disbanded on grounds of negligence, incompetence, and corruption. It was admitted in 1981 that the organization had not become firmly established among the rank and file of youth. Social and work centers had not become organized and, where units did exist, they were not effective. Young people were said to regard the OJM with indifference and in some places with hostility. Many factors were adduced for this alienation, among them arrogance and indifference of the OJM leadership and the tendency to emulate the formalism and operating methods of FRELIMO itself.

Organization of the labor force was begun in 1977 with the introduction of production councils designed to involve the workers in questions of production and management planning and to lead the struggle against indiscipline and sabotage in the work force. The production councils thus supplanted the GDs as the main instrumentality for mobilizing factory workers in support of FRELIMO's goals. In 1979 the remaining labor unions were dissolved as colonial vestiges, and their assets were transferred to the production councils. New responsibilities were imposed on the councils, including the conduct of social emulation campaigns to meet higher production targets, organizing voluntary work, recruiting for the militia, upgrading plant cadres, and ensuring healthy and safe working conditions.

Seven years after their launching, the production councils were in turn replaced by a new trade union body, the Organization of Mozambican Workers (Organização dos Trabalhadores de Moçambique—OTM). Machel declared that the councils had achieved important successes but had become overly bureaucratized and had occupied themselves with winning immediate benefits for workers instead of stressing the fulfillment of production goals.

At the organizing conference of the OTM in November 1983, Machel emphasized that the new trade unions would not be constituted as autonomous bodies representing the interests of the workers as in capitalist societies. The unions, he said, would form an arm of the party for organizing the laboring classes. Accordingly, they would not be permitted to act as instruments of confrontation or to make wage demands. (The right to strike, to organize freely, and to bargain collectively is not recognized in Mozambican law and practice.) The statutes adopted at the opening conference defined the purpose of the OTM as the mobilization of workers for increased production and productivity in carrying out the nation's social and economic development plans. The OTM was also to promote an active participation by the workers in the planning, direction, and control of the economy. One union was to be formed in each work place, and all workers, whether manual or white-collar, would have the right to join. The 93-member Central Council of the OTM elected Augusto Macamo, a member of the party's Central Committee and former head of the production councils, as general secretary of the OTM.

### Role of the Information Media

The information media in Mozambique are regarded as ideological tools of the party in mobilizing the workers and peasants for the tasks of building a socialist society, exercising power in their class interests, and conducting the struggle against "imperialism." All authorized publications and the radiobroadcasting system are owned and operated by the state. Owing to the poverty of the country and the low rate of literacy, the full potential of the media in the service of FRELIMO has not been realized. Newspaper circulation per capita is believed to be among the lowest in the world. Ownership of radio receivers, estimated at 255,000 in 1981, is also relatively restricted as a consequence of the scarcity of equipment and the weak buying power of the public. As of early 1984 television broadcasts were still conducted on an experimental basis while technicians were being trained pending its introduction on a regular schedule.

One approach taken to deal with the problem of communication has been the introduction of amplified public sound systems in a number of communal villages. Installed with financial assistance from the United Nations International Children's Fund (UNICEF), these systems have included a generator, loudspeakers mounted on poles, amplifiers, record and cassette players, and, in some cases, a film projector and a shortwave radio. Begun in 1977, the project's impact remained limited as of 1983 and was available only to 40 villages and four urban neighborhoods. A larger number of communities were served by four mobile communication units, each of which could visit 12 to 15 villages a month.

Soon after FRELIMO came to power, four of the six private newspapers in Mozambique were closed down. The remaining two were turned over to FRELIMO. As of 1984 there were still only two dailies in the country: *Notícias* (estimated circulation 38,000), published in Maputo, and *Diário de Moçambique* (estimated circulation 16,000), published in Beira. These were supplemented by a Sunday newspaper, *Domingo*, and a weekly magazine, *Tempo*, as well as specialized publications for the military and other groups. *Voz da Revolução*, the organ of the Central Committee, focused on the application of Marxism to FRELIMO's policies.

*Mozambican wall newspaper in 1976, modeled on the Chinese counterpart; an important means of propagating FRELIMO's views and policies during the early days of the revolution, they continue to be found in factories, offices, and gathering places in rural areas.*
*Courtesy Mozambique Information Office, London*

The public media are actively involved in propagating the government's viewpoint on issues and in promoting FRELIMO's social philosophy. A moderate amount of African and other world news is presented, although it is generally selected and treated in a manner supporting the government's outlook on international issues. Within limits, accounts of shortcomings in the implementation of the government's plans are tolerated, as are individual abuses and failings—especially when such criticisms are in accord with official campaigns. *Tempo* features letters from readers asking for investigation of bungling by government offices. Writers for the newspapers are aware of their duty to emphasize party themes and practice self-censorship in treating sensitive topics. The government has nonetheless expressed dissatisfaction at times, condemning journalists who see information as neutral and distinct from the "class struggle," those who exhibit a lack of class feeling, and those who look on the media as a means of drawing to the attention of the public and the leadership the shortcomings in the party and state. Membership in the journalists' association, the ONJ, is compulsory. The ONJ is the government's instrument for bringing ideological pressure on the press, although it has been criticized by the political leadership as lifeless and inactive at the level of its local committees.

An official news-gathering organization, the Information Agency of Mozambique (Agência de Informação de Moçambique—AIM), disseminates domestically and abroad government-approved reports on developments in the country. AIM is responsible for gathering information by employing a network of correspondents in communities throughout the country, a system that remained at a developmental stage as of 1983. Local news collecting was hampered by a lack of vehicles, the poor and dangerous road system, and unreliable telephone service. Portugal, the Soviet Union, and the German Democratic Republic (East Germany) maintained bureaus in Maputo. Along with other nations of southern Africa, Mozambique decreed a ban on visits by Western correspondents based in South Africa. This restriction was not, however, strictly enforced.

## Politics

The paramount political problem of Mozambique's leaders has been to devise an effective strategy for surmounting repeated economic setbacks without abandoning its chosen Marxist-Leninist path. The turmoil surrounding the sudden transition to independence in 1975, accompanied by the flight of most trained personnel and considerable capital, brought the economy to a virtual standstill. The government could not meet even its modest goal of restoring 1973 production levels by 1980. Successive shocks to the economy and misdirected policies have only accentuated the new nation's initial handicaps. Cycles of floods and droughts coupled with ill-advised emphasis on state and communal farming have necessitated rising imports of food to a country in which 90 percent of the inhabitants live in rural areas. Purchases of grain, which depleted the country's scarce foreign exchange, supplemented by massive aid shipments—mostly from Western donors—were barely sufficient to stave off famine.

Efforts to restore order to the economy and launch it on a growth track have been impeded by the destabilizing effect of violence and terrorism in the region. Sacrifices that the country could ill afford were entailed in Mozambique's support for the black nationalist struggle in neighboring Zimbabwe until that country's independence was won in 1980. Since then the rising incidence of insurgency and sabotage has battered the already stricken Mozambican economy.

### New Economic Directions, 1980–83

Initially, the course charted by the government was dictated both by its avowed Marxist-Leninist inspiration and by the circumstances in which the country found itself at independence. The reorganization of agriculture was undertaken on a basis of state farms, cooperatives, and communal villages. Existing large-scale industry, financial institutions, and infrastructure were nationalized. Priority in future development was to be assigned to heavy industry as communist orthodoxy demanded. Portuguese owners of large plantations and factories were gradually squeezed out, facilitating the adoption of these policies. The state took over vacated homes and apartments as well as private rental property. In similar fashion the government found itself operating shops, restaurants, hotels, and other services.

In the face of mounting economic stress, the government continued to regard the areas of health, especially preventive medicine, human services, and education, as deserving of priority attention. Progress was recorded in combating disease, ignorance, and illiteracy (see Education; Health, ch. 2). The breakdown of the basic food supply had, however, reached such a state in many areas of the country that by 1981 malnutrition and hunger had overshadowed all other domestic issues.

It had become clear that FRELIMO and its subsidiary organs of control and mobilization were failing to bring about the reorientation of social and economic life demanded of it during the Third Party Congress in 1977. Launching an "offensive" during the first part of 1980 to restore momentum, Machel conceded that the party had shown itself to be too weak to fulfill its functions of participating in managing, planning, producing, motivating workers, and controlling the state apparatus. He demanded renewed efforts to ensure party direction over the day-to-day activities of the state, especially by its most dynamic members who had become preoccupied with their parallel responsibilities as government officials. Machel personally spearheaded a campaign to expose corruption, bureaucratic negligence, indiscipline, and inertia. In a series of unannounced visits to factories, ports, warehouses, and clinics, Machel found stockpiles of food, medicines, and other goods unavailable in retail shops. He uncovered corrupt practices in the state housing office and in the people's shops, as well as chronic apathy and inefficiency.

In March 1980 a decisive change of emphasis was announced with respect to the consumer sector and the role of foreign capital.

The so-called people's stores run by the government were to be turned over to private shopkeepers and to cooperatives. The former operators of restaurants, hotels, garages, repair shops, and hairdressing establishments were invited to return to Mozambique to operate their enterprises. The private sector in agriculture was to be encouraged by raising the price for crops offered by the state. The state would, however, continue to reserve for itself the major development sectors and would not retreat from its fundamental commitment to centralized planning and control of the economy.

Corresponding changes were introduced in the political field. Several key ministers were removed and ministries reorganized. Each government agency was required to establish an office of control and discipline to stimulate efficiency and to act as a public ombudsman. Two senior members of the Political Bureau, dos Santos and Rebelo, were relieved of their ministerial assignments to devote all of their efforts to revitalizing the FRELIMO party.

These announced changes did little to slow the economic decline. Appeals for foreign investment brought a minimal response owing to uncertainty over the terms under which private firms would be allowed to operate and doubts over the viability of new enterprises under deteriorating economic conditions. Productivity in the small industry sector continued to suffer in part because of a lack of raw materials and equipment breakdowns. Inefficient state companies continued to proliferate. Food rationing had to be introduced in Maputo in March 1981. A new wage and salary scale was imposed in late 1980, which raised the wages of unskilled agricultural and industrial workers relative to trained workers and placed the economy under further pressure. The state farms and other socialized units continued to be favored over the much larger private agricultural sector in the allocation of resources, accentuating the crisis in food supply.

### Reforms of the Fourth Party Congress of FRELIMO

As preparations got under way in 1982 for the Fourth Party Congress, it was acknowledged that the weaknesses of the party had not been overcome. The "theses," distributed for internal discussion before the congress convened, maintained that the party had been too lax in its membership criteria. The result was that many cells had lapsed into passivity. FRELIMO, it was acknowledged, had allowed itself to become office bound, compiling reports and memorandums instead of moving energetically to solve the problems of production, training, and efficient use of resources. Unlike the Third Party Congress, the critical issues were not to be the idelogical model to be followed but rather the practical problems of overcoming hunger and defeating the anti-FRELIMO guerrillas.

Addressing the Fourth Party Congress with characteristic bluntness when it met in April 1983, Machel enumerated the difficulties faced by the country. According to the president, these included the disintegration of the trading network in rural areas, the failure of the cooperative movement to take hold among the peasants, the persistent bottlenecks in agricultural marketing, inexperienced and lethargic management cadres, and ineffectual local governing bodies. At the same time, Machel claimed credit for setting in motion a broad transformation of Mozambican society, notably in the form of social benefits for the mass of people who had been ignored by the colonial regime. The popular assemblies and popular tribunals had, he asserted, created conditions for the ordinary citizens to govern themselves and to obtain justice. The armed forces had been strengthened, and militia and village vigilance groups had been formed. Machel declared that water supplies had reached new areas and that new schools, local factories, clinics, and town services had been provided. Mozambicans had received training in leading and managing their own economy, and ordinary workers had been brought into the planning process.

Machel did not ignore the disastrous situation in the agriculture sector, which had caused hunger and even starvation in some areas and had dragged down other sectors of the economy. Rural delegates were outspokenly critical of the disorganization in the countryside and the deficiencies in the state and cooperative farms. The congress endorsed a shift in emphasis to the family farm and called for action to improve the distribution and marketing of crops. In a further departure from Marxist orthodoxy, Machel underscored the need for development projects based on local initiative—fisheries, exploitation of wildlife resources, and small factories to supply simple consumer items.

Machel promised a reallocation of resources and new policies to favor individual family farms, along with encouragement of the private sector and cooperatives in establishing small-scale local manufacturing in activities such as building materials, food processing, domestic tools, and household implements. In other respects Machel held out little promise of relaxing the policy of economic development centered on the state sector. He noted with apparent satisfaction that the government companies already produced 70 percent of the goods sold in the country, predominating in the industrial, energy, mining, transportation, communications, and construction sectors. In addition these firms held a monopoly over foreign trade and insurance and were dominant in banking.

A number of major personnel changes were announced in conjunction with the Fourth Party Congress. Four of the most prominent figures in Mozambican politics—dos Santos, Vieira, Minister of Defense Alberto Joaquim Chipande, and Minister of Planning Mário de Graça Machungo—were to be assigned as provincial heads. All except Vieira were also members of the Political Bureau. José Oscar Monteiro, in addition to joining the Political Bureau, was relieved from a temporary governorship to become minister of justice. Another member of the Political Bureau, Jacinto Veloso, was brought into the cabinet in the newly created position of minister of economic affairs in the presidency. In addition, over 100 officials of the central government were transferred to the district level to reinvigorate local planning and administration.

The assumption of provincial responsibilities by four of the most eminent FRELIMO figures was at first interpreted as an effort to remove them from the national scene as part of a major shift in relationships. They did not, however, take up full-time residence in the provincial capitals. Machel asserted that they were not to be regarded as governors but as members of the central leadership vested with special authority to supervise the materialization of congressional decisions at the provincial level. The president said they were needed in sections of the country of strategic importance for their food and industrial production. In the case of the distant northern province of Cabo Delgado, a greater effort was said to be necessary because it was far behind the rest of the country in development.

### Opposition to FRELIMO

No public opposition to the government or to FRELIMO has been permitted under Mozambique's authoritarian one-party system. In early 1984 there were few specific indications that anti-FRELIMO sentiment among the general public had been translated into seditious activity or the formation of groups hostile to the government. Alienation was undoubtedly widespread owing to the decline in living standards, the severe shortages of basic foodstuffs, and the breakdown in the supply of ordinary goods and services. FRELIMO's failed policies had contributed to its unpopularity in the countryside, as had its efforts to coerce individual farmers into joining communal villages and cooperatives and its partiality for state farms over private holdings. In the cities discontent was said to be found among many intellectuals, who faced the threat of reeducation camps if they voiced dissenting opinions, among those offended by the government's antireligious attitude, and among technocrats critical of economic policies. A further source of the government's unpopularity was the suspicion that it was under the influence of nonblacks driven by communist orthodoxy and out of touch with the real needs of the society, particularly in the agricultural sector. There was also a feeling that it was dominated by officials from the southern region and that the problems of other areas consequently were little understood and neglected. The government's security forces, neighborhood informers, and other means of surveillance had either succeeded in suppressing public protests, or evidence of the existence of unrest and internal opposition had failed to come to the attention of foreign observers because of strict control over the news media.

A persistent threat to the security of the country and to FRE-LIMO rule, however, has been posed by the guerrilla organization, the Mozambican National Resistance (Resistência Nacional Moçambicana—RNM, sometimes referred to as RENAMO), which has pursued a strategy of raids and sabotage directed initially at less populated areas of the central and southern provinces—Manica, Sofala, Inhambane, and Gaza—but which by 1984 had reached nearly every region of the country (see The Mozambican National Resistance, ch. 5). The RNM was purportedly formed in 1976 by disaffected former FRELIMO military commanders unreconciled to domination of the liberation front by Marxist elements. The RNM was the successor to an underground group, the United Democratic Front of Mozambique (Frente de Unidade Democrática de Moçambique—FUMO), formed among exiles in Europe. FUMO claimed that its policies, reflecting the true thoughts of FRELIMO's founder, Mondlane, were aimed at creating a racially integrated state composed of ethnic segments in a federal format.

In addition to defectors from FRELIMO, the ranks of the RNM have included former members of the colonial security forces and other opponents of the government of Maputo. Its financial backing was widely ascribed to Portuguese businessmen, particularly Jorge Jardim, a prominent publisher and influential political figure in Beira before Mozambican independence. A secret source of support, including both funds and training, was the white government of Southern Rhodesia. Bases and training areas were provided on Rhodesian territory, as was a site for the RNM radio station, Voice of Free Africa. After Southern

Rhodesia became independent Zimbabwe under a black-majority government in April 1980, South Africa reportedly became the main source of RNM's arms, supplies, and training.

The RNM's political program has been defined in only general terms. Claiming to represent the original FRELIMO doctrines of Mondlane, it has called for the dissolution of the communist system "without vindictiveness" and for a free vote on the future political and social system. The private sector would become the dynamic force in the economy, with the caveat that exploitation of groups or classes would not be permitted. Nationalized property would be reviewed for "reprivatization." A future constitution, to be drawn up by a national assembly and put to a referendum, would guarantee fair trials and due legal process. The RNM's international policies have stressed cooperation in the region and nondiscrimination against any country on account of its domestic system.

In 1983 the RNM's propaganda broadcasts claimed that liberated and operational areas had been established and that health, educational services, and other infrastructure had been introduced. There was, however, no independent evidence that the RNM had been able to occupy territory except on a temporary basis or that any effort had been made to impose a political administration. Its indiscriminate attacks and sabotage presented the government an opportunity to deflect blame to the guerrillas for the deteriorating conditions in the countryside. The gradual enlargement of the RNM's area of operations did appear to demonstrate that it had met with some support arising from resistance to the government's policies among the peasantry. Nevertheless, the insurgency movement had not fully succeeded in escaping the stigma of being under the control of former Portuguese colonists in collaboration with the white government of South Africa.

## Foreign Relations

Mozambique has regularly aligned itself with the more militant nations of the Third World, as well as the Soviet Union and its allies, on major issues before the world community. It has, however, followed a moderate and pragmatic course on African regional issues of most direct concern to it. A participant in the full range of international, continental, and regional groupings, Maputo's activity in these bodies is subordinated to the primary goal of its foreign policy: the quest for material aid, financing, and technical assistance in relieving acute economic distress. A central problem of its bilateral relations is the management of its differences with South Africa, a neighbor whose racist policies are anathema to Mozambique but a country that is economically and militarily dominant in southern Africa. In its advocacy of an end to colonialism and white majority rule in Africa, Mozambique provided refuge to the forces of the Zimbabwe African National Union (ZANU) before Zimbabwean independence and has been a haven for members of the African National Congress (ANC), whose goal is to topple the white-dominated government of South Africa. As one of the front-line states (see Glossary), Mozambique participates in negotiations over the independence of Namibia (South West Africa).

Mozambique is a member of the United Nations (UN), the Organization of African Unity (OAU), and the Nonaligned Movement (see Glossary). The country turns to these bodies in its search for political, material, and moral support in what FRELIMO calls "the struggle against colonialism, imperialism, racism, and inequality." Mozambique's voting record in the UN has shown a consistent bias against positions of the Western and capitalist nations. The United States Department of State has estimated that the Mozambican delegation has voted on the same side as the United States less than 10 percent of the time. Mozambique often joins the more radical OAU members—Algeria, Angola, Ethiopia, Libya, and Zimbabwe—on issues before that body. It regards many countries of Africa, particularly those that formerly were French colonies, as victims of "neoimperialism," having failed to achieve full economic liberation. Mozambique was one of the countries backing the demand of the Polisario (see Glossary) guerrilla movement in the Western Sahara to be recognized in the OAU as the Saharan Arab Democratic Republic, rejecting the position of Morocco that the area is an integral part of its territory.

Mozambique's concept of nonalignment is not one of neutralism or of equidistance between the great powers. Machel has stated that the "socialist community," i.e., the communist world, is the natural ally of the people of the developing countries in overcoming what he has perceived as flagrant injustices in the world economic order. Mozambique has been among a small group of countries that has defended the conduct of the Soviet Union even on such actions as the invasion of Afghanistan and is joined with the Soviet Union in a 20-year treaty of friendship and cooperation. The Soviet Union and its allies have been the principal sources of military equipment and training and have been important suppliers of economic and technical assistance. Mozambique has not, however, permitted the Soviets to establish a naval base in its territory. The government in Maputo has advocated that the Indian Ocean be declared a nuclear-free zone of peace and that existing bases be dismantled.

The preponderant share of economic assistance reaching Mozambique has been from the Scandinavian countries and other Western nations. Owing to strains in political relations between the two countries, help from the United States has been limited to humanitarian aid in the form of food shipments. Efforts to moderate differences with the United States and Western Europe have both political and economic motives. A stronger commitment by the West is recognized as indispensable to the achievement of objectives of the Black African states in their confrontation with South Africa. The greater resources of the West in helping Mozambique with its intractable economic problems and in support of regional development have been acknowledged. Differences have been composed with Portugal, which—as the former colonial power—is a potentially valuable economic partner. Reluctance to join the Lomé Convention of Third World states associated with the European Economic Community (EEC) has been overcome, and a decision to apply for membership in the International Monetary Fund and World Bank (see Glossary) was announced in 1984.

As of early 1984 Mozambique had entered into diplomatic relations with 80 countries; 52 of them had permanent representatives in Maputo. Embassies had been established by Mozambique in only 10 countries in addition to its permanent missions to the UN and OAU. They included all contiguous countries of southern Africa (with the exception of South Africa), the Soviet Union, the German Democratic Republic (East Germany), Cuba, China, the United States, and Portugal. The office of the Palestine Liberation Organization (PLO) representative was accorded full embassy status. Although Israeli funds and equipment were provided at an early stage of the guerrilla movement, Mozambique conformed to an OAU resolution by refraining from establishing diplomatic ties with Israel. It declared that its actions were a gesture of solidarity with the PLO and other Arab states whose territories were occupied by Israel. Although their economic aid to Mozambique has been limited, various Arab nations have furnished oil at concessional rates.

### Neighboring Black African States

Mozambique has been able to maintain harmonious relations

*Tanzania's president Julius K. Nyerere (left) and Zambia's
president Kenneth Kaunda (right) receiving recognition
from President Machel during Victory Day celebrations in Maputo
in September 1983; during their visit, Kaunda and Nyerere
were awarded the Eduardo Mondlane Order, first class,
Mozambique's highest honor.
Victory Day commemorates the anniversary of
agreements with Portugal signed in Lusaka, Zambia, in 1974
granting Mozambican independence nine months later.
Courtesy AIM/Anders Nilsson*

with all five of the Black African countries with which it has common
borders. In 1984 its ties with Zimbabwe and Tanzania were secure,
as a consequence both of having a degree of ideological affinity and
of having cooperated in struggles against colonial rule. Relations
with Swaziland, Zambia, and Malawi, although less intimate, were
still friendly and cooperative. All of these countries, plus three additional states (Angola, Botswana, and Lesotho) formed the Southern
African Development Coordination Conference (SADCC), which
first came together in 1979 for the purpose of reducing South
Africa's economic domination in the area and promoting economic
development of its members. The transportation and communication sectors were adopted as priority areas of cooperation. The
Southern African Transport and Communications Commission was
set up with its secretariat in Maputo to supervise a series of projects,
among the first of which were the rehabilitation of the railroad line

from the port of Nacala to the border with Malawi and increased capacity of the ports of Beira and Maputo to facilitate their use by other SADCC members.

Mozambique played a prominent supportive role in the Zimbabwean independence struggle, allowing the ZANU forces under Robert Mugabe to use its territory for military bases, acting as a conduit for arms shipments from the communist countries, and receiving civilian refugees from the fighting. In 1976 Mozambique closed its border with Southern Rhodesia in observance of the UN embargo against the latter's illegal white regime. Southern Rhodesia's rail links to Beira and Maputo were thereby severed; the cost to Mozambique in lost revenues and jobs was estimated at the equivalent of over US$500 million. It was partly the economic distress brought on by the Rhodesian civil war that induced Machel to bring pressure on the Patriotic Front coalition of Mugabe's ZANU and Joshua Nkomo's Zimbabwe African People's Union to accept the compromises that preceded adoption of a British-sponsored constitution and Zimbabwean independence in April 1980.

Less than a year later, in January 1981, Zimbabwe and Mozambique negotiated a defense and security agreement, which stated that an attack by South Africa on either country would be regarded as an attack on both. Rebels of the RNM concentrated their operations against transport links between Mozambican ports and landlocked Zimbabwe and repeatedly damaged the oil pipeline that delivered products from the refinery at Beira. Several hundred Zimbabwe troops were introduced into Mozambique in 1982 to help protect the pipeline from attack.

Tanzania, under the leadership of Julius K. Nyerere, has continued to be a close ally of the FRELIMO leaders in spite of different interpretations of how socialist principles should be applied in an African setting. It is doubtful that FRELIMO could have existed, let alone flourished, during the long years of guerrilla warfare without Tanzanian support, based on its intense opposition to colonial rule in Africa. The northern neighbor provided a haven in its capital for senior FRELIMO officials, camps and education centers for the war's refugees, training bases and supply routes for its army, and some forms of military aid.

Tanzania and Mozambique have established a Joint Cooperation Commission with eight cabinet ministers on each side to strengthen bilateral cooperation in such areas as banking, health, finance, and trade. The two countries planned to introduce a free-trade area on a progressive basis beginning in 1984. The significance of such a step is likely to be limited at first, in part as a consequence of poor land communications between them. Tanzania is also reported to be helping Mozambique in its struggle against the RNM by supplying instructors for the military academy at Nampula.

Relations with Zambia have also evolved in a harmonious manner. The use of Zambia as a secure base was of strategic importance to FRELIMO's military victories in the early 1970s. The ideology of Zambia's ruling party has had little affinity, however, with the Marxism-Leninism of FRELIMO. The strongest bond between the two countries has been mutual interest in secure access to the sea for Zambia's trade through Mozambique. Agreement on a joint cooperation commission similar to the one with Tanzania was concluded in 1976.

FRELIMO resented the absence of support from Malawi during the liberation struggle and Malawi's continued diplomatic relations with Portugal under the threat of Portuguese interference with Malawi's external trade through Mozambican ports. Since independence there have been recurrent reports that Malawi was lending support to FUMO, Africa Livre, or other anti-FRELIMO groups. The two countries have remained at opposite ends of the African political spectrum; Malawi's president, H. Kamuzu Banda, has been one of the most conservative of Africa's leaders and the only one who has maintained relations with South Africa. As of 1983 Malawi was reported to be cooperating with Mozambique against the insurgents of the RNM, although Mozambican officials conceded that the lengthy mountainous boundary area between the two countries, inhabited by the same ethnic group on both sides of the border, made policing difficult.

A special kinship is felt with the other Portuguese-speaking countries of Africa. Two of these, Angola and Guinea-Bissau, are tied to Mozambique by a common colonial experience and a common struggle to overthrow Portuguese rule. The FRELIMO leaders have regarded the Popular Movement for the Liberation of Angola (Movimento Popular de Liberação de Angola—MPLA) as Africa's only other true Marxist-Leninist movement, and therefore the two have been close ideological partners. The five former Portuguese African colonies—Angola, Cape Verde, Guinea-Bissau, Mozambique, and São Tomé and Príncipe—have held several summit conferences in an effort to coordinate their diplomatic policies and to agree on measures for economic and trade collaboration.

### South Africa
At independence in 1975 Mozambique found itself in a paradoxical relationship with South Africa, a state whose political, social, and economic system was radically at odds with its own.

South Africa was a capitalist-oriented country ruled by the white minority of its inhabitants; its nonwhite majority was consigned to an inferior status. In the light of its own history, Mozambique could hardly refuse its support to black nationalist forces ranged against South Africa's apartheid system. Economic considerations, however, made a total breach impracticable. Maputo had long served as a seaport for the major industrial and mining zone of South Africa. This transit trade, combined with the use of Mozambique's rails and ports by Zimbabwe and other countries of the region, was a decisive factor in Mozambique's colonial economy. Moreover, South Africa had long been Mozambique's second-ranking trading partner. Mozambique's foreign exchange earnings were dependent to a considerable degree on the wages paid to over 100,000 of its citizens working under contract in South African mines. Under a long-standing arrangement, a portion of the miners' earnings was remitted in gold to the government in Maputo. Owing to the surging free market price of gold during the mid-1970s, gold was for a time the young nation's primary source of foreign exchange, offsetting the postindependence decline in exports (see Economic Overview, ch. 3).

After its initial dismay at the assumption of power by a communist movement in a neighboring country where it had so many interests, South Africa found it advantageous to maintain selective economic ties. Although continued contact with the despised Pretoria government was even more distasteful for the Maputo authorities, they too felt constrained to adopt a pragmatic course. Diplomatic relations were out of the question; South African shipments were allowed to continue through Maputo, although on a reduced scale owing to a combination of political and technical problems. A handful of South African specialists were stationed at the port to expedite transshipments. An agreement reached in 1979 provided a large South African credit for rehabilitation of the railroad and loading facilities and for the purchase of new equipment. An increase in transshipments well in excess of preindependence levels was foreseen. The number of miners offered contracts was sharply reduced but was eventually stabilized at about 40,000. In addition, perhaps as many as 100,000 Mozambicans were illegally in South Africa as farm and domestic laborers. The reimbursement terms for the miners were renegotiated in 1978 to prevent the Mozambican government from taking further advantage of the skyrocketing market price of gold. Another factor in the relationship was the giant Cahora Bassa hydroelectric project, which could supply South Africa with up to 10 percent of its total electrical energy needs—although not on a regular basis because of RNM attacks. (It seemed paradoxical that South Africa would fail to use its influence with the RNM to prevent sabotage of the power line. One possible explanation was that the harm done to Mozambique's economy outweighed the inconvenience to South Africa.)

Mozambique had become a haven for exiled activists of the outlawed ANC, notably its president, General Oliver Tambo, and Joe Slovo, the white communist heading the military wing. Maputo officials claimed that neither training bases nor transit camps had been granted to ANC followers in its territory. Moreover, ANC members could be accepted as refugees, but it was too risky to allow them to use Mozambican territory as a launching pad for guerrilla operations against South Africa. However, the growing number of ANC bombings and sabotage in South Africa during the early 1980s had led to South African reprisals in the form of commando raids and air strikes on sites in the Maputo area claimed to be centers for ANC agents and saboteurs. Mozambique accused South Africa of being responsible for heightened RNM activity as part of the pressure on it to curb ANC activity.

In early 1984 the security situation in southern Africa suddenly assumed a new shape. South Africa had adopted a more aggressive diplomacy aimed at moderating conflict with its black neighbors while at the same time denying foreign sanctuaries to the ANC and other dissident groups. Mounting economic distress and the advances by the RNM compelled Mozambique to be receptive to the South African approaches. Talks that had begun in late 1982 had shown little progress until January 1984 when four working groups composed of high officials from both sides were established to consider security questions, tourism, economic matters, and the existing agreement on the Cahora Bassa power complex. Subsequent meetings of cabinet-level delegations in Maputo and Cape Town culminated in an agreement of nonagression and good neighborliness, known as the Nkomati accord, on March 16, 1984. The intent of the accord was to prevent operations by the ANC from originating on Mozambican soil and to terminate South African support to the RNM (see External Concerns, ch. 5). Initially at least, attacks by the RNM did not abate, although Mozambican leaders declared that they were satisfied that the South African government was living up to its commitments under the agreement.

*Government leaders meeting in a special railroad coach before signing the Nkomati accord; seated (left to right) are Mozambique's foreign minister Chissano, President Machel, an interpreter, South Africa's foreign minister Roelof F. ("Pik") Botha, Prime Minister P.W. Botha, and interpreter.*

*President Machel introducing Prime Minister Botha to members of the Mozambican cabinet at the Nkomati accord ceremony*

*President Machel and Prime Minister Botha acknowledge a salute
at the colorful ceremony that followed the signing of the
Nkomati accord on the two countries' common border*

*Rail line at Mozambican-South African border near
Komati River, March 16, 1984*

*Photographs courtesy Embassy of South Africa, Washington*

231

## Portugal

A foundation for generally good relations between Portugal and Mozambique was established by the accord on Mozambican independence signed at Lusaka on September 7, 1974, and the Treaty of General Cooperation, concluded after independence, dealing with economic assistance and cooperation in scientific and technical affairs. Political and ideological differences nevertheless hindered the normalization of relations. Most black Mozambicans found it hard to forget the injustices of colonial rule. The government in Maputo objected to the fact that Lisbon was a center of RNM propaganda activity. Another major source of tension was the existence in Portugal of a large community of former residents of Mozambique who had fled FRELIMO's rule or had been forced to leave suddenly during the mass expulsions of 1977. Resentful of the losses they had suffered, they formed a bloc capable of influencing Portuguese politics. The leaders of the Portuguese Socialist Party had long supported self-determination for Portugal's African colonies, even when such a stand exposed them to harassment and accusations of treason from the government of longtime dictator António de Oliveira Salazar. Nevertheless, when the Socialists came to power, the FRELIMO leaders regarded them as "reactionary," openly preferring to associate with the Portuguese Communist Party.

The cool and sometimes tense relations between the two governments began to thaw in 1980 when Portugal dropped claims for compensation for nationalized property as part of its policy of reconciliation with former African colonies. Mozambique had vigorously rejected these demands, making counterclaims based on "150 years of colonial pillage." Portuguese president António Ramalho Eanes had won the gradual cooperation of the right-of-center government for these policies after it came to power in 1979, in spite of the influence of former settler elements still hostile to FRELIMO. The symbolic turning point was the state visit to Mozambique by Eanes, accompanied by a large contingent of Portuguese businessmen, in November 1981. A joint commission was formed to encourage cooperation on trade, health, and other matters. Agreement was reached on Portuguese investment in a glass factory, management of tourist hotels, a credit line for the import of consumer goods and pharmaceuticals, and participation by Portugal and other West European countries in rehabilitating a key rail line. A line of credit was set up to cover the wages of Portuguese "cooperants" (technicians) and to construct housing for them.

In a step interpreted as revealing Mozambique's dissatisfac-

tion with the level and suitability of military assistance from the
Soviet Union and Eastern Europe, Machel concluded a protocol
on military cooperation with Lisbon as well. Initially, Portugal
was to accept Mozambican cadets for an officer training course, to
build barracks in Mozambique, and to supply a limited amount of
light weapons and other equipment.

### Other West European Countries

In its dealings with the West, Mozambique at first regarded
without suspicion only the Scandinavian nations, for these countries alone had provided aid in substantial amounts to FRELIMO
during the war years and had consistently opposed Portugal's position at the UN in defense of its colonial policies. The United
States and other member states of the North Atlantic Treaty
Organization (NATO) were looked on by Maputo as sympathetic
to Portugal, and their supply of armaments to enable Portugal to
meet its NATO commitments was deemed to be contributing to
Portugal's ability to deal with the FRELIMO insurgency.
Ideologically, the Scandinavian countries were considered to be
socialist inclined and therefore sympathetic to the FRELIMO
movement, whereas other NATO countries were identified with
the capitalist bloc.

Sweden and, to a lesser extent, other Scandinavian countries
remained leading suppliers of assistance in the early 1980s, concentrating their activities on projects in energy, agriculture,
forestry, education, and telecommunications. Sweden reportedly
provided Mozambique more grant aid than any other country.
Among other major projects in which they were involved, France
and Italy were providing the equivalent of US$120 million in
credits for construction of a power line to link Cahora Bassa to the
northern reaches of Mozambique. A large SADCC project being
carried out by France and Portugal (with credit financing equal to
US$200 million from France, Portugal, and Canada) involved
rehabilitation of the 615 kilometers of rail line between the port of
Nacala and the Malawi border.

British relations with Mozambique were favorably affected
by London's decisive role in ending the war in Southern Rhodesia
and the successful transition to independence of Zimbabwe under
a black-majority government. Britain, in turn, acknowledged the
practical contribution of Machel in urging the Patriotic Front to
accept the proposed settlement. London has extended aid to
Mozambique on the basis of interest-free loans for use in the
transport sector, for power plants, and for rehabilitation of the
sugar industry; grants of food have been provided to help deal

with problems of famine and malnutrition.

The Netherlands had also committed itself to a significant level of aid to Mozambique, providing engineering services and equipment in support of SADCC plans to build modern storage and loading facilities at Beira and to enable the port to handle large-capacity coal carriers. Assistance from the Federal Republic of Germany (West Germany) was delayed by Maputo's reluctance to accept treaty language acknowledging the status of West Berlin in the form insisted on by the Bonn authorities. After the Mozambicans acceded to the West German position in 1982, both bilateral assistance and aid from the EEC were unblocked. In the same year about 44,000 tons of cereals plus other foodstuffs were committed by the EEC. Maputo also declared its intention (along with Angola) to participate in negotiations on the 1986–90 Lomé Convention (Lomé III), which will be the main framework for aid from the EEC to developing countries of Africa, the Caribbean, and the Pacific. Mozambique had previously remained aloof from this group, apparently out of concern that closer association implied a political commitment to West.

**The United States**

The United States extended diplomatic recognition to Mozambique upon its independence in 1975. (During Portuguese colonial rule, it had been represented at Lourenço Marques by a consul general.) FRELIMO leaders did not invite United States officials to attend the independence ceremony, although Americans considered friendly to the country were invited personally. The initial reserve in the Mozambican attitude was attributed in part to resentment over the ties that the United States maintained with Portugal. Although United States military equipment supplied to Portugal was limited to that needed to fulfill the latter's NATO obligations, FRELIMO objected that insufficient effort was made to prevent Portugal from diverting this aid to its colonial wars in Africa. United States Export-Import Bank loans and other aid announced in conjunction with renewal of United States base rights in the Azores in 1971 were also regarded as indirectly supporting the Portuguese campaign against the liberation forces.

An initial grant of US$10 million in aid was made to Mozambique in 1976 as part of an effort to compensate Mozambique for losses incurred by the closure of its borders in support of UN sanctions against Southern Rhodesia. The United States foreign aid act of 1978, however, was passed with a prohibition against the use of funds for Mozambique. This action was taken at the initiative of a number of congressmen who contended that Mozambique was falling under Soviet control and that FRELIMO was guilty of political repression and harassment of Portuguese residents.

Nevertheless, in December 1980 the United States secretary of state, Edmund Muskie, signed a waiver of the prohibition on the grounds that such aid would be in the foreign policy interests of the United States. This action had been preceded by a number of indications from Maputo of a greater readiness to cooperate with the West. Mozambique's constructive participation in the negotiations leading to Zimbabwean independence and its subsequent role among the front-line states in negotiations over Namibia further improved the atmosphere between the two countries. In March 1981 the expulsion of four members of the staff of the American embassy in Maputo on charges of "espionage, subversion, and interference" caused the United States to suspend plans to provide development aid and to assign a new ambassador. The Maputo authorities claimed that embassy officials had been supplying South Africa with information on ANC residences and during the Zimbabwean conflict had supplied information on the location of refugee camps to the Rhodesian government. The United States denied the charges, saying the expulsions were linked to an incident in which an American diplomat in Maputo was kidnapped by Cuban officials in a failed attempt to recruit him as a spy.

Relations between the two countries have slowly reverted to a more normal pattern. Assistant Secretary of State for African Affairs Chester A. Crocker said in early 1983 that "the utter incapacity of Marxist economics to cope with the problems of a developing country, and the conspicuous inability of the Soviet Union to assist Mozambique with security and political problems stemming from its isolation, led to indications that the Mozambican government wished to reestablish communication with the United States. We responded by making clear that we were interested in a positive relationship based upon respect for each other's interests and were willing to engage in building bridges between us based on mutual respect." In late 1983 the ambassadorial post in Maputo was again filled, and a Mozambican embassy was opened in Washington. This would, said Crocker, "help foster this fragile dialogue" between the two nations.

The United States has continued to supply humanitarian aid in the form of emergency grains and dairy products, valued at about US$10 million annually, to help Mozambique overcome the ravages of the worst drought in its history. Supplemental shipments were expected to be provided in fiscal year (FY) 1984 in the light of reports of actual starvation. The United States was the most important customer for Mozambique's exports, chiefly in the form of cashew nuts and sugar. In spite of efforts by Mozambique to interest foreign investors, the only direct American investment was a nominal share and a technical assistance agreement by the General Tire Company in a tire factory that began operations in 1979. In 1983 it was announced that a partnership of Esso Oil Exploration Company and Royal Dutch Shell would begin test drillings for oil in Cabo Delgado Province.

## Communist Countries

On most international questions aside from those of the African continent, Mozambique has associated itself with the position of the Soviet Union. It has been the beneficiary of a considerable amount of military assistance from the Soviet Union and the countries of Eastern Europe. The Soviet Union has provided most of FRELIMO's arms since independence, although China was a prime supplier of both matériel and training during the decade of guerrilla warfare that preceded national sovereignty (see Foreign Military Assistance, ch. 5). In addition to the tangible contributions it has received, Mozambique acknowledges the importance of its ideological affinity with the communist nations. This kinship is recorded in the Constitution, which states that "Mozambique consolidates and develops solidarity with its natural allies, the socialist countries, solidarity forged in the struggle for national independence."

The treaty of friendship and cooperation signed in March 1977 is the cornerstone for Maputo's relations with the Soviet Union. Similar agreements have subsequently been negotiated with Cuba, Bulgaria, East Germany, Romania, and the Democratic People's Republic of Korea (North Korea). The agreement with Moscow pledges that, in the event of "situations arising that threaten peace or lead to an outbreak of war," both countries will immediately get in touch to "coordinate their positions in the interests of eliminating the threat that has arisen or restoring peace." In spite of the RNM insurgency and several violations of Mozambican borders by South Africa, this clause has had little practical effect, although some observers have interpreted periodic visits by Soviet naval units as reminders of Moscow's commitment to Mozambique's security.

Soviet economic aid has been modest, focusing more on technical assistance, although it has furnished some emergency foodstuffs. In cooperation with Bulgaria the Soviet Union has developed a 200,000-hectare irrigated area in the Limpopo River

*President Machel (center) meeting with Soviet leader Leonid
Brezhnev (second from right) and his government
advisers during a visit to Moscow in November 1980
for economic discussions*

valley. It has engaged in mineral exploration and has helped
launch several industrial projects. A floating dry dock has been
installed at the port of Matola adjacent to Maputo for the overhaul
of domestic vessels and ships of the Soviet fishing and naval fleets.
The valuable fishing rights granted to the Soviets in Mozambican
waters have been compensated for by deliveries of lesser quality
frozen fish to Mozambique.

   The quantities and financial terms of Soviet aid are not made
public. It is believed, however, that the exchange of goods (which
totaled US$60 million, or less than 10 percent of Mozambique's
two-way trade in 1981) favors the Soviet Union; the deficits
accrued by Mozambique are transformed into hard currency
credits on favorable terms. Moscow supplies trucks, agricultural
equipment, and industrial machinery in return for cashew nuts,
sisal, citrus fruit, tea, and other products.

   As of 1981 a total of 550 Soviet and East European military
trainers and technicians, as well as 1,000 Cuban military personnel, were estimated to be in the country. A further 1,800 techni-

cians and specialists from the Soviet Union and Eastern Europe were engaged in economic aid and development activities. Roughly 1,000 Cubans were active in the economic sector, principally in sugarcane production and in the building industry. Cuban doctors have helped relieve the critical shortage of medical personnel. More than 2,500 Mozambican students were in the Soviet Union and Eastern Europe at the end of 1981, a large proportion of them located in East Germany. Another 1,000 Mozambican youth of primary- and high-school age were studying in Cuba. In 1984 longer term professionals and technical training of five to six years' duration was being provided in the Soviet Union for 300 Mozambicans. Trade and aid relationships with East Germany appeared to be developing particularly rapidly in the early 1980s. Among other projects, an East German contingent of 100 specialists was reported to be supervising the opening of a coal mine at Moatize in northwest Tete Province. An East German loan on favorable terms, equivalent to US$32 million, was provided for equipment and technical assistance in connection with a large new textile plant at Macuba in Zambezia Province.

Mozambique's association with China has not advanced at the same pace as with other communist countries, owing in part to political differences and in part to China's inability or unwillingness to supply aid on a scale similar to that of the Soviet Union and Eastern Europe. China's support of the opponents of Machel's close allies of the MPLA during the Angolan civil war of 1975–76 had soured relations for a time. The 1977 treaty with the Soviet Union and the identification of Machel with virtually all Soviet foreign policy positions were also found provocative by the Chinese. The Chinese were conspicuously absent from the Third Party Congress of FRELIMO in 1977, although they were represented at the Fourth Party Congress in 1983 at a less senior level than other communist countries. During the Fourth Party Congress Machel referred to the "traditional fraternal relations of cooperation" with China, but the expression chosen lacked the warmth of his references to the Soviet Union, Eastern Europe, North Korea, and Cuba.

Moscow's reaction to the Nkomati accord between Mozambique and South Africa was muted. The Soviet media expressed suspicion over the fact that South Africa was pursuing a policy of reconciliation with the black nations of southern Africa and that the United States was encouraging this trend. Nevertheless, cooperation, exchanges, and official visits between Mozambique and the Soviet Union and other communist states continued as though no breach had occurred.

\*   \*   \*

In *Mozambique: From Colonialism to Revolution, 1900–1982*, Allen and Barbara Isaacmani provide a sympathetic account of Mozambique's emergence as an independent nation, including such aspects as the FRELIMO party, the conduct of elections, the legal system, and foreign relations. The chapter on Mozambique in David and Marina Ottaway's *Afrocommunism* analyzes the distinctive features of FRELIMO within the spectrum of Marxist-Leninist systems. Among numerous press treatments of internal conditions in Mozambique, the series by Jean-Pierre Langellier appearing in the *Guardian* in late 1980 and early 1981 is especially informative. Material from Mozambican journals, official releases, and addresses by political leaders is available in ongoing issues of the Foreign Broadcast Information Service's *Daily Report: Middle East and Africa*. Mozambique's foreign policy can be traced through two articles in *World Today*, one by Robert DA. Henderson (July 1978) and one by Norman Mac-Queen (January 1984). (For further information and complete citations, see Bibliography.)

# Chapter 5. National Security

*Walls of São Sebastião fortress built by the Portuguese on Ilha de Moçambique in the sixteenth century*

DURING THE TWO DECADES since its insurrection against colonial rule, Mozambique has enjoyed only brief respites from violence and conflict. Soon after independence in 1975, the revolutionary regime was plunged into a three-year involvement on the side of other black nationalists in their guerrilla warfare against the white minority government of neighboring Southern Rhodesia. In retaliation, Rhodesian intelligence agents operating in collusion with former Portuguese settlers organized an opposition movement, the Mozambican National Resistance, which mounted counterinsurgency actions against Rhodesian guerrillas in Mozambique as well as more conventional operations against the new Marxist-Leninist government in Maputo. When Southern Rhodesia became black-ruled Zimbabwe in 1980, the main source of support for the Mozambican insurgents shifted to South Africa. In spite of several successful individual operations by the Mozambican armed forces, by early 1984 the fighting had extended to every area of rural Mozambique except the far north. Acts of sabotage and attacks on communication facilities and the transport system had had a disabling effect on the already weakened economy.

To compound Mozambique's security problems, South Africa had repeatedly demonstrated its ability to mount damaging raids against the capital city of Maputo and its suburbs. Aimed primarily at discouraging the African National Congress from using Mozambican territory as a base for its terrorist actions in South Africa, these raids nevertheless underscored Mozambique's vulnerability to South Africa's overwhelming military power. In an effort to gain a respite from the insurgents' pressure in order to deal with the country's mounting economic distress, Mozambique's president Samora Moises Machel came to a formal agreement, known as the Nkomati accord, with the South African government in March 1984. Both sides committed themselves to denying the use of their territory for violence or agression against the other. For the government in Pretoria, this meant abandoning its support for the Mozambican insurgents. For the administration in Maputo, it meant curbing the use of its territory as a sanctuary for black nationalists from South Africa. It was not immediately apparent whether the accord between the two countries would prove to be a decisive landmark for the security of southern Africa or only a pause in a prolonged struggle.

Dependent mainly on the Soviet Union, Eastern Europe, and other communist countries for equipment and training during the liberation struggle, Mozambique continued to receive similar aid after independence in remodeling its armed forces along conventional lines. The resulting structure and armaments have not proved to be well adapted, however, to dealing with guerrilla operations carried out by insurgents in remote areas of the country. Accordingly, the national military establishment's conventional forces have been supplemented by new counter-insurgency units under the direct control of provincial military commanders. Militia units of increasing size and unknown effectiveness have been formed to aid in containing the insurgency. Soviet, East European, and Cuban advisers have been present in substantial numbers, but the low level of education and the inadequate training among the two-year conscripts who have formed the bulk of the armed forces have remained serious problems. Apparently dissatisfied with the variety and amount of Soviet aid, Mozambique initiated efforts in the early 1980s to supplement it by seeking contributions from certain countries of Western Europe. Initially, only Portugal had responded positively to these overtures.

## State of National Security

By the end of 1983 the country faced a spreading threat from the Mozambican National Resistance (Resistência Nacional Moçambicana—RNM, sometimes referred to as RENAMO), a force purportedly composed of disaffected elements of Mozambican society and of the ruling party itself but generally regarded to be dependent on external support. The RNM was still few in number in relation to the size of the country and inferior to the Mozambique military and security forces in personnel, weaponry, and equipment. In individual engagements, however, it was often better armed than the government units and more effective on a man-to-man basis. Operating as small guerrilla units, the RNM had been able to conduct damaging hit-and-run operations aimed at the country's vulnerable rail, road, power, and communications lines and the state farms and communal villages. One security analyst has suggested that the Mozambican armed forces would need about 85,000 troops to suppress the growth of the RNM.

Since independence Mozambique has been associated with the other black-ruled countries of southern Africa through a series of multilateral and bilateral understandings that have a common objective of reducing their dependency on South Africa, a country that exercises a dominant influence in the region owing to its economic and military superiority. Mozambique has been used as a safe haven by the African National Congress (ANC), the group of South African black nationalists leading the resistance against the apartheid system. Subjected to sporadic terrorist-style attacks from the ANC, South Africa has retaliated by violating Mozambican territory in raids aimed at ANC centers. At the same time, it had contributed assistance to the RNM with the presumed purpose of deterring the Machel government from harboring the ANC and perhaps contributing to destabilization of Mozambique as a country dangerous to South African interests because of its Marxist ideology and Soviet ties.

The March 1984 agreement on nonagression and good neighborliness between South Africa and Mozambique, known as the Nkomati accord, in effect committed South Africa to refraining from further incursions and from supporting the RNM; Mozambique was to restrain the ANC. Together with new measures of economic cooperation being discussed by the two countries, the accord was expected to bring much needed relief to the government in Maputo. South Africa's termination of its aid to the RNM was expected to be a crippling blow to the Mozambican insurgents, whose ability to sustain themselves without a foreign patron had not been tested. But the RNM's attacks intensified in the period following the signing of the accord.

### The Mozambican National Resistance

Until early 1984 the RNM accounted for most of the guerrilla opposition to the ruling political party, the Front for the Liberation of Mozambique (Frente de Libertação de Moçambique—FRELIMO). The FRELIMO regime and many of its non-Mozambican supporters claimed that the RNM was a puppet of the South African government and, before 1980, of the Southern Rhodesian government and that it existed only to further the goals of these white minority regimes. The insurgents and their supporters argued that the RNM was an indigenous movement opposed to communist totalitarianism. In spite of the stigma of its connection with the apartheid government in Pretoria, the RNM's existence was in part a response to widespread dissatisfaction with FRELIMO's performance. The RNM seemed to be demonstrating that it could function despite the loss of South Africa's military and financial support that resulted from the Nkomati accord. But unless it could take greater advantage of the disenchantment with the Mozambican government, the movement's continued viability was uncertain.

## The Rhodesian Phase

In conjunction with Portuguese who had fled independent Mozambique, the Central Intelligence Organization (CIO) of Southern Rhodesia established the RNM in 1976. The CIO's interest lay in gathering information about the Zimbabwe African National Union (ZANU), which was infiltrating Southern Rhodesia from bases within Mozambique. The Portuguese included Jorge Jardim, a wealthy businessman; Orlando Christina, a former secret police officer and personal secretary to Jardim; and Domingos Arouca, a plantation owner. These men and others like them were not ready to concede FRELIMO's dominance in Mozambique, and they were not prepared to renounce their long association with Mozambique. The CIO and the Portuguese recruited still other Portuguese settlers, black troops who had served in colonial police and counterinsurgency units, and disgruntled former members of FRELIMO. The last group included such men as Andre Matzangaissa, an ex-FRELIMO platoon commander, and Afonso Dhlakama, both of whom would soon gain public recognition as leaders of the RNM.

The Rhodesians furnished a base in Bindura and radio facilities for the insurgents' Voice of Free Africa. Operating initally from Bindura and later from two other camps in Southern Rhodesia, the RNM established bases in two mountainous, forested areas in Mozambique—along the western border zone and in the Gorongosa Game Reserve. Most of the RNM's operations in this period occurred in Manica, Tete, and Gaza provinces, all adjacent to the 600-kilometer frontier with Southern Rhodesia. Occasionally the RNM would attempt operations well beyond the border, e.g., in Beira or Maputo, but it spent much of its time attacking commercial settlements and so-called reeducation camps, using small sabotage teams for these purposes. Employing peaceful means, such as offering food, the RNM infiltrated ZANU camps and "worked" villages to gather intelligence for the CIO. At other times in cooperation with Rhodesian special forces, the RNM engaged ZANU forces in Mozambique and helped the Rhodesians by masking their cross-border incursions. Such incursions were generally regarded as RNM guerrilla attacks and thus served to deflect some international criticism of Southern Rhodesia.

Despite its general success, the RNM encountered several setbacks before early 1980 when Robert Mugabe's newly independent Zimbabwe put an end to that country's support of the insurgents. These setbacks curtailed RNM activity for a time, but they lulled

FRELIMO into believing that the RNM threat had passed. In October 1979 Mozambique's army, known as the People's Forces for the Liberation of Mozambique (Forças Populares da Libertação de Moçambique—FPLM), supported by artillery and aircraft, had successfully attacked the RNM's main camp in the Gorongosa Game Reserve, and the RNM's leader, Matzangaissa, was killed in action. Disputes over leadership in the next months led to a shoot-out between rival factions at a Zimbabwean base in June 1980. In early 1984 Evo Fernandes, previously the RNM's European director, became the movement's secretary general; Dhlakama directed ground operations. Fernandes succeeded Orlando Christina, who was killed by unknown assassins.

### The South African Phase

Zimbabwe officially became independent in April 1980, thus depriving the RNM of bases in and support from that country. But it was not until October 1980 that the RNM and its Voice of Free Africa were firmly established in South Africa's Transvaal Province, having been airlifted there by South African military aircraft. South Africa had been giving the RNM support during the Rhodesian phase, but it had now become the dominant supplier of matériel, training, and technical help. Its support reportedly included establishing bases at a number of places in Transvaal Province, setting up radio links between various RNM units, conducting aerial reconnaissance of government forces, and infiltrating RNM units into and out of Mozambique. Other sources of support probably included wealthy former colonists living in Portugal. The Mozambique government claimed that South Africa not only aided the insurgents but also determined its targets, offering in evidence RNM prisoners and documents it reportedly had captured that told of the South African Defense Forces (SADF) imposing strategy on the RNM.

RNM groups based in South Africa entered Mozambique by land (usually through South Africa's Kruger National Park), by air in SADF transport aircraft or helicopters, and by sea via submarines or fast patrol boats that took advantage of Mozambique's long coastline and the limited Mozambican naval capability. In mid-1983 Mozambican officials claimed that RNM units were operating out of four Malawian bases, apparently without the permission of the Malawian authorities.

A number of observers have suggested that South Africa supported the RNM only to harass the Mozambicans and was not necessarily interested in toppling the FRELIMO regime. In this view, its interest lay in reaffirming Mozambique's economic

*Insurgency forces of the*
*Mozambican National Resistance movement*
*Courtesy RNM*

dependence on South Africa and in ending Mozambique's role as a base for and a supporter of the ANC. To this end, South African-supported RNM operations had the effect of amplifying the economic pressure on Mozambique, diverting money and manpower to a costly and protracted conflict, disrupting a fragile rural economy, and sabotaging the transportation infrastructure. From this perspective the Nkomati accord of March 1984 was precisely the best reward Pretoria could have wished for in undertaking sponsorship of the RNM.

### Organization and Operations

As of early 1984, Dhlakama was both commander in chief of the RNM's forces and head of the RNM governing body, the 12-member executive council. According to the RNM, the movement's deputy leader (and, in 1984, information director) was Lieutenant Adriano Bomba, a former Mozambican air force pilot. Christina, the RNM's principal contact with South Africa, had been given the title of secretary general as head of the political wing of the movement in early 1983. Not long thereafter, he was found shot to death at his home near Pretoria, South Africa. Evo Fernandes, the Lisbon-based spokesman for the RNM, subsequently assumed the post of secretary general. Under the commander in chief were generals for the northern, central, and southern sections of Mozambique; commanders of regional and subregional sectors; operational zone commanders; company commanders; platoon commanders; and section commanders, whose rank was apparently equivalent to that of a sergeant. Estimates in late 1983 and early 1984 placed the RNM's total personnel strength at about 12,000, of which two-thirds were combatants; all but a few were black Mozambicans. Included among the porters, radio operators, and other noncombatants were a number of women. White South African personnel apparently did not fight alongside the RNM, although they were said to have carried out specialized operations. For example, several waterborne raids against Beira's oil storage tanks and navigation buoys seemed too sophisticated to have been accomplished by RNM personnel, although the insurgents claimed responsibility.

The RNM usually traveled in groups of 30 to 200 men, hitting isolated targets, burning crops, and physically intimidating villagers before disappearing. There had been a tendency in late 1983 to operate with smaller forces, presumably to permit a larger number of sorties and to avoid the possibility of a large-scale defeat at the hands of government forces. There were few extended battles or front lines, and movement within Mozambique was usually by foot, aided by sophisticated communications between units. Before the Nkomati accord, movement was often aided by South African air reconnaissance and air drops of supplies.

The RNM's concentration on disrupting the economic infrastructure has included attacks on development projects (where European expatriates have been kidnapped), state farms and communal villages, and difficult-to-defend targets, such as the Beira-Mutare oil pipeline, railroad lines, and highway traffic. One of the insurgents' major goals has been to cut off food supplies in order to increase urban discontent and to force FRELIMO to use precious foreign exchange to purchase imports. When attacking villages, the insurgents have generally appropriated foodstuffs and have targeted FRELIMO officials or anyone possibly affiliated with the national government, such as nurses and teachers. By relying on light weapons, by concentrating on lightly populated areas or poorly defended targets, e.g., rail lines or pipelines, and by not occupying the villages, the insurgents have usually avoided sustained contact with government troops. The assaults on communal villages and the state farms may have had a symbolic purpose, but they were mounted to confiscate food and to secure new recruits from disaffected areas. The RNM has tended to see these villages and farms as the expressions of FRELIMO's rural policies and, therefore, legitimate targets for attack.

### Constituency of the Resistance

The range and depth of the RNM's appeal to segments of the Mozambican population has been a matter of some controversy. The government and observers sympathetic to FRELIMO have argued that the Africans who have voluntarily joined the insurgency or positively supported it were interested in immediate rewards after FRELIMO's victory but did not obtain them or that they were persons of traditional status who were threatened by the policies of the regime. Included among these voluntary members or supporters were FRELIMO veterans who could not tolerate the rigid morality that characterized the party after independence or who expected and did not receive the benefits of FRELIMO's coming to power. Still others may have been deserters or persons who were placed (or feared being placed) in reeducation camps; some were candidates defeated in the 1977 elections. According to regime sympathizers, at least some of those who have fought with the RNM have done so only because they had been kidnapped and then forced to engage in antigovernment acts that made them vulnerable to FRELIMO retribution. They therefore continued to fight with the RNM for lack of an alternative. A few observers believe that some members of the RNM forces have been recruited by the simple expedient of paying high wages and bonuses for specific operations to young men who had not been able to get work in the South African mines and had little other prospect of earning money.

Observers who have noted a presumed RNM appeal to the self-interest of persons having traditional status also point to a tendency of the RNM to make explicitly ethnic appeals. The two kinds of appeals apparently were joined in the region of northern Manica and Sofala provinces where the RNM had made its first impact and where it continued in early 1984 to wield a good deal of influence. Before 1980, when the RNM operated among the largely Shona-speaking peoples of the area, they stressed the Shangaan leadership of FRELIMO. (In fact, the Shona-speaking area had neither contributed significant numbers of personnel to FRELIMO at any level during the struggle for independence nor had it been the locus of important encounters between FRE-LIMO and colonial forces.) The resistance movement's ethnic appeal had some force, particularly among chiefs and various religious figures who were scorned by the new regime. The RNM also emphasized the government's publicized opposition to bride-price, polygyny, and other indigenous practices. As the insurgents extended their operations to other provinces after 1980, they could no longer make a specific appeal to the Shona. It has been noted by some observers, however, that in early 1984 many of the commanders of RNM units in other provinces were Shona. It was also asserted that the Shona-speaking area in northern Manica and Sofala provinces, i.e., above the rail line between Beira and Mutare, was dominated by the RNM. Information of this kind could not be corroborated.

Most of the efforts to explain such appeal as the RNM is said to have for Mozambicans emphasized self-interest, ethnicity, and traditionalism or sheer coercion. The RNM, however, has claimed to be based on an anticommunist ideology and a non-authoritarian political order (see Opposition to FRELIMO, ch. 4). There have been no indications of the Mozambican population's responding to an abstract political appeal by the RNM. It was possible, however, that many Mozambicans were giving the resistance movement a degree of passive support simply as a response to the government's ineptness in the economic domain, to the RNM's distribution of scarce food and clothing supplies, and to FRELIMO's efforts to change the social order too quickly and radically (see Interethnic Relations; The Social Order, ch. 2).

**External Concerns**

The Machel regime's external security concerns have necessarily focused on South Africa, the dominant military power in southern Africa. The government in Pretoria has repeatedly demonstrated a willingness and capability to employ its forces in pursuit of political objectives outside its own territory. Relations between Mozambique and the five other states with which it shares common borders have been largely harmonious, based on closely meshed foreign policy interests, similar perceptions of the political situation in the region, and a lack of contentious issues of significant proportions. Political relations have been strengthened by joint participation in the Organization of African Unity (OAU), the informal alliance of African front-line states (see Glossary), and the Southern African Development Coordination Conference (SADCC), supplemented in some cases by bilateral treaties (see Neighboring Black African States, ch. 4). None of the black-ruled countries of southern Africa have ever had sufficient military strength to present Mozambique even a contingent source of concern, particularly taking into account the difficult terrain and transport factors that would discourage the movement of major bodies of conventional forces.

In the early 1980s the military superiority of the SADF over the other southern African countries, singly or combined, was especially apparent in such categories as combat aircraft, artillery, and armored fighting vehicles. But the superiority in numbers was less significant than the SADF's greater experience, higher level of education and training, and the quality of its arms (fig. 14). The SADF had demonstrated its ability to mount offensives over long distances and to occupy large areas against hostile forces. Mozambique shares about 500 kilometers of common border with South Africa, most of it close to the most heavily populated Mozambican areas and important transport lines, and Maputo lies less than 90 kilometers by rail and 120 kilometers by road from the frontier. Most of the land on the South African side of the border is encompassed within Kruger National Park, a vast game reserve easily patrolled by the SADF. Two major installations—the operational air base at Hoedspruit, equipped with figher aircraft, and the infantry training and reconnaissance commando base at Phalaborwa—are adjacent to the border area immediately west of the game park.

The SADF has acknowledged responsibility for three attacks against Mozambique between 1981 and 1983. These incursions were justified as being in self-defense, intended to discourage the ANC from mounting operations against South Africa from posi-

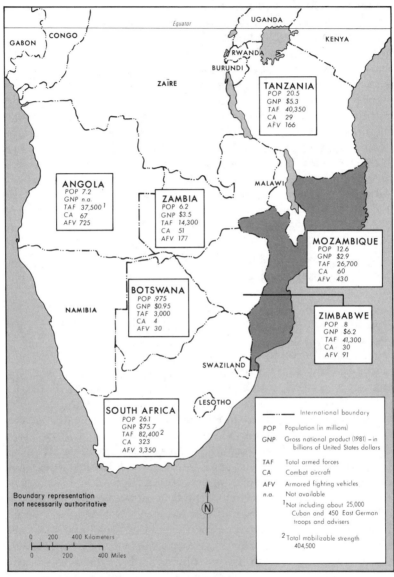

Source: Based on information from The Military Balance, 1983-84,
    London, 1983

*Figure 14. Balance of Power in Southern Africa, 1983*

tions in Mozambique. The first overt attack occurred in January 1981 when members of a South African reconnaissance commando unit drove across the Mozambican border to the Maputo suburb of Matola. The commandos killed 11 alleged ANC members before being airlifted back to their own country by helicopter. The SADF struck twice more at ANC complexes in 1983, both times declaring that its actions were in repsonse to terrorist bombings in South Africa. Although the damage from these attacks was narrowly contained and minimal casualties were inflicted, the extreme vulnerability of Mozambican defenses was fully demonstrated. Machel admitted that South Africa had complete information on his force's combat readiness, its deployments, and its defense systems. The first of the attacks in 1983, carried out by Impala fighter-bombers and Mirage fighters, employed low-altitude flight procedures, following a flight path similar to that of DC-10 commercial aircraft, thus preventing the use of Mozambique's heat-seeking missiles.

South Africa made its superiority over Mozambique's defenses manifest in other ways. The Machel government documented numerous violations of its country's airspace by the South African Air Force. Between January 1981 and July 1982, it claimed more than 70 air violations, most of which were presumably in connection with the supplying of the RNM. In spite of the fact that several of its squadrons were equipped with Soviet MiG fighters, the Mozambican air force did not attempt to become involved in air engagements. Ground fire was, however, directed at the SADF attackers. Early evidence of South Africa's direct support for RNM sabotage operations came in October 1981 when a reconnaissance commando operating out of Phalaborwa was killed while laying explosives on the Beira-Mutare rail line. The destruction in December 1982 of a depot at Beira used to store fuel for the Zimbabwean pipeline was ascribed to South African demolition experts. In 1982 Ruth First, a South African communist, prominent sociologist, and the wife of ANC military leader Joe Slovo, was killed by a letter bomb; it was widely assumed that South Africa was responsible. In early 1984 FRELIMO estimated that direct aggression by South Africa and the RNM had caused the equivalent of US$333 million in damage.

Before the Nkomati accord, the ANC had offices in Mozambique, and leading ANC officials (including Slovo) often transited through Maputo. During his visits, ANC president general Oliver Tambo was accorded honors similar to those for a head of state, and Mozambique had hailed the ANC as the sole legitimate representative of the South African people in international forums. In 1982 Machel stated that Mozambique and the ANC would "fight shoulder to shoulder until apartheid falls."

Up to 50 South African refugees entered Mozambique in any given month; some ANC members and recruits were usually among them. Most ANC members and sympathizers then traveled to Tanzania, Zambia, or Angola for military training. Estimates of the total number of ANC guerrillas ranged between 1,500 and 2,000. The Machel government claimed that it granted humanitarian, political, and diplomatic support to the ANC but that it did not permit the establishment of training bases and transit camps or the possession of weapons while ANC members were in Mozambique. South Africa, however, claimed that Mozambique had previously allowed the operation of two ANC military camps, one in the Mozambican lowlands near Ponta do Ouro and another 60 kilomters north near the Olifants River.

On March 16, 1984, Machel joined P.W. Botha, the prime minister of South Africa, at the frontier between the two countries to sign the Nkomati accord. By this treaty both countries agreed to resolve future disputes by peaceful means and undertook not to resort to threats or force against each other's territory. Specifically forbidden were sabotage, unwarranted concentrations of forces near each other's borders, and assistance to any state or group of states deployed against either signatory. Neither party was to allow its territories or air space to be used or transited by any other military forces, organizations, or individuals intent on committing acts of violence, terrorism, or aggression against the other. In executing this commitment, both parties were to prevent the use of bases, training centers, arms depots, command posts, telecommunications facilities, and broadcasting stations by such elements. Recruitment, abductions, the provision of logistic facilities, and acts of propaganda were similarly to be banned. The treaty provided for the appointment of a joint security commission to monitor its application. Meetings were held alternately in the two capitals under Mozambique's deputy defense minister, Sergio Vieira, and the South African police commissioner, General Johan Coetzee. In the first sessions the protection of the power line between the Cahora Bassa hydroelectric project and South Africa was the priority topic.

The signing of the accord had been preceded by more than a year of intermittent negotiations between Mozambique and South Africa that had focused primarily on economic issues. The scope of the nonaggression pact nevertheless came as a surprise in the region. Leaders of the other countries of southern Africa avoided associating themselves with Mozambique's rapproch-

*The signing of the Nkomati accord between Mozambique and*
*South Africa, March 16, 1984;*
*FPLM honor guard in background*
*Courtesy Embassy of South Africa, Washington*

ment with South Africa, and ANC leaders denounced it as helping
to perpetuate the detested white minority regime in South Africa.
Describing the accord as a "unique and significant movement in
our history [which] guarantees a solid and lasting peace between
the two neighboring countries," Machel portrayed it as a victory
for Mozambique and as acknowledgement by Pretoria that its
campaign of regional destablization and the overthrow of Mozambique's progressive, socialist system had failed.

The FRELIMO regime acted promptly to fulfill its obligations under the treaty. ANC members were ordered to move to
refugee camps or be resettled in other countries. Raids were conducted against ANC houses in search of weapons. It appeared that
none of the other black-ruled states bordering South Africa was
prepared to permit the ANC to use its territory for bases or infiltration, leaving the ANC with the dangerous prospect of having to
direct its campaign of subversion from within South Africa itself.

Machel saw the Nkomati accord as bringing peace to Mozambique and enabling the country to shift resources from military
spending to reconstruction and development. He described it as a
basic prerequisite to the healthy and normal development of

economic relations between the two countries. There was widespread understanding that Mozambique's strained economic and military circumstances had left it little alternative to seeking accommodation with South Africa, but some independent observers evaluated the treaty as a success for South Africa's policy of using military means to achieve political ends. Through the SADF's direct incursions of Mozambique and its aid to the RNM, the government in Pretoria had brought about a decisive setback to the ANC and a tightening of Mozambique's economic reliance on South Africa.

The Nkomati accord could lead to a prolonged period of peace and stability, enabling Mozambique to restore its economy and increase the effectiveness of its armed forces. It was by no means certain, however, that this would be the case. The question of whether South Africa would act in good faith to end its interference had not been tested, nor had the ability of the RNM to survive in the absence of substantial outside help. South Africa's apartheid policies had long generated unstable conditions in the region. It seemed unlikely, although not impossible, that two countries whose political interests and systems were ultimately incompatible could avoid future clashes during an extended period of mutually cooperative relations.

## The Armed Forces

The Machel government signed the Nkomati accord with Pretoria partly because Mozambique, using limited resources, was fighting against a guerrilla insurgency as well as guarding against conventional, South African-mounted military incursions. For some time Mozambique's dilemma had been that, whether it placed emphasis on developing conventional or counterinsurgency forces, South Africa had the resources and the political motivation to mount a counteracting effort.

The FPLM has demonstrated only limited capacity to conduct either conventional or counterinsurgency operations. FRELIMO won the liberation struggle not by defeating the Portuguese forces militarily but, along with liberation groups in other Portuguese colonies, by imposing economic and military strains on the colonial regime until a military-led coup in Portugal displaced the government in power. Although its capabilities improved during the Rhodesian civil war (1972-79), the FPLM was clearly no match for the forces of the Ian Smith government. There has never been a question of superiority in comparison with the forces of South Africa.

### General Development

FRELIMO began its military operations in 1964, carrying on the struggle until a cease-fire in 1974. Outmanned and outgunned by the Portuguese armed forces, FRELIMO relied during its liberation campaign on traditional guerrilla tactics, e.g., recoilless rifle or long-range mortar attacks, ambushes, and extensive use of landmines. Quick guerrilla strikes attempted to inflict the maximum damage in a minimum time before the attackers fled to the bush.

Eduardo Chivambu Mondlane, FRELIMO's founder and first president, and Machel, his successor, deliberately mixed troops of different Mozambican regions and ethnic groups during both training and operations. This integration lessened potential division arising from the fact that the majority of FRELIMO commanders came from the south—mostly Gaza and Maputo provinces. Most of the soldiers, often Maconde, came from Cabo Delgado, Tete, and Niassa provinces.

FRELIMO began simultaneously as a guerrilla army and a political party, and the army represented the state in liberated areas. The army, in Machel's words, was "the most dynamic and conscious sector . . . the ideological arm" during the liberation war. This dual role did not persist after the war, although the military was still expected to assist with civilian reconstruction and crop growing and to carry out certain political tasks.

FRELIMO's guerrilla army relied almost entirely on external support. It fought with communist-supplied weapons—both Soviet and Chinese—as well as whatever it captured from the Portuguese forces. Its heavier equipment included Soviet 12.7mm Degtyrev Shpagin and 14.5mm ZPU-4 antiaircraft guns, 75mm recoilless rifles, 122mm rockets, 82mm mortars, and various Chinese RPG rockets. Lighter weapons included Soviet AK-47 and AK-S assault carbines and RPD light machine guns. The Soviets and Chinese supplied most of the arms and training both in their own countries and in Tanzania, a close ally of FRELIMO. Tanzania apparently supplied some combat troops and training bases, served by both Soviet and Chinese training advisers. The African Liberation Committee of the OAU was based in Dar es Salaam and supplied much of FRELIMO's financial aid. In the 1960s FRELIMO relied on Tanzania for external bases and sanctuary. In the 1970s it acquired bases in Zambia.

During the liberation struggle FRELIMO established a militia that linked the guerrillas to the Mozambican peasants.

Generally noncombatants, these women, children, and older men aided in logistics and reconnaissance. FRELIMO's first military operation occurred in September 1964 when guerrillas attacked a Portuguese administration post near Mueda, in Cabo Delgado District. For the next two years FRELIMO forces fought mostly in Niassa and Cabo Delgado districts (called provinces after independence). In 1966 FRELIMO created a military staff, the National Command Council, to provide central command, control, and coordination. The Portuguese countered with more men and matériel and exploited some ethnic divisions while separating many Africans from FRELIMO by consolidating rural people in *aldeamentos* (fortified village complexes) in Tete and other northern districts. In 1970 Operation Gordian Knot in Cabo Delgado District strongly damaged FRELIMO's combat ability by destroying large amounts of supplies.

Learning from its loss, FRELIMO established a larger number of small bases and managed to withstand the last large Portuguese effort, Operation Frontier, in 1971. Late that year guerrillas moving south crossed the Zambezi River. FRELIMO assassinated at least 82 village headmen and a number of white farmers and Portuguese administrators to destroy rival figures of authority and to demonstrate its own strength. By the end of 1973 guerrillas, using shoulder-fired SA-7 surface-to-air missiles of Soviet origin, were within striking distance of Beira. This southward movement, which stretched Portuguese resources and morale, contributed to the April 1974 coup in Portugal, which, in turn, contributed to the September 1974 peace agreement between Portugal and FRELIMO. FRELIMO forces had won the war by surviving, by spreading revolt throughout the northern half of the country, and by avoiding the Portuguese rather than by defeating them militarily.

The FPLM continued to face serious problems after national independence in June 1975. In December 400 rebellious soldiers and policemen in Maputo attempted to capture FPLM headquarters, a nearby airport, and Radio Mozambique. After two days of fighting loyal government troops, the rebellion collapsed. It had been instigated because of rules of strict behavior imposed by the new national government. FRELIMO's task of establishing order was complicated by hostilities with neighboring Southern Rhodesia. Relations with the British colony's white rulers had been antagonistic ever since the regime's unilateral declaration of independence in 1965. The government in Salisbury aided the Portuguese armed forces by supplying troops for operations, especially in Mozambique's Tete and Vila Pery (later Manica) districts. Relations worsened after FRELIMO came to power. In February 1976 Rhodesian aircraft, artillery, and infantry engaged the FPLM, and in March 1976 Mozambique closed the common border and confiscated Rhodesian property. This move in accord with United Nations sanctions against Rhodesia dramatically hurt both countries. Rhodesia lost the use of port and shipping facilities of a country through which it had been defying the international sanctions, and Mozambique reported that it had lost the equivalent of US$500 million in transit fees during the four years the sanctions were in effect.

The Rhodesian operations against FRELIMO were motivated by the fact that Mozambique was providing sanctuary to ZANU forces, lending Soviet equipment to them, and guarding their bases against Rhodesian preemptive strikes. Most of the FPLM's actions were defensive, but the Mozambican forces did at times shell the border town of Umtali (present-day Mutare) and send small units to fight within Southern Rhodesia. Besides wanting to help ZANU by providing manpower, FPLM leaders felt that their forces would benefit from the combat experience. The contact also enabled Mozambique to collect information on the RNM and Rhodesian troop movements. FPLM troops in Southern Rhodesia were reguarly rotated; at the time of the December 1979 cease-fire at least 500 Mozambican troops were attached to ZANU forces.

Many observers felt that the Rhodesians, using such elite units as their Special Air Service and Selous Scouts along with superior air power, faced little opposition in their operations. Rhodesian strikes inflicted increasing damage on ZANU soldiers and civilians within Mozambique and on the Mozambican economy. Several of Southern Rhodesia's more destructive attacks occurred in 1976 at the Nyazonia refugee camp 40 kilometers from the border. Between 500 and 1,000 refugees and ZANU troops were killed. In November 1977 strikes by the Special Air Service and the Rhodesian Air Force killed over 1,000 ZANU personnel at Chimoio. Nevertheless, by mid-1979 the Rhodesian military was forced to step up operations to interdict an increasing flow of ZANU and FPLM troops crossing over the border from Mozambique. Between 1975 and 1979 Southern Rhodesia staged over 350 attacks within Mozambique. Nonetheless, the FPLM's air defense capabilities improved during these three years of mounting hostilities after the input of significant Soviet and Cuban military aid. During a major Rhodesian raid in Gaza Province in 1979, Mozambican forces downed two enemy helicopters. During a second raid on Chimoio, the FPLM counterattacked quickly with its Soviet-supplied 122mm rocket launchers.

Facing both the Rhodesian incursions and the South African threat, Mozambique, with Soviet encouragement, began to transform the FPLM into a conventional defense force. Soviet trainers taught conventional techniques while Moscow supplied weaponry that was fairly modern by African standards. Besides combating Rhodesian strikes, Mozambique sent an artillery battalion to join Tanzanian forces in the overthrow of Uganda's despotic head of state, Idi Amin Dada, in 1979. After Zimbabwe's independence in 1980 the Mozambican government continued its plans for a conventional force and discharged most of the experienced FRELIMO guerrillas. Even after this reorganizational move, the FPLM had not found the means to contain the RNM threat or to defend its borders against occasional South African incursions. The same geography that benefited FRELIMO during the liberation struggle similarly aided its enemies.

Yet despite problems of geography, manpower, and equipment, the FPLM has at times operated effectively against the RNM. It scored initial victories against the base camps at the Gorongosa Game Reserve and in Sitatonga, and in June 1982 in Manica Province the FPLM mounted a 5,000-man offensive supported by armored units and light infantry as well as Mozambican and Zimbabwean air power. In September the FPLM captured a key RNM base at Tome, and in November the RPLM captured the RNM's base in Zambezia Province. Two months later the FPLM defeated an RNM force of several hundred that had come within 140 kilometers of Maputo. In this Gaza Province campaign General Sebastião Marcos Mabote, chief of the army's General Staff, assumed personal control of operations, bringing in several extra battalions and some 1,000 Zimbabwean troops. The campaign destroyed a series of RNM bases, forcing the insurgents to pull out of Gaza Province. By early 1984 the FPLM units, bolstered by the recent addition of some 1,500 former FRELIMO guerrillas and some former counterinsurgency troops of the colonial army, were reportedly operating with increasing effectiveness.

### Place in the National Life

FRELIMO and its army started as a unified entity, and the guerrillas carried out political tasks during the liberation struggle. The army created the first party committees and the first party school for the study of Marxism-Leninism. Guerrillas identified themselves with the peasants because they often maintained farms to raise their own food supplies, and the guerrilla army sought to transform social attitudes by introducing women into its ranks.

This nexus between political and military elements, however, began unraveling shortly after national independence. In reaction to various reports of military indiscipline and complaints over low pay, a FRELIMO meeting with FPLM officers and enlisted personnel led to a proposed tightening of rules governing military behavior. One major change was the revocation of the army's power to arrest civilians. The directives developed by FRELIMO made subordination of the military explicit: all future orders to civilians were to come only from the party and the national government authorities. Civilian control of the military establishment has continued. In March 1977 FRELIMO dismissed seven high-ranking army officers (including the commanders and deputy commanders of two infantry battalions), the Third Party Congress described the army as a "problem," and Vice Minister of Defense Armando Emilio Guebuza was appointed as a political commissar to reinforce party control over the FPLM. Since then, attempts have been made to revitalize party cells within the armed forces.

On September 25, 1980—Armed Forces Day—a resolution of the FRELIMO Political Committee announced that a formal system of ranks had been introduced into the FPLM. Before this time, the FPLM did not have a rank hierarchy comparable to that found in other armies but had an informal system of commanders. Later, three classes of officers were recognized (high, middle, and low), but still without indentification by insignia. It was explained that the decision to adopt a conventional rank structure denoted the fact that the FPLM had been transformed into a "powerful, modern, disciplined, and regular army," which had been cleansed of "class infiltration." The failure to create an officer corps earlier was said to reflect lack of political reliability and professionalism among former guerrilla commanders, many of whom had taken advantage of their new power by engaging in corrupt activities. It was only later that FRELIMO felt sufficiently confident of its political control to introduce a system of ranks (see fig. 15). The highest rank was marshal (*marechal*), a grade that was conferred on Machel by the Political Committee. FRELIMO also assigned military ranks of major general or colonel to top party civilians, some of whom had never fought in the liberation struggle.

The 1980 proclamation announced that a military council of the armed forces and military regions was to be established. The military council was to be headed by Machel as commander in chief and was to include the defense minister, the chief of the General Staff, the national political commissar, the minister of interior, the minister of security, the deputy ministers of defense,

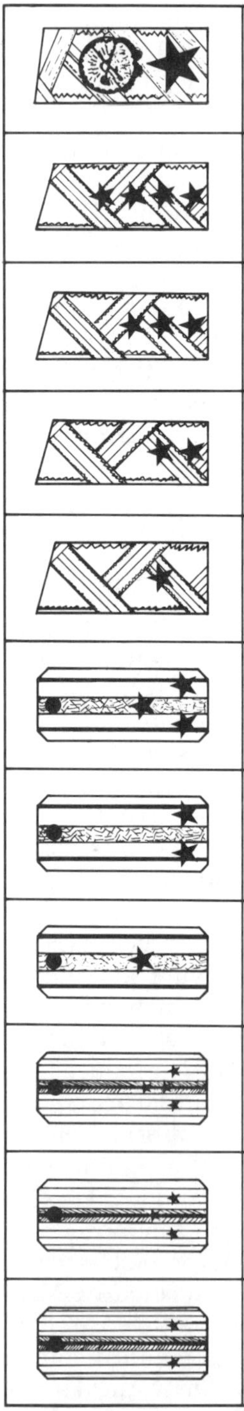

| | | Portuguese | United States |
|---|---|---|---|
| | | Marechal | General of the Army |
| | | General do Exército | General |
| | | Coronel General | Lieutenant General |
| | | Tenente General | Major General |
| | | Major General | Brigadier General |
| | | Coronel | Colonel |
| | | Tenente Coronel | Lieutenant Colonel |
| | | Major | Major |
| | | Capitão | Captain |
| | | Tenente | First Lieutenant |
| | | Alferes | Second Lieutenant |

UNITED STATES EQUIVALENT

*Figure 15. Ground Force Officer Ranks, Insignia, and United States Equivalents*

and the commanders of the three branches of the armed forces.

South Africa's successful Matola raid in 1981 contributed further to a public loss of confidence in the FPLM. Machel, remembering the importance of the peasantry to FRELIMO's past successes, worried publicly about the growing separation of Mozambique's civilians from the military forces. Compulsory political education occurs throughout the armed forces and is more intensive for troops guarding the country's borders. In a May Day speech Machel noted that "defense and economy are two muzzles of the same gun" and that "the gun [the soldiers] are bearing has the same value as the peasant's hoe or plough. . . ." He stated that each soldier should work in a village commune, cooperative, or state farm. At the Fourth Party Congress in April 1983 Machel noted that FPLM officers, noncommissioned officers (NCOs), and soldiers had constructed communal villages, helped revive areas devastated by insurgents, aided and evacuated people in areas affected by natural disasters, and were involved in the national campaign to increase food production.

Despite its subordinated status, the military retains influence within the government. The minister and vice minister of defense sits on the Council of Ministers, Mozambique's governing body. Both Alberto Joaquim Chipande, the long-time minister of defense, and Mabote, the vice minister of defense, have been closely allied with Machel since the liberation strugle, and both also have served on the 11-member Political Bureau at the apex of FRELIMO. Machel, however, assumed personal responsiblity for defense in 1983 when Chipande was reassigned to head Cabo Delgado Province. Members of the armed forces are also represented on the Central Committee and the People's Assembly. Yet indicative of civilian dominance over the military have been the effects of FRELIMO's permanent "legality campaign" (see Public Order and Internal Security, this ch.). Soldiers who have abused their position have been disciplined, and Machel has dismissed or shifted high-ranking officers he has considered inept.

As in other sectors, Mozambique has had to balance within the FPLM and the police force the two (often conflicting) qualities of loyalty and ability. By placing the FPLM under strong political control, Machel has attempted to avoid the disloyalty that rose to the surface in the 1975 attempted coup and South Africa's 1981 raid on Matola. By emphasizing political allegiance—all officers must be communists and FRELIMO members, and political indoctrination is an integral part of army life—Machel has rejected the Western model of a strong, semiautonomous hierarchy and has possibly lessened the operational effectiveness of the FPLM.

**Manpower: Sources and Quality**

Most of the FPLM manpower needs have been satisfied through a national system of conscription, which draws selectively from the pool of Mozambican men and women above the age of 18. *The Military Balance, 1983–1984*, published by London's International Institute for Strategic Studies, indicated that about 75 percent of the army's personnel had been conscripted. Mozambique has always had an ample supply of manpower for its military needs. Out of a population estimated at 13.1 million in 1983, roughly 2.9 million were males between the ages of 15 and 49; of these an estimated 1.7 million were considered fit for military service. Women also serve in the armed forces, the security service, and the national police. The required three months of training at the Military Preparation Center at Moamba, northwest of Maputo, reportedly has equal proportions of political and military instruction.

Ethnic dissension, a problem common to many African armed forces, apparently has not been a source of concern for the FPLM. Preindependence FPLM soldiers were predominantly Maconde from the north, while their commanders came from various southern ethnic groups. African colonial forces were drawn largely from the Macua and the Yao groups. The apparently successful ethnic and regional integration may have resulted from Machel's decision during the liberation struggle to mix potential factions in both training and combat situations.

The quality of the FPLM soldiers is probably poor, as evidenced by low educational levels, inadequate selection methods, and ineffective discipline, as well as by occasional disloyalty and desertion. The FPLM has frequently shown reluctance to act aggressively in seeking out the RNM and has angered local residents by arbitrary and punitive actions that have been counterproductive in a conflict against an insurgent group dependent on the rural populace for food and information.

Since its inception the FPLM has been seriously deficient in the skills required to use sophisticated weapons. At independence, Mozambique's adult literacy rate was about 10 percent; in response to what Machel terms "the low scientific and educational levels of the majority of the [military] candidates," the FPLM has apparently established primary schools for military conscripts, and FRELIMO has announced that well-educated soldiers will serve as tutors within the armed forces. The extent of foreign advisers attached to military units has indicated, in part, the inability of most FPLM personnel to absorb technically sophisticated material (see Foreign Military Assistance, this ch.).

The first officer class from Nampula Military Academy graduated in 1981 after three years of training. In the final examination, 24 percent were rated as "very good," 49 percent as "good," and 27 percent as "sufficient." There were no failures at the school, but the government has admitted that the institution has operated with deficient administrative and development requirements.

Selection of FPLM cadres sometimes has been poorly administered, and unenthusiastic manpower has often been the result. Although the conscription system has required compulsory registration and partial call-up, many conscripts have been picked from crowds because they appeared unemployed or because they lacked the required registration papers. Machel has acknowledged that the recruitment system's arbitrariness has brought "damaging" and "incapacitating" results and the induction of soldiers without the correct political attitudes. He declared that the effect of expanding the FPLM after 1975 with new recruits who had not participated in the liberation struggle had "opened the door to bourgeois ideas."

The FPLM has also faced a serious problem of disloyalty among high-ranking security officials and army officers who have defected from Mozambique or have been charged with being agents of South Africa. After the 1981 attack against Matola, in which the South Africans used FPLM trucks and uniforms, Machel admitted that South Africa had obtained inside knowledge of Mozambique's security. Eight high-ranking FPLM officers were arrested, including four key members of the General Staff. Shortly thereafter, two of the latter escaped, reportedly with the help of a domestic underground network. In mid-1982 four senior Mozambican officials defected; the most notable of them was Jorge da Costa, a high-level employee of the Ministry of Security. After obtaining political asylum in South Africa, da Costa reportedly conveyed detailed information on ANC activities in Mozambique. After da Costa's flight, the FRELIMO government arrested a number of highly placed Ministry of Security officials.

One analyst stated that in 1984 the FPLM's most serious problem was poor training, which had been accentuated by the rapid growth of the FPLM, the People's Militia, and the Border Guard. The army was hampered by a lack of NCOs and junior officers. Transportation was also a problem, including fuel shortages, mediocre maintenance, and poor resupply and medical evacuation capabilities. It has been claimed that the FPLM has suffered extensive desertions caused by insufficient food, inadequate weapons, low pay, and continuing attacks by the RNM insurgents. Reports of low morale may explain the hesitation of FPLM officers and enlisted personnel to engage the RNM. Machel has disciplined several officers who did not lead their troops against the RNM during a one-year period in contested provinces. Public meetings, some of which Machel has presided over, have featured accusations regarding the undisciplined conduct of FPLM soldiers. The president has ordered troops to vacate illegally occupied apartments and has decreed that nearby towns be closed to off-duty soldiers and police because of the "confusion" their presence created. In Zambezia Province doctors and priests complained about the killing of innocent civilians. In late 1983 some reports indicated that FRELIMO had undertaken a campaign to revitalize the FPLM through political training and motivation in an effort to overcome indiscipline and inefficiency.

### Defense Spending

In early 1984 little information was available regarding the specifics of Mozambique's defense spending. Reflecting the dual requirements of preparing for both conventional and unconventional threats, the defense budget for 1982 was the equivalent of US$177.4 million, or 29 percent of the total government expenditures. Mozambique spent almost the same amounts each year for defense as for health and education until 1982, which marked the first year that health and education received more government funds. In view of the paucity of government financial data available in the early 1980s, it was not clear whether the 1982 figure included all allocations for the People's Militia, the Border Guard, and other FPLM elements. Large equipment items and some construction assistance furnished by the Soviet Union and other countries presumably were not included in the total. Low wages paid to conscripts probably have also helped to keep military costs at a manageable level.

Nevertheless, defense spending has undoubtedly strained the Mozambican economy. The RNM's renaissance in the early 1980s occurred as FRELIMO was struggling to rebuild an economy depleted by the Portuguese exodus, the closing of the common border with Southern Rhodesia from March 1976 to December 1979, and a series of natural catastrophes. Military requirements not only diverted scarce financial resources but also absorbed skilled manpower needed in the modern sector of the economy. FRELIMO has attempted to lessen the military's drain on manpower by ordering soldiers to perform civil action tasks, e.g., picking cotton in Nampula Province, constructing a fishing complex near Lake Nyasa, working at the oil refinery on the outskirts of Maputo, and laboring on various reclamation projects.

*Regular troops of the*
*Mozambican armed forces*
*on parade*
*Courtesy AIM, Maputo*

## Mission, Organization, and Training

Since national independence Mozambique's military establishment—the FPLM—has had the dual missions of defending the country against threats posed by potential external aggressors and of providing backup to the police in the maintenance of public order and internal security. During the late 1970s the FPLM's size grew steadily in response to the threats presented to Mozambique by Southern Rhodesia and the RNM. In mid-1981, as RNM activity increased, the Mozambican government began a series of substantial changes in the national security structure to improve both its conventional capability and to achieve a credible counterinsurgency posture. Lacking the foreign exchange to purchase sufficient counterinsurgency equipment, such as helicopter transports and gunships, Machel strove instead to enlarge his armed forces, to develop new counterinsurgency elements, and to move toward the eventual integration of all national security forces. The president also imposed several restrictions on specific units and reshuffled the leaders of various security forces.

In March 1982 the FPLM positioned a motorized infantry brigade on the Mozambique-Malawi frontier to counter RNM infiltration from that country. Elswhere special counterinsurgency units began to be formed. In the same month, Machel announced the formation of a new decentralized force known as the People's Militia, designed to guard villages, factories, and state farms, thus freeing regular FPLM troops for offensive response to the insurgents. After four to eight weeks of training,

269

new militia personnel received rifles. At least one army base, at Dondo in Sofala Province, provided assistance in the training of militia personnel. The steady growth of the militia indicated Mozambique's move toward an increased war footing. According to several reports, more than 40 percent of the adult population in Sofala Province, one of the more contested areas, was armed.

Machel appointed provincial military commanders to all of the provinces except Maputo. Most of the officers were major generals who had been born in the provinces to which they were assigned and had led FRELIMO guerrilla units during the liberation struggle of the early 1970s. The principal task of these new provincial commanders was to organize and lead local units of the militia and the newly formed counterinsurgency elements. FRELIMO hoped that the new leadership and these unconventional forces would be sufficiently motivated and versed in the techniques of bush warfare to defend their own territories. In May 1982 the president reactivated 1,500 former FRELIMO fighters, some of whom joined the armed forces while others helped in the development of village militia units. This action by the government followed an earlier one that integrated some soldiers from the former colonial security units into the FPLM. Some observers believed that the return of these two elements to combat status was the key to several FPLM successes against the RNM in 1983.

There has been a dearth of publicly available information regarding the size, organizational structure, and training of the Mozambican military and security establishments. It was beleived in early 1984, however, that the restructured FPLM consisted of three separate elements: a regular force of at least 26,700 officers and enlisted personnel trained for employment using both conventional and unconventional equipment and tactics; the People's Militia of approximately 30,000 members; and the Border Guard of some 6,000. Few whites or Asians had been conscripted into the FPLM. Mozambican officials either perceived them to be a security threat or considered their critical skills more useful in bolstering the flagging economy. No information was available on the percentage of conscripts or volunteers that had opted for reenlistment in the FPLM when their two-year active-duty commitments were fulfilled.

The FPLM's conventional force was organized into an army of about 25,000 personnel, an air force of approximately 1,000, and a navy of roughly 700. The army consisted of eight or nine infantry brigades, each of which was composed of two to four infantry battalions of 300 to 400 troops each and variable numbers of armored, artillery, and support battalions. In addition, the FPLM had a tank brigade—the elite Presidential Guard—that could be depended on to back up the infantry units. The size of full-strength Mozambican battalions and brigades corresponded roughly to that of comparable Soviet or Cuban units.

The army's inventory of weapons was largely of Soviet and East European origin. By early 1984 these suppliers were probably providing significant amounts of newer and more sophisticated matériel, but because of the Nkomati accord between Mozambique and South Africa, future delivery trends were difficult to predict. The army was updating its tank inventory, phasing out its nearly 200 Soviet T-34s and replacing them with significant numbers of T-54s and T-55s. It was thought that the army also had some 50 PT-76 light tanks, 250 to 300 BTR-60/152 armored personnel carriers, and roughly 40 BRDM-1/2 armored scout cars. Artillery included 100 or fewer 105mm and 122mm howitzers; some 200 guns ranging in size from 76mm to 130mm; an unknown number of 75mm and 82mm rocket launchers and Sagger antitank guided weapons; some 300 antiaircraft guns, including 20mm, 23mm, 37mm, and 57mm towed models and ZSU-23/24 self-propelled versions; and fewer than 30 SA-3 and SA-7 surface-to-air missiles.

The FPLM's air defense units were controlled by the army, which operated SA-3 missile emplacements near major cities, such as Maputo. Mozambique's radar capabilities were sharply limited except for the area around the capital city by Rhodesian forces and South African reconnaissance commando units. Subsequently, Soviet-supplied tracking radar and guidance systems have increased the SA-3 capabilities.

The air force was developed as an element of the FPLM shortly after independence, using a small collection of obsolete aircraft left behind by the departing Portuguese. To provide an operational capability to deter attacks by both the RNM and Rhodesian forces, the government in Maputo sought military assistance from Moscow and received the first MiG fighter aircraft in March 1977 together with missiles, other equipment, and Soviet advisers who trained Mozambican personnel in weapons use and air doctrine. Air matériel support has subsequently continued. These aircraft and the organizational units necessary for their employment were believed by foreign observers to be assigned to the two air bases constructed near Nacala and Beira in the late 1970s. Subsequent training of pilots and technicians has been conducted at a base near Maputo with the assistance of East European and Cuban military advisers. Cuban and Soviet pilots probably flew many of the MiG aircraft in the inventory.

In early 1984 the air force had at least 60 Soviet-built combat aircraft that had been used more for close air support of FPLM forces operating against the RNM insurgents than for interdicting incursions by foreign aircraft, such as those from neighboring South Africa. Six squadrons charged with fighter-interceptor and forward ground attack roles formed the air arm's offensive thrust. More than 25 MiG-21 fighter-bombers were divided between two of the squadrons, and a third squadron operated by an unknown number of MiG-17 and MiG-19 fighters. Approximately 35 MiG-17s (many of them nonoperational) were parceled out to the remaining three fighter-interceptor squadrons.

In addition to the combat aircraft, the air force had at least eight Soviet Mi-8 helicopters divided between two squadrons and an unknown number of more sophisticated models, as well as several French light helicopters. A transport squadron was equipped with a variety of aircraft that included the French Noratlas, the American Cessna 182, and the Soviet AN-26. Light airplanes assigned to the training squadron (and for possible dual use in counterinsurgency operations) included the Czechoslovak Aero L-39, the Czechoslovak Zlin single piston-engine trainer, and the American Cessna 152.

Little information was available regarding the small Mozambican navy, which operated largely in a border surveillance role on Lake Nyasa and offshore with a limited coastal patrol capability. Its bases were at Maputo, Beira, Nacala, Pemba, and Metangula. Equipment included about 14 light coastal patrol craft of Soviet, Portuguese, and Dutch origin.

Similarly, detailed information was not generally available regarding the structure and operational doctrine of the other elements of the FPLM that had been formed outside the conventional force structure. The People's Militia, directed and controlled from its central headquarters within the Ministry of Defense in Maputo, and a counterinsurgency force that operated as light infantry units in the provinces appeared to be FRELIMO's main response to the damaging attacks of the RNM. These capabilities were augmented by the Border Guard's four brigades, whose mission was to protect the country's frontiers against unfriendly intruders. These brigades, which lacked artillery or a mechanized capability, also functioned more as light infantry than as paramilitary units.

The militia, formed of workers organized in their work and residential areas, was under the political leadership of the party organs and operational leadership of the FPLM. Its mission was to combat the guerrillas and to assist in maintaining public order. The militia was reportedly incapable of dealing with the RNM; its purpose was more psychological and political than military. Some of the militia was armed with Portuguese-supplied G3 automatic rifles, but others reportedly carried only machetes. In early 1984 a start had been made in organizing the city of Maputo on a block basis, purportedly to help strengthen the city's defenses against infiltration by terrorists. Each city block was to have an elected head, a deputy, a woman's representative, and "vigilance organizers."

## Foreign Military Assistance

Mozambique reportedly had little if any arms industry. As a consequence, it has relied almost exclusively on the Soviet Union and countries of Eastern Europe for military equipment and has received training and advisory assistance from the Soviet Union, Eastern Europe, the African front-line states, the Democratic People's Republic of Korea (North Korea), Cuba, and China. Shortly after Mozambican independence the Soviet Union replaced China as the FRELIMO regime's main military suppliers. In 1983, however, Mozambique began looking increasingly to the West for military assistance.

Military equipment and agreements, as well as the presence of foreign advisers, have underscored Mozambique's continuing reliance on the communist states. Its weapons inventory has indicated that almost all of the FPLM's heavy equipment, including its air defense gear, has come from communist sources. Portuguese equipment, notably coastal vessels, was given to Mozambique when the Portuguese departed in 1975.

In 1977, when its aid program began, the Soviet Union supplied mostly howitzers, guns, and tanks. From 1978 to 1980 it provided armored cars and jet aircraft. In 1980 alone, deliveries included 110 T-54/55 tanks, some MiG-21s, about 43 transport planes, and two coastal patrol boats. Communist countries also have supplied substantial amounts of smaller weaponry: Tokarev and Stechkin pistols; AK, AKM, and Simonov SKS rifles; and KPV/ZPU carbines. The financial arrangements for the weapons have not been publicly announced; information sources have disagreed over whether Moscow sold the matériel at concessionary rates, whether it bartered weapons for agricultural goods, or whether it donated at least some of the weapons to the FRELIMO government.

Besides its political interest in seeing a successful Marxist-Leninist state in Africa, the Soviet Union has hoped to monitor traffic moving through the Mozambique Channel, a potential chokepoint for Western shipment of petroleum and other strategic goods. The Soviet fleet has enjoyed access to Maputo and other Mozambican ports. The first Soviet naval visits occurred in 1977 and included 14 arrivals and departures. Fourteen additional visits were made by Soviet ships from 1978 through 1980. These visits accounted for 271 days in Mozambican ports. In 1981 Moscow supplied the country's only naval repair facility, a floating dry dock. The dock accommodated both Mozambican and Soviet vessels, although Moscow's desire for a naval base in Mozambican waters has been resisted by Machel.

Treaty agreements have emphasized the reliance on the communist countries. In 1977 Mozambique and the Soviet Union signed a 20-year treaty of friendship and cooperation, which contained a standard military commitment clause. Other military cooperation agreements have been concluded with Bulgaria, Czechoslovakia, Cuba, and the German Democratic Republic (East Germany), which has supplied Mozambique's radar and telecommunications system. China, North Korea, Libya, and Ethiopia also have furnished some military assistance.

As of 1981 more than 500 Mozambicans had received military training in the Soviet Union and Eastern Europe. A mix of about 600 Soviets and East Germans, some 1,000 Cuban military technicians, and about 400 Tanzanians have trained and advised the Mozambican security forces. Soviet advisers have been prevalent throughout the security forces; 60 of them have been the training nucleus at the Nampula Military Academy, which was established in 1978 and graduated its first class in 1981. Subjects have ranged from tank warfare to political studies. Some 200 Tanzanians have trained Mozambican NCOs near Maputo, and at least 200 more have trained militia personnel. Some reports have indicated the presence of small numbers of Chinese, Hungarian, and North Korean advisers and technicians. East Germans have reorganized the police force, and Cubans have advised the army's mechanized battalions and supplied mechanical expertise. Cuba and East Germany built two air bases near Nacala and Beira. Pilots have been trained to operate jet aircraft in East Germany. North Korea has trained a brigade of Mozambicans in counterinsurgency operations; the unit became operational in 1983. Since Mozambique has expanded the size of its regular forces as well as its militia, the need for military training both at home and abroad has also increased in 1984.

The front-line states have provided assistance in the belief that their own security is tied to defense of the FRELIMO government, which has been exposed to direct and indirect aggression from South Africa, their common adversary. Moreover,

Mozambique has aided Angola, Tanzania, and Zimbabwe in the past and has shared many ideological perceptions with them. Zimbabwe has also allocated troops because RNM attacks have disrupted that country's foreign trade and petroleum shipments and because Mozambique, at considerable expense, once allowed ZANU to establish bases in its territory during the Rhodesian civil war. Tanzania's current aid was a form of reciprocity, in part for Mozambique's having supplied an artillery battalion for the Tanzanian invasion of Uganda in 1979. The economic agreements for training assistance have varied. Zimbabwe has paid for its own troops, whereas Tanzania probably has received compensation from either Mozambique or the Soviet Union. Close military cooperation existed with Angola and Tanzania. Mozambicans claim that Tanzania has supplied all regular training and ordinary weapons, but the Soviet Union has furnished more advanced training and matériel. Angola may have furnished nine Noratlas transport aircraft.

An agreement in January 1981 between Mozambique and Zimbabwe covered "all the vital areas of defense and security." By early 1984 Zimbabwe was probably the only country that had supplied combat soldiers to Mozambique. Upwards of 2,000 Zimbabweans, possibly with helicopter backup, have patrolled the common border and have guarded both the Maforga petroleum pumping station and the Beira-Mutare pipeline. Zimbabwe's North Korean-trained Fifth Brigade, as well as air support forces, reportedly have been used in at least one major offensive against the RNM. The agreement between the two countries probably permitted unlimited hot pursuit of insurgents across the common border and facilitated an exchange of information. The two countries coordinated their counterinsurgency activities, and Zimbabwe turned over to Mozambique captured RNM guerrillas who had crossed the border. By the summer of 1981 Zimbabwe was providing Mozambique the results of its aerial reconnaissance of the border areas.

A hint by Foreign Minister Joaquim Alberto Chissano in 1983 that Mozambique might turn to Cuban troops drew a quick response from South Africa that such aid would not be tolerated. After the South African raid on Matola in 1981, several Soviet warships visited Maputo, and Soviet ambassador Valentin P. Vdovin spoke of possible escalations: "If anyone attacks us or our friends, we will give a suitable response." Yet the Soviets did not appear to be prepared to augment their aid substantially enough to stop the RNM advances or South African incursions. Future Soviet aid was expected to include improved air defense hardware and transport aircraft; Mabote requested MiG-21 fighter-bombers and Mi-8 helicopters, as well as T-54 and T-55 tanks, during his visit to Moscow in 1982. There were no immediate indications that the nonagression pact with South Africa in early 1984 would be regarded as a reason for Moscow to cut back on deliveries or to reduce other public symbols of support, such as naval visits. Mozambique's long-term reliance on Soviet equipment made it unrealistic for the Machel government to contemplate a rapid shift to other sources of military matériel.

Among Mozambique's other allies, notably Zimbabwe, domestic considerations have limited further increases in military assistance. Zimbabwe has continued to face smoldering discontent in its own Matabeleland area and might worry that increased aid to Mozambique would invite South African retaliation. Moreover, service in Mozambique might be unpopular among Zimbabwean soldiers.

Lacking sufficient Soviet and African aid and faced with continuing threats from the RNM, Machel was forced to turn to the West. In 1982 Mozambique signed a defense agreement with Portugal. Lisbon subsequently supplied small amounts of light weapons, uniforms, and ammunition for the village-level People's Militia units and was expected to provide logistics and engineering assistance. The FPLM also hoped to receive counterinsurgency instruction from Portugal's Commando Regiment, including paratroop training. Mozambique has raised its military needs in discussions with Britain and France, as well as with Yugoslavia and Brazil, but reportedly has received no significant commitments. Machel and Chipande displayed special interest in paratroop and counterinsurgency units when visiting Britain and France in October 1983. The Mozambican president apparently hoped that the British Military Training and Advisory Team in Zimbabwe might assist in training elements of the FPLM.

Machel has broadened his group of possible donors for several reasons. The FPLM was aware that obsolete Soviet equipment had not been effective in dealing with the security threats to Mozambique. The FPLM apparently has been unhappy about the utility of its outdated Soviet weapons. But Mozambique may be tied to future shipments of conventional Soviet equipment, at least partially reimbursed by Mozambican exports, because of long-term agreements made during the Rhodesian war. Soviet advisers were instrumental in the late 1970s in persuading FPLM authorities to switch from guerrilla operations to conventional tactics, a shift that left Mozambique unprepared for the RNM threat. Soviet training reportedly has continued to emphasize the conventional warfare approach and heavy weapons, ignoring such aspects as close combat and bush survival techniques.

By early 1984 Western nations had not undertaken significant training of FPLM personnel. The military establishment desired counterinsurgency equipment and hoped to obtain dual-use troop transport/gunship helicopters (such as the Alouette-IIIs), more surface-to-air missiles, better radar, and a more sophisticated missile control system. In 1983 the air force placed an order with a British firm (Rediffusion) for a sophisticated radio communications system connecting three military fields and facilitating ground-to-air communications. In 1984 Britain reportedly was supplying Land Rovers. The FPLM leaders also had sought Western assistance for improvements in Mozambique's transportation infrastructure, especially the construction of all-weather roads.

## Public Order and Internal Security

By the beginning of 1984 the FRELIMO regime had not only confronted the rural-based RNM insurgency and South African military incursions, but it had also faced potential security problems from growing urbanization, certain business and foreign groups, former colonial officials, and religious organizations. Fortunately for FRELIMO, no widely accepted personality, ideology, or organization had appeared around which these affected groups could coalesce. In facing these threats, the government was hampered by an often inefficient police system or disloyal personnel, a situation that angered many Mozambicans. The rising discontent and economic disorder had induced the regime to toughen and broaden the scope of its security legislation.

The government has regarded rapid urbanization as a potential threat to internal security. In the nine years since independence, Maputo's population had grown to about 1 million residents; the unemployed have strained the country's social services. In reaction, the Ministry of Interior organized "Operation Production" in early 1983 to relocate 100,000 urban residents to rural areas—away from RNM activity—to help with agricultural production (see Demography, ch. 2).

When signs of the RNM presence first appeared in Maputo in the form of graffiti and pamphlets in mid-1982, the regime responded with roadblocks, a late-night curfew, arming of trusted FRELIMO activists, and implementation of a food rationing system that required proof of legal residence in the capital city. By

January 1983 the government was issuing resident cards in Maputo, Beira, Chimoio, Tete, and Quelimane. A year later the RNM claimed that it had quietly organized urban cells and would begin operations within the major urban centers later in the year.

In addition to the implicit threat posed by RNM sympathizers, FRELIMO officials have harbored a long-standing suspicion of foreigners. This attitude has arisen from the regime's forced reliance on numerous individuals who once worked for (or sympathized with) the colonial authorities before the massive pullout of the Portuguese when Mozambique attained independence. Despite the European exodus, foreigners have dominated much of the local business scene, and some have been suspected of passing information to South Africa to facilitate military raids against a government that harbored and assisted the ANC. In April 1983 a Mozambican court convicted the director of Beira's largest shipping and forwarding firm on charges that he was the leader of an RNM unit. The regime's distrust has also extended at certain times to representatives of foreign governments, particularly those of the West. The expulsion of four United States embassy personnel in March 1981 was based on Mozambican charges that they were part of a Central Intelligence Agency "spy ring" that had been operating since Mozambique's independence—ostensibly in collaboration with South African agents—to gather information on the ANC, the FPLM, and other groups.

Government officials, particularly Machel, have branded all individuals or groups opposed to the regime's policies as the compromised (*comprometidos*). The regime has usually refrained from violent retribution against the so-called compromised but has deprived them of certain civil rights, e.g., the right to vote. The government has allowed some to admit their guilt publicly and then permitted them to return to their work places, where their pictures and descriptions of their past collaboration have been displayed openly. Others of those implicated have been dispatched to reeducation centers. In 1982 Machel met with several thousand individuals labeled as the compromised, including former members of the colonial security forces who were being welcomed back into Mozambican society with restored civil rights. It is not known whether people accused of "compromising" have continued to present a threat as potential dissidents or whether they have sought to reestablish themselves through loyal service to FRELIMO.

Not surprisingly, the country's religious organizations have also come under the suspicion of the Marxist-Leninist government and its party. During the colonial era, the Roman Catholic

Church had been influential in the Portuguese society in Mozambique, and, with few exceptions, church officials had strongly supported Portuguese rule (see Religion, ch. 2). Since coming to power, Machel has referred to "[imperialist] agents camouflaged in cassocks." Probably because of the church hiearchy's past loyalty to Portuguese authority, the president reacted bitterly in 1983 when the bishop of Beira suggested that FRELIMO should negotiate with the RNM.

By early 1984 FRELIMO had neutralized any perceived threat to its regime posed by the Roman Catholic church. FRELIMO nationalized the church's former responsibilities for health and education, as well as its substantial landholdings. The state also closed some churches and placed travel restrictions on priests. According to FRELIMO, the church was too strong to be tolerated and too pro-colonial to be pardoned.

The perceived threat posed by the Jehovah's Witnesses had also been neutralized. By early 1984 the remaining members of the sect apparently were in state reeducation centers.

In 1977 and 1978 students were the target of heavy criticism by Machel. They were accused of indiscipline, indifference to FRELIMO's policies, and susceptibility to foreign propaganda. He threatened to send to reeducation camps those older students who continued to resist the party's teachings. Perhaps as a result of intimidation of this kind, there were few subsequent indications that university and high school students have been a significant source of unrest. Those attending the Eduardo Mondlane University in Maputo appeared to represent little threat to the government, although in early 1983 six students each received 48 whip lashes and eight years in prison for starting a "subversive group."

A particular problem disturbing FRELIMO has been its own security forces. The FPLM has apparently suffered a large number of defections; some have joined the RNM while others, perhaps 5 to 10 percent of the deserters, have become bandits within the interior of the country. But these bandits, whose actions probably have been confused by observers with those of the RNM, have posed no real security threat to FRELIMO. At the same time, however, the military and police forces have engaged in arbitrary actions against civilians, a pattern that could lessen public support for the security forces and FRELIMO. In November 1981 numerous public complaints prompted Machel to announce a "legality campaign," which encouraged citizens to report and act against inefficient or corrupt security personnel. The campaign also placed checks on arbitrary police power, notably imprisonment, beatings, and torture. The legality campaign established an outlet known as the Office of Control and Discipline under the police command in each province. Citizens could complain about police behavior to the new authority or at public meetings conducted by it. Subsequently, police officers or soldiers have been required to produce identification cards when requested to do so. Machel also announced that any police officer or private citizen could arrest a security force member observed committing a crime, and, if found guilty, the security officer would receive a stiffer fine than would a civilian. Local and country councils have formed special committees to which accused personnel of the local police, security police, and the FPLM must report. The committees also investigated complaints lodged by the public against activities of security force members. In 1982 a high-ranking security official acknowledged that most of the public complaints were valid. As part of the legality campaign, political instruction within the police system was increased, and departments conducting criminal investigation received more technical and legal training. These problems apparently had not been resolved as of early 1984 when the Central Committee again criticized "deviations from and violations of the Constitution" by members of the police, the military establishment, and other security services.

Between November 1981 and October 1982 approximately 150 police personnel were suspended under the legality campaign. In February 1982 Machel announced that 406 members of the country's security police had been dismissed and that 18 others had been arrested during the previous year. The president made clear his displeasure, noting that Mozambique "must send contingents of policemen to reeducation camps." At the Fourth Party Congress he accused some police officers of being "racist, regionalistic, or tribalistic."

Mozambique's security forces have faced a dilemma in obtaining reliable, qualified personnel. Many of the best educated and trained Mozambicans received preferential training during colonial rule, a factor that raised questions about their loyalty to the revolutionary regime. Although acknowledging the need for skilled individuals and modern equipment, Machel has stressed that "the important thing is the political and ideological quality of the security cadres." As in the case of FRELIMO's relations with the military, the trade-off for political loyalty might be a loss of efficiency.

**The Police**

In early 1984 two police organizations had major responsibility for the maintenance of public order and internal security. The smaller one, the People's Police of Mozambique (Polícia Popular de Moçambique—PPM), was responsible primarily for public order in the urban areas. Figures denoting the PPM's personnel strength and details of its exact organizational structure were not available. The larger force was known as the National Service of People's Security (Serviço Nacional de Segurança Popular—SNASP), an organization that devoted its attention to problems of internal security. It also operated mainly in the urban environment but had spread slowly into the rural areas. Further expansion was hindered by the country's size, the inadequate transportation infrastructure, and a shortage of manpower, vehicles, and fuel. The SNASP had approximately 1,500 full-time officers and a much larger number of informants.

The PPM was responsible in its operations to the Ministry of Interior, which shared supervisory authority for prisons and reeducation centers with the Ministry of Justice and the Ministry of Security. The Ministry of Security controlled and directed the operations of the SNASP forces. Overall responsibility for public order and security thus was shared by the ministries of defense, interior, security, and justice. In view of their overlapping jurisdictions, these governmental bodies were required to coordinate closely with each other. It appeared that FRELIMO had deliberately established the overlapping nature of these responsibilities, believing that shared authority prevented any one agency or individual from accumulating too much power.

The SNASP was established by presidential decree in October 1975, four months after independence. Responsible only to the head of FRELIMO (who was also president of the republic), the organization was instituted to detect and combat subversion and sabotage. It operated from the outset much in the manner of a secret police force. In 1984 its director, who was a member of the FRELIMO Political Bureau, enjoyed cabinet rank as minister of security. Acting on his own authority, this official could decide whether an individual apprehended on suspicion of a security offense would be turned over to a court for trial or sent directly to a reeducation camp. SNASP decisions were not subject to appeal, and its authority had been made retroactive to September 1974.

FRELIMO guerrillas of proven loyalty staffed the SNASP initially, but by 1984 its increased personnel complement probably included conscripts who had been called up for national service. High-ranking officers received training in East Germany and the Soviet Union, and personnel of lower rank were trained in

Mozambique by Soviet, East German, and Mozambican instructors. A secretariat within the SNASP controlled a series of units known as People's Vigilance Groups that were used for conducting surveillance and gathering intelligence. It was estimated that about 300,000 Mozambicans belonged to these groups, but the number of active members was much smaller.

FRELIMO had little need for police during its liberation struggle in the early 1970s, and Mozambican independence came too suddenly for the immediate formation of a force that could deal with ordinary criminal activity. A lack of trained manpower and the urgent need to maintain order during the uncertain period after independence forced the new government to retain the services of the Mozambique Police Corps (Corpo Policial de Moçambique), which had existed during the colonial era. That organization was abolished in June 1979 when the PPM was introduced. The small force has always been armed with light weapons and in 1984 consisted of both male and female officers.

Mozambique also had a number of quasi-police organizations. The customs, immigration, and port authorities employed their own guards, but they lacked the power to make arrests. During "Operation Production," so-called Identification Brigades were empowered to stop Mozambicans, request identification documents, and, if necessary, deliver the citizens to verification points.

### The Prison System

At the end of the war of liberation, the FRELIMO government took over existing colonial prisons. Included in the system were maximum and minimum security facilities located near urban centers and penal colonies or correctional farms sited in rural areas where inmates engaged in supervised agricultural production. There was less constraint at the rural facilities, but the inmates were still prisoners and still under guard. During the new government's first year in power, Machel made a number of reforms in criminal justice procedures after a series of visits to prisons in June 1976. He found that too many prisoners were assigned to cells and that reform of the system was needed. But the government was hampered in its efforts at improvement because no one in FRELIMO had experience with modern penal administration. Moreover, the prison system the government had inherited was so outdated that it was believed to be beyond reform. The few capable administrators who had remained in Mozambique after independence could not be easily retrained to adopt the revolutionary methods proposed by the FRELIMO regime.

By 1976, in accordance with its hopes for rehabilitation

through reeducation and collective labor, FRELIMO was sending most minor offenders to newly established "reeducation centers" rather than to older prisons that housed persons who had committed serious crimes. In 1980 it was believed that 12 of these camps were in operation in remote parts of the country. Inmates included political prisoners and other "antisocial elements" (prostitutes, black marketeers, vagrants, and others who failed to cooperate with FRELIMO policies). Both the Ministry of Interior and the Ministry of Justice have sent internees to the camps for offenses deemed simply as antisocial; those confined by Ministry of Justice authority usually have had the benefit of some legal safeguards, but this was generally not the case among persons confined by the Ministry of Interior.

According to the United States Department of State's *Country Reports on Human Rights Practices for 1983*, the conventional prisons suffered from overcrowding and were characterized by inadequate food, sanitation, and medical care for prisoners. These conditions were attributed to insufficient resources that had resulted from the country's low level of economic development. Many of the inmates at the so-called reeducation centers have been confined under sentences of indeterminate length. Conditions in the camps in 1983 were described in the Department of State's report as "harsh, and prisoners must feed and shelter themselves." Some of the inmates were organized into brigades that were partly responsible for discipline within the centers. Reports by some observers have indicated that cruel treatment by guards was common at the more isolated camps.

Journalists who have occasionally been allowed to visit the camps have described the spartan living conditions. One such facility was the reeducation center for women at Masauize in Niassa Province, to which female Mozambicans from different parts of the country were sent. The camp, administered by a FRELIMO political commissar, held 500 inmates and was operated by a brigade of 36 female guards. The prisoners engaged mainly in farm work. Political instruction was a major part of the program. Food, sanitation, and health services were inadequate. The Masauize facility was one of five similar centers in Niassa Province in the late 1970s.

As of early 1984 no data had been released on the number of people still in detention, although estimates ranged up to 10,000 or more in 1980. On two subsequent occasions, the mass release of more than 1,000 detainees was announced. In 1981 Machel acknowledged that many inmates were being held in violation of the law. Whether a subsequent investigation by the government's inspector general had produced reforms was not made clear. Earlier tours of prisons and reeducation centers had produced the same conclusion: one of the major problems in both kinds of institutions appeared to be the lack of trained penal and legal personnel. In June 1980, according to Amnesty International, Mozambican courts prosecuted three prison officials for maltreatment of inmates. Convictions were obtained, and the three men were fined and sentenced to short terms of imprisonment. One of the convicted offenders was the penal officer at Maputo's Machava Central Prison.

\* \* \*

There are no definitive works available that deal expressly with Mozambican national security concerns, policies, or institutions, but certain information is available in various publications and in several books and periodical articles dealing with Mozambican politics.

Useful information on military and security affairs can be garnered from the International Institute for Strategic Studies' annual *The Military Balance*, as well as from the periodicals *Africa, New African, Defence Africa, Africa Confidential, Afrique Défense,* and *Africa Research Bulletin. Africa Contemporary Record,* produced annually by noted Africanist Colin Legum, the Foreign Broadcast Information Service's *Daily Report: Middle East and Africa,* and the Joint Publications Research Service's foreign periodical translations in its *Sub-Saharan Africa Report* are indispensable for research on Mozambican national security developments. Occasionally, useful information can also be gleaned from the Mozambican press, particularly Maputo's daily, *Notícias.* (For further information and complete citations, see Bibliography.)

# Appendix

## Table 1.    Metric Conversion Coefficients

| When you know | Multiply by | To find |
|---|---|---|
| Millimeters . . . . . . . . . . . . . . | 0.04 | inches |
| Centimeters . . . . . . . . . . . . . . | 0.39 | inches |
| Meters . . . . . . . . . . . . . . . . | 3.3 | feet |
| Kilometers . . . . . . . . . . . . . . | 0.62 | miles |
| | | |
| Hectares (10,000 m²) . . . . . . . . | 2.47 | acres |
| Square kilometers . . . . . . . . . . | 0.39 | square miles |
| | | |
| Cubic meters . . . . . . . . . . . . . | 35.3 | cubic feet |
| Liters . . . . . . . . . . . . . . . . . | 0.26 | gallons |
| | | |
| Kilograms . . . . . . . . . . . . . . | 2.2 | pounds |
| Metric tons . . . . . . . . . . . . . . | 0.98 | long tons |
| . . . . . . . . . . . . . . . | 1.1 | short tons |
| . . . . . . . . . . . . . . . | 2,204 | pounds |
| | | |
| Degrees Celsius . . . . . . . . . . . | 9 | degrees Fahrenheit |
| (Centigrade) | divide by 5 and add 32 | |

## Table 2.   Area, Population, and Population Density by Province, 1980

| Province | Area (in square kilometers) | Population Males | Females | Total | Per Square Kilometer |
|---|---|---|---|---|---|
| Cabo Delgado . | 82,625 | 445,300 | 494,700 | 940,000 | 11.4 |
| Gaza . . . . . . | 75,709 | 469,300 | 521,600 | 990,900 | 13.1 |
| Inhambane . . . | 68,615 | 458,100 | 539,500 | 997,600 | 14.5 |
| Manica . . . . . | 61,661 | 307,200 | 334,000 | 641,200 | 10.4 |
| Maputo . . . . . | 25,756 | 235,700 | 256,100 | 491,800 | 19.1 |
| Maputo (city) . | 602 | 404,000 | 351,300 | 755,300 | 1,254.7 |
| Nampula . . . . | 81,606 | 1,189,200 | 1,213,500 | 2,402,700 | 29.4 |
| Niassa . . . . . . | 129,056 | 246,300 | 267,800 | 514,100 | 4.0 |
| Sofala . . . . . . | 68,018 | 535,200 | 530,000 | 1,065,200 | 15.7 |
| Tete . . . . . . . | 100,724 | 393,100 | 437,400 | 831,000 | 8.3 |
| Zambezia . . . . | 105,008 | 1,224,600 | 1,275,600 | 2,500,200 | 23.8 |
| MOZAMBIQUE . | 799,380 | 5,908,000 | 6,221,500 | 12,130,000 | 15.2 |

Source:  Based on information from Mozambique, Comissão Nacional do Plano, *Moçambique: informação estadística, 1980–81*, Maputo, June 1982, 29.

*Table 3.* Selected Marketed Agricultural Products, 1980 and 1981*

| Product | Unit | 1980 | 1981 |
|---|---|---|---|
| Agricultural | | | |
| Cashews . . . . . . . . . . . . . . . | 1,000 tons | 17.6 | 16.9 |
| Sugar . . . . . . . . . . . . . . . . | -do- | 170.0 | 177.7 |
| Seed cotton . . . . . . . . . . . . | -do- | 63.9 | 73.6 |
| Rice . . . . . . . . . . . . . . . . . | -do- | 42.9 | 28.9 |
| Maize . . . . . . . . . . . . . . . . | -do- | 65.0 | 78.3 |
| Sunflower seeds . . . . . . . . . | -do- | 11.8 | 12.0 |
| Potatoes . . . . . . . . . . . . . . | -do- | 9.0 | 13.9 |
| Fruits (other than citrus) . . . . . | -do- | 6.3 | 2.2 |
| Beans . . . . . . . . . . . . . . . . | -do- | 9.6 | 14.1 |
| Copra . . . . . . . . . . . . . . . . | -do- | 37.1 | 54.4 |
| Tea (green leaf) . . . . . . . . . . | -do- | 94.7 | 99.2 |
| Citrus fruit . . . . . . . . . . . . | -do- | 32.0 | 36.7 |
| Livestock | | | |
| Beef . . . . . . . . . . . . . . . . . | tons | n.a. | 6,768.5 |
| Pork . . . . . . . . . . . . . . . . . | -do- | n.a. | 1,162.8 |
| Chicken meat . . . . . . . . . . . | -do- | n.a. | 5,375.0 |
| Other meat . . . . . . . . . . . . | -do- | n.a. | 87.1 |
| Eggs . . . . . . . . . . . . . . . | 1,000 tons | n.a. | 48,008.0 |
| Milk . . . . . . . . . . . . . . . . . | 1,000 liters | n.a. | 4,093.0 |

n.a.—not available.

*Total products marketed by commercial and subsistence sectors; earlier comparable data not available.

Source: Based on information from Mozambique, Comissão Nacional do Plano, *Moçambique: informação estadística, 1980/81*, Maputo, June 1982, 48.

Table 4. *Principal Exports, Selected Years, 1975-82*
(in millions of meticais)[1]

| Product | 1975 | 1977 | 1979 | 1981 | 1982 |
|---|---|---|---|---|---|
| Cashews and products . . | 780 | 1,468 | 1,445 | 1,890 | 1,647 |
| Shrimp . . . . . . . . . . . | 276 | 366 | 753 | 1,852 | 1,454 |
| Sugar . . . . . . . . . . . | 575 | 260 | 952 | 888 | 331 |
| Tea . . . . . . . . . . . . . | 177 | 409 | 680 | 502 | 870 |
| Timber . . . . . . . . . . | 375 | 154 | 206 | 260 | 124 |
| Cotton . . . . . . . . . . . | 439 | 288 | 761 | 881 | 653 |
| Tires . . . . . . . . . . . . | --- | --- | -.- | 62 | 259 |
| Cement . . . . . . . . . . | 16 | 178 | 147 | 109 | 121 |
| Coal . . . . . . . . . . . . | 177 | 148 | 158 | 344 | 158 |
| Petroleum and petroleum products . . . . . . . . | 370 | 329 | 1,111 | 1,848 | 1,421 |
| Other . . . . . . . . . . . | 1,865 | 1,323 | 2,089 | 1,290 | 1,517 |
| TOTAL . . . . . . . . . . | 5,050 | 4,923 | 8,311[2] | 9,926 | 8,655[2] |

---means none.
[1] For value of the metical—see Glossary.
[2] Total as published.

Source: Based on information from Mozambique, National Planning Commission, *Economic Report*, Maputo, January 1984, 25.

## Table 5. Imports by Major Categories, Selected Years, 1975-82 (in millions of meticais)*

| Product | 1975 | 1977 | 1979 | 1981 | 1982 |
|---|---|---|---|---|---|
| Consumer goods, food, and other commodities . . . . . . . . . | 3,127 | 2,639 | 4,798 | 6,303 | 6,362 |
| Raw materials Petroleum and petroleum products . . . . . . . . . . . . | 1,585 | 1,738 | 4,470 | 5,906 | 8,044 |
| Other . . . . . . . . . . . . . . . . | 2,870 | 3,283 | 3,539 | 7,070 | 6,248 |
| Total raw materials . . . , | 4,455 | 5,021 | 8,009 | 12,976 | 14,292 |
| Spare parts . . . . . . . . . . . . . . | 1,365 | 1,601 | 1,634 | 3,690 | 4,061 |
| Equipment . . . . . . . . . . . . . . | 1,798 | 1,560 | 4,134 | 5,348 | 6,859 |
| TOTAL . . . . . . . . . . . . . . . . | 10,745 | 10,821 | 18,575 | 28,317 | 31,574 |

* For value of the metical—see Glossary.

Source: Based on information from Mozambique, National Planning Commission, *Economic Report*, Maputo, January 1984, 24.

Table 6. Destination of Exports, Selected Years, 1974–82
(in millions of United States dollars)

| Destination | 1974 | 1976 | 1978 | 1980 | 1982 |
|---|---|---|---|---|---|
| Industrialized countries | | | | | |
| United States . . . . . . . . . . . . | 31.5 | 40.3 | 38.0 | 102.6 | 51.3 |
| Japan . . . . . . . . . . . . . . . . . | 6.9 | 32.5 | 39.8 | 17.3 | 20.2 |
| European Economic Community[1] | 46.7 | 104.3 | 77.9 | 84.4 | 60.2 |
| Other . . . . . . . . . . . . . . . . . | 19.9 | 18.0 | 20.6 | 15.4 | 17.2 |
|    Total industrialized | | | | | |
|     countries . . . . . . . . . | 105.0 | 195.1 | 176.3 | 219.7 | 148.9 |
| Developing countries | | | | | |
| Europe | | | | | |
|   Portugal . . . . . . . . . . . . . . | 99.5 | 45.4 | 18.7 | 19.7 | 12.3 |
|   Other . . . . . . . . . . . . . . | 0.1 | 0.2 | 0.1 | 0.3 | --- |
|     Total Europe . . . . . . . | 99.6 | 45.6 | 18.8 | 20.0 | 12.3 |
| Western Hemisphere . . . . . . . | 0.3 | 2.8 | 0.4 | 0.8 | 13.1 |
| OPEC[2] . . . . . . . . . . . . . . . | 1.7 | 3.5 | 60.5 | 68.5 | 29.8 |
| Middle East, (non-OPEC) . . . . | 2.5 | 1.1 | 5.9 | 24.3 | 21.6 |
| Africa | | | | | |
|   South Africa . . . . . . . . . . | 27.8 | n.a. | n.a. | n.a. | n.a. |
|   Other . . . . . . . . . . . . . . | 28.5 | 21.4 | 15.7 | 55.1 | 21.3 |
|     Total Africa . . . . . . . . . | 56.3 | 21.4 | 15.7 | 55.1 | 21.3 |
| Asia | | | | | |
|   Singapore . . . . . . . . . . . . | 0.2 | 3.0 | 25.8 | 43.1 | 17.6 |
|   Other . . . . . . . . . . . . . . | 18.1 | 8.5 | 9.5 | 25.2 | 12.6 |
|     Total Asia . . . . . . . . . | 18.3 | 11.5 | 35.3 | 68.3 | 30.2 |
|   Total developing | | | | | |
|     countries . . . . . . . . . | 178.7 | 85.9 | 136.6 | 237.0 | 128.3 |
| Unspecified and special | | | | | |
|   category . . . . . . . . . . . . . . | 14.9 | 11.0 | 15.3 | 30.6 | 26.1 |
| TOTAL[3] . . . . . . . . . . . . . . . . | 298.7 | 292.1 | 328.2 | 487.7 | 303.2 |

---means none.
n.a.—not available.
[1] Includes Belgium, Denmark, France, West Germany, Ireland, Italy, Netherlands, and United Kingdom.
[2] Organization of Petroleum Exporting Countries.
[3] Figures may not add to total because of rounding.

Source: Based on information from *Direction of Trade Statistics Yearbook, 1981*, Washington, 1981, 270–71; and *Direction of Trade Statistics Yearbook, 1983*, Washington, 1983, 281–82.

*Appendix*

### Table 7.   Sources of Imports, Selected Years, 1974–82
(in millions of United States dollars)

| Source | 1974 | 1976 | 1978 | 1980 | 1982 |
|---|---|---|---|---|---|
| **Industrialized countries** | | | | | |
| United States | 27.1 | 13.4 | 22.2 | 76.3 | 29.0 |
| Japan | 31.1 | 14.7 | 34.4 | 39.0 | 19.5 |
| European Economic Community[1] | 154.5 | 118.1 | 139.2 | 199.8 | 195.7 |
| Other | 24.4 | 31.8 | 70.3 | 59.0 | 83.8 |
| Total industrialized countries | 237.1 | 178.0 | 266.1 | 374.1 | 328.0 |
| **Developing countries** | | | | | |
| Europe | | | | | |
| Portugal | 77.6 | 29.9 | 37.9 | 41.0 | 63.1 |
| Other | --- | 1.3 | 0.3 | 6.3 | 2.1 |
| Total Europe | 77.6 | 31.2 | 38.2 | 47.3 | 65.2 |
| Western Hemisphere | | | | | |
| Brazil | 2.5 | 4.4 | 5.5 | 79.5 | 108.6 |
| Other | 0.3 | 2.3 | 5.0 | 1.9 | 0.9 |
| Total Western Hemisphere | 2.8 | 6.7 | 10.5 | 81.4 | 109.5 |
| OPEC[2] | | | | | |
| Iraq | 1.1 | 45.9 | 4.6 | --- | --- |
| Saudi Arabia | 23.9 | 21.3 | --- | 4.1 | 19.1 |
| United Arab Emirates | --- | --- | --- | 29.5 | 84.6 |
| Other | 11.3 | 4.1 | 2.2 | 4.6 | 6.8 |
| Total OPEC | 36.3 | 71.3 | 6.8 | 38.2 | 110.5 |
| Middle East, (non-OPEC) | 1.3 | 12.4 | 1.0 | --- | 5.7 |
| Africa | | | | | |
| Kenya | ... | 0.6 | 0.5 | 1.7 | 21.8 |
| South Africa | 91.4 | n.a. | n.a. | n.a. | n.a. |
| Zimbabwe | --- | 44.6 | --- | --- | 27.5 |
| Other | 11.7 | 7.1 | 14.4 | 21.9 | 3.8 |
| Total Africa | 103.1 | 52.3 | 14.9 | 23.6 | 53.1 |
| Asia | | | | | |
| Bangladesh | --- | 22.3 | 19.3 | 29.1 | 39.0 |
| Malaysia | 0.5 | 1.7 | 5.2 | 9.3 | 10.1 |
| Other | 7.6 | 7.2 | 19.6 | 18.9 | 24.4 |
| Total Asia | 8.1 | 31.2 | 44.1 | 57.3 | 73.5 |
| Total developing countries | 229.2 | 205.1 | 115.5 | 247.8 | 417.5 |
| Unspecified and special category | 0.5 | — | 25.7 | 51.3 | 43.6 |
| **TOTAL[3]** | 467.0 | 383.9 | 411.2 | 673.7 | 792.2 |

---means none.
... means less than one-half of the unit.
n.a.—not available.
[1] Includes Belgium, Denmark, France, West Germany, Ireland, Italy, Netherlands, and United Kingdom.
[2] Organization of Petroleum Exporting Countries.
[3] Totals as published.

Source: Based on information from *Direction of Trade Statistics Yearbook, 1981,* Washington, 1981, 270–71; and *Direction of Trade Statistics Yearbook, 1983,* Washington, 1983, 281–82.

Table 8.    *Balance of Payments, 1980–83*
(in billions of meticais)[1]

| | 1980 | 1981 | 1982 | 1983[2] |
|---|---|---|---|---|
| Merchandise | | | | |
| Exports . . . . . . . . . . . . | 8.20 | 7.88 | 7.50 | 4.40 |
| Imports . . . . . . . . . . . | 22.34 | 24.34 | 24.37 | 19.62 |
| Net merchandise . . . . . | − 14.14 | − 16.46 | − 16.87 | − 15.22 |
| Productive services and invisibles | | | | |
| Income . . . . . . . . . . . . | 5.41 | 6.05 | 6.24 | 6.94 |
| Expenditures . . . . . . . . | 2.08 | 2.87 | 2.84 | 2.65 |
| Net productive services and invisibles . . . . . . | + 3.33 | + 3.18 | + 3.40 | + 4.29 |
| Donations . . . . . . . . . . | + 1.81 | + 1.73 | + 2.70 | + 2.98 |
| Current account balance . . | − 9.00 | −11.55 | − 10.77 | − 7.95 |
| Capital account | | | | |
| Receipts . . . . . . . . . . . | 13.16 | 23.81 | 21.66 | 13.32 |
| Payments | | | | |
| Principal . . . . . . . . . | 4.50 | 10.93 | 12.44 | 4.75 |
| Interest . . . . . . . . . . | 0.20 | 1.27 | 2.28 | 1.02 |
| Total payments . . . . . | 4.70 | 12.20 | 14.72 | 5.77 |
| Capital account balance . . | + 8.46 | +11.61 | + 6.94 | + 7.55 |
| Errors and omissions . . . . . . | − 0.51 | − 0.85 | − 0.61 | − 0.49 |
| Balance of payments . . . . . | − 1.05 | − 0.79 | − 4.44 | − 0.89 |

[1] For value of the metical—see Glossary.
[2] Preliminary.

Source: Based on information from Mozambique, National Planning Commission, *Economic Report*, Maputo, January 1984, 44.

## Table 9.  Council of Ministers, 1984

| Position | Incumbent |
| --- | --- |
| President . . . . . . . . . . . . . . . . . . . . | Samora Moises Machel |

Ministers
Agriculture . . . . . . . . . . . . . . . . . . Joāo dos Santos Ferreira
Defense . . . . . . . . . . . . . . . . . . . Alberto Joaquim Chipande
Economic affairs in the presidency . . . . Jacinto Veloso
Education and culture . . . . . . . . . . . Graça Machel
Finance . . . . . . . . . . . . . . . . . . . Rui Baltazar dos Santos Alves
Foreign affairs . . . . . . . . . . . . . . . Joaquim Alberto Chissano
Foreign trade . . . . . . . . . . . . . . . . Joaquim Ribiero de Carvalho
Health . . . . . . . . . . . . . . . . . . . . Pascoal Mocumbi
Industry and power . . . . . . . . . . . . Antōnio Lima Rodrigues Branco
Information . . . . . . . . . . . . . . . . . José Luis Cabaço
Interior . . . . . . . . . . . . . . . . . . . . Armando Emilio Guebuza
Internal trade . . . . . . . . . . . . . . . Manuel Jorge Aranda da Silva
Justice . . . . . . . . . . . . . . . . . . . . José Oscar Monteiro
Mineral resources . . . . . . . . . . . . . José Carlos Lobo
Planning . . . . . . . . . . . . . . . . . . . Mário da Graça Machungo
Ports, railways, and merchant marine . . Luis Alcantara Santos
Posts and telecommunications . . . . . . Rui Lousā
Public works . . . . . . . . . . . . . . . . Júlio Zamith Carrilho
Security . . . . . . . . . . . . . . . . . . . Mariano de Araujo Matsinhe

Governor of the Bank of Mozambique . . . Prakash Ratilal

Vice minister of defense and chief of the
General Staff of the army . . . . . . . . . Sebastião Marcos Mabote

Source: Based on information from Mocambique, National Planning Commission, *Economic Report*, Maputo, January 1984, Appendix 1, 1–2.

Table 10.    *Leading FRELIMO Officials, 1984\**

| Political Bureau of the Central Committee | Government Position |
|---|---|
| Samora Moises Machel, president of FRELIMO | President of Mozambique |
| Marcelino dos Santos | Resident minister to Sofala Province |
| Joaquim Alberto Chissano | Minister of foreign affairs |
| Alberto Joaquim Chipande | In charge of Cabo Delgado Province; minister of defense |
| Armando Emilio Guebuza | Minister of interior |
| Jorge Rebelo | none |
| Mariano de Araujo Matsinhe | Minister of security |
| Sebastião Marcos Mabote | Vice minister of defense and chief of the General Staff of the Army |
| Jacinto Veloso | Minister for economic affairs in the presidency |
| Mário da Graça Machungo | In charge of  Zambezia Province; minister of planning |
| José Oscar Monteiro | Minister of justice |

*Secretariat of the Central Committee*
Samora Moises Machel
Marcelino dos Santos
Joaquim Alberto Chissano
Jorge Rebelo
Armando Panguene
José Luis Cabaço

*Control Committee of the Central Committee*
Mariano de Araujo Matsinhe, secretary
Raimundo Pachinaupa, assistant secretary

\*  FRELIMO—Frente de Libertação de Moçambique
(Front for the Liberation of Mozambique).

Source:  Based on information from Foreign Broadcast Information Service, *Daily Report: Middle East and Africa*, May 17, 1983, U2.

# Bibliography

## Chapter 1

Abshire, David M., and Michael A. Samuels (eds.). *Portuguese Africa: A Handbook*. New York: Praeger with the Center for Strategic and International Studies, Georgetown University, 1969.

Allen, James de Vere. "Swahili Culture and the Nature of East Coast Settlement," *International Journal of African Historical Studies*, 14, No. 2, 1981, 306–34.

Alpers, Edward A. "Dynasties of the Mutapa-Rozwi Complex," *Journal of African History* [London], 11, No. 2, 1970, 203–20.

————. "Ethnicity, Politics, and History in Mozambique," *Africa Today*, 21, No. 4, Fall 1974, 39–52.

————. *Ivory and Slaves in East Central Africa: Changing Patterns of International Trade to the Late Nineteenth Century*. Berkeley and Los Angeles: University of California Press, 1975

————. "The Struggle for Socialism in Mozambique, 1960–72." Pages 267-95 in C.G. Rosberg and T.M. Callaghy (eds.), *Socialism in Sub-Saharan Africa*. Berkeley: Institute of International Studies, University of California, 1979.

————. "Towards a History of the Expansion of Islam in East Africa: the Matrilineal Peoples of the Southern Interior." Pages 172–201 in Terence O. Ranger and I.N. Kimambo (eds.), *The Historical Study of African Religion*. Berkeley and Los Angeles: University of California Press, 1972.

————. "Trade, State, and Society among the Yao in the Nineteenth Century," *Journal of African History* [London], 10, No. 3, 1969, 405–20.

Alpers, Edward A., and C. Ehret. "Eastern Africa." Pages 469-536 in Richard Gray (ed.) *The Cambridge History of Africa, IV (from c. 1600 to c. 1790)*. Cambridge: Cambridge University Press, 1975.

Axelson, Eric. *Portuguese in Southeast Africa, 1498–1600*. Mystic, Connecticut: Verry, 1973.

————. *Portuguese in South-East Africa, 1600-1700*. Johannesburg: Witwatersrand University Press, 1960.

Birmingham, David, and Shula Marks. "Southern Africa." Pages 567-620 in Roland Oliver (ed.), *The Cambridge History of Africa, III (from c. 1050 to c. 1600)*. Cambridge: Cambridge Unviersity Press, 1977.

Boxer, Charles R. *Four Centuries of Portuguese Expansion, 1415–1825: A Succinct Survey*. Berkeley and Los Angeles: University of California Press, 1972.

———. *The Portuguese Seaborne Empire, 1415–1825*. New York: Knopf, 1969.

———. *Race Relations in the Portuguese Colonial Empire, 1415-1825*. Oxford: Clarendon Press, 1963.

Breytenback, W.J. *Migratory Labour Arrangements in Southern Africa*. (Communications at the Africa Institute, No. 20) Pretoria: Africa Institute of South Africa, 1972.

Bruce, Neil. *Portugal: The Last Empire*. New York: Wiley, 1975.

Chanaiwa, David. "Politics and Long-Distance Trade in the Mwene Mutapa Empire During the Sixteenth Century," *International Journal of African Historical Studies*, 5, No. 3, 1972, 424–35.

Chittick, H. Neville. "The East Coast, Madagascar, and the Indian Ocean." Pages 183-231 in Roland Oliver (ed.), *The Cambridge History of Africa, III (from c. 1050 to c. 1600)*. Cambridge: Cambridge University Press, 1977.

Curtin, Philip D. *The Atlantic Slave Trade: A Census*. Madison: University of Wisconsin Press, 1969.

De Oliveira Marques, A.H. *History of Portugal*. 2 vols. New York: Columbia University Press, 1972.

Duffy, James. *Portugal in Africa*. Cambridge: Harvard University Press, 1962.

———. *Portuguese Africa*. Cambridge: Harvard University Press, 1959.

———. "Portuguese Africa, 1930 to 1960." Pages 171–93 in L.H. Gann and Peter Duignan (eds.), *Colonialism in Africa, 1870–1960, Vol. 2: The History and Politics of Colonialism, 1914–1960*. Cambridge: Cambridge University Press, 1970.

Fagan, Brian M. "Early Trade and Raw Materials in South Central Africa," *Journal of African History* [London], 10, No. 1, 1969, 1-13.

Fieldhouse, D.K. *The Colonial Empires: A Comparative Survey from the Eighteenth Century*. New York: Delacorte Press, 1967.

First, Ruth. *Portugal's Wars in Africa*. London: Christian Action, 1971.

Freeman-Grenville, G.S.P. "The Coast, 1498–1840." Pages 129-68 in Roland Oliver and Gervase Mathew (eds.), *History of*

*East Africa*. Oxford: Clarendon Press, 1963.

Freyre, Gilberto. *The Portuguese and the Tropics*. Lisbon: Executive Committee for the Commemoration of the Fifth Centenary of the Death of Henry the Navigator, 1961.

————. *Portuguese Integration in the Tropics*. Lisbon: Realização Gráfica da Tipografia Silva, 1961.

Gann, L. H. "Portugal, Africa, and the Future," *Journal of Modern African Studies* [London], 13, No. 1, 1975, 1-18.

Gray, Richard. "Portuguese Musketeers on the Zambezi," *Journal of African History* [London], 12, No. 4, 1971, 531-33.

Gutteridge, William F. "Military and Police Forces in Colonial Africa." Pages 286–319 in L. H. Gann and Peter Duignan (eds.), *Colonialism in Africa, 1870–1960, Vol. 2: The History and Politics of Colonialism, 1914–1960*. Cambridge: Cambridge University Press, 1970.

Hammond, Richard J. *Portugal and Africa, 1815–1910: A Study in Uneconomic Imperialism*. Stanford: Stanford University Press, 1966.

————. "Race Attitudes and Policies in Portuguese Africa in the Nineteenth and Twentieth Centuries," *Race* [London], 9, No. 2, October 1967, 205-16.

————. "Some Economic Aspects of Portuguese Africa in the Nineteenth and Twentieth Centuries." Pages 256–82 in Peter Duignan and L. H. Gann (eds.), *Colonialism in Africa, 1870–1960, Vol. 4: The Economics of Colonialism*, Cambridge: Cambridge University Press, 1969.

————. "Uneconomic Imperialism: Portugal in Africa Before 1910." Pages 352–82 in L. H. Gann and Peter Duignan (eds.), *Colonialism in Africa, 1870–1960, Vol. 1: The History and Politics of Colonialism, 1870–1914*. Cambridge: Cambridge University Press, 1969.

Hastings, Adrian. *A History of African Christianity, 1950–1975*. Cambridge: Cambridge University Press, 1979.

Henriksen, Thomas H. "Angola and Mozambique: Intervention and Revolution," *Current History*, 71, No. 421, November 1976, 153-57.

————. *Mozambique: A History*. London: Collings, 1978.

————. "People's War in Angola, Mozambique, and Guinea-Bissau," *Journal of Modern African Studies* [London], 14, No. 3, September 1976, 377-99.

————. "Portugal in Africa: A Noneconomic Interpretation," *African Studies Review*, 16, No. 3, December 1973, 405-16.

————. *Revolution and Counterrevolution: Mozambique's War of Independence, 1964–1974*. Westport, Connecticut:

Greenwood Press, 1983.

――――. "Revolutionary Thought of Eduardo Mondlane," *Génève-Afrique* [Geneva], 12, No. 1, January 1973, 37–52.

Hodges, Tony. "Mozambique: The Politics of Liberation." Pages 57–92 in Gwendolen M. Carter and Patrick O'Meara (eds.), *Southern Africa: The Continuing Crisis*. Bloomington: Indiana University Press, 1979.

Huffman, T. N. "The Rise and Fall of Zimbabwe," *Journal of African History* [London], 13, No. 3, 1972, 353–66.

Isaacman, Allen F. *A Luta Continua: Creating a New Society in Mozambique*. (Southern Africa Pamphlets, No. 1) Binghamton, New York: Fernand Braudel Center for the Study of Economies, Historical Systems, and Civilizations, State University of New York, 1978.

――――. "Madzi-Manga, Mhondoro, and the Use of Oral Traditions: A Chapter in Barue Religions and Political History," *Journal of African History* [London], 14, No. 3, 1973, 395–409.

――――. *Mozambique: From Colonialism to Revolution, 1900–1982*. Boulder: Westview Press, 1983.

――――. *Mozamibique—The Africanization of a European Institution: The Zambezi Prazos, 1750–1901*. Madison: University of Wisconsin Press, 1972.

――――. "The Origin, Formation, and Early History of the Chikunda of South Central Africa," *Journal of African History* [London], 13, No. 3, 1972, 443–61.

――――. "The Tradition of Resistance in Mozambique," *Africa Today*, 22, No. 3, July-September 1975, 37–50.

――――. *The Tradition of Resistance in Mozambique: The Zambesi Valley, 1850–1921*. Berkeley and Los Angeles: University of California Press, 1976.

Katzenellenbogen, Simon E. *Southern Africa and Southern Mozambique: Labour, Railways, and Trade in the Making of a Relationship*. Manchester: Manchester University Press, 1982.

Latham, S. F. "About-Turn in Mozambique?" *World Today* [London], 37, No. 2, February 1981, 69–73.

Liesegang, Gerhard. "Dingane's Attack on Lourenço Marques in 1833," *Journal of African History* [London], 10, No. 4, 1969, 565–79.

Livermore, H. V. *A New History of Portugal*. Cambridge: Cambridge University Press, 1969.

Maier, F.X. *Revolution and Terrorism in Mozambique*. New York: American African Affairs Association, 1974.

Marks, Shula. "Southern Africa and Mozambique." Pages 384–

468 in Richard Gray (ed.), *The Cambridge History of Africa, IV (from c. 1600 to c. 1790)*. Cambridge: Cambridge University Press, 1975.

Mathew, Gervase. "The East African Coast until the Coming of the Portuguese." Pages 94–128 in Roland Oliver and Gervase Mathew (eds.), *History of East Africa*, 1. Oxford: Clarendon Press, 1963.

Middlemas, Keith. *Cabora Bassa: Engineering and Politics in Southern Africa*. London: Weidenfeld and Nicolson, 1976.

———. "Independent Mozambique and Its Regional Policy." Pages 213–33 in John Seiler (ed.), *Southern Africa since the Portuguese Coup*. Boulder: Westview Press, 1980.

———. "Twentieth Century White Society in Mozambique," *Tarikh* [Lagos], 6, No. 2, 1979, 30–45.

Mondlane, Eduardo C. "Struggle for Independence in Mozambique." Pages 195–210 in John L. Davis and James K. Baker (eds.), *Southern Africa in Transition*. London: Pall Mall Press, 1966.

———. *The Struggle for Mozambique*. Baltimore: Penguin Books, 1969.

Moreira, Adriano. *Portugal's Stand in Africa*. New York: University Publishers, 1962.

Mudenge, S.I. "The Role of Foreign Trade in the Rozvi Empire: A Reappraisal," *Journal of African History* [London], 15, No. 3, 1974, 373–91.

Newbury, Colin W. "Historical Aspects of Manpower and Migration in Africa South of the Sahara." Pages 523–45 in Peter Duignan and L.G. Gann (eds.), *Colonialism in Africa, 1870–1960, Vol. 4: The Economics of Colonialism*. Cambridge: Cambridge University Press, 1975.

Newitt, M.D.D. "Angoche, the Slave Trade, and the Portuguese, c. 1844–1910," *Journal of African History* [London], 13, No. 4, 1972, 659–72.

———. "The Early History of the Maravi," *Journal of African History* [London], 23, No. 2, 1982, 145–62.

———. "The Early History of the Sultanate of Angoche," *Journal of African History* [London], 13, No. 3, 1972, 397–406.

———. "The Massingire Rising of 1884," *Journal of African History* [London], 11, No. 1, 1970, 87–105.

———. *Portugal in Africa: The Last Hundred Years*. London: Longman, 1981.

———. "The Portuguese on the Zambezi: An Historical Interpretation of the Prazo System," *Journal of African History*

[London], 10, No. 1, 1969, 67–85.

―――. "The Portuguese on the Zambezi from the Seventeenth to the Nineteenth Centuries," *Race* [London], 9, No. 4, April 1968, 87–105.

―――. *Portuguese Settlement on the Zambezi: Exploration, Land Tenure, and Colonial Rule in East Africa*. London: Longman, 1973.

Nowell, Charles E. "Portugal and the Partition of Africa," *Journal of Modern History*, 19, No. 1, March 1947, 1–17.

O'Ballance, Edgar. "To Turn His Coat—or Not?" *Journal of the Royal United Services Institute for Defence Studies* [London], 1, No. 118, March 1973, 85–87.

Oliveira Marques, A.H. de. *History of Portugal*. 2 vols. New York: Columbia University Press, 1972.

Oliver, Roland. "The Problem of the Bantu Expansion," *Journal of African History* [London], 7, No. 3, 1966, 361–76.

Oliver, Roland, and Anthony Atmore. *Africa since 1800*. Cambridge: Cambridge University Press, 1972.

Oliver, Roland, and Brian M. Fagan. *Africa in the Iron Age: c. 500 B.C. to A.D. 1400*. Cambridge: Cambridge University Press, 1975.

―――. "The Emergence of Bantu Africa." Pages 342–409 in J.D. Fage (ed.), *The Cambridge History of Africa, II (from c. 500 B.C. to A.D. 1050)*. Cambridge: Cambridge University Press, 1978.

Oliver, Roland, and J.D. Fage. *A Short History of Africa*. Baltimore: Penguin Books, 1962.

Omer-Cooper, John D. "Aspects of Political Change in the Nineteenth-Century Mfecane." Pages 207–29 in Leonard Thompson (ed.), *African Societies in Southern Africa*. New York: Praeger, 1969.

―――. "The Nguni Outburst." Pages 319–52 in John E. Flint (ed.), *The Cambridge History of Africa, V (from c. 1790 to c. 1870)*. Cambridge: Cambridge University Press, 1976.

Opello, Walter C., Jr. "Pluralism and Elite Conflict in an Independence Movement: FRELIMO in the 1960s," *Journal of Southern African Studies* [London], 2, No. 1, October 1975, 66–82.

Ottaway, David, and Marina Ottaway. *Afrocommunism*. New York: Africana, 1981.

Payne, Stanley G. *A History of Spain and Portugal*. 2 vols. Madison: University of Wisconsin Press, 1973.

Phillipson, D.W. "The Chronology of the Iron Age in Bantu Africa," *Journal of African History* [London], 16, No. 3, 1975,

321–42.

Rasmussen, R. Kent. *Historical Dictionary of Rhodesia/Zimbabwe*. (African Historical Dictionaries, No. 18) Metuchen, New Jersey: Sacrecrow Press, 1979.

Rennie, J.K. "The Ngoni States and European Intrusion." Pages 302–31 in Eric Stokes and Richard Brown (eds.), *The Zambesian Past: Studies in Central African History*. Manchester: Manchester University Press, 1966.

Rita-Ferreira, António. "The Ethno-history and the Ethnic Grouping of the Peoples of Mozambique," *South African Journal of African Affairs* [Pretoria], 3, 1973, 56–76.

Robinson, K.R. "The Archaeology of the Rozwi." Pages 3–27 in Eric Stokes and Richard Brown (eds.), *The Zambesian Past: Studies in Central African History*. Manchester: Manchester University Press, 1966.

Saul, John S. *The State and Revolution in Eastern Africa*. New York: Monthly Review Press, 1979.

Serapião, Luís Benjamin. "Church and State in Mozambican Politics, 1960–1980," *Lusophone Areas Studies Journal* [Ile-Ife, Nigeria], 1, No. 1, January 1983, 67–86.

―――. "The Roman Catholic Church and the Principle of Self Determination: A Case Study in Mozambique," *Journal of Church and State*, 23, No. 2, 1981, 323–35.

Serapião, Luís Benjamin, and Mohamed A. El-Khawas. *Mozambique in the Twentieth Century: From Colonialism to Independence*. Washington: University Press of America, 1979.

Shinnie, Margaret. *Ancient African Kingdoms*. New York: New American Library, 1970.

Smith, Alan K. "António Salazar and the Reversal of Portuguese Colonial Policy," *Journal of African History* [London], 15, No. 4, 1974, 653–67.

―――. "Delagoa Bay and the Trade of South-Eastern Africa." Pages 265–90 in Richard Gray and David Birmingham (eds.), *Pre-Colonial Trade: Essays on Trade in Central and Eastern Africa Before 1900*. London: Oxford University Press, 1970.

―――. "The Peoples of Southern Mozambique: An Historical Survey," *Journal of African History* [London], 14, No. 4, 1973, 565–80.

―――. "The Trade of Delagoa Bay as a Factor in Nguni Politics." Pages 171–89 in Leonard Thompson (ed.), *African Societies in Southern Africa*. New York: Praeger, 1970.

Sutherland-Harris, Nicola. "Trade and the Rozwi Mambo." Pages 243–64 in Richard Gray and David Birmingham (eds.), *Pre-Colonial African Trade: Essays on Trade in Central and East-*

*ern Africa Before 1900*. London: Oxford University Press, 1970.

————. "Zambian Trade with Zumbo in the Eighteenth Century." Pages 231–42 in Richard Gray and David Birmingham (eds.), *Pre-Colonial African Trade: Essays on Trade in Central and Eastern Africa Before 1900*. London: Oxford University Press, 1970.

Vail, Leroy. "Mozambique's Chartered Companies: The Rule of the Feeble," *Journal of African History* [London], 17, No. 3, 1976, 389–416.

Vail, Leroy, and Landeg White. *Capitalism and Colonialism in Mozambique: A Study of the Quelimane District*. Minneapolis: University of Mininesota Press, 1980.

Warhurst, Philip R. *Anglo-Portuguese Relations in South-Central Africa, 1890–1900*. London: Longmans for the Royal Commonwealth Society, 1962.

————. "The Scramble and African Politics in Gazaland." Pages 47–62 in Erik Stokes and Richard Brown (eds.), *The Zambesian Past: Studies in Central African History*. Manchester: Manchester University Press, 1966.

Wheeler, Douglas L. "African Elements in Portugal's Armies in Africa (1961–1974)," *Armed Forces and Society*, 2, No. 2, Winter 1976, 233–50.

————. "Gungunhana." Pages 165–220 in N.R. Bennett (ed.), *Leadership in Eastern Africa*. Boston: Boston University Press, 1968.

————. "Gungunyane the Negotiator: A Study in African Diplomacy," *Journal of African History* [London], 9, No. 4, 1968, 585–602.

## Chapter 2

Abshire, David M., and Michael A. Samuels (eds.). *Portuguese Africa: A Handbook*. New York: Praeger with the Center for Strategic and International Studies, Georgetown University, 1969.

Alpers, Edward A. "Ethnicity, Politics, and History in Mozambique," *Africa Today*, 21, No. 4, Fall 1974, 39-52.

Balmes, Pierre. "Le Mozambique," *Afrique contemporaine, 1978–79* [Paris], 18, No. 106, November-December 1979, 8–15.

Barnes, Barbara. "Education for Socialism in Mozambique," *Comparative Education Review*, 26, October 1982, 406–19.

Barrett, David B. (ed.). *World Christian Encyclopedia*. New York: Oxford University Press, 1982.

Bruno, David. "Mozambique's True Christians Put Themselves at Risk," *Johannesburg Star* [Johannesburg], December 13, 1980, 15.

*Casting New Molds—First Steps Toward Worker Control in a Mozambique Steel Factory: Conversation with Peter Sketchley and Francis Moore Lappé*. San Francisco: Institute for Food and Development Policy, 1980.

Constantin, François, and Christian Conlon. "Minoritiés Musulmanes et pourvoir politique en Afrique Orientale," *Annuaire des pays de l'Océan Indien* [Aix-en-Provence], 6, 1979, 19–47.

Dias, Jorge, and Margot Dias. *As Macondes de Moçambique, III: vida social e ritual*. Lisbon: Junta de Investigaçoes do Ultramar, Centro de Anthropologia Cultural, 1970.

Dimsdale, John. "Tanzania/Mozambique: Two Roads to Socialism," *Africa Report*, 27, No. 5, September-October 1982, 14–17.

Economist Intelligence Unit. *Quarterly Economic Review of Tanzania, Mozambique* [London], First Quarter, 1981.

————. *Quarterly Economic Review of Tanzania, Mozambique* [London], Second Quarter, 1982.

————. *Quarterly Economic Review of Tanzania, Mozambique* [London], Third Quarter, 1983.

————. *Quarterly Economic Review of Tanzania, Mozambique* [London], Fourth Quarter, 1983.

Ehret, Christopher, and Margaret Kinsman. "Shona Dialect Classification and Its Implications for Iron Age History in Southern Africa," *International Journal of African Historical Studies*, 14, No. 3, 1981, 401–43.

Fauvet, Paul. "Cholera: Killer Disease that Is Haunting Beira's Shantytown," *New African* [London], No. 167, August 1981, 89.

Federal Republic of Germany. Statistisches Bundesamt. *Länderkurzbericht: Mosambik, 1983*. Wiesbaden: September 1983.

"Fighting Killer Diseases," *Africa* [London], June 1979, 73–75.

First, Ruth. *Black Gold: The Mozambican Miner Proletarian and Peasant*. New York: St. Martin's Press, 1983.

Fivaz, Derek, and Patricia Scott. *African Languages: A Genetic and Decimalised Classification for Bibliographic and General Reference*. Boston: G.K. Hall, 1977.

Foy, Felician A. (ed.) *1983 Catholic Almanac*. Huntingdon, Indiana: Our Sunday Visitor, 1982.

Frankel, Glenn. "Mozambique Evicts Urbanites in Bid to Raise Productivity," *Washington Post*, October 9, Al.

Hanlon, Joseph. "A Country of Illiterates," *New African* [London], No. 149, January 1980, 31–32.

―――. "Machel Rounds on Rome," *Guardian* [London], January 14, 1983, 5.

―――. "Mozambique 'Villagisation': Hiccups Galore," *New African* [London], September 1982, 19–20.

―――. "Too Little, Too Late," *New Statesman* [London], February 3, 1984, 18.

―――. "Where Concrete Meets Crane," *New Scientist* [London], August 31, 1978, 627–29.

Harris, Laurence. "Agricultural Co-operatives and Development Policy in Mozambique," *Journal of Peasant Studies* [London], 7, No. 3, April 1980, 338–52.

Harris, Marvin. "The Assimilado System in Portuguese Mozambique," *African Report*, 3, No. 11, November 1958, 7–10.

―――. "Labor Migration among the Moçambique Thonga: Cultural and Political Factors." Pages 91–106 in Immanuel Wallerstein (ed.), *Social Change: The Colonial Situation*. New York: Wiley and Sons, 1966.

―――. "Race, Conflict, and Reform in Mozambique." Pages 157– 83 in Stanley Diamond and Fred G. Burke (eds.), *The Transformation of East Africa: Studies in Colonial Anthropology*. New York: Basic Books, 1966.

Hastings, Adrian. "The Christian Churches and Liberation Movements in Southern Africa," *African Affairs* [London], 80, No. 320, July 1981, 345–54.

Henriksen, Thomas H. *Mozambique: A History*. London: Collings, 1978.

―――. "People's Republic of Mozambique." Pages 527–52 in Bogdan Szajkowski (ed.), *Marxist Governments—A World Survey, Vol. 3: Mozambique-Yugoslavia*. New York: St. Martin's Press, 1981.

Hodges, Tony. "Mozambique: the Politics of Liberation." Pages 57–92 in Gwendolen M. Carter and Patrick O'Meara (eds.), *Southern Africa: The Continuing Crisis*. Bloomington: Indiana University Press, 1979.

Isaacman, Allen F. *A Luta Continua: Creating a New Society in Mozambique*. (Southern Africa Pamphlets, No. 1) Binghamton, New York: Fernand Braudel Center for the Study of Economies, Historical Systems, and Civilizations, State University of New York, 1978.

―――. "The Origin, Formation, and Early History of the Chikunda of South Central Africa," *Journal of African History* [London], 13, No. 3, 1972, 443–61.

Isaacman, Allen F., and Barbara Isaacman. *Mozambique: From Colonialism to Revolution, 1900–1982*. Boulder: Westview Press, 1983.

―――. "South Africa's Hidden War," *Africa Report*, 27, No. 6, November-December 1982, 4–8.

Isaacman, Barbara, and June Stephen. *Mozambique: Women, the Law, and Agrarian Reform*. Addis Ababa: United Nations Economic Commission for Africa, 1980.

Joint Publications Research Service—JPRS (Washington). The following items are from the JPRS series:

*Sub-Saharan Africa Report*.

"Activities of 'Operation Production' in Sofala," *Tempo*, Maputo, November 6, 1983. (JPRS 85000, No. 2886, December 22, 1983, 25–29).

"Article Examines Nation's Domestic Difficulties," *Le Monde*, Paris, May 25, 1983. (JPRS 83890, No. 2820, July 14, 1983, 30–33).

"The Bourgeoisie We Have," *Notícias*, Maputo, October 20, 1982. (JPRS 82309, No. 2725, November 23, 1982, 20–21).

"Census Results Provide Data on Literacy, Housing," *Tempo*, Maputo, October 3, 1982. (JPRS 82266, No. 2723, November 18, 1982, 8–11).

"First Hand Report on Mozambique by SA Journalist," *Rand Daily Mail*, Johannesburg, July 18, 19, 20, 22, 1983. (JPRS 84251, No. 2840, September 2, 1983, 19–25).

"GDR Solidarity School to Be Inaugurated in Stassfurt," *Notícias*, Maputo, September 14, 1982. (JPRS 82423, No. 2733, December 8, 1982, 48–50).

"Mozambique—Neither Western Democracy nor a Concentration Camp System," *O Jornal*, Lisbon, April 23–29, 1980. (JPRS 75775, No. 2257, May 20, 1980, 68–73).

"Portrait of Typical Petit Bourgeois Drawn," *Notícias*, Maputo, September 8, 1982. (JPRS 82215, No. 2718, November 10, 1982).

"Racism Is Not Dead," *Notícias*, Maputo. (JPRS 82215, No. 2718, November 10, 1982, 33–34).

"We Don't Want to Be Headed by Mahumos," *Tempo*, Maputo, June 8, 1980. (JPRS 76009, No. 2265, July 8, 1980, 117–19).

Kaplan, Irving, et al. *Area Handbook for Mozambique*. (DA Pam 550-64.) Washington: GPO for Foreign Area Studies, The American University, 1977.

Kettani, Ali. "Muslims in East Africa: An Overview," *Journal of the Institute of Muslim Minority Affairs*, 4, Nos. 1–2, 1982,

133–144.

Kuder, Manfred von. *Moçambique: Eine Geographische, Soziale, und Wirtschaftliche Landeskunde*. Darmstadt: Wissenschaftliche Buchgesellschaft, 1978.

Langellier, Jean-Pierre. "Mozambique Five Years On: Africa's El Dorado?" *Guardian* [London], January 4, 1981.

———. "Mozambique Five Years On: Words, Deeds, and Demons," *Guardian* [London], December 21, 1980, 9–10.

Legum, Colin (ed.). *Africa Contemporary Record: Annual Survey and Documents, 1980–1981*. New York: Africana, 1981.

———. *Africa Contemporary Record: Annual Survey and Documents, 1981–1982*. New York: Africana, 1981.

Luke, Timothy W. "Angola and Mozambique: Institutionalizing Social Revolution in Africa," *Review of Politics*, 44, No. 3, July 1982, 413–36.

Machel, Graça. "The National System of Education," *AIM Bulletin* [Maputo], No. 66, December 1981 (supplement).

"Machel Addresses Rally," Foreign Broadcast Information Service, *Daily Report: Middle East and Africa*, 5, No. 131 (FBIS-MEA-83-131), July 7, 1983, U4–U9.

"Maputo Opts for Family Planning," *New African* [London], No. 163, April 1981, 25.

Mattelart, Armand. *Mass Media, Ideologies, and the Revolutionary Movement*. Atlantic Highlands, New Jersey: Humanities Press, 1980.

Medeiros, Eduardo. *Bibliografía etnográfica Macua*. Maputo: Faculdade de Letras, Universidade Eduardo Mondlane, 1980.

Meyns, Peter. "Liberation Ideology and National Development Strategy in Mozambique," *Review of African Political Economy* [Sheffield, England], No. 22, October-December 1981, 42–64.

Middlemas, Keith. "Independent Mozambique and Its Regional Policy." Pages 213–33 in John Seiler (ed.), *Southern Africa since the Portuguese Coup*. Boulder: Westview Press, 1980.

———. "Twentieth Cenitury White Society in Mozambique," *Tarikh* [Lagos], 6, No. 2, 1979, 30–45.

Mozambique. Comissão Nacional do Plano. *Moçambique: informação estadística; 1980–81*. Maputo: June 1982.

Mozambique. National Planning Commission. *Economic Report*. Maputo: January 1984.

"Mozambique: Who Runs What?" *Africa* [London], No. 121, September 1981, 30, 33.

Museu de Historia Natural. *Galeria de Etnográfia*. Maputo:

1975–78.

Newitt, M.D.D. "The Early History of the Maravi," *Journal of African History* [London], 23, No. 2, 1982, 145–62.

Nicholson, Brenden. "Mozambique 'Barefoot Doctors,'" *Johannesburg Star* [Johannesburg], December 1, 1979, 13.

Opello, Walter C., Jr. "Pluralism and Elite Conflict in an Independence Movement: FRELIMO in the 1960s," *Journal of Southern African Studies* [London], 2, No. 1, October 1975, 66–82.

———. "Revolutionary Change in Mozambique: Implications for the Emerging Postindependence Society." Pages 256–300 in J.R. Scarrett (ed.), *Analyzing Political Change in Africa*. Boulder: Westview Press, 1980.

Penvenne, Jeanne. *The Unmaking of an African Petite Bourgeoisie: Lourenço Marques, Mozambique*. (Working papers, No. 57.) Boston: African Studies Center, Boston University, 1982.

Rita-Ferreira, António. "The Ethno-history and the Ethnic Grouping of the Peoples of Mozambique," *South African Journal of African Affairs* [Pretoria], 3, 1973, 56–76.

Serapião, Luís Benjamin. "Church and State in Mozambican Politics, 1960–1980," *Lusophone Areas Studies Journal* [Ile-Ife, Nigeria], 1, No. 1, January 1983, 67–86.

———. "The Roman Catholic Church and the Principle of Self-Determination: A Case Study in Mozambique," *Journal of Church and State*, 23, No. 2, 1981, 323–35.

Sketchley, Peter. "Fishing Co-operatives on Lake Niassa: Seeds of a New Socialist Society or New Roots for an Old Exploiting Class?" *Review of African Political Economy* [Sheffield, England], No. 24, May-August 1982, 85–95.

"Southern Africa's Drought," *Economist* [London], February 11, 1984, 70–71.

Srivastava, R.K., and I. Livingstone. "Growth and Distribution: The Case of Mozambique." Pages 249-80 in Dharam Ghai and Samir Radwan (eds.), *Agrarian Policies and Rural Poverty in Africa*. Geneva: International LAbour Office, 1983.

Statistisches Bundesamt. *Länderkurzbericht: Mosambik, 1983*. Wiesbaden: 1983.

Talbot, Stephen. "Marxism in Mozambique," *Progressive*, No. 43, May 1981, 39–43.

United Nations Educational, Scientific and Cultural Organization. *World Guide to Higher Education* (2d ed.) New York: Bowker, 1982.

United States. Department of State. *Country Reports on Human Rights Practices for 1983*. (Report submitted to United States Congress, 98th, 2d Session, House of Representatives, Committee on Foreign Affairs, and Senate, Committee on Foreign Relations.) Washington: GPO, February 1984.

"Views on Traditional Social Practices Sought," Foreign Broadcast Information Service, *Daily Report: Middle East and Africa*, 5, No. 230 (FBIS-MEA-83-230), November 29, 1983, U2.

Walt, Gill. "Commitment to Primary Health Care in Mozambique: A Preliminary View," *Rural Africana*, Nos. 8–9, Fall-Winter 1980–81, 91-98.

Webster, D.J. "The Origins of Migrant Labour, Colonialism, and the Underdevelopment of Southern Mozambique." Pages 236–79 in P.L. Bonner (ed.), *Working Papers in Southern Africa*. Johannesburg: African Studies Institute, University of Witwatersrand, 1977.

Wuyts, Marc. "Peasants and Rural Economy in Mozambique." (Discussion paper.) Maputo: Centro de Estudos Africanos, Universidade Eduardo Mondlane, August 1978.

(Various issues of the following publications were also used in the preparation of this chapter: Joint Publications Research Service, *Sub-Saharan Africa Report*, January 1980-April 1984; *Kessing's Contemporary Archives* [London], 1976; *New York Times*, January 1980-April 1984; and *Washington Post*, January 1980-April 1984.)

## Chapter 3

Aitken, Thomas. "Mozambique: Prospering from the Peace," *Development Forum, Business Edition* [Geneva], December 17, 1980, 1–2.

Almeyra, Guillermo. "Cooperatives in Mozambique," *Ceres* [Rome], 11, No. 3, September-October 1978, 37–42.

Azevedo, Mario J. " 'A Sober Commitment to Liberation?' Mozambique and South Africa, 1974–79," *African Affairs* [London], 79, No. 317, October 1980, 567–84.

Balmes, Pierre. "Le Mozambique," *Afrique contemporaine, 1978–79* [Paris], 18, No. 106, November-December 1979, 8-15.

Caplan, Basil, "Mozambique Beckons the West," *Banker* [London], No. 130, December 1980, 33–39.

Christie, Iain. "Mozambique's Three Years of Independence," *Africa: An International Business, Economic, and Political Magazine* [London], No. 82, June 1978, 62–69.

Dimsdale, John. "Tanzania/Mozambique: Two Roads to Socialism," *Africa Report*, 27, No. 5, September-October 1982, 14–17.

*Direction of Trade Statistics Yearbook, 1981*. Washington: International Monetary Fund, 1981.

*Direction of Trade Statistics Yearbook, 1983*. Washington: International Monetary Fund, 1983.

Economist Intelligence Unit. *Quarterly Economic Review of Tanzania, Mozambique* [London], Annual Supplement, 1981.

————. *Quarterly Economic Review of Tanzania, Mozambique* [London], Annual Supplement, 1982.

————. *Quarterly Economic Review of Tanzania, Mozambique* [London], Annual Supplement, 1983.

*FAO Production Yearbook, 1981*, 35. Rome: Food and Agriculture Organization, 1982.

Federal Republic of Germany. Statistisches Bundesamt. *Länderkurzbericht: Mosambik, 1983*. Wiesbaden: September 1983.

Fitzpatrick, J. "The Economy of Mozambique: Problems and Prospects," *Third World Quarterly* [London], 3, No. 1, January 1981, 75–87.

"Focus on Mozambique," *Africa: An International Business, Economic, and Political Magazine* [London], No. 107, July 1980, 51–68.

Food and Agriculture Organization. *Forest Resources of Tropical Africa, Part II: Country Briefs*. Rome: 1981.

FRELIMO. Departamento do Trabalho Ideológico da FRELIMO. *Directivas econômicas e sociais*. (Documentos do Terceiro Congresso da FRELIMO.) Maputo: 1977.

Güdel, Christoph. "Report from Mozambique," *Swiss Review of World Affairs* [Zurich], 32, No. 5, August 1982, 11–19.

Harris, Laurence. "Agricultural Co-operatives and Development Policy in Mozambique," *Journal of Peasant Studies* [London], 7, No. 3, April 1980, 338–52.

Henriksen, Thomas H. "People's Republic of Mozambique." Pages 527–52 in Bogdan Szajkowski (ed.), *Marxist Governments—A World Survey, Vol. 3: Mozambique-Yugoslavia*. New York: St. Martin's Press, 1981.

Hodges, Tony. "Mozambique: FRELIMO's Test of Stamina," *African Business* [London], No. 64, December 1983, 12–15.

Isaacman, Allen F. "The Mozambique Cotton Cooperative: The Creation of a Grassroots Alternative to Forced Commodity

Production," *African Studies Review*, 25, Nos. 2–3, June-September 1982, 5–25.

————. "Transforming Mozambique's Rural Economy," *Issue*, 8, No. 1, Spring 1978, 17–24.

Isaacman, Allen F., and Barbara Isaacman. *Mozambique: From Colonialism to Revolution, 1900–1982*. Boulder: Westview Press, 1983.

————. "Mozambique: On the Road to Economic Recovery," *Africa Report*, 25, No. 3, May-June 1980, 4–7.

Kgarebe, Aloysius (ed.). *SADCC2-Maputo. The Proceedings of the Second Southern African Development Co-ordination Conference, Held in Maputo, People's Republic of Mozambique, on 27–28 November 1980*. London: SADCC Liaison Committee, July 1981.

Kihle, R. "Recent Surveys Outline New Potential for Offshore Mozambique," *Oil and Gas Journal*, 81, No. 9, February 28, 1983, 126–34.

Kofi, Tetteh A. "Prospects and Problems of the Transition from Agrarianism to Socialism: The Case of Angola, Guinea-Bissau, and Mozambique," *World Development* [Oxford, England], 9, Nos. 9–10, 1981, 851–70.

Latham, S.F. "About-Turn in Mozambique?" *World Today* [London], 37, No. 2, February 1981, 69–73.

Legum, Colin (ed.). *Africa Contemporary Record: Annual Survey and Documents, 1980–1981*. New York: Africana, 1981.

————. *Africa Contemporary Record: Annual Survey and Documents, 1981–1982*. New York: Africana, 1981.

Machel, Samora Moises. *A Nossa Luta*. n. pl.: Imprensa Nacional de Moçambique, 1975.

————. *Produzir é um acto de Militância*. Maputo: Departamento do Trabalho Ideológico da FRELIMO, October 1979.

Middlemas, Keith. *Cabora Bassa: Engineering and Politics in Southern Africa*. London: Weidenfeld and Nicolson, 1976.

Missão de Bioceanologia e Pescas de Moçambique. *Relatório científico, 1969*. Lourenço Marques: 1972.

Mozambique. Assembleia Popular. Quarta Sessão. *Lei do Comércio privado*. Maputo: May 1980.

Mozambique. Assembleia Popular. Quinta Sessão. *Lei das cooperativas*. Maputo: Imprensa Nacional, March 1980.

————. *Lei orçamental*. Maputo: Imprensa Nacional, March 1980.

Mozambique. Centro de Documentação Económica. Ministério do Desenvolvimento e Planificação Económica. *Valorização do carvão*. Maputo: 1977.

Mozambique. Comissão de Implementação dos Conselhos de Produção. *Organização dos Conselhos de Produças*. Maputo: April 1977.

————. *Resoluções do IV Plenário dos C.P. sobre Restrutaração dos Sectores e Estruturas (II)*. Maputo: 1977.

Mozambique. Comissão Nacional do Plano. *Moçambique: informação estadística, 1980–81*. Maputo: June 1982.

Mozambique. Departamento de Estradas e Pontes. *Mapa rodoviário de Moçambique*. Maputo: 1983.

Mozambique. Departamento de Turismo. *Estradas e pontes de Moçambique*. Maputo: 1976.

Mozambique. Direcção Nacional dos Portos e Caminhos de Ferro de Moçambique. *Boletim trimestral, outubro-dezembro 1976*. Maputo: 1976.

Mozambique. Direcção Provincial dos Serviços de Indústria. *Auxiliar do investor*. Lourenço Marques: 1973.

Mozambique. Ministério de Desenvolvimento e Planificação Económica. *Orientações para a preparação do programa de governo para 1978*. Maputo: 1977.

Mozambique. National Planning Commission. *Economic Report*. Maputo: January 1984.

Mozambique. Secretaria Provincial de Economia. *A Economia de Moçambique em números*. Lourenço Marques: 1973.

Mozambique. Serviços de Planeamento Económico. *Moçambique informação econômica*. Lourenço Marques: December 1975.

*Mozambique Land Law*. Cambridge: Committee on African Studies, Harvard University, 1981.

"Mozambique's Farm Machinery Graveyards," *African Business* [London], No. 63, November 1983, 77, 79.

Mühlemann, Christoph. "Pragmatism, Progress, and Problems in Mozambique," *Swiss Review of World Affairs* [Zurich], 29, No. 1, April 1979, 25–29.

Ottaway, David, and Marina Ottaway. *Afrocommunism*. New York: Africana, 1981.

Portugal. Agência-Geral do Ultramar. *Cabora-Bassa: The Signing of the Cabora Bassa Agreement on the 19th of September 1969*. Lisbon: 1970.

Portugal. Junta de Investigações Científicas do Ultramar. Missão de Estudos Agronómicos do Ultramar. *Fertilidade dos solos de Moçambique*. Lisbon: 1981.

Sketchley, Peter. "Fishing Co-operatives on Lake Niassa: Seeds of a New Socialist Society or New Roots for an Old Exploiting Class?" *Review of African Political Economy* [Sheffield, England], No. 24, May-August 1982, 85–95.

Srivastava, R.K., and I. Livingstone. "Growth and Distribution: The Case of Mozambique." Pages 249–80 in Dharam Ghai and Samir Radwan (eds.), *Agrarian Policies and Rural Poverty in Africa*. Geneva: International Labour Office, 1983.

Steiner, Herbert R. *Mozambique's Agricultural Economy in Brief*. (Foreign Agricultural Economic Report, No. 116.) Washington: Department of Agriculture, March 1976.

Torp, Jens Erik. *Industrial Planning and Development in Mozambique: Some Preliminary Considerations*. (Research Report, No. 50.) Uppsala: Scandinavian Institute of African Studies, 1979.

United Nations. Economic Commission for Africa. *African Economic Indicators, 1980*. Addis Ababa: n.d.

United Nations. General Assembly. Security Council. *Special Economic and Disaster Relief Assistance. Assistance to Mozambique. Report of the Review Mission to Mozambique*. (Document No. A/35/297, S/14007, June 30, 1980.) New York: 1980.

————. *Special Economic and Disaster Relief Assistance. Assistance to Mozambique. Report of the Review Mission to Mozambique*. (Document No. A/36/267, S/14627, August 21, 1981.) New York: 1981.

United States. Department of State. Agency for International Development. Bureau for Program and Policy Coordination. *U.S. Overseas Loans and Grants and Assistance from International Organizations. Obligations and Loan Authorizations, July 1, 1945-September 30, 1983. Washington: n.d.*

United States. Department of State. Agency for International Development. Economic and Social Data Services Division. *All Data Currently Available on Mozambique. Washington. June 1983*.

United States. Department of State. International Trade Administration. *Foreign Economic Trends and Their Implications for the United States: Mozambique*. (International Marketing Information, FET 82-106.) Washington: GPO, November 1982.

United States. Embassy in Maputo. *Investment Climate Statement*. Maputo: October 1982.

Washington, Shirley. "Portugal's New Initiatives," *Africa Report*, 27, No. 6, November-December 1982, 9–13.

World Council of Churches. Programme to Combat Racism. *Cabora Bassa and the Struggle for Southern Africa*. Geneva: n. d.

Wuyts, Marc. *Camponeses e economia rural em Moçambique*.
Maputo: Centro de Estudos Africanos, Universidade
Eduardo Mondlane, 1978.

―――. "The Mechanization of Present-Day Mozambican Agriculture," *Development and Change* [London], 12, 1981, 1–
27.

Zafiris, Nicos. "The People's Republic of Mozambique: Pragmatic
Socialism." Pages 114–64 in Peter Wiles (ed.), *The New Com-
munist Third World: An Essay in Political Economy*. New
York: St. Martin's Press, 1982.

(Various issues of the following publications were also used in
the preparation of this chapter: *African Business* [London],
January 1979–April 1984; *Africa Research Bulletin* (Economic,
Financial, and Technical Series) [Exeter, England], January
1973-April 1984; Joint Publications Research Service, *Sub-Saharan Africa Report*, January 1980-April 1984; and *Quarterly
Economic Review of Tanzania, Mozambique* [London], 1981–83.

## Chapter 4

Azevedo, Mario J. " 'A Sober Commitment to Liberation?'
Mozambique and South Africa, 1974–79," *African Affairs*
[London], 79, No. 317, October 1980, 567–84.

Clough, Michael. "American Policy Options," *Africa Report*, 27,
No. 6, November-December 1982, 14–17.

Egero, Bertil. "Mozambique Before the Second Phase of Socialist
Development," *Review of African Political Economy* [Lon-
don], No. 25, September-December 1982, 83–91.

"FRELIMO Fights for the Future of Mozambique," *African
Communist* [London], No. 95, 4th Quarter, 1983, 37–47.

Güdel, Christoph. "Report from Mozambique," *Swiss Review of
World Affairs* [Zurich], 32, No. 5, August 1982, 11–19.

Henderson, Robert D'A. "Principles and Practices in Mozambique's Foreign Policy," *World Today* [London], 34, No. 7,
July 1978, 276–86.

Henriksen, Thomas H. "Angola, Mozambique, and the Soviet
Union: Liberation and the Quest for Influence." Pages 56–75 in
Warren Weinstein and Thomas H. Henriksen (eds.), *Soviet and
Chinese Aid to African Nations*. New York: Praeger, 1980.

―――. "Marxism and Mozambique," *African Affairs* [Lon-
don], 77, No. 309, October 1978, 441–62.

―――. "Mozambique: The Enemy Within," *Current History*,

81, No. 473, March 1982, 111–14.

―――. "People's Republic of Mozambique." Pages 527–52 in Bogdan Szajkowski (ed.), *Marxist Governments—A World Survey, Vol. 3: Mozambique-Yugoslavia*. New York: St. Martin's Press, 1981.

Hill, Christopher R. "Regional Co-operation in Southern Africa Reviewed," *African Affairs* [London], 82, No. 327, April 1983, 213–39.

Hodges, Tony. "Mozambique: The Politics of Liberation." Pages 57–92 in Gwendolen M. Carter and Patrick O'Meara (eds.), *Southern Africa: The Continuing Crisis*. Bloomington: Indiana University Press, 1979.

Isaacman, Allen F., and Jennifer Davis. "U.S. Policy Towards Mozambique, 1946–1976: 'The Defense of Colonialism and Regional Stability.'" Pages 18–61 in René Lemarchand (ed.), *American Policy in Southern Africa: The Stakes and the Stance*. Washington: University Press of America, 1978.

Isaacman, Allen F., and Barbara Isaacman. "Creating a New Legal System," *Africa Report*, 26, No. 1, January-February 1981, 19–22.

―――. "In Pursuit of Nonalignment," *Africa Report*, 28, No. 3, May-June 1983, 47–54.

―――. *Mozambique: From Colonialism to Revolution, 1900–1982*. Boulder: Westvieww Press, 1983.

―――. "South Africa's Hidden War," *Africa Report*, 27, No. 6, November-December 1982, 4–8.

Isaacman, Barbara, and Allen F. Isaacman. "A Socialist Legal System in the Making: Mozambique Before and After Independence." Pages 281–323 in Richard L. Abel (ed.), *The Politics of Informal Justice—Vol. 2: Comparative Studies*. New York: Academic Press, 1982.

"Joaquim Chissano, Foreign Minister of Mozambique," *Africa Report*, 28, No. 1, January-February 1983, 42–45.

Langellier, Jean-Pierre. "Mozambique Five Years On: Guerrillas Worry, but Don't Frighten, the Machel Regime," *Guardian* [London], December 28, 1980, 8.

―――. "Mozambique Five Years On: Machel's Uneasy Partnership with the East," *Guardian* [London], January 11, 1981, 8–9.

―――. "Mozambique Five Years On: Words, Deeds, and Demons," *Guardian* [London], December 21, 1980, 9–10.

Latham, S.F. "About-Turn in Mozambique?" *World Today* [London], 37, No. 2, February 1981, 69–73.

Legum, Colin (ed.). *Africa Contemporary Record: Annual Sur-*

*vey and Documents, 1980–1981*. New York: Africana, 1981.
————. *Africa Contemporary Record: Annual Survey and Documents, 1981–1982*. New York: Africana, 1981.
Luke, Timothy W. "Angola and Mozambique: Institutionalizing Social Revolution in Africa," *Review of Politics*, 44, No. 3, July 1982, 413–36.
"Machel Reads Report to Party Congress," Foreign Broadcast Information Service, *Daily Report: Middle East and Africa*, 5, No. 092 (FBIS-MEA-83-092), May 11, 1983, U1–U23.
MacQueen, Norman. "Mozambique's Widening Foreign Policy," *World Today* [London], 40, No. 1, January 1984, 22–28.
Matatu, Godwin. "Machel's New War," *Africa: An International Business, Economic, and Political Magazine* [London], No. 105, May 1980, 14–20.
Middlemas, Keith. "Independent Mozambique and Its Regional Policy." Pages 213–33 in John Seiler (ed.), *Southern Africa since the Portuguese Coup*. Boulder: Westview Press, 1980.
Mittelman, James H. "The Dialectic of National Autonomy and Global Participation: Alternatives to Conventional Strategies of Development—Mozambique Experience," *Alternatives*, 5, No. 3, November 1979, 307–28.
Mozambique. National Planning Commission. *Economic Report*. Maputo: January 1984.
"Mozambique." Pages 1089–91 in George Thomas Kurian (ed.) *World Press Encyclopedia*. New York: Facts on File, 1982.
"Mozambique: How South Africa Is Supporting the MNR," *New African* [London], No. 179, August 1982, 22.
Munslow, Barry. *Mozambique: The Revolution and Its Origins*. London: Longman, 1983.
"Notícias Lists Central Committee Members," Foreign Broadcast Information Service, *Daily Report: Middle East and Africa*, 5, No. 096 (FBIS-MEA-83-096), May 17, 1983, U1–U2.
Ottaway, David, and Marina Ottaway. *Afrocommunism*. New York: Africana, 1981.
Ottaway, Marina. "The Theory and Practice of Marxism-Leninism in Mozambique and Ethiopia." Pages 118–44 in David E. Albright (ed.), *Communism in Africa*. Bloomington: Indiana University Press, 1980.
Papp, Daniel S. "The Soviet Union and Southern Africa." Pages 69–96 in Robert H. Donaldson (ed.), *The Soviet Union in the Third World: Successes and Failures*. Boulder: Westview Press, 1981.
Pélissier, René. "Mozambique." Pages 708–26 in *Africa South of the Sahara, 1982–83*. London: Europa, 1982.

Serapião, Luís Benjamim, and Mohamed A. El-Khawas. *Mozambique in the Twentieth Century: From Colonialism to Independence*. Washington: University Press of America, 1979.

"The State Department Perspective," *Africa Report*, 28, No. 1, January-February 1983, 46–48.

United States. Congress. 95th, 2d Session. House of Representatives. Committee on International Relations. Subcommittee on Africa. *Perspectives on Mozambique*. Washington: GPO, May 1978.

United States. Department of State. *Background Notes: Mozambique*. Washington: 1983.

――――. *Country Reports on Human Rights Practices for 1981*. (Report submitted to United States Congress, 97th, 2d Session, House of Representatives, Committee on Foreign Affairs, and Senate, Committee on Foreign Relations.) Washington: GPO, February 1982.

――――. *Country Reports on Human Rights Practices for 1982*. (Report submitted to United States Congress, 98th, 1st Session, Senate, Committee on Foreign Relations, and House of Representatives, Committee on Foreign Affairs.) Washington: GPO, February 1983.

――――. *Country Reports on Human Rights Practices for 1983*. (Report submitted to United States Congress, 98th, 2d Session, House of Representatives, Committee on Foreign Affairs, and Senate, Committee on Foreign Relations.) Washington: GPO, February 1984.

――――. *Reagan Administration's Africa Policy: A Progress Report*. (Statement by Chester A. Crocker, Assistant Secretary for African Affairs, Current Policy, No. 527.) Washington: 1983.

――――. *Soviet and East European Aid to the Third World, 1981*. Washington: 1983.

Washington, Shirley. "Portugal's New Initiatives," *Africa Report*, 27, No. 6, November-December 1982, 9–13.

Zafiris, Nicos. "The People's Republic of Mozambique: Pragmatic Socialism." Pages 114–64 in Peter Wiles (ed.), *The New Communist Third World: An Essay in Political Economy*. New York: St. Martin's Press, 1982.

(Various issues of the following publications were also used in the preparation of this chapter: *Africa* [London], January 1980-March 1984; *Africa Research Bulletin* [Exeter, England], January 1980-March 1984; Agência de Informação de Moçambique, *Information Bulletin* [Maputo], January 1981-December 1982;

*Christian Science Monitor*, January 1980-April 1984; Foreign Broadcast Information Service, *Daily Report: Middle East and Africa*, January 1983-April 1984; Joint Publications Research Service, *Sub-Saharan Africa Report*, January 1980-March 1983; *Keesing's Contemporary Archives* [London], 1978–84; *New African* [London], January 1982-March 1984; *New York Times*, July 1978-April 1984; *Quarterly Economic Review of Tanzania, Mozambique* [London], 1981–83; and *Washington Post*, January 1980-April 1984.)

## Chapter 5

*Amnesy International Report, 1981*. London: Amnesty International, 1981.

"Botha's Terrorist Raid," *Africa* [London], No. 115, March 1981, 39–40.

"Country's Military Capabilities Against South Africa: MNR Guerrillas Described," *Africa Now* [London], December 1983, 86–88.

"Dissidents by Proxy," *Africa* [London], No. 133, September 1982, 20.

Dove, Fancis. "How South Africa Is Supporting the MNR," *New African* [London], No. 179, August 1982, 22.

Economist Intelligence Unit. *Quarterly Economic Review of Tanzania, Mozambique* [London], Second Quarter, 1982.

——. *Quarterly Economic Review of Tanzania, Mozambique* [London], Third Quarter, 1982.

Fauvet, Paul. "Mozambique: Bitter Dawn at Matola," *Africa Now* [London], April 1981, 35–37.

——. "Mozambique 'Rebels' Shift to a New Master," *New African* [London], No. 159, December 1980, 28–30.

Fauvet, Paul, and Alves Gomes. "The So-Called 'Mozambique National Resistance' (MNR)," *Sechaba* [London], June 1982, 12–19.

"First Officers Graduate in Nampula," *Tempo* [Maputo], January 10, 1982, 5–9.

Fowler, Will. "Battlefield Firepower," *Defence Africa* [Winchester, England], 10, No. 2, January 1984, 28–30.

"Frelimo Draws the Battleline," *Africa* [London], No. 116, April 1981, 38–39.

"Frelimo's Ruthless Enemies," *New African* [London], No. 141, May 1979, 38–40.

"Frelimo Woos the West and Rallies Anti-MNR Support," *Afri-*

*can Business* [London], No. 58, June 1983, 21–22.

"Guerrillas Use Malawi as Base," *Africa Economic Digest* [London], October 8, 1982, 25.

"The Guerrilla War in Mozambique," *Foreign Report* [London], No. 1652, October 22, 1980, 3–4.

"Hands (and Arms) Across the Border," *Economist* [London], June 12, 1982, 26.

"The Hand that Feeds the Dissidents," *Africa* [London], No. 123, November 1981, 65–67.

Hanlon, Joseph. "Adjusting Course," *Africa News*, July 20, 1981, 4–5, 9–10.

———. "Draconian Punishments to Deter MNR," *New African* [London], No. 190, July 1983, 35.

———. "Frelimo Gets Tough," *New African* [London], No. 186, March 1983, 31–32.

———. "Machel Speaks Out on Defections," *Africa News*, June 14, 1982, 3–4.

———. "Mozambique," *Africa News*, February 9, 1981, 2–10.

———. "New Battles with the MNR," *Africa News*, August 30, 1982, 3–4.

———. "The Saboteur Who Blew Himself Up," *New African* [London], No. 187, April 1983, 35–36.

———. South Africa Adopts Israeli Military Tactics," *New African* [London], No. 191, August 1983, 29–30.

Isaacman, Allen F., and Barbara Isaacman. "Creating a New Legal System," *Africa Report*, 26, No. 1, January-February 1981, 19–22.

———. "Mozambique: On the Road to Economic Recovery," *Africa Report*, 25, No. 3, May-June 1980, 4–7.

———. "South Africa's Hidden War." *Africa Report*, 27, No. 6, November-December 1982, 4–8.

Isaacman, Barbara, and June Stephen. *Mozambique: Women, the Law, and Agrarian Reform*. Addis Ababa: United Nations Economic Commission for Africa, 1980.

Jacobs, G. "Soviet Activity in the Indian Ocean (Part One)," *Defence Africa* [Winchester, England], 10, No. 1, November 1983, 36–38.

———. "Soviet Activity in the Indian Ocean (Part Two)," *Defense Africa* [Winchester, England], No. 2, January 1984, 22–24.

Jasper, Robert S. *A Regional Security Role for Africa's Front-Line States: Experience and Prospects*. (Adelphi Papers, No. 180.) London: International Institute for Strategic Studies,

1983.

Joint Publications Research Service—JPRS (Washington). The following items are from the JPRS series:

*Sub-Saharan Africa Report.*

"Anti-Government Forces Suffer Setbacks," *Star*, Johannesburg, February 7, 1983. (JPRS 83075, No. 2772, March 16, 1983, 64–65).

"Article Examines Nation's Domestic Difficulties," *Le Monde*, Paris, May 25, 1983. (JPRS 83890, No. 2820, July 14, 1983, 30–33).

"Faced with the RMN Rebellion, Maputo Is Looking for More Effective Western Aid," *Le Monde*, Paris, May 17, 1983. (JPRS 83634, No. 2808, June 8, 1983, 31–33.)

"Hawkish New Policy Toward ANC Threat," *Sunday Express*, Johannesburg, June 5, 1983. (JPRS 83743, No. 2814, June 22, 1983, 63–64).

"Interim Minister Comments on Results of Legality Campaign," *Tempo*, Maputo, November 14, 1982. (JPRS 82587, No. 2743, January 5, 1983, 27–30).

"Korean Officials Visit, Pledge More Assistance," *Notícias*, Maputo, February 18, 1983. (JPRS 83309, No. 2788, April 21, 1983, 63–66).

"Machel-Botha Talks Said Aimed at Reducing Tension," *Le Monde*, Paris, May 11, 1983. (JPRS 83687, No. 2811, June 15, 1983, 3).

"Need Stressed for More Party Members in Armed Forces," *Notícias*, Maputo, December 20, 1982. (JPRS 82747, No. 2755, January 27, 1983, 45–46).

"RNM Chief Christina Shot and Killed in South Africa," *Afrika-Post*, Bonn, June 1983. (JPRS 84139, No. 2833, August 17, 1983, 41–43).

"2ndo Caderno," *O Jornal*, Lisbon, October 21, 1983, (JPRS 84896, No. 2880, December 7, 1983, 64–74).

"Soldiers Praised for Participation in Civilian Activities," *Combate*, Maputo, November 28, 1982. (JPRS 82725, No. 2753, January 25, 1983, 41).

"Zimbabwe Veterans Promoted," *PANA*, Dakar, December 30, 1983, (JPRS 84007, No. 2749, January 17, 1984, 26).

Komba, Marcelino. "Mozambique's Return to Arms," *Africa* [London], No. 118, June 1981, 52, 61–62.

Legum, Colin. "Mozambique-South Africa: Is It a Deal?" *New African* [London], No. 198, March 1984, 15–17.

——. "Resistance in Mozambique," *Times of India* [Bombay], March 30, 1983, 8.

————. "South Africa's Power Game," *New African* [London], No. 186, March 1983, 11–14.

Legum, Colin (ed.). *Africa Contemporary Record: Annual Survey and Documents, 1980–1981*. New York: Africana, 1981.

————. *Africa Contemporary Record: Annual Survey and Documents, 1981–1982*. New York: Africania, 1981.

"Machel in Moscow," *New African* [London], No. 187, April 1983, 13.

"Machel Postpones European Tour," *African Economic Digest* [London], June 11, 1982, 23–24.

Martin, David, and Phyllis Johnson. *The Struggle for Zimbabwe: The Chimurenga War*. London: Faber and Faber, 1981.

Matthews, Lloyd. "Mozambique." Pages 407–408 in John Keegan (ed.), *World Armies*. New York: Facts on File, 1983.

"Message from Mozambique," *India Today* [New Delhi], April 10, 1982, 71.

*The Military Balance, 1981–1982*. London: International Institute for Strategic Studies, 1981.

*The Military Balance, 1982–1983*. London: International Institute for Strategic Studies, 1982.

*The Military Balance, 1983–1984*. London: International Institute for Strategic Studies, 1983.

"Mozambican Armed Forces," *Indian Ocean Newsletter* [Paris], No. 104, November 5, 1983, 7–10.

"Mozambique Explains Its Stand," *New African* [London], No. 198, March 1984, 17.

"Mozambique: MNR Seeks a Leader," *Africa Now* [London], No. 28, August 1983, 25.

"Mozambique: No 'Victory' but Concessions Won," *Africa Now* [London], No. 36, April 1984, 27.

"Mozambique's Air Arm," *Flight International* [Sutton, England], 24, No. 3874, August 1, 1981, 361.

"New South African Manoeuvres in Angola, Mozambique," *African Business* [London], No. 66, February 1984, 5–6.

Ottaway, David, and Marina Ottaway. *Afrocommunism*. Africana, 1981.

Owen, John (ed.). *Brassey's Infantry Weapons of Armies of Africa, the Orient, and Latin America*. London: Brassey's, 1980.

Pachter, Elise Forbes. "Contra-Coup: Civilian Control of the Military in Guinea, Tanzania, and Mozambique," *Journal of Modern African Studies* [Cambridge, England], 20, No. 4, December 1982, 595–612.

"Policing the Police," *Africa* [London], No. 128, April 1982, 32–

33.

"The Price of Solidarity," *Africa* [London], No. 105, May 1980, 17.

"Purge of Security Forces," *Africa* [London], No. 124, December 1981, 39–40.

"Radio Notes: The Issuing of Residents' Cards in Mozambique," *Facts and Reports* [Amsterdam], January 9, 1983, 12.

"Rebels in Limbo," *Africa* [London], No. 109, September 1980, 25–26.

Sivera, Filipe. "Need Stressed for More Party Members in Armed Forces," *Noticias* [Maputo], December 20, ;1982, 45–46.

Somerville, Keith. "MNR Still Active Despite Peace Talks," *New African* [London], March 1984, 34.

"Spreading Trouble," *Economist* [London], March 26, 1983, 45.

Thomashausen, Andre E. "The National Resistance Movement of Mozambique." *Africa Insight* [Pretoria], 13, No. 2, 1983, 125–29.

United States. Department of State. *Country Reports on Human Rights Practices for 1983*. (Report submitted to United States Congress, 98th, 2d Session, House of Representatives, Committee on Foreign Affairs, and Senate, Committee on Foreign Relations.) Washington: GPO, February 1984.

Ward, David, and Martin Plaut. "The True Story Behind the Bombing of Mozambique," *New African* [London], No. 191, January 1982, 24.

"War of Words," *Economist* [London], March 21, 1981, 44–45.

Whitaker, Mark. "Swordpower and Diplomacy," *Newsweek*, February 6, 1984, 3.

(Various issues of the following publications were also used in the preparation of this chapter: *Africa Confidential* [London], January 1980-March 1983; *Africa Report*, January 1978-March 1984; *Africa Research Bulletin* [Exeter, England], March 1978-March 1984; *Afrique défense* [Paris], February 1981-April 1983; *Christian Science Monitor*, December 1983-April 1984; *Facts and Reports* [Amsterdam], December 1983-April 1984; *Financial Times* [London], December 1983-April 1984; Foreign Broadcast Information Service, *Daily Report: Middle East and Africa*, January 1983-April 1984; *Guardian* [London], May 1979-January 1984; *Keesing's Contemporary Archives* [London], May 1983-March 1984; *New York Times*, March 1981-April 1984; *Noticias* [Maputo], December 1982-January 1984; *Observer* [London], September 1982-March 1983; *Summary of World Broadcasts—*

BBC [London], September 1980-October 1983; and *Washington Post*, January 1980-April 1984.)

# Glossary

Asian—Term used in Mozambique for a resident of Indian or Pakistani origin. The term succeeded the word *Indian* in East African and southern African usage after the partition of India in 1974.

clan—A descent group (*q.v.*), the members of which are commonly accepted as having descended from a common ancestor; often comprises several subclans, which in turn consist of lineages (*q.v.*), or the clan may comprise lineages and lack subclans.

descent group—A human unit whose members are commonly accepted as having descended from a common ancestor. For most Africans in Mozambique, descent occurs exclusively through males (patrilineal) or through females (matrilineal); peoples south of the Zambezi River are patrilineal; peoples north of the Zambezi are matrilineal. The largest descent group is the clan (*q.v.*), which may be divided into subclans and lineages (*q.v.*).

dynamizing group (*grupo dinamizadore*—GD)—Local unit composed of political activists led by members of FRELIMO (*q.v.*). Formed in villages, town wards, factories, and commercial farms, the GDs were intended to indoctrinate the people with FRELIMO's ideology. They also served as a major means of communication between the national leadership and the people.

fiscal year (FY)—Corresponds to the calendar year.

FRELIMO—*Frente de Libertação de Moçambique* (Front for the Liberation of Mozambique). Organization that carried out the bulk of guerrilla warfare against the Portuguese colonial regime, beginning in 1964, and took power at independence in June 1975. In theory an anticolonialist front during that period, it formally became a Marxist-Leninist vanguard party in February 1977.

front-line states—Countries of southern Africa (Tanzania, Zambia, Zimbabwe, Angola, Mozambique, and Botswana) whose leaders have maintained common policies on transfers of power in white-ruled states and territories of the region.

gross domestic product (GDP)—The total value of goods and services produced within a country's borders during a fixed period, usually one year. Obtained by adding the value contributed by each sector of the economy in the form of compensation of employees, profits, and depreciation (consumption of capital). Subsistence production is included and consists of the imputed value of production by the farm family for its own use and the imputed rental value of owner-occupied dwellings.

gross national product (GNP)—GDP (*q.v.*) plus the income received from abroad by residents, less payments remitted abroad to nonresidents.

International Monetary Fund (IMF)—Established along with the World Bank (*q.v.*) in 1945, the IMF is a specialized agency affiliated with the United Nations and is responsible for stabilizing international exchange rates and payments. The main business of the IMF is the provision of loans to its members (including industrialized and developing countries) when they experience balance of payments difficulties. These loans frequently carry conditions that require substantial internal economic adjustments by the recipients, most of which are developing countries.

lineage—A descent group (*q.v.*), the members of which can, in principle, trace their descent from a common ancestor; lineages of great generational depth may include lineages of lesser depth.

*mestiço*—A person of mixed ancestry, usually European and African but sometimes Indian (specifically Goan) and African. Term may be considered derogatory.

metical (pl., meticais)—Unit of currency introduced on June 16, 1980, to replace the Mozambique escudo. Like the latter, the metical also consists of 100 centavos. The unit's initial value was the same as that for the escudo (at the time, the equivalent of about US$0.035; US$1 equaled 28 meticais). Depreciation against the dollar occurred gradually during 1981, and value declined to US$0.033 at the end of that year, when US$1 equaled 30.05 meticais. The rate averaged about US$0.033 through mid-1983 but increased thereafter to approximately 41 meticais to the dollar (1 metical equaled about US$0.023). It stood at this figure in April 1984.

Nonaligned Movement—A grouping of countries that have deliberately chosen not to be associated politically or militarily with either the West or the communist states. Member countries are expected to pursue independent foreign policies, support national liberation movements, and refrain from participating in multilateral or bilateral military alliances with the major powers. The movement's seventh summit meeting, held in New Delhi in March 1983, was attended by 97 nations.

Organization of African Unity (OAU)—Formal organization of all independent African states except those considered "colonial" in character—specifically the Republic of South Africa.

Polisario—Frente Popular para la Liberación de Saguia el Hamra y Río de Oro (Popular Front for the Liberation of Saguia el Hamra and Rio de Oro); independence movement in North Africa's Western Sahara.

*prazeros*—Recipients of land (*prazo, q.v.*) leased from the Portuguese crown. *Prazeros* in Mozambique were initially Portuguese, but after generations of intermarriage with local Africans and immigrating Indians, they became Africanized; they played a major role in Mozambique from 1630 through 1890.

*prazo*—Land leased by the Portuguese crown to individuals either in perpetuity or for a fixed number of generations. The leases were renewable. The *prazos* became the major bases of economic and political power along the Zambezi River from 1630 through the late nineteenth century. They continued to exist through the early years of the twentieth century but had lost their significance after 1890.

RNM—Resistência Nacional Moçambicana (Mozambican National Resistance). Referred to variously in English-language publications as the MNR, MRM, MNRM, and RENAMO. A dissident group that has carried out guerrilla warfare since 1976 in opposition to FRELIMO (*q.v.*) with backing from South Africa and wealthy Portuguese formerly resident in Mozambique. The movement's political program calls for elimination of communism from the national society and easing of the stress placed on the private sector; further, it demands respect for tradition and ethnic bonds within a federal structure.

World Bank—Informal name used to designate a group of three affiliated international institutions: the International Bank for Reconstruction and Development (IBRD), the International Development Association (IDA), and the International Finance Corporation (IFC). The IBRD, established in 1945, has the primary purpose of providing loans to developing countries for productive projects. The IDA, a legally separate loan fund but administered by the staff of the IBRD, was set up in 1960 to furnish credits to the poorest developing countries on much easier terms than those of conventional IBRD loans. The IFC, founded in 1956, supplements the activities of the

IBRD through loans and assistance designed specifically to encourage the growth of productive private enterprises in the less developed countries. The president and certain senior officers of the IBRD hold the same positions in the IFC. The three institutions are owned by the governments of the countries that subscribe their capital. To participate in the World Bank group, member states must first belong to the International Monetary Fund (IMF—*q.v.*).

# Index

# Published Country Studies

## (Area Handbook Series)

| | | | |
|---|---|---|---|
| 550–65 | Afghanistan | 550–151 | Honduras |
| 550–98 | Albania | 550–165 | Hungary |
| 550–44 | Algeria | 550–21 | India |
| 550–50 | Angola | 550–154 | Indian Ocean |
| 550–73 | Argentina | 550–39 | Indonesia |
| | | | |
| 550–169 | Australia | 550–68 | Iran |
| 550–176 | Austria | 550–31 | Iraq |
| 550–175 | Bangladesh | 550–25 | Israel |
| 550–170 | Belgium | 550–182 | Italy |
| 550–66 | Bolivia | 550–69 | Ivory Coast |
| | | | |
| 550–20 | Brazil | 550–177 | Jamaica |
| 550–168 | Bulgaria | 550–30 | Japan |
| 550–61 | Burma | 550–34 | Jordan |
| 550–83 | Burundi | 550–56 | Kenya |
| 550–50 | Cambodia | 550–81 | Korea, North |
| | | | |
| 550–177 | Cameroon | 550–41 | Korea, South |
| 550–159 | Chad | 550–58 | Laos |
| 550–77 | Chile | 550–24 | Lebanon |
| 550–60 | China | 550–38 | Liberia |
| 550–63 | China, Republic of | 550–85 | Libya |
| | | | |
| 550–26 | Colombia | 550–172 | Malawi |
| 550–91 | Congo | 550–45 | Malaysia |
| 550–90 | Costa Rica | 550–161 | Mauritania |
| 550–152 | Cuba | 550–79 | Mexico |
| 550–22 | Cyprus | 550–76 | Mongolia |
| | | | |
| 550–158 | Czechoslovakia | 550–49 | Morocco |
| 550–54 | Dominican Republic | 550–64 | Mozambique |
| 550–52 | Ecuador | 550–35 | Nepal, Bhutan and Sikkim |
| 550–43 | Egypt | 550–88 | Nicaragua |
| 550–150 | El Salvador | 550–157 | Nigeria |
| | | | |
| 550–28 | Ethiopia | 550–94 | Oceania |
| 550–167 | Finland | 550–48 | Pakistan |
| 550–155 | Germany, East | 550–46 | Panama |
| 550–173 | Germany, Fed. Rep. of | 550–156 | Paraguay |
| 550–153 | Ghana | 550–185 | Persian Gulf States |
| | | | |
| 550–87 | Greece | 550–42 | Peru |
| 550–78 | Guatemala | 550–72 | Philippines |
| 550–174 | Guinea | 550–162 | Poland |
| 550–82 | Guyana | 550–181 | Portugal |
| 550–164 | Haiti | 550–160 | Romania |

| | | | | |
|---|---|---|---|---|
| 550–84 | Rwanda | 550–89 | Tunisia |
| 550–51 | Saudi Arabia | 550–80 | Turkey |
| 550–70 | Senegal | 550–74 | Uganda |
| 550–180 | Sierra Leone | 550–97 | Uruguay |
| 550–184 | Singapore | 550–71 | Venezuela |
| | | | |
| 550–86 | Somalia | 550–57 | Vietnam, North |
| 550–93 | South Africa | 550–55 | Vietnam, South |
| 550–95 | Soviet Union | 550–183 | Yemens, The |
| 550–179 | Spain | 550–99 | Yugoslavia |
| 550–96 | Sri Lanka (Ceylon) | 550–67 | Zaïre |
| | | | |
| 550–27 | Sudan | 550–75 | Zambia |
| 550–47 | Syria | 550–171 | Zimbabwe |
| 550–62 | Tanzania | | |
| 550–53 | Thailand | | |
| 550–178 | Trinidad and Tobago | | |

☆U.S. GOVERNMENT PRINTING OFFICE: 1985 -0- 461-018 (10033)